W9-ACV-461

NOTES OF AN APPRENTICESHIP

NOTES OF AN APPRENTICESHIP

(Texts collected and presented by Paule Thévenin)

Pierre Boulez

Translated from the French by

HERBERT WEINSTOCK

ALFRED · A · KNOPF

New York · 1968

THIS IS A BORZOI BOOK
PUBLISHED BY ALFRED A. KNOPF, INC.

First American Edition

Published in the United States by
Alfred A. Knopf, Inc., New York, N.Y.
Distributed by Random House, Inc., New York, N.Y.
Library of Congress Catalog Card Number: 67-18625
Manufactured in the United States of America

Originally published in French as
Relevés d'apprenti by Editions du Seuil,
Paris, 1966. © by Editions du Seuil.

CONTENTS

I

IN VIEW OF A MUSICAL ESTHETIC

A Time for Johann Sebastian Bach

Since 1920 the musical world seems to have been living with an obsession about "classicism." "Style," "objectivity": two major epithets of that adventure.

One could say without fear of going astray that as a matter of fact two tendencies coexist in this "classicism": one of them aims to rediscover total objectivity in "pure music"; the other, based more validly on a historical dialectic, tries to characterize a new "universality" of style. I need not speak of certain appeals marked as much by ingenuity as by naïveté: measures from a two-voice canon by Johann Sebastian Bach have been summoned to the support of polytonality; right now, such-and-such a "Mediterranean" composer is combing Mozart's *Don Giovanni* for a twelve-tone row; such-and-such another—not Mediterranean—is making a parallel analysis of Webern and Beethoven expositions . . .

All musical activity means to play the game under the sign of absolute security. In both camps, therefore, the term "romantic" is strongly tinged with scorn because of its instability and disarray. From the neoclassic side, anathema is hurled upon the dodecaphonic experience, which is called an ultra-individualistic endeavor, the final hypertrophy of Wagnerism. On the dodecaphonic side, with the firm support of historic evolution, neoclassicism is treated as a nostalgia for the past, its pretended return to "pure" music as a notoriously subjective illusion.

Do we want precise testimony? To recall some of Stravinsky's phrases should suffice: "I consider music, by its essence, as powerless to *express* anything whatever: a sentiment, an attitude, a psychological state, a phenomenon of nature. *Expression* never has been the immanent property of music . . ." And again: "The phenomenon of music is given to us for the sole purpose of instituting order among things. To be realized, it therefore necessarily and uniquely demands a construction. The construction made, the order attained, everything has been said. It would be vain to search in it or await from it anything else." Let us put beside these declarations such works as the Violin Concerto and the "Dumbarton Oaks" Concerto.

From another camp we have a text by Berg, paraphrasing Riemann in order to claim for Schoenberg a position symmetrical with that of Bach:

> . . . One of the great masters of all time, one of those who can never be surpassed because they incorporate equally the sensibility and the musical wisdom of an epoch; a master who owes his particular significance and unparalleled greatness to the fact that two sorts of styles belonging to two distinct eras flower in him simultaneously, so that he rises between the two like a powerful landmark, participating in two worlds in a gigantic way.

Bach belongs with equal right to the earlier period of polyphonic music, of the contrapuntal, "imitative" style, and to the period of harmonic music . . .	Schoenberg belongs with equal right to the earlier period of the harmonic style and to the one that re-begins with him—that of polyphonic music, of the contrapuntal, "imitative" style . . .

> . . . and also to the system—now established for the first time—which replaces:

The ancient modes with the modern tonalities.	The major and minor tonalities with the series of twelve tones.

He lived in a transitional epoch—that is to say, at a time when the older style had not died out, but when the new style was in only the first stages of its development and still bore the marks of incompleteness. His genius combined the particular qualities of the two sorts of styles . . .

In Berg, more precisely, we find the varied chorales of the Violin Concerto and of *Lulu,* the big passacaglia of *Wozzeck.* Webern would have been even happier making a magnificent orchestration of the big six-voice fugue in *Das musikalisches Opfer* had he not been followed by numerous disciples of the "dodecaphonic school" who, in turn, felt themselves obliged to bedizen Bach or Mozart with sickly, though adroit, tinsel. Webern's moving, inimitable homage remains the quartet in which the series is based on the four notes B–A–C–H.

Midway between these two headstrong positions, is it possible to designate the completely empirical position of Bartók, the *chaconne* of whose Sonata for Unaccompanied Violin is full of reminiscences of his illustrious predecessor? The no less empirical position of a Hindemith, who enlisted many adepts not long ago? Shall we recall that a similar heritage weighed heavily on Roussel? Shall we, finally, forget the unexpected *rapprochement* between Bach and jazz at the hands of a pianist-composer who had his hour of syncopated fame?

Note that if the common tendency of the neoclassic and dodecaphonic positions is toward security, they are nonetheless results of essentially different philosophies: the former is founded upon an esthetic of reconstitution, whereas the latter obeys an evolutionary dialectic. A priori, the latter should enlist all our sympathy . . . But, subversively, I have no unbounded belief in a new "collective" language—the phenomena of revolution appear to me illusory, to say the least.

For the great justification of these estheticizing and historicizing programs resides above all in the return of the idiom to the "universality" that was lost, principally because of Beethoven, at the turn of the nineteenth century. Boris de Schloezer, in fact, tells us: "Style has been dead since the beginning of the nineteenth century." And by "style" he means "the product, to some extent collective, in which are crystallized certain ways of thinking, of feeling, of acting on the part of a century, a nation, even a group, when it succeeds in imposing its spirit upon a society." I believe that everyone will agree to accept those premises. But after that beginning the most violent misunderstandings start to cut away the best part.

We still must come to some agreement about what is called the "universality" of a style. I shall take the neoclassic definition from Paul Collaer's *Stravinsky*, which seems to me the most nearly complete formulary that one could find of that inchoate period from 1920 to 1930. He speaks of *Pulcinella*, a score written "after Pergolesi," as everyone knows: "Henceforth, a completely renewed classical style, active and alive, is restored to music . . . The particular character of *Le Sacre* or *Les Noces* allowed of no 'continuation.' The universality of the language of *Pulcinella* permits others to assimilate it . . . From *Pulcinella* on, one can say of Stravinsky what is true of Mozart: that his personality is not owing to the elements of his style, but rather to their execution, their use in the work." Farther along, Collaer also says: "His music was to become more and more abstract. It passes beyond all initial pretext, however remote. It is of absolute purity, and its spirit can be compared only to that of Bach's Inventions and Suites." There, certainly, is a "chef-d'oeuvre-ish" definition of the universality of a style. But what the definition carefully does not do is demonstrate the necessity of such universality. For, aside from some considerations of a "positive, realistic conception of the art" proper to a postwar generation, it leads to our being told that by rejoining the classic spirit Stravinsky "adds the final link that closes the cycle of evolution, always the same under its special appearance in every century." May we not attempt to find a less conventionally feeble explanation?

I should be inclined to think that this *return* has technical as well as esthetic causes. In an earlier essay,[1] I said that Stravinsky's weakness resides in the inconsequence—call it the inconsistency—of his vocabulary: having exhausted a certain number of expedients intended to palliate the tonal breakdown, but not having discovered a syntax, he found himself greatly deprived. It is usually in such periods of disarray that one notes immense nostalgias for lost paradises—let me say, more prosaically, regrets for salutary comforts. Incapable by himself of reaching the coherence of a language other than the tonal one, and frightened by that impotence. Stravinsky dropped the unwisely attempted struggle and began to employ his expedients—which became arbitrary and gratuitous gestures intended to delight the already "perverted" ear—in a vocabulary for which he was not responsible. Let us say that he transferred the responsibility. Is it necessary to add that such a masquerade is to be found in his instrumentations—as varied as they are small in value, though always impeccably carried out? Up to here, I have been discussing only the powerlessness of the vocabulary. But it would be equally proper to point out that until then Stravinsky did not know how to "compose," properly speaking. The great works like *Le Sacre* and *Les Noces* were compacted by juxtaposition, repetition, or successive superimpositions, procedures clearly of limited bearing. Perhaps it was the need for an architecture of imbrecation (and not of juxtaposition), the need for an architecture-function, which led Stravinsky to discover the formal virtues of classicism—that is, the ternary form, the sonata form, and all the familiar repertoire of musical scholasticism. And let me add that if those architectures were clearly functional in the works in which they were created, the use of them a posteriori clearly has deprived them of any trace whatever of necessity.

Do these technical debits suffice to explain the declarations cited above about "pure music"? It does not seem so: further-

[1] "Trajectories." —ED. See page 242.

more, it is clear that almost all of Stravinsky's works—in any case, his major works—up to his neoclassic period were in response to a spectacle or at least to a literary text. And when one tallies the instability of the tendencies that come to light in *Petrushka, Le Sacre, Le Rossignol, Les Noces, Histoire du soldat,* one realizes that the illusion of "pure music" appeared as the sole prop of an activity organized afterward. Those constant declarations about music's impotence to "express," that desire to refer constantly to abstraction, to construction in itself, to the play of forms—could they be merely a vexed reaction to a series of works that did nothing but "express," and in the most extreme way?

A reaction, one may suppose, whose technical or esthetic anteriority is very difficult to discern. But the most amusing element in that adventure is having taken Bach as the model "bachelor of pure musics" in the limited sense in which the term clearly was intended. For Bach, one should not forget, wrote the Passions. Furthermore, his contemporaries—whose testimony we can trust to give us a notion of that epoch's musical sensibility [2]—reproached him for the violence of his sentiments, the excess of his "Gothic" genius. In turn, I could cite Johann Gotthilf Ziegler, who wrote in 1746: "My master, Kapellmeister Bach, who is still alive, taught me to play the chorale in such a way that I do not play chorales simply as such, but according to the feeling indicated by the words." For the rest, I gladly say that to me it seems narrow—if not mistaken or misunderstanding—to think of Bach solely as a particularly balanced product of formalism; for it seems evident—even in the Variations on "*Vom Himmel hoch*" or *Die Kunst der Fuge*—that the formal beauty is not alone in engendering the emotion. I am not pleased by the too fantastic interpretations of Pirro and Schweitzer of a Bach inordinately expressionistic and symbolistic, but I still cannot subscribe to

[2] Which does not at all signify that I give those *impressions* the character of a value judgment.—P. B.

an ultrarationalistic conception of him. For the rest, the problem of "form" has been clearly evaluated by Boris de Schloezer in a passage—a very important one, I think—in his *Introduction à Jean-Sébastien Bach*, in which he demonstrates the vanity of formal objectivity.

Musical literature offers us many examples of works in which the means that composers habitually employ to confer logic and coherence upon their productions, to weld together the various phases so that they may seem necessary, so as to render their unity easily perceptible—in which these means, I say, turn out to be inoperative.

Therefore, then, a well-organized work . . . is not necessarily well composed—that is to say, composed in conformity to the rules of the genre; and, on the other hand, a work correctly and even ably composed (judicious use of procedures meant to reinforce the compositional unity) is not necessarily well organized. It often happens that the perfection of the concrete forms demands that the artist sacrifice the schema and obliges him to renounce symmetry, the periodic return of motifs, and other like artifices. If, out of timidity, routine, respect for tradition, lack of confidence in his creative power, he refuses . . . he ends up with a scholastic conception of form which, for failure to distinguish between form and formula, between organization and composition, treats form as an inert thing, as a world indifferent to what is put into it. Therefore so many fragmentarily significant and moving works, works in which the musical thought is not in accord with the construction . . . In that case, so-called thematic analysis is nothing but a snare.

I have cited Boris de Schloezer at length because his text seems to me the best indictment there is of both the neoclassicists and the "disciples" of dodecaphony, who are so generous with exhaustive assurance in a particularly inconsequential certainty about form.

But before facing the problem of "dodecaphonic classicism," I must see whether Berg's position, which places Bach and Schoenberg in parallel positions—a point of view echoed by René Leibowitz in his *Introduction à la musique de douze sons*—is valid simply from the historic point of view. (For I think it entirely illusory if it deals with Bach as an individual in comparison with Schoenberg as an individual.) They would have us believe that Bach's position between the modal and tonal worlds is identical to Schoenberg's position between the tonal and dodecaphonic concepts: just as some references to the modes will be found in Bach, so one will see Schoenberg essaying the synthesis of tonality and dodecaphonism. One quickly detects that this seductive, reassuring view of the spirit is partially false.

When Bach steps into the musical world, the tonal language is already completely constituted: in Germany, Buxtehude, Pachelbel, Kuhnau are its direct predecessors; in Italy, Corelli and, above all, Vivaldi. Bach brings no new element to this working tool, but he raises it to its optimum productivity. If he reaches back to the Renaissance, that is because of his taste for complex polyphony, not because of any element in his morphology or syntax. He does not live—in the way in which we read it in Riemann—"in a transitional epoch," unless it is in considering—and there is no lack of this—harmonic functions as the only proper expansion of the tonal language. (This does not at all explain Mozart and Beethoven as contrapuntalists; but then, one considers their efforts destructive interludes, a view that resolves the discontinuous phenomena by situating them between abusively arbitrary parentheses.) It is precisely because Bach has at hand a syntactical and morphological organization that is not transitory, but perfectly established—the theoretical works of Rameau are its contemporary transcription—that he can concentrate completely on the possibilities of productivity implied by that organization. In one sense, we can consider *Das wohltemperirte Clavier* and its preludes and fugues on the twelve semitones, as well as Bach's works in general, less a manifestation of conquest than a manifestation of *extension*—of occupation, if that word had not been spoiled. For if the forms that his precursors used—prelude, fugue, chorale, recitative, aria, etc.—had made evident a structuration proper to tonality (in particular the tonic-dominant dominant-tonic relations, modulations to the relative and to nearby keys, loans to the subdominant), Bach brought to that structuration a precise perfection and an enlargement that would play a preponderant role in the stabilization of musical forms. (Bithematicism itself is included here: the trio sonatas and the big organ preludes.) Only Beethoven's last works put this heritage in doubt; still, they had no immediate consequences.

Schoenberg, on the contrary, is the very model of a search for language. Arriving during a period of dissolution, he pushed that breaking-up to its extreme result: "suspension" of the tonal language. That expression—which I borrow from René Leibowitz—seems to me, in fact, to fit better than "atonal" language, for it points to Schoenberg's first wish, which is to "avoid" tonality, differentiating it from the second, constructive phase of his thinking. Schoenberg's work thus rests on two elevations separated by seven years of silence. Which certainly does not mean that the two elevations are unconnected, as many well-intentioned spirits would have us suppose. Unlike Bach's work, Schoenberg's departs in search of a new constitution for the sound-world; and I believe that this is truly his principal and only virtue. An important discovery, as important as any in the story of the morphological evolution of music. For the true measure of the Schoenberg phenomenon cannot be taken from the fact of his having instituted a rational organization of chromaticism by means of the twelve-tone series; rather, it seems to me, it must be taken from the fact of his institution of the serial principle itself, a principle that could, I should gladly be inclined to think, rule a sound-world of intervals more complex than the semitone. For just as the modes or the tonalities engender not only musical morphologies, but also—out of them—syntax and forms, so the serial principle also conceals new morphologies departing from that new distribution of the sound-space, in which the idea of sound itself comes to occupy the preponderant position—a new syntax and specific new forms. I must admit freely that I find nowhere in Schoenberg a consciousness of the serial principle as generative, of serial FUNCTIONS properly speaking, but only of their embryonic state—for example, the use of the four possible variants of a series; the use of regions common to series; organization inside the series of selected spaces. In Berg, furthermore, that consciousness appears rarely; one can cite as the sharpest examples of that state of mind the *allegro misterioso* of the *Lyrische Suite* and the metamorphosis of the initial series in *Lulu*. (This is inquiry, not indictment.) With Webern, on the other hand, the SOUND-CLARITY is achieved by the birth of the structure out of the material. I am speaking of the fact that the architecture of the work derives directly from the ordering of the series. To say it another way, schematically, whereas Berg and Schoenberg in some manner limit the role of serial writing to the semantic level of the idiom—the invention of elements that will be combined by a nonserial rhetoric—with Webern the role of that writing is understood as extending to the rhetoric itself. It is with Webern, then, that there irrupt into the acquired sensibility the first elements of a kind of musical thought irreducible to the fundamental schemata of earlier sound-worlds. Here one seems to be dealing with a basic change comparable to what the passage from monodic to polyphonic must have been—that is, with a radically new concept of the utilizable sound-space. Whereas melody remained the fundamental element in the very interior of polyphony, one now can say that with the serial system the polyphonic element itself becomes the basic element. In fact, to an ordering that had to take account of harmonic relationships (vertical) in order to organize monodic elements (horizontal), there succeeds a universe in which the structural laws are based on the relations among polyphonies conceived as distributions of sound determined by the utilizable sound-space; one result of which is the fact that this manner of thinking transcends notions of vertical and horizontal. It is remarkable to see Webern preoccupied as early as his nonserial works with the functional use of intervals (*Bagatelles* for string quartet), whereas with Schoenberg the dodecaphonic principle appears instead to come from ultrathematization (third piece of opus 23). One realizes that the two procedures can be essentially antinomic; one also sees why, having met in the series itself, they can only diverge within the new organization. Webern, moreover, because of his firm determination to observe rigorous purity and tactical modesty, will never attempt—as Schoenberg the deceiver and Berg the prestidigitator attempted—aleatory syntheses of the tonal language and the serial principle, with the latter taking the former into account. One should emphasize, then, the fact that the significance of Webern's *oeuvre*, the reason for its being historic, independent of its indisputable intrinsic value—is its introduction of a new manner of musical "being."

It becomes evident that the parallel between Bach and Schoenberg is devoid of any real significance. Were there place for such a comparison, it could be only with Webern. Considering the respective positions of Bach and Webern—the one in relation to the tonal language, the other with regard to the serial language—one could state that they were situated symmetrically; we could even borrow from geometry the word "antiparallel" to define more exactly the relationships that could be conceived between Bach and Webern. The former displays chiefly an activity of extension, as I remarked above; the latter is involved essentially in the conquest of a new world.

That, at the present time, one has been able to engage in such an adventure leads one to reflect upon the reality of works that, at the same time, accept as their only justification the maintenance at whatever cost, by a fluke, of a mode of thought transmitted and received with a priori submissiveness. Aside from the inherited technique that Webern leaves us, one should, then, take account of that passionate determination to install a constantly questioned musical order, a fact that does not appear to have been understood very clearly by the dodecaphonic "disciples," whether "classicizers" or "neoclassicizers." It allows us to use these disharmonious terms—for these tendencies, both inspired by a taste for comfort, do not deserve more agreeable terms.

The phenomenon common to the two tendencies, in fact, is that species of nostalgia which is nourished toward a "universal" language. A nostalgia of another order, for—as I remarked at the beginning of this essay—the one leads to a false reconstitution, the other to an arbitrary parallelism. Well, can a "universal" language be established now?

By means of "neoclassicism"? One scarcely needs to deny it, given the total gratuity of the game thus played, its historical necessity not being at all evident. The distracting sudden movements—as distracted as distracting—from Bach to Tchaikovsky, from Pergolesi to Mendelssohn, from Beethoven to the Renaissance polyphonists, mark off the steps toward an eclectic, miserable insolvency without the smallest embryo of a language being forced into birth. Intellectual laziness, pleasure taken as an end in itself—or, if one wishes, a morose hedonism—we can agree that one would not find serious tools for such research in them; they have produced the result that might have been foretold.

Much more difficult to grasp is the aspect of dodecaphonic "classicism." Let us try to analyze it in the behavior of Berg and Schoenberg. I spoke earlier, apropos of Webern, of tactical modesty, which I understand in relation to the complexity of the work. Said otherwise, I mean that in order to be able to think out the problems of polyphonic writing as developing from the serial principles, Webern was obliged somehow to "limit" the problems of structure and invention (relative brevity of the works, wholly relative simplicity of the musical material, clarity of the architecture; as he succeeds in his enterprise, he employs material of greater richness, a more complex rhetoric; the proportions become larger). On the other hand, Berg and Schoenberg, once the serial principles are established, pass at once to the building of musical works at least as complex as the works that preceded them. And that naturally leads them to lean upon principles of composition anterior to those of the serial technique (sonata form, rondo, or such preclassical forms as gigue, passacaglia, chorale)—serial writing being considered as a consolidation and codification of chromaticism and as a possibility of uniting the separate sections of the musical discourse through a sort of smaller common denominator. In a certain sense, the principle of serial writing here is at the service of musical thought that disavows nothing of the anterior mentality that gave it birth. (The limiting cause, evidently, is the tonal language reconstituted inside the series.) There we find an artful overlapping of presumption and timidity. Presumption, certainly, that desire to set out swiftly upon the business of aiming at the big form immediately, with all of its inherent complexity, but in a language whose articulative means still are ill defined. Timidity no less, for to give the new language a pre-established support that was put into play outside it is not to display great confidence in its specific properties. (With Berg, one even notices the intention of opposing a serial structure, properly speaking, to a nonserial structure. Thus the third movement of the *Lyrische Suite* is formed as a nonserial structure—*trio estatico*—flanked by two serial structures—the *allegro misterioso* and its retrograde. In an opposite sense, the fifth movement also has such an opposition as its basis. This can even lead to a generalization about the movements themselves: second and fourth movements, nonserial, in relation to the first and sixth movements, serial. One even is driven to the ambiguity of writing dodecaphonic variations on themes belonging to the frankest tonality. Thus, in Schoenberg's opus 29, the third movement is built on a popular melody; in Berg's Violin Concerto, too, we find the scherzo amalgamating a popular theme and dodecaphonic variations on a Bach chorale. The most extreme manifestation of this state of mind goes so far as to try reintegrating tonal functions within the dodecaphonic technique, as I have already said. This same Berg Violin Concerto, for example, is based on a characteristic oscillation from a minor tonality to its relative major (G minor—B-flat major). Beginning with his "American" period, Schoenberg showed great instability, a hesitation between a more or less purely dodecaphonic determination and a more or less frankly avowed tendency toward tonality.

To compare that wavering position to the modal reminiscences that can be found in Bach seems to me an exaggeration, to say the least. For Bach's use of certain Gregorian *cantus firmus* (the first three "Catechism" chorales of Part III of the *Clavierübung*, for example) is not comparable in importance to Schoenberg's hesitation. In those chorales, the tonal functions are firmly established; they are even contrary to the mode implied by the *cantus firmus*. At the beginning of this century, the modal purists—Vincent d'Indy and Maurice Emmanuel, among others—remarked on that fact more or less acrimoniously; all the modal notes that do not form part of the corresponding tonality are treated as *modulating*. That is to note, justly, the strength with which Bach imposed the tonal functions until they destroyed the characteristic of plain chant; the method followed in certain of Schoenberg's dodecaphonic works is exactly the opposite: they take procedures of tonal writing into account and impose them upon the serial principle. Bach's tonal language corrodes the modal functions; tonal functions corrode Schoenberg's dodecaphonic language. Here one encounters again the antiparallelism of situation which I mentioned earlier. Here, too, we find again that mélange of presumption and timidity with regard to the serial principle which presides over these eclectic syntheses; a strange need, in any case, for reassurance about the potential of the new language through proof that it is capable of remaining aware of the world that it just has left.

It is no part of my intention to discuss the psychology that lies behind such a need. I limit myself to asserting that such a persistence of old habits of thought with the new means of expression is one element of a transitional attitude; and that this attitude, linked as it is to composers incarnating that transition, is bound to disappear when the situation is clarified. It is logical, in effect, that a new syntax, a new rhetoric, and a new sensibility should correspond to a new morphology. "Dodecaphonic classicism," then, is unthinkable and carries its own defeat in the incoherence that brought it into being.

Should one, then, forget even the face of the past for that reason? On the contrary, I think that a work revealed as necessary is rich as much beacuse of its realization as because of the eventuality that it may enclose. That is the way I regard Bach, certain of whose traits are particularly dear to me because they seem to me more effective than others—without my therefore wanting to give that preference the value of a criterion.

In the very first place, my taste for the contribution of Bach's writing to the architectural phenomenon is manifest. (A century of romanticism has turned us away from this problem, and Debussy himself is not exempt—how much not!—from that lack of interest.) With Bach, in fact, one can consider the canons, the imitations, not as simple artifices of writing, but as generators of the structure: the variations for organ on the chorale "*Von Himmel hoch*"—called the "Mizler Variations"—are the most astonishing example. The progressive complexity of the canonic structure, the progressive increase in the number of real parts, the increasing difficulty of the canons, the procedure of augmentation—that is to say, the rhythmic progression—and, finally, the renewal in the disposition of the canons within a single variation and their disposition in *stretti* define the architecture of this chorale. Therefore one sees the rigor and the necessity with which these variations are linked together—thanks solely to the writing and to a superimposed structure from which the schema can be abstracted.

I should like to emphasize equally the chorale "*Vor Deinen Thron tret'ich hiermit,*" which Bach dictated some days before his death. Everyone has noted its exceptional contrapuntal richness. One could not indicate more clearly that the structure of the chorale melody engenders the structure of the chorale itself. This chorale, in fact, is made up of four *sequences*—developments corresponding to the four members of the melodic phrase. Let us notice that each of these four sequences utilizes as the contrapuntal element only the fragment of the figured chorale within it, and that therefore we are dealing with an entirely special technique of development which is reinforced by the writing: a technique that rejects any useless figure and occupies itself exclusively (thanks to the multiple resources of the counterpoint—imitations, inversions, augmentations) with the phrase that it develops; that is to say, all automatism is excluded. Let me sum up by saying that here the "theme" engenders all the sound-figures of its development and its own architecture, the second flowing from the first.

I think that with these two chorales I have defined what is most necessary for us to look for in Bach's work—that is to say, a technique of form, powerfully unitarian, of uterine relationship between the writing itself and the architecture. The form is essentially variable and is put to the question in each work. (Let us recall in this regard the statement often made, that even fixed forms are presented by Bach under extremely various aspects: no two fugues, for example, have identical plans.)

Finally, I should like to point out a particularly astonishing aspect of Bach which I find best described in François Florand's *Jean-Sébastien Bach:*

> In constructing a movement, Bach came to prefer a means that consists of developing the concert of the voices without going out-

side the *tessiture* that he had assigned them in the beginning, keeping them as though by force within the same limits—never more than an octave for each part—and leading to a progression that had come entirely from the melodic current itself, a little like a stream that one sees increasing without apparent external cause, without affluents or glaciers or storms, solely by the contributions of mysterious subterranean springs. This is something different from a simple esthetic of repetitions in the Oriental and Hindu manners. It is a procedure very personal to Johann Sebastian Bach, which is formed of an interior accumulation of energy, of emotional force, to the point at which the composer and listener are saturated as though intoxicated.

François Florand also speaks of Bach's disposition toward musical intoxication: "One surely should not," he adds, "search for anything brutal or gross. But in the end a moment arrives at which, by dint of his having turned and returned his motif, the composer's head seems to turn. *Es schwindelt* . . . And this is the apex of his work." He defines this musical "vertigo" as an "interior fermentation of the polyphony itself." He concludes this analysis by demanding that we not forget that Bach's "delirium" is "lucid, his intoxication conscious, his abdications deliberate and always contained within the background of the creative consciousness by a will and an intelligence that never for a second sleep." (I would add that I have found similar intoxication in Webern when he is caught up in a single registration from which his polyphony seems unable to escape because of the purity of his writing; the exposition in the first movement of the *Symphonie*, opus 21, the second movement of the Piano Variations, opus 27, and the exposition in the second movement of the String Quartet, opus 28, are notable in this regard.)

In Bach's many-faceted work, these are my preferences. It nonetheless remains impossible to associate oneself with the undertakers who have used Bach as a guarantee of their gravedigging activities, thanks to more or less gross misunderstanding. How believe in these prophets of a "return to" or various "reactivations," when their most evident aim is security, their moving principle a want of courage? If, furthermore, one must reject neoclassicism in the name of a historic dialectic, one cannot, by referring to it, encourage a tendency toward a new "collective" style, the ably prepared camouflage of a pointless academicism. Whether one is pleased or not, it is not possible to reintegrate the collective domain, properly speaking, with what we call the classical style, for it would be illogical, to say the least, to make an abstraction of the violent individualism that came to light more than a century ago. Furthermore, in adopting such conduct, one considers the phenomena of the evolution only superficially when one assimilates them in a continuity of successive acquisitions that have established a tradition. That seems not to take account of the discontinuity of the evolution, in the sense that the necessary work, the consolidation of that living tradition, cannot be foreseen by it, but integrates itself with it and justifies it a posteriori. (Webern was not foreseeable; in order to live usefully after him, one does not continue him: one must dispense with him. The eventual writers of dodecaphonic grammars will take off from his work to display their own lacks of strength.) Amid semblances of logic in which we shall be able, by means of apriorisms devoid of critical intelligence, by means of a "tradition" of go and stop resulting from all the more or less shameful causes—in the midst of these contemptible activities of the needy in quest of "authenticity," we shall finally restore its potential to what Mallarmé called the *Hasard.*

We are indebted to the poet for that famous phrase: "One does not make verses with ideas, but with words"—a phrase that, taken literally, has served as a pretext for all compromises. But that is no reason to forget that:

Toute pensée émet un coup de dés.[3]

[3] Literally, "Every thought gives forth a cast of the dice." —TRANS.

Today's Searchings

Enlightened manifestoes cannot pretend to be objects of great delight; as to professions of faith, they may have no imperative except to deceive those who embrace them.

And to what does this preamble relate? To current discussions about music.

What do these discussions deal with? Articles of faith. One believes or does not believe in the "system." The commentary is deployed; "technique" becomes a screen, the wished-for protection from questions that it is extremely delicate to face.

The chief word around which all these skirmishes take place—how ridiculous a word—is dodecaphony; it clearly displays its garden of Greek roots. But it is very vague—twelve tones, with an approximate manner of using them. More precisely, then: the series.

What is dodecaphony? What is the series? The explainers vie with one another; they give examples; they establish relationships with classical definitions of counterpoint. And after that? Armed with that police card, one could add to it: Distinguishing mark: nullity . . .

In our illuminated era—what is . . . what is . . . —we do not hold dear the work born of perpetual assertions, of serene historical comparisons or elucidations with scientific tendencies. "*Quel siècle à mains!*"

If, in the words of a distinguished old humorist, we should "subvert the poetic exhalation"? . . .

In the meantime, is it to be believed that music is made of notes? Certainly . . . The art of sounds . . . But one already has discussed at length the new hierarchy enthroned by the three Viennese of illustrious memory. We should so much love to get out of this specialized domain and play truant, even though we should be blamed, and to remind ourselves that we are, after all, only musicians.

Our "art," then, has undergone—one begins to understand—a technical overthrow of which only a minority of the consequences is now in play. One must admit that a composer's position is not all repose; the problems present themselves, all at once, in a way that does not brook evasion. The writing, properly speaking, in its most elementary though most inescapable stage: form, in which deception inevitably means catastrophe; instrumental realization, the indispensable condition if there is one.

Certain acquisitions having been made precise in these domains, it seems that now—after these acquisitions and as a result of them—we are faced with new demands that are more difficult to satisfy because they are infinitely more subtle, being linked in a less showy, less secure way to the famous "technique." Not everything is for the best in the realm of the series . . .

Contemporary painting rejects the anecdote; that is understood; music also, fraternally. How avoid the exhausting monotony of the abstract productions that overwhelm painting and music in our day? Lack of personality? Certainly. The encephalitis of the somnambulists on their high wires is evident. But we are fastidious in unmasking that sterile mannerism. The chosen masters are excellent; the negative conclusions deduced from contact with them are above reproach; neither good will nor the desire to do good is lacking . . .

Let us go back to music itself . . . The chief elected predecessor: Webern; the essential object of the investigations into him: organization of the sound-material. One reaches certain conclusions and hastens to exploit them by amplification; one rushes frenetically into organization; one senses unexploited worlds in one's ear—the Promised Land or Babel would scarcely be misplaced comparisons. Webern had organized nothing but pitch; one organizes rhythm, timbre, dynamics; everything is fodder for that monstrous polyvalent organization, the volume of which must be lowered quickly unless one wishes to be condemned to deafness. One will soon perceive that compoistion and organization cannot be confused—something that Webern himself never dreamed of doing—under pain of maniacal inanity.

Nevertheless, despite arithmetical excesses, one has acquired certain "punctual" functions of sound—let us use the term in the sense of discovering diverse functional possibilities at a given point. What has led to this "punctual" style? The justified rejection of thematism. That was, however, to give a slightly naïve solution to the problem of composition itself—charging a simple hierarchy with substituting in the role formerly played by thematic relations. Those relations are specific, whereas the sound-hierarchy by itself is highly ineffective because it includes all the possibilities. Utilized in its rough state, that hierarchy can give—during a passing utilization—an impression of "weightlessness," which will take on its full value when one opposes it to other managed structures.

This "punctual" style presents another considerable inconvenience. The structural plans renew themselves in parallel fashion identically; at each new pitch, a new duration affected by a new intensity. The perpetual variation—on the surface—has engendered a total absence of variation on a more general level. An exasperating monotony has taken possession of the musical work, putting all the means of renewal into play at each moment.

Let me also point out in parentheses that the confidently adopted series do not take into account a phenomenon of perception that is extremely important: many arithmetic phenomena are perceived logarithmically, whereas logarithmic phenomena—among others, intervals, durations, and intensities—may be perceived arithmetically.

The anecdote—the theme—having been rejected as referring to a method of composition that contradicts the current hierarchy, how—and on what basis—are we to articulate development? In general, by certain transformations of primitive *données*, quantitative or qualitative transformations, renewal of means being a constant demand. About these transformations the question was posed: are they perceptible? Always the same argument, the same doubts, from the *ars nova* through *Die Kunst der Fuge* to the Viennese: accusations of esotericism have played a large part. However, it will not do to see only certain rigorous works in the history of music, to the detriment of all the others; that would be to falsify singularly the equilibrium of musical creation. Asceticism serves no purpose except that of masking or misleading the imagination—pious crutches.

Now the great effort in the domain proper to us is that of seeking a dialectic that will establish each moment of a composition between a rigorous total structure and a momentary structure submissive to free will. Let me make a summary acoustical comparison. The timbre of a sound results chiefly from the distribution of its harmonics; these harmonics are distributed in groups that are more or less important because of their relationships to the fundamental tone in intensity and pitch. One calls these the "constituents" of a timbre. Can not one envisage the "constituents" of a work? Related, certainly, to the organization of the sound-universe native to the work, but not depending upon it at all? Nothing would less resemble a "theme," for a theme consists of particularities already integrated. However, the "constituents"—particularities not integrated—would be responsible for the work's physiognomy, for its unique character. Whereas, by the law of large numbers, in confiding oneself to the organization one can only return to chance.

Just as certain painters want a canvas to be a flat surface to cover with nonfigurative signs, but also use their ingenuity to find a new idea corresponding to the abolished "perspective," so must music discover a new way to distribute the developments in a work without appealing for it to the formal ideas and "architecture" of the past.

A parenthesis on this subject: Debussy's last works—at least, certain of them—will be almost more astonishing than the final works of Webern as pointers along such a road.

What one does not want in these quests, above all, is a "return" to perspective or to architecture; we want to have recourse to entirely new ideas; neoclassicism's resounding failures have put us on guard with sufficient brutality to preserve us from any temptation to re-begin such a mockery.

These reflections on the composition of the musical work make me hope for a new poetics, a different way of listening. Perhaps it is precisely at this point that music manifests its greatest lag in relation, for example, to poetry. Neither the Mallarmé of the "*coup de dés*" nor Joyce was paralleled by anything in the music of their epoch. Is it sensible or absurd to use these points of comparison this way? (If one thinks of what they loved: the one, Wagner, the other, Italian opera and Irish songs . . .)

Although I do not want to refer too closely to their investigations, they having dealt with language, to see them as having been marked by a search for a new musical poetics is not illusory.

Even when the most essential contemporary works reject formal classical schemes, they do not really abandon at all a general idea of form which has not varied since the development of tonality. A musical work is made up of a series of separate movements; each of them is homogeneous in both structure and tempo; it is a closed circuit (a characteristic of Occidental musical thought); balance among its different movements is established by a dynamic distribution of tempos. The exception of the finale of the Ninth Symphony—but that is, above all, a citation! The generative themes of a work: Debussy's *La Mer*, a subtle example; there is nevertheless an integration of the generative themes with the homogeneous time of a movement. Berg, finally—*Wozzeck*, the *Lyrische Suite*, principally—manifests an obsession with citations from one movement to another; in *Wozzeck*, the dramatic action demands them; in the *Lyrische Suite*, a sort of imaginary dramatic action.

For the moment, I merely want to suggest a musical work in which this separation into homogeneous movements will be abandoned in favor of nonhomogeneous distribution of developments. I demand for music the right to parentheses and italics . . . ; a notion of discontinuous time, thanks to structures that will be bound together rather than remaining divided and airtight; finally, a sort of development in which the closed circuit will not be the only solution envisaged.

I want the musical work not to be that series of compartments which one must inevitably visit one after the other; I try to think of it as a domain in which, in some manner, one can choose one's own direction.

Utopias? Let us realize . . . exactly the time to pulverize certain already ancient habits.

As for grammar and pedantries, I shall always abstain from them—isn't proselytizing exasperating?

Corruption in the Censers

Ouïs toute la lumière
Qu'y soufflera Debussy . . .

If we separate these lines from their specific reference to the *Prélude*, we shall have the most striking enunciation of Debussy's role in the music of his times. This point of view may remain linked to extramusical considerations: no sense in denying that! Despite that, it will not do to overlook the fact that one of the forces driving Debussy was Mallarmé—symbolism aside—and that some of the poet's vertiginous attainments still have not been caught up with. We cannot forget that Debussy's time was also that of Cézanne, whose scope is still measured prudently—impressionism aside. Ought we, for these reasons, to establish a Debussy-Cézanne-Mallarmé reality at the root of all modernity? One would gladly have recourse to such an undertaking if it did not have a slightly autarchic character. After those three illustrious men, other illustrious men appeared and upset things in the showiest way.

Contemporary truth—or creation—has demanded violence almost as its proof: necessary surface shocks that have profoundly modified its various re-beginnings. Fashioned by means of abrupt proposals, a new configuration has arisen, but one has been prey to strange surprises in the relief and the revolution; in the beginning one remains skeptical about the fact that these brusque, brutal mutations have kept us unaware of changes felt less immediately, but more upsetting in the long run. Symbolism was dissipated by Apollinaire, then by the surrealist revolution; cubism was set at nought by Cézanne; the bassoon of *Le Sacre* replaced the flute of the *Faune* while *Pelléas* was emigrating from Paris to Vienna. Meanwhile, the bolts of the "*coup de dés*" set certain surrealist flashes vibrating for pallid people; the *Montagnes Sainte-Victoire* preserves a haughtier, more secret prestige than most of the avatars of cubism and abstraction; finally, when bristling barbarisms have been weakened and the paroxysms of hypnosis mitigated, the resonance emanating from *Jeux* continues to seem obstinately mysterious.

That Debussy-Cézanne-Mallarmé reality? A "luminosity" that withstands refraction by any prism of simple analysis. They are "outside." What do they show us? Perhaps this: that their revolution must be not only constructed, but also dreamed.

Shock in return for certain conquests in the realm of creation: audacious madmen mingle in a curious conservatism; in reverse, a not very rebellious holder of the line establishes a novelty that some lustra keep outside assimilation. Happily or unhappily, history is not a well-greased toboggan; it is not spectacular in the style of those scenic railways rebuilt by bitter workers in closed, mephitic rooms. Let us remember the discontinuity of individuals as well as that of phases of evolution: perhaps a similar point of view accidentally engenders acidity. It does not matter: the face of discovery is mistaken for that of growth or aging. This means that in trying to encompass Debussy's actuality, I shall not make use of the morphological approach, but not because it was a paradox freely introduced, a clever constraint, or a simple tactical ruse. Moreover, we have for some years been sufficiently burdened with compactly opaque morphological studies. One tries a component; one selects that other component; one adds, a thematic is proposed; one adds again, which gives a form; one always adds, a structure results. What will dissolve the monotony and platitude of these hexahedral forms? "Ah let the time come . . ."

Negatively, Debussy? This "*musicien français*," a dimension chosen in the semi-ecstasy of a wartime patriotism and which one dreams of lessening. Nothing remains of it but a legion of ambitions tasting of nationalist ashes from which the semi-ecstasy has evaporated; after Couperin and Rameau, the epigoni have discovered, in the proper time and place, Marc-Antoine Charpentier and Lalande. Miserable recourses! No longer an "impressionist," that label which remains vexatiously implanted on his misshapen forehead. The misunderstanding has risen from epithets, often, and from the fact that "Monsieur Croche spoke of an orchestral score as of a picture": a simple question of antidilettantism. In fact, the "impression" is dissipated by the "*Clavecin*."

On the other hand, Debussy remains that force of refusal opposed to the Schola. He is for the "sounding alchemy," wildly, furiously opposed to "the beaver's technique." That position remains an actuality that is not contradicted by our venerated *d'indouilles*, our *indouilles-witz*, or our *indouilles-mith*.[1]

In depth or in relief, these stipplings mark the outside dimensions of a more subtle teaching. We shall try to propagate that subtlety by breathing it in three directions: determined autodidacticism; modernism; a break in the Occidental circle.

The autodidact is formidable because in him and through him an uncertain will to power is working on the basis of lacunae and ignorance; this sort of autodidact, an original, perpetually discovers certain simple academicisms, to his own astonishment. More than that the procedure permits a naïve and

[1] These portmanteau-pun words are untranslatable. *Indouille* signifies a variety of pork and, by extension, an imbecile. Thus, "*d'indouille*" criticizes Vincent d'Indy, "*indouille-witz*" René Leibowitz, and "*indouille-mith*" Paul Hindemith. —TRANS.

flavorful freshness in the sudden prospecting of the banal; it admits of a sterility lacking expedients, an inventiveness based on ruses, anemic inspiration. No, Debussy *knows;* but at the same time he rejects this inherited knowledge and pursues a dream of vitrified improvisation. He is strongly repelled by those shabby constructive jugglings which transform the composer into an infantile architect. For him, form is never *given;* his whole life was a search for the unanalyzable, for development that, even in its procedures, would incorporate the surprises of the imagination. He mistrusted architecture in its petrified sense; he preferred structures that mixed precision and free will. That is why, with him, those words and keys with which teaching saturates us become denuded of sense and object; the habitual mental categories of an exhausted tradition cannot be applied to his work even in an attempt to adjust them at the cost of some torsion. It is what the Ubus, from the lofty perches of their anniversary cathedra, call corrupting morals . . .

Debussy's shades have to drink a bitter hemlock while taking part in the savage debauch of "classicism" which raged after his death; all those ill-tempered clavecins on which were let loose an orgy of fugues, variations, sonatas, and still other things!—forms that, always in relation to that damned impressionism, were said to be "constructed." In that great withdrawal to the torches of history, did not Debussy himself hold aloft for an instant a dubious torch salvaged from the accessories of weary youth? Certainly there was some trace of "pre-Raphaelitism" in that love which made him attach himself to Villon and Charles d'Orléans; but that *poetic* deviation did not in any way unite him to the later "constructors." No considerations of style, certainly, furnish us with the justification of the *title "Hommage à Rameau";* at most, the musical content is "in the style of a Saraband, but without strictness . . ."

Must what Debussy did, being incommensurable with all academicism, incompatible with all experienced order, with all disposition not created instantaneously—must that doing remain a foreign body in the music of the Occident, having remained there, impermeable in its later developments: a veritable mercury bath? One sees too clearly what has caused that isolation: Debussy rejects every hierarchy not found implicated in the musical instant. With him, and often, the significance of musical time changes, above all in his last works. Thus the creation of his technique, his vocabulary, his form led him to the total overthrow of notions that had remained static up to his time: the unstable, the instant, irrupt into music; not only the impression of the momentary, of the fugitive, to which it has been reduced, but also really an irreversible relative conception of musical time, of the musical universe more generally. For in the organization of sounds, that conception, translated as a rejection of existing harmonic hierarchies, was the only *donnée* of the facts of sound; the relations of object to object are established in a context following inconstant functions. As for the rhythmic writing, it participates equally in a like manifestation with the same will toward variability in the metrical conception, just as the solicitude for an adequate timbre will profoundly modify the instrumental writing, the instrumental combination the sonority of the orchestra. The courage of willing to be an autodidact forced Debussy to rethink all the aspects of musical creation; doing that, he carried out a radical, though not always spectacular, revolution. The two portraits of M. Croche testify to that endowment. In black: "They salute you with sumptuous epithets, and you are only a rogue"; in white: "One must seek discipline in liberty and not in the formulas of a philosophy that has become decrepit and good for the weak." An undeniable offense in the eyes of the lumpish constructors. Nothing was promulgated. Behold, nevertheless, the most fascinating chimera.

Another Debussyan chimera, no less troubling: modernity in the sense that Baudelaire attached to the word. Will this criterion perhaps be found very trivial? "It is an immutable fact that after a knife has sliced a fruit, its segments never will be rejoined." Evidence: after the flute of the *Faune* or the English horn of *Nuages*, music has breathed differently. It is equally just to point out that with Mussorgsky, principally the Mussorgsky of *The Nursery* and *The Marriage*, modernity irrupted vigorously. Of what does it consist? That question is not easy to answer precisely. "Modernity," Baudelaire says, "is the transitory, the fugitive, the contingent, that half of art of which the other half is the eternal and the immutable." With Debussy, it remains in close contact with the form of his music, a form tied to the instant, as we have seen. It remains curious, moreover, to realize how, writing of *The Nursery*, Debussy defined himself with strange precision. I transcribe: ". . . it resembles the art of an enquiring savage discovering music step by step through his emotions; nor is it ever a question of any particular form; or, at all events, that form is so multiple that it cannot be related to established—one should say administrative—forms; it struggles toward birth by means of successive minute touches mysteriously held together by a mysterious connection and by a gift of luminous clairvoyance."

If one wanted to interest oneself in discovering the sources of that modernity in music, Mussorgsky aside, one would doubtless have to turn to the painters and poets whose influence over the young Debussy's emerging spirit was preponderant: Manet, Whistler, Verlaine . . . That is to believe that music was saved from the post-Wagnerian engulfment by its hardier, more experienced sisters: the vitality of the painting and poetry of that period in French intellectual life parallel, to a certain degree, the radically new esthetic sense of the Debussyan creation, thanks to which the romantic conflicts were reabsorbed: the unique dress that this music imposes among all the others, as the revelation of an unknown, "modern" sensibility, a condition of all later development.

How insert into the renewal of the sound-world which Debussy proposes the breaking of the occidental circle? This has nothing to do with an exoticism intended to pile up nostalgias for the picturesque at bargain prices. There has been enough commentary on the surprise and impressions that Debussy experienced during the Exposition of 1889 in the Annamite theater—the Javanese dancing, the sonority of the gamelan. Paradoxically, it was the shock of a tradition that was differently, but just as powerfully, codified as the occidental tradition which was to precipitate the new music's rupture with the European elements: one may ask if it is not ignorance of those other conventions which provokes such an impression of freedom. Certainly, the sound-scales are richer in particularities than the European scales of that era, and the rhythmic structures reveal a different suppleness; furthermore, the acoustic power of the instruments themselves differs completely from that of our instruments. However, it is, above all, the poetics of the Far Eastern musics which imposes its corrosive influence. This calls to mind, moreover, the adventure of Van Gogh with the Japanese painters. At the other extreme of the circuit, did not Paul Klee exclaim: "It is necessary to be reborn and to know nothing, absolutely nothing, of Europe"? If one also thinks of Claudel, one becomes aware that Europe was stewing within its hopelessly stabilized confines, that it was growing skeptical about the supremacy of its culture. Since then, this contact with the Orient has not been circumscribed by a banal question of exotic scales or brilliant sonorities. It has united, on one hand, the "modern" direction that esthetics has taken and, on the other, the search for a constantly revivified hierarchy. Strictly conjugated, these three phenomena gave Debussy his irreplaceable physiognomy at the edge of the whole contemporary movement: a certain, solitary position. Debussy remains one of the most isolated of all musicians, and his epoch sometimes forced him into fleeting, feline solutions. Nevertheless, in his incommunicable experience and his sumptuous reserve, this unique, universal Frenchman preserves a hermetic and disturbing power of seduction.

Moved by "that desire always to go farther which for him took the place of bread and wine," he corrupted in advance every attempt to relate to the old order. Yes, thanks be rendered to him, he was a corrupter of musical "good manners" . . . Apropos, did he himself not write that "it is necessary to disdain the bad exhalation of the censers and that in a pinch it is not useless to spit into them"? In short, at the hour of choosing and disorder, he is a famous, an excellent ancestor!

Alea

Notable in several composers of our generation at the present time is a constant preoccupation, not to say obsession, with chance. This is, at least to my knowledge, the first time that this notion has entered Western music, a fact that surely makes it worth while to tarry here a little, for it is too important a bifurcation in the idea of composition for us to underestimate it or unconditionally reject it.

Can one find one's way back to the sources of this obsession? On the exterior, one could suggest various causes not lacking an appearance of solidity, variables according to the temperaments of the different creators. The most elementary form of the transmutation of chance is located in the addition of a philosophy dyed with Orientalism and masking a fundamental weakness in the technique of composition; this would be a recourse against the asphyxia of invention, recourse to a more subtle poison that destroys every embryo of artisanship; I should willingly qualify that experience—if it is one—in which the individual, not feeling responsible for his work, simply throws himself into a puerile magic out of unavowed weakness, out of confusion, for temporary assuagements—I should willingly qualify that experience as chance by inadvertence. Said otherwise, the event arrives as it can, uncontrolled (voluntary absence, though not meritorious, resulting from impotence), BUT inside a certain established network of probable events, it being very necessary for chance to dispose of some sort of contingency. Why, then, choose the network so meticulously rather than leave the network itself to inadvertence? That is what I never have been able to clarify. One plays a half-franc game, but has the merit of never hiding the fact. It is an artificial paradise prettily laid out, in which, I think, the dreams are never very miraculous; this sort of narcotic protects one, in fact, from the sting that all inventiveness inflicts; one should realize that its action is exaggeratedly calming, at times exhilarating, in the image of that described by the amateurs of hashish. Peace to the souls of these angelic beings! One is sure that they will never steal any lightning, that not being what they are up to. Inadvertence is droll to begin with, but it very quickly becomes boring, the more quickly because it is condemned never to renew itself. Our preference, then, uncontestably goes to natural inadvertence, which does not need *instruments* to manifest itself. The "non-art," the "anti-art" still have some reference to the "art," and in our quest, what it has been agreed to name is thus never the center of our efforts. Beauty has been found bitter for some lustra now . . . Let us situate the A-Beauty, the Anti-Beauty, etc., etc., with that intoxicant and toss on some shovelfuls of earth. Chance will do the rest!

However, a more venomous, subtler form of intoxication exists. I have spoken of it several times because that form has continuing life; each time one believes it surmounted, it arises again. Composition desires to reach for the most nearly perfect, the smoothest, the most untouchable objectivity. And by what means? Schematization, simply, takes the place of invention; the imagination—ancillary—strains to give birth to a complex mechanism that is then charged with engendering microscopic and macroscopic structures until the exhaustion of possible combinations has indicated the end of the work. Admirable security and powerful signal of alarm! As for the imagination, it is careful not to intervene along the way: it would trouble the absolute of the developmental *processus*, introducing human error into so perfectly deduced an ensemble; a fetichism of numbers which leads to pure and simple bankruptcy. We are plunged into a statistical display that has no more value than any other. In its All-Objectivity, the work represents—or we dream that it represents—a fragment of chance as justifiable (or as little justifiable) as any other fragment whatever. One perceives the difference from the form described earlier with that new temptation, just as pernicious; there we find more knavery, and the spontaneous avowal of weakness is changed into a distractedly sterile search for the combining strength in an angry rejection of the arbitrary, that new *diabolus in musica.* In the meantime, one arrives at the paradox that the more one flees from that hated and repudiated arbitrary, the more one finds it again. At each moment, objectivity vanishes before your eyes like a sort of irritating, fragile mirage that exhausts and dries up all living force; these slices of chance are unsuitable for consumption because, in the beginning, one asks oneself why one consumes them!

That overt objectivity having failed, one is then driven like a maniac in search of the arbitrary. One is going to search for the devil and then lead him, duly escorted, imprisoned, chained by a thousand snares, to a work that he is to vivify by his omnipresence. The devil will be there, bashful, or he won't be. Did one complain of lack of subjectivity? One is going to have it in every structure, in every note; that ferociously dislocated, dismembered, dispersed subjectivity—it is going to force us to take a part, *hypocrite auditeur*, to be as subjective as the composer. As for the interpreter, it is up to him to transmit to you the demon's assaults; he will compromise you; an interpreter-medium who will be installed as the high officiator of that intellectual diablerie.—What then? Much less sootily than you—hypocrite—may be inclined to suppose. Notation will become sufficiently—but subtly—imprecise, to allow the passage through its mesh—a diagram of a hypothesis—of the interpreter's instantaneous and changing reflection. One *could* prolong this silence, one *could* suspend this sound, one *could* accelerate, one *could* . . . at every moment . . . ; in short, one has chosen henceforth to be meticulous in imprecision.

Do you see whither we are tending? Always to a rejection of choice. The first conception was purely mechanistic, automatic, fetichistic; the second is fetichistic again, but delivers one from choice, not by numbers, but by means of the interpreter. One transfers one's choosing to that of the interpreter. Thus one is wrapped under cover, camouflaged; not very cleverly, though, for the arbitrary or, rather, a superficial arbitrary imposes its presence. What a relief! The hour of choice is postponed again; a superficial subjectivity has been grafted onto an aggressive conception of initial objectivity. No! Chance is too bashful to be diabolic . . .

Between benign parentheses, let us note that a certain analytic procedure has borrowed the same dead ends. A sort of sanctimoniously statistical legal trial has replaced a means of investigation that was more intelligent and more shocking. One uses one's brain as though it were a photoelectric cell selecting various components by specialties: thanks to a formulation of intervals or figures, one registers that the *vice* is as good as the *versa*—which, it must be said, is a poor teaching. As for the composer's choosing, it is done away with in an absence of virtuosity that is painful to watch. How can analysis be confined to vulgar census-taking, gross bookkeeping? Despite the best intentions and the most praiseworthy projects, I have never been able to discern the exact reason for this fear of approaching the real problem of composition. Perhaps the phenomenon is owing equally to a sort of fetichism regarding numerative selection, a position that is not only ambiguous but also totally out of line because it deals with investigation of a work that structurally rejects such procedures, which above all are excessively gross and primary.

Face to face with chance by inadvertence, we thus find

chance by automatism, whether that automatism is desired pure or a notion of supervised bifurcations is introduced into it. Meanwhile, the obsession with what *can* happen is taking the place of what *should* happen, but not owing solely to the feebleness of the means of composition put into play, or solely to a determination to introduce the interpreter's or listener's subjectivity into the inside of the work and thus to create for others the constant need to make instant choices. One could give still other apparent reasons, all of them also justifiable. And to begin with, concerning the structure of the work, the rejection of any preestablished structure, the legitimate determination to erect a sort of labyrinth of several circles; on the other hand, the desire to create a complexity that will be moving, renewed, specifically characteristic of the music played, *interpreted*, as opposed to the fixed, unrenewable complexity of the machine. Certainly, in a musical universe in which all notion of symmetry tends to disappear, in which an idea of variable density occupies a more and more primordial position in all the echelons of construction—from the material to the structure—it is logical to seek an unfixed form, an evolving form that, rebellious, will reject its own repetition; in short, a virtuality. We arrive at the idea active behind that research which, in my view, can concentrate on the necessity of destroying every kind of immanent structure.

How has this necessity been able progressively to define itself more and more precisely? For, classically, composition is the result of constant choice. Have I myself said it enough? Inside of certain networks of probabilities, it is to be led—from solution to solution—to choose. The composer's "arbitrary" intervenes, rendering effective certain propositions of structures that remain amorphous until, thanks to their elaboration, they acquire a character of lived necessity. In the meantime, outside that elaboration, chance still, and always, intervenes. Is that possibility more productive of results than another? That is because you have found it so at this point in your development. My own experience has been that it is impossible to foresee all the meanderings and virtualities contained in the material supplying the point of departure. However much genius may exist in that premonitory vision, in that glance of estimation—of expertise—in the beginning it seems to me that composing will be deprived of its most eminent virtue: surprise. One can imagine without effort the boredom of an omniscience and an omnipotence that would have nothing to unveil along the way. Composition should, at each step, conceal a surprise and a "good pleasure," despite all the rationality to be imposed otherwise in order to achieve a certain solidity. I arrive, then, again, after another shift, at the irrational: it is thus that, by interrogating oneself, one comes back to that obsession which crouches in even the most rigorous arrangements. One seeks desperately to dominate the material by arduous, sustained, vigilant effort, but chance desperately subsists, introducing itself through a thousand crevices that it is impossible to stop up . . . "And it is good that way!" Nevertheless, will the composer's ultimate ruse be to *absorb* this chance? Why not tame this potential and force it to an account of itself, an accounting?

Introduce chance into composition? Is that not a madness or, at best, a vain attempt? Madness perhaps, but it will be a *useful madness*. In any case, to adopt chance out of weakness, for ease, to give oneself over to it, is a way of renouncing to which one will subscribe only by denying all the prerogatives and hierarchies that a created work implies. How, then, reconcile composition and chance?

Being a function of duration, of its physical time of unfolding, musical development can allow "chances" to intervene at several stages, on various levels of composition. In short, the result will be a linking, of greater probability, of aleatory events within a certain duration, itself indeterminate. This may appear absurd in the context of our Occidental music, but

Hindu music, for example, combining a sort of structural "forming" with instantaneous improvisation, very easily accepts this sort of problem and solves it daily. Evidently, it relates to a different sort of listening, and that in an open cycle, whereas we consider the elaborated work as a closed cycle of possibilities.

Let us see if, by surmounting certain contradictions, it is possible to absorb chance.

The most elementary level, that of giving the executant a certain freedom. Let us not be at all deceived: this will be, if it is made use of summarily, no more than a sort of generalized *rubato*, a little more organized than formerly (I mean, of course, a *rubato* that can be extended to intensities, registers, and tempo). If the interpreter can modify the text in his own image, it is necessary that this modification be implied in the text, that it not be solely imposed upon it. The musical text should include this interpreter's "chance" in filigree. If, for example, in a certain succession of sounds, I write between them a variable number of little notes, it is very clear that the *tempo* of these sounds will be kept constantly moving by the intrusion of the little notes, which provoke each time a different interruption or, more exactly, a different rupture of tension. They could concur in giving an impression of nonhomogeneous time. In the same way, if, in a rapid succession of notes and chords of the same rhythmic duration which in turn necessitate very different displacements (very near or very remote registers) of very different densities (aggregates of from two to eleven sounds), of attacks, and of excessively differentiated intensities—if in such a succession I demand that the executant adjust his *tempo* to the difficulty of the performance, it is evident that this series will not have a regular rhythmic pulsation, that the rhythm will be physically linked to the mechanical differentiation that I demand. Another example: I can demand of the interpreter not that he slow down or accelerate, but that he oscillate around a given *tempo* within more or less strait limitations. I can also rather freely make certain caesuras dependent upon a dynamic without always specifying a rigid boundary for the *ad libitum.* I thus introduce into the text a necessity for chance in the interpretation: a directed chance. But here we must be on our guard: the words *rubato* and *ad libitum* are used here only for ease in speaking, it being understood that the notions thus newly introduced into composition do not at all correspond to the conceptions generally covered by these terms, conceptions related simply to suppleness of articulation (one could also make use here of organ point and the *fermata*, the use of which has changed direction completely). Here I have taken the example of a single performer, but one can picture the kaleidoscope offered the imagination by several performers or several groups of performers. For one should dare to make use of the entire play between the two dimensions of the text: the one rigorous, the other interpreted. In that way, one reaches a pragmatic realm that is worth examining, as the performance or conducting of such music poses still unthought-of problems (notation also participates in this causation); but already experience has proved that scores thus conceived can be realized. I shall speak of them later; for the moment I want to concentrate on the "theoretical" aspect of the question.

Although implied by the musical text, this "chance," let us say again, is on an elementary level. It already presents appreciable possibilities for aerating, for liberating interpretation; it seems to resolve the dilemma posed by strict and liberal interpretation. Perhaps, then, it requires the executant to be more daring than formerly in putting himself in tune with the composer's invention, but one can—without excessive optimism—hope for good results from such a more effective collaboration. Let us recall, meanwhile, that this liberty needs to be directed, to be projected, the "instantaneous" imagination being more susceptible to failures than to illuminations, just as this liberty does not operate on invention, properly speaking, but on the pragmatism of the invention. Everyone, I think, can agree to the prudence of that proposition.

On the level of putting the structures themselves into play, I think that at the beginning one could "absorb" chance by establishing a certain automatism of relationships among various previously established probabilities. But, I shall be told, you are contradicting your initial proposal, in which you rejected this automatism, this objectivity, as a fetichism of number. I perfectly understand that this automatism should not be extended to all of creative thought, but that it can take part as a particularly efficacious means at a given moment in the elaboration of a work. Nothing of a kind to give an impression of nondirection, of nonweight, to impose the sensation of an undifferentiated universe. Nevertheless, according to whether this automatism shall be more or less preponderant, there will be a more or less tempered solution for chance. The proliferation of these automatic structures will have to be watched carefully if one does not want an anarchy of ordered appearance to lay waste the composition completely and thus deprive it of all its privileges. Given the greater or lesser rigor assigned to the networks of probabilities, one will obtain a unique conjuncture or multiple conjunctures of varying degree, depending upon whether the chance is single or multiple. How will we translate this practically? Suppose that I select series of durations and intensities and that—the result of the meeting of these two series being taken as fixed—I want to affect a series of pitches. If I give the series of pitches determined registers, there clearly will be only one solution for a given note; that is to say, this note will be fixed ineluctably in its register (absolute frequency), intensity, and duration: a unique chance for a meeting of these organizations at this "point" of sound. But suppose that we maintain the same series of sounds but do not impose a register upon it, that the register be left to the improvisation in the writing; immediately we have a "right" of registers, a geometric place for all the "points" that answer to the other three characteristics: relative generic frequency, intensity, and duration. Progressively giving the relativity of the registration to the duration and then to the intensity, I shall have obtained a determined "plan" and then "volume" within which my "point" of sound will find its justification. If I have adopted this geometric convention, it is solely so as to have a term of comparison, and not so as to be able to refer to an exact similarity in situation. For the different ensembles of characteristics, then, there are fields of encounter in which the chance of the definitively fixed musical event lies.

Such manipulation of these ensembles demands a total absence of choice in the putting into play, the choice being insinuated to the degree to which the probabilities multiply. One thus reaches this phenomenon: the less one chooses, the more the unique chance depends upon the coefficient of chance implied by the composer's subjectivity. What will sustain interest in a passage within a work thus composed is the more or less loose play of that antinomy.

I clearly specified that in the preceding instance we were dealing with the most elementary stage of automatism, voluntarily nondirected. If we want to integrate chance into the notion of structure itself in a directed ensemble, then we must appeal to subtler differentiations and introduce such notions as that of defined or undefined structure, amorphous or directional structure, divergent or convergent structure. Undeniably, this development of chance in composition will create a much more clearly differentiated universe than we had before and will mark a sharper development of a renewed perception of form. In a directed ensemble, these various structures will have to be controlled obligatorily by a general "phrase," to carry necessarily an initial and a final signature, to be allowed accessory appeal to species of platforms of bifurcation; this is in order to obviate total loss of the global sense of form as well as to avoid giving way to improvisation with no necessity but that of free will. For, as I said above, the liberty—or liberation—of the performer does not at all change the notion of structure; the problem, in fact, is only brought back a little farther on, and the solutions always remain to be found. Here, I think, an objection that seems to me well founded can be raised: will not such a form entail an enormous danger of fragmentation? Is one not going to fall foul of one of the defects most prejudicial to composition properly speaking, the defect that consists of the juxtaposition of "sections" centered upon themselves? This is a justifiable argument only in the case where, as a matter of fact, one does not think of a general form but develops one gradually. In order to mitigate that disappearance of the composition, one must have recourse to a new notion of development—development as being essentially discontinuous, but of a foreseeable and foreseen discontinuity: as a result, one must necessarily introduce "formatives" into a work and the indispensable "phrase" into the interrelation of structures of varying nature.

In such a form, then, one will conceive points of junction, platforms of bifurcations, types of mobile elements susceptible in an arbitrary fashion to adaptation (with certain modifications to be set down in the eventual score) to the eligible fixed structure, with the restriction that along the "routes" of development, a given event shall not occur more than once. Finally, thanks to an aggrandizement of that simple notion, in order to oppose the horizontal and the vertical, certain structures will be juxtaposable or superimposable totally or in part—that is to say, from or just to a given point of junction—with the positive or negative criteria that will be imposed on the writing by the necessity or the absence of superimposition. And here we are, led by this fact, at the demand of the writing: how, in fact, can we manifest the demands of these structures in the realization itself? Very evidently this will be translated from the beginning by the timbres, the most graspable phenomenon in the immediate exterior; by turning to certain instrumental groups or, less categorically, to certain instrumental combinations, one singularly clarifies for the listener the crisscrossing and multiplicity of the developments; this will be one of the most effective means to make them live, to make them constantly skim the sensitive comprehension. But if one does not wish to base it chiefly on timbre—a desire for monochromy might prevail—one will have the *tempo*, fixed or changing, intervene as the predominant characteristic; in fact, as the speed of the unfolding of a structure varies more or less, it contributes most powerfully to characterizing it. I have just spoken of two such "enveloping" phenomena as *tempo* and timbre; the third "enveloping" phenomenon, similarly, will be the type of writing, by which I mean the exterior aspect of the writing itself in its horizontal, vertical, or oblique aspect. Thus carried out, encompassed by these three external characteristics, a structure would respond to the nomenclature that I have developed above.

I have spoken of defined and undefined, divergent or convergent structures; those terms characterize two dialectically opposed families. Taking up again the comparison made above in relation to the probabilities of a musical "point," we can extend it to the structure itself. One will go from the undefined to the defined, from the amorphous to the directional, from the divergent to the convergent, according to the greater or lesser degree of automatism allowed to the factors in the development, in proportion to the negations placed in opposition in larger or smaller number, in proportion to the unlimited multiplication of their possibilities; thus one goes from free play to the strictest choice, a classical opposition that has always governed the strict style in relation to the free style. I have selected these various terms so as to underline the importance that I assign not only to the internal constitution of a structure but also to its possibilities for linkage, be it by isomorphism or polymorphism, be it from nucleus to nucleus of development. Undeniably, these terms apply rather poorly to music; lacking more directly appropriate appellations—it is up to the musicology of the future to discover them—we shall have to be content with a vocabulary in which scientific incidences risk being misunderstood because their significance has not been carried over. Meanwhile, we shall have to run this temporary risk if we want to clarify notions that are just dawning. From that moment one sees how the "formatives" of composition could link these different types of structures in families more intrinsically than such linkage could be accomplished by the circumstantial "envelopers" I spoke of earlier; one also sees how a general notion of phrase can forecast in some manner the ordering and agogics of the composed work. Starting from an initial signature, ending at an exhaustive, conclusive sign, the composition comes to put into play what we were seeking at the outset of our search: a problematic "route," a temporal function—a certain number of chance events registered within a mobile duration—always having a developmental logic, a directed over-all sense—caesuras being allowed to interpose themselves there, caesuras of silence or plateaux—sound-forms—routes going from a beginning to an end. We have respected the "finish" of the Occidental work, its closed cycle, but we have introduced the "chance" of the Oriental work, its open unfolding.

However, what I just have described is applied to a homogeneous sound-space of timbres, tempos, intervals. If I try to reach total variability and relativity of structure, I must make use of a nonhomogeneous space with reference to tempo and intervals. Present-day music shows in its development that it appeals more and more to variable notions from its inception, obedient to evolving hierarchies. It is for that reason that already we have seen the series of twelve equal tones replaced with series of sonorous blocs always of equal density; that we have seen meter replaced by series of durations and rhythmic blocs (rhythmic cells or superimpositions of several durations); and that, finally, we have seen intensity and timbre no longer content with their decorative or pathetic virtues, but acquiring instead, beyond those preserved privileges, functional importance that reinforces their powers and dimensions. Thanks to electroacoustic means and to various instrumental artisanries, we can break apart the homogeneity of the sound-space within the changing distribution of frequencies, either creating various forms of temperament or excluding temperament totally; in the same way, the machine's continuity and the discontinuity of the interpreter's inner pulsation shatter the homogeneity of musical time at its base. My aim here is not to show how one achieves these nonhomogeneous spaces; I content myself with noting the fact so as to seize upon those effects which it may have on the notion of structure: it imposes a new—and certainly the most discrepant—"chance" into its basis.

The danger of these researches, should they, out of weakness or inadvertence, be diverted from their real aim—the danger, then, consists of the possibility that the composer may flee his own responsibility, escape the choice inherent in all creation. The *ossia* must not, even upon a superior level, be the last word in invention. For, on the other hand, one can adapt to composition the notion of series itself—I mean to say that one can endow structure with the most general notion of permutation, permutation in which the limits are rigorously defined by restriction of powers imposed upon it by autodetermination: there you have a logical evolution fully justified because the same organizing principle simultaneously governs morphology and rhetoric.

From the practical point of view of performance, what is implied for the interpreter by these unprecedented dimensions of a work created in such an esthetic and poetic context? Is the only possibility that of reconciling the work and the instrumentalist? the work and the conductor who is going to direct it? Certainly yes: The examples to prove it are already here, in the works that inaugurate this new mode of musical being. If there is only a single performer, there is no difficulty, except that he must have more initiative than formerly, that initiative—that collaboration—being demanded by the composer. A certain number of signals, varying typographical characteristics lead the interpreter with assurance among the choices that he must make. (Let us remember well that these choices are not necessarily selections, but can be limited to a variable freedom of performance.)

When there are two instrumentalists—such as two pianists—the problem remains practically unchanged, with the supplementary adoption of signals, common guide marks, or both. If one is presenting the superimposition of a fixed tempo at one piano and a variable tempo at the other—an accelerando, for example—it will suffice to indicate the points of meeting—departure and arrival—of the two structures, points at which coordinates will have been calculated by the composer with the greater or lesser precision that he requires at the given moment. It can even be that, the composer having chosen appropriate registers, the two structures of tempo can be totally independent: it will be necessary then to indicate the interval of time during which he wishes those sequences to be played. A simple familiarity with such landmarks and signals quickly brings about the impression of "abandon" which one can have vis-à-vis one's partner when one is no longer linked to him by a strictly synchronous metric.

When, finally, one must conduct music thus conceived, the conductor's role consists essentially of giving signals that a convention clearly established with his musicians will diversify into specialized signals to indicate departure from the principal tempo, return to that tempo, or periodic coincidence with it. If the musicians must deviate individually from the general tempo, a single leader "centralizes" the indications. But when—with an orchestra—a group of musicians must adopt a variable tempo, one has recourse either to a first-desk leader or to a secondary conductor, who will take his references for all the fluctuations from the indications given by the principal conductor. These problems of group performance are not so very far from the difficulties met with daily in the theater: their solution is relatively simple. The only obstacle to be surmounted from the beginning is that of getting the musicians to feel freed in their relationship to the conductor and not "abandoned" by him; consequently it is necessary to make each of them conscious of his individual tempo in relation to the individual tempo of each of the others, demonstrating that the divergences are based upon a balanced whole.

"Toward that supreme conjunction with probability" one certainly cannot proceed with inalienable security. Certainly we will not fail to be accused, in this regard, with "dehumanization"; . . . the exalted absurdities circulating on this subject are of inexhaustible monotony: they can be reduced, all of them, to a very low conception of what is understood by "human." Lazy nostalgia, a predilection for potpourris, very *pourris* [rotten], which are sometimes baptized with the name of syntheses—such are the strained schemes of the "heart" of these vigilant detractors. On the most elementary level, I can reply that, far from denying or annihilating the interpreter, we bring him back into the creative circle after many years during which he has been asked merely to play the text as "objectively" as possible. What am I saying? That what we are leading to is even a glorification of the interpreter. And not at all of an interpreter-robot of bewildered precision, but of an involved interpreter freed to make his choices.

As for those who are disturbed by that dynamite introduced into the heart of the work, that chance which is not "composed," and who want to demonstrate to us that the human poetic and the extrahuman chance are inalienable, irreducible enemies and that their amalgamation cannot produce a positive result, I shall cite to them this passage from Mallarmé's *Igitur:*

"In brief, in any act in which chance is in play, it is always chance that achieves its own Idea by affirming or denying it. Faced with its existence, negation and affirmation run aground. It contains the Absurd—implies it, but in latent state, and prevents its existence: which allows the Infinite to be." Perhaps some unconsciousness—and insolence—is involved in broaching this periplus plunged in incertitude, but is it not the only means for attempting to *fix the Infinite?* The unavowed aim of whoever refuses pure and simple hedonism, limited artisanry, in a creative universe burdened with lowly deceptions. Every dilettante will find himself wounded by a responsibility beyond these ruses; every worker—horrible—will be annihilated by the inanity, the vacuity of his labor. After all, will this not be the only means of killing the *Artist?*

Sound and Word

It is generally conceded that the evolution of music shows a serious lag in relation to the developments of other means of expression; this admission goes so far as to establish precise relations tending to prove that the delay can be localized in a defined interval of time. If the relations of music and painting are necessarily rather distant, it is quite otherwise with poetry, which is in part linked to music or, at least, to a realm of music which rests upon putting the vocal element into play. For, even without taking the permanence of the theatrical fact into account, music is always confronting the word. Taking examples only from the closest of our occidental traditions, I may cite plain chant, the polyphonic music of the Middle Ages or the Renaissance, opera and church music, and, finally, the abundant literature of the song. One has often observed that when musicians select texts, they make choices on the basis of poetic tenor rather than of the quality of the poem. One has not failed to attribute this misunderstanding of poetic quality to frequently evident lack of culture; but one has also explained that the reasons moving the musician in his election of such and such a text do not necessarily coincide with the larger or smaller literary value of that text.

My purpose is not to analyze the complex connections that relate musical and poetic values; I simply want to recall the degree to which certain forms of expression intrinsically link these two phenomena: sound and word. Is this to go so far as to say that the evolution of language corresponds to a similar evolution of music? To me it does not seem possible to assert that this problem is posed in terms of a simple parallelism. It is almost superfluous to recall that musical evolution involves, before everything else, technical conceptions, and that it carries with it important modifications of vocabulary and syntax, mutations much more radical than those which language undergoes; but, undeniably—and especially after the past century—the great poetic currents have resounded strongly in the esthetic development of music—musical technique being so specific that it automatically elbows aside all direct influence. One may note that poets who worked on language itself are the ones who left the most visible imprint upon the musician; surely there come to mind immediately the names of Mallarmé rather than Rimbaud, of Joyce rather than Kafka. Thus we can quickly reach a classification—very fluid, to be sure—that will separate the precise, direct influences and the more diffuse influences by osmosis. Which does not mean that the first of these two categories is more important or operates more deeply then the second; what differs is their way of working. In one case, certain acquisitions pass from one form of language to the other, undergoing an essential translation; in the other case, the relationship is infinitely more complex and can be established only upon the basis of very general structural considerations or in a like esthetic direction.

Structure, one of our epoch's words. It seems to me that if there is to be a connection between poetry and music, it is to this concept of structure that one can appeal most effectively; and I mean from basic morphological structures to the vastest structures of definition. If I choose a poem in order to make it something more than a point of departure for ornamentation that will weave arabesques around it, if I choose a poem to employ it as a source of irrigation for my music, and by that fact to create an amalgam, so that the poem will be the "center and absence" of the sound-body, then I cannot limit myself to just the affective relationships linking the two entities; in such a case, a tissue of conjunctions imposes itself, which, among other things, includes those affective relationships, but also englobes all the mechanisms of the poem from pure sonority to intelligent ordering.

When one envisages the "putting to music" of the poem—I stay outside the theater—a series of questions relating to declamation, to prosody is posed. Is one going to sing the poem, "recite" it, speak it? All the vocal means enter into play, and upon these diverse particularities of emission depend the transmission and the more or less direct intelligibility of the text. One knows that after Schoenberg and *Pierrot lunaire* these problems have aroused great interest among musicians, and it is scarcely necessary to recall the controversies that have been aroused by *Sprechgesang.* As for a consideration of the type: one should "prosodize" the sung poem by approaching as closely as possible to spoken poetry—henceforth I can only find that rather summary. When a good poem is recited, it has its own sonorities; on that level it is useless to try to compete with a perfectly adapted means. If I sing the poem, I enter upon a *convention;* it is more expedient to take advantage of that convention as such, with its specific laws, than to ignore it deliberately or want to dodge it and cheat it in order to diverge from its real purpose. Singing implies a relationship of the poem's sonorities with intervals and rhythm that differ fundamentally from spoken intervals and rhythm; it is not a power of aggrandized diction, but a transmutation and—let us admit it—a destruction of the poem. The poet doubtless will not at first recognize his text as thus treated, not having written it with that aim; even its sonorities will become strange and alien to him because they have been grafted onto an unforeseeable support not foreseen by him; at best, and the poem's always existing autonomy having been taken into account, he will recognize that if there had to be intervention, the invervention would necessarily be this one. From that extremity of pure *convention* to that of spoken language, properly so-called, a very rich gamut of intonations extends which only now are we starting to know how to take advantage of consciously; Schoenberg was the initiator of this, as I said above. Since then, knowledge of Far Eastern theaters has revealed to us the point of perfection to which technique can be pushed in utilizing the resources of the vocal fact; on the part of Schoenberg and Berg, to be sure, certain questions have not been brought fully to light—such as the nature and speed of vocal emission according to the different effects desired, the duration of support of a sound or *tessitura* that various modes of emission imply; all questions that can be replied to empirically. Surely a new vocal technique, in which precisely these problems will be encompassed, will be forged.

But prosody in this enterprise? That famous prosody which each one boasts of possessing better than his neighbor? Should one place accents and voice movements by approaching as close as possible to spoken inflections? That essentially depends upon the zone of vocal emission in which one is moving, and certain rules cannot be transgressed without detriment and sometimes without becoming ridiculous; it goes without saying that punctuation—in the most general meaning of that word—must be respected; otherwise, instead of magnifying the poetry and transmuting it, one pillages it as much of its substance as of its sonorities. From that point on, one can consider the music-poem coincidence as a sort of function having as a variable the mode of vocal emission employed.

The musical text having thus been structured in relation to the poetic text, the obstacle of its intelligibility arises. Let us, without evasion, ask: is the fact of "not understanding" —supposing that the interpretation has been perfect—an absolute, unconditional sign that the work is not good? Contrary to this generally held opinion, it seems that one may act upon the intelligibility of a text as a "center or absence" of music. If you wish to "understand" the text, then read it, or *speak* it: there can be no better solution. The subtler effort that

I am now proposing implies that knowledge of the poem already has been acquired. I reject the "reading in music" or, rather, the reading with music—that is to say, the merely apparent solution, in which the real problem is given the slip because one is refusing, there again, to envisage a convention and the obligations that it entails. All arguments in favor of the "natural" are only stupidities, the natural being irrelevant (in all civilizations) when one considers amalgamating text and music.

But then, I shall be told, if you place the largest importance upon sonorities, work with a text whose significance is not important, or even with a text devoid of significance, made up of onomatopeias or imaginary vocables forged especially to enter the musical context; you will no longer knock yourself against practically insurmountable contradictions. Certainly onomatopoeia and pulverized words can express what constructed language cannot propose to touch upon; also, abundant use of those procedures has not been lacking, whether in learned music or in popular music; the fact that this usage can be an instinctive act will be used by some to disarm the conscientious objectors. For example, ritual chants in a large number of liturgies use a dead language that keeps direct understanding of the chanted text remote from a large number of the participants; that dead language, such as Latin in the Catholic liturgy, may still be known and translatable, its sense perfectly decipherable, but in some African rites the dialect employed during important rites has fallen into disuse so that its meaning is totally obscure to those employing it (especially when there has been transplantation, as with Brazilian Negroes). The Greek theater and the Japanese *noh* also furnish us with example of "sacred" language in which archaicism singularly or utterly limits comprehensibility. In popular songs, at the other extreme, who has not been surprised to hear successions of onomatopoeias and ordinary words deprived of their purpose? All that is admitted is the necessity and pleasure of rhythm; they allow for a certain logic of the absurd, which is enchanting. Such are counting songs, such are many folkloric songs. (Stravinsky used these resources admirably in such works as *Les Noces*, *Renard*, and *Pribaoutki.*)

According to Novalis, "to speak in order to speak, that is the formula of deliverance"; deliverance in religion or deliverance in play, the examples are never lacking. Do not dream, then, of astonishing us with the fact that composers have recourse to that dissociation of sense and language; nevertheless, to pursue that objective alone would be equivalent to restraining ourselves purposelessly and renouncing many other richnesses of expression that alone permit an organized text to give a comprehensible message.[1] To that gamut, which stretches from the word, organized with a view to logical sense, to the pure phoneme, I would gladly compare the gamut of possibilities in the sound-body, which furnish us with sounds as well as with noises—but this is, in any question of causation, only a comparison. Through the ensemble of procedures which I have just evoked, the needs of music will recover almost completely the demands of the text, morphologically speaking; what remains to be done is to make the large structures of organization and composition coincide, but it is no part of my purpose to study that problem here, I having wished to limit myself to language properly speaking.

Artaud's name comes to mind promptly when one evokes questions of vocal emission or of dissociation of words and their fragmentation; actor and poet, he naturally has been impelled by material problems of interpretation, just as a composer is who performs or conducts. I am not qualified to examine Antonin Artaud's language thoroughly, but I discover the fundamental preoccupations of present-day music in his

[1] At the risk of arousing astonishment, I want to add that composers ought not to ignore the researches in communication which scholars have been making for some time, researches that have brought into this field certain clarifications that could be helpful in illuminating and ordering some present-day musical researches. —P. B.

writings; having heard him read his own texts, accompanying them with cries, noises, rhythms, has showed me how to bring about a fusion of sound and word, how to make the phoneme splash when the word can do no more—in short, how to organize delirium. What nonsense, what an absurd conjunction of terms, it will be said! And so? will you have faith only in the vertigoes of improvisation? Only in the powers of an "elementary" sacralization? More and more I imagine that an effective creator must take delirium into account and—yes—organize it.

II

TOWARD A TECHNOLOGY

Proposals

In criticizing Olivier Messiaen's *Technique de mon langage musical,* René Leibowitz said that one cannot separate rhythm and polyphony. I am astonished that the man who pointed out so many *lapalissades* in that book should make a statement of this sort. For analysis of the compositional elements of a polyphony obliges us to dissociate those elements temporarily in any attempt to investigate them. Did not Leibowitz himself offer a display of the ridiculous in analyzing—and in what a droll way—the rhythm of the tango used by Berg in the cantata *Der Wein?* As my point of departure for the present essay I shall take the lesson learned from Messiaen, the only one interested in the material.

The first composer to make an immense conscious effort in the rhythmical direction was Stravinsky. From the outset, his technique was one of using cells. Let us take the very simple case of the opening of *Petrushka.* Here we have a melodic line harmonically accompanied and made up of different cells. The melodic cells correspond to the rhythmic cells, which are repeated in variation—this by juxtaposition. That method, if one seeks a comparison, is clearly related to Hindu *ragas.* Later, Stravinsky made use of the oppositions of two or several variable cells, as in the *Danse sacrale* of *Le Sacre du printemps.*

Section A: the rhythmic cell corresponding to the repetition of chord I; B: a melodic-harmonic complex II; C: a complex III. At the outset, we shall have:

A–7,[1] B–7, A–5, B–7, A–3, C–8, A–4, B–7, C–5, A–5, B–7, A–8,

B–4, A–2, B–4, A–8, B–4, C–7.

EXAMPLE I—Stravinsky: *Danse sacrale*

I have given this schematic enumeration of the rhythmic scheme of the beginning of the *Danse sacrale* because it has very remarkable properties. One notices immediately that it is divided into two sections. The B rhythm retains its relation to the others; in the first part it lasts for a duration of seven sixteenth-notes, in the second for one of four sixteenth-notes, whereas A and C are mobile and vary irregularly. Stravinsky also utilized the system of superimposed rhythmic pedals—that is to say, his polyphonic apparatus being made up to some degree of clearly characterized stages, he gives each of them an independent rhythmic period. The linkings of these several superimpositions will not be reproduced at the same intervals, but so as to obtain a varied disposition. There you have the chief lessons that Messiaen has helped us to learn from Stravinsky.

[1] In this way I indicate that A may contain seven sixteenth-notes, etc. —P. B.

Bartók's influence was also very great, but it was manifested much more simply and in a way more closely connected to tradition. Above all, Bartók used the popular rhythms of central Europe, made up of unequal rhythms or of simple measures with accents on weak beats or weak sections of the time. Equally, he made use of—especially in developments—short elisions, very stressful, coinciding with contrapuntal responses. We find all of this in the quartets, the Sonata for Two Pianos, and the Music for Percussion, Strings, and Celesta.

Following Varèse, André Jolivet tries to advance the rhythmic inquiry. But his empirical technique prevents him from going very far. With him, the greatest effort is directed toward monody, as in his *Incantations pour flûte*, where again we find the system of the *ragas.* He merits mention because of his particularly welcome use of rational values in relation to irrational values (triplet, group of five, etc.), which can be used as a point of departure for effective construction in this direction.

Finally, Messiaen's research posits certain basic facts that it is indispensable to consider as acquisitions. To begin with, there is the added value, which Messiaen defines this way: "Half of the smallest value of any rhythm whatever added to a rhythm, whether by a note or by a dot." Thus we can obtain irregular rhythms even in rapid passages. Then there is the extremely important base of the rhythmic canon, exact, augmented, diminished, or dotted. One knows that contrapuntal definition of canon sufficiently well to apply it to pure rhythm. The dotted canon is founded on this principle: in the canonic figure, a dotted value will correspond to every value in the model. Augmentation thus becoming irregular, the dot adding a shorter or longer value to the note according to the note's duration. This, therefore, brings incontestable enrichment to the classic diminution or augmentation—usually going from the simple to the double, quadruple, etc. We thus find the principle of rhythmic pedals entirely organized and employed as a means of development. Finally, the diminution or augmentation of cells in their interrelationships is clearly seen to be defined and enlarged in view of greater effects.

On the other hand, we encounter only total indifference to these problems on the part of Schoenberg and Berg, who remain attached to the classic measure and the old conception of rhythm. At times they may displace accents in a variation, but nothing in their music detaches one's attention from the regular meter. Only Webern—despite his loyalty to the tradition of rhythmic writing—came to dislocate the regular measure by an extraordinary use of counterrhythms, syncopations, accents on weak beats, weakenings on strong beats, and all the other artifices adapted to making us forget the squareness.

Thus we have been traversing a period of gropings and of various attempts, in which the sporadic and sometimes gratuitous aspect is evident and disagreeable. I believe that this is owing to lack of cohesion between the elaborations of the polyphony, properly speaking, and those of the rhythm. With Messiaen in particular, in whom the purely harmonic side will irritate the most indulgent, the quest remains in the state of a sketch covered indifferently with a mass of chords. When Messiaen produces a rhythmic canon, for instance, it is at once made noticeable by a debris of absolutely unnecessary chords; it intervenes in the construction without motivation; it disappears unceremoniously. In short, Messiaen's searchings are not integrated into his discourse, because he does not compose; he juxtaposes; and because he always has recourse to exclusively harmonic—I should almost say accompanied melodic—writing.

How, then, can one coordinate and enrich the novelties of Messiaen and his predecessors? Admitting the principle of a contrapuntal writing in which all the parts must have equal importance—I shall explain this later in another discussion—I should say that we must integrate rhythm into polyphony in a more or less independent fashion: that the rhythmic must be independent of or dependent upon the contrapuntal figures according to the development in view. It is clear that dynamism or stasis within the gradation of sounds can correspond to rhythmic dynamism and stasis, parallel or contrary.

At the outset, the question is to define what I understand by dynamism or stasis in the scale of sounds. It seems to me imperative that, in the technique of twelve tones, in order to obtain kinds of values corresponding to such tonal values as modulation, one should have recourse to totally different procedures based upon the mobility or fixity of the notes. This is to say that in mobility, each time a note occurs it will be in a different register; and in fixity, the contrapuntal scheme will be formed within a certain disposition in which the twelve tones will each have a well-determined place. That having been established, it remains for us to dispose the rhythm in relation to these values. Let us take an example:

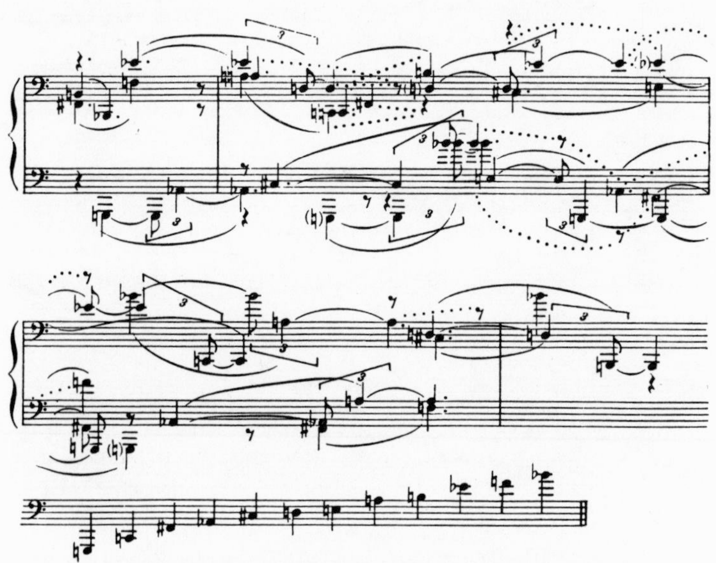

Example II—Boulez: Second Piano Sonata

One sees that the contrapuntal response (being made by a group of two) fixes the sound-scale in the order indicated in bottom line. The rhythms will be in long values and on the basis of:

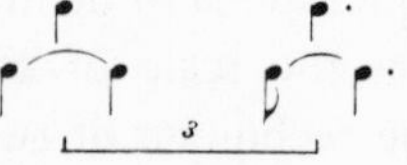

We can also make rhythmic canons that rest or do not rest upon contrapuntal canons. To vary the presentation to the maximum, we ban long, exact rhythmic canons, which are merely repetition, and admit only irregular canons. We shall take into account the fact, stressed by Messiaen, that there are retrograde rhythmic figures. I shall give the following as an example of irregular rhythmic canon:

EXAMPLE III—Boulez: *Visage nuptial*, poem by René Char

This is a retrograde melodic canon to which an irregular retrograde rhythmic canon responds: to short values, it will reply with long values, and vice versa; the medial values will remain unaltered. Thus, the first triplet remains a triplet (a), the quarter-note becomes an eighth-note (b), the dotted eighth-note becomes a dotted quarter-note (c), etc.

Similarly, I shall give an example of rhythmic canon independent of the polyphony:

EXAMPLE IV—Boulez: Sonatina for Flute and Piano

We are in an athematic passage in which the development is made without any support from marked contrapuntal cells. One sees that the rhythmic cells are closed by a ternary rhythm in rational or irrational values:

an embryonic rhythm propitious to multiple combinations. With different linkings of these cells I form three different rhythms:

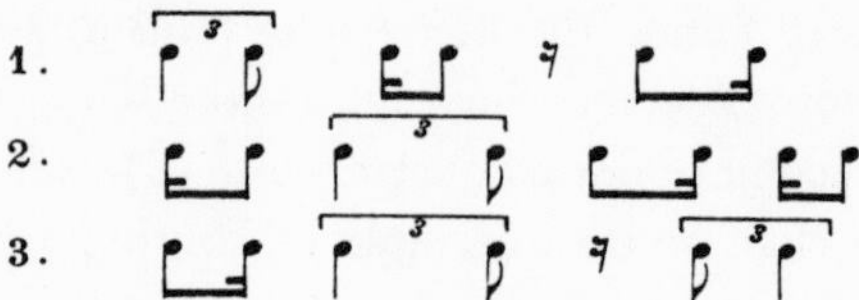

the third being linked to the first by the transposition of rational values into irrational values and vice versa. I superimpose

$\overleftarrow{1}\quad \overleftarrow{2}\quad \overrightarrow{2}$

$\overrightarrow{2}\quad \overleftarrow{3}\quad \overleftarrow{1}$

$\overrightarrow{3}\quad \overleftarrow{1}\quad \overleftarrow{3}$ (the arrows indicate the direction of the rhythm, forward or retrograde)

Because these rhythms are not of equal lengths (the third exceeding the first by a sixteenth-note, the second exceeding the third by a sixteenth-note), their successive superimpositions do not exactly correspond, and we thus have pushed to the maximum the variations that can be extracted from this ternary variation.

As a third and final example of rhythmic canon, I shall give this:

EXAMPLE V—Boulez: *Symphonie* [2]

in which the canon makes rational values out of irrational values (as we have already seen in the preceding example), equal values, and unequal values; but here it is directly related to the contrapuntal cell. The responses are made on the following motive: melodically linked, two minor thirds at a half-tone, then two fifths at a half-tone, and again two minor thirds at a half-tone:

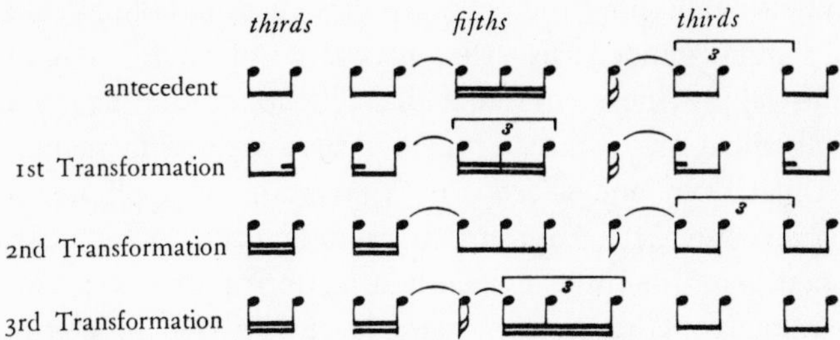

Furthermore, the silences between the respective entries are dysymmetrical; the first transformation comes three eighth-notes after the preceding one; the second transformation one eighth-note after the first transformation; the third transformation a dotted eighth-note after the second transformation.

If I have dwelt very specifically on the technical aspect of rhythmic canon and its employment parallel to, contrary to, or

[2] This is not from an incomplete or abandoned work, but unhappily, from one composed in 1947 and lost during a journey in 1954. —ED.

independent of, the polyphony, that is because it is the only aspect I think it possible to convey. Someone now might ask me how I choose the rhythms—and that is a question to which no verbal reply is possible; it is one that can be answered only by the music that one writes. I shall say, however, that one should make use of all the forms developed up to now. I can try to apply brief definitions to them. In doing so, I do not at all pretend that I am discovering new terrain; I am simply condensing what seems most evident to me.

I shall designate as *rhythm-bloc* the rhythm that rules all parts of the polyphony as placed in vertical aggregate (as in the *Danse sacrale*); as *rhythm-counterpoint* what rules independently each of the counterpoints in the polyphony. The *regular rhythm* will be that within which the values remain simple multiples of the unit; *irregular rhythm* will be that in which the values are uneven or irrational in relation to the unit.

When establishing the counterpoints of a polyphony, then, we should—guided by the necessity of these counterpoints—apply these rhythmic differentiations to them while mixing them or, to the contrary, clearly separating them. At the time when one selects the registration of a phrase, one should register the rhythms. It is difficult to give a strict method here, for this is evidently a matter of strictly personal equation. Nonetheless, the principle of variation or constant renewal will guide us unrelentingly.

After all this, one more difficulty remains: how adapt the measure to complex combinations, especially in orchestral scores. I think that again the best way is to follow as closely as possible the metric and its writing, and not to fear, even with the orchestra, irregular measures, and to employ the notations (⊓ for two and △ for three of the units of value previously established) conceived by Desormière and Messiaen. This permits the transcription of writing that is already very complex. I must acknowledge that at times the resulting complexity exceeds this simple way of notation: I shall then propose putting dots before the notes that coincide (see Example III).

Why try for such complexity? In order to make a rhythmic element also of perfect "atonality" responsive to writing methods as varied as those of dodecaphony. It is clear that researches into rhythm are not of serious worth unless they necessarily take place in the musical text. In this connection, the case of Varèse is striking in its gratuity: he does away with the problem by doing away with the writing itself so as to devote himself to nothing but the rhythm. It is an easy solution that solves nothing.

I have, finally, a personal reason for giving so important a place to the rhythmic phenomenon. I believe that music should be collective hysteria and spells, violently of the present time—following the lead of Antonin Artaud and not in the direction of simple ethnographic reconstruction in the likenesses of civilizations more or less remote from ours. But, here too, I have a horror of dealing in words with what is complaisantly called the esthetic problem. I shall therefore prolong this essay no longer; I prefer to return to my staff paper.

Stravinsky Remains

Any attempt to assess Stravinsky's *œuvre* is disconcerting and vain. It seems more and more evident that, despite constant "renewals" pursued with less happiness than disenchantment, there is no composer whose name is more narrowly attached to a single work or, let us say, a single series of works. Stravinsky is, in the first place, *Le Sacre; Petrushka, Renard, Les Noces,* and *Le Chant du rossignol* form a constellation of which the importance cannot be denied, but the magnetic pole always remains that *Sacre,* yesterday scandalous, today a pretext for animated cartoons! It is curious to realize that the two great "scandals" of contemporary music—that is, *Le Sacre* and *Pierrot lunaire*—have had a noticeably similar fate: just as *Le Sacre* remains THE Stravinsky phenomenon in most people's eyes, so *Pierrot lunaire* remains THE Schoenberg phenomenon. *Grosso modo,* I can only ratify that opinion, for in one case as in the other there has in fact been no greater coalescence between the resources of the language and poetic force, between the means of expression and the will to express.

Especially with regard to Stravinsky, his admirers and his detractors have drawn this chef d'oeuvre to themselves and have wanted to see in it either the origin of all his glorious epics of rejuvenation or, very intrinsically, the point of departure for all of his turpitudes. There have been imprudent words about a chef d'oeuvre scarcely conceivable by the human spirit and about precocious expression by a young composer lacking maturity. There has been talk about a wrought-iron lyre and a Russian bard. In short, a certain number of stupidities on both sides.

One is inclined to think that this composition is worth more than all the praise that has been heaped upon it; as for those who discern Stravinsky's incapacities in it, one feels that they do so mostly by retroactive prophecy.

Would it not be more serious to deal with *Le Sacre* as a musical product and to apprehend the realm in which we can make fruitful exploration after having jettisoned a certain exclamatory, sentimental, and Pythian vocabulary, to which there seems no need to abandon musical exegesis?

One emerges from a hearing of this score with immediate awareness that, the Introduction aside, *Le Sacre* is thickly written, by which I mean to say that essentially it makes use of highly contrasted levels, of a global writing. That impression is not inexact. In fact, it is justified by all of the work's tonal structures, but is contradicted paradoxically by its rhythmic constructions. What most astonishes a listener to *Le Sacre* is the massiveness of those repeated chords, of those scarcely varied melodic cells; nonetheless, it is in them that there is manifest in the highest degree Stravinsky's inventiveness, difficult to imagine in 1913 and unequaled during the following twenty-five or thirty years. One is content to imitate the writing, the irregularity and number of changes of measure, not preoccupied at all with any reality in their use. Also, ought we not be amazed to see that *Le Sacre* has had no true descendants except a tendency toward the dionysiac and toward "wicked" music, as has been said, to see that the best-known work of contemporary music is also a work without issue? To such a degree that jazz has been credited with having brought music a considerable rhythmic renewal through its poor and unique syncopation and its inseparable four-beat measure? (Did not Stravinsky himself give a wrong direction with his *Ragtime*?) Why, after so long a time, that inexplicable insolvency? Perhaps I might say that the encounter with Stravinsky's complexity of rhythmic vocabulary and syntax could lead to valuable deductions only through an equally complex morphological and syntactical vocabulary such as was perfected by Webern.[1]

I should remark right away that Stravinsky's language, far from being a liberation from the tonal point of view, in fact consists of powerful attractions created around certain poles, the most classic poles there are—that is, the tonic, dominant, and subdominant. Greater or lesser tension is obtained by means of unresolved appoggiaturas, passing chords, the superimposition of several modalities upon a single attractive note, the disposition of different forms of chords on compartmentalized levels. But in a general sense the large themes of the work are diatonic, very primitively diatonic; one realizes that some of them are even in defective five-tone modes. Themes with chromatic tendencies are notably few, and except for frequent major-minor play, the chromaticism assumes only harmless aspects in relation to the attractive notes, where it can be aimed only at assuring sonorous dysymmetry in slightly used linkages (I think in particular of the series of parallel thirds in the *Jeu du rapt* and the *Jeux des cités rivales*, accompanied by a like parallelism of thirds or sixths in which now the bottom note, now the upper note, is raised a half-tone.) Also, it is necessary throughout the score to oppose a certain horizontal diatonicism to a vertical chromaticism, but without excluding the opposite disposition. Stravinsky gives a solution to the entire sound-vocabulary by means of complexities grafted onto the old organization, which is why this attitude can take on an aspect of timidity or confusion once we are aware of the experiences undergone in Vienna at the same time.

[1] Let us note, however, Berg's use of a rhythmic structure organized by means of what he called "*Monoritmica*" or "*Hauptrhythmus*." —P. B.

Equally, it is undeniable that Stravinsky had little sense of development—that is, of the sound-phenomenon in constant renewal. Perhaps this will be found a weakness—and in truth it is; shall I let myself think that it is one of the chief reasons for that rhythmic force which he is obliged to deploy in order to face the difficulties of writing? I do not think that I am being paradoxical when I affirm that because these horizontal or vertical coagulations are simple, easily manageable materials, one can attempt much sharper rhythmic experience. The opposite, furthermore, of what happened in Vienna, where the writing was on the way toward undergoing a radical transformation inside of a rhythmic organization that was scarcely more than traditional, in which the complexities were shored up on the unshaken principle of regular meter.

In the course of the following analysis, I shall have several occasions to verify this rhythm-sound antimony, which I have merely wanted to point out here.

I shall not go through the score page by page and discover the means of expression one by one; I think that it will be more profitable to proceed by increasing order of complexity, by going from the structure of a simple phrase to the "polystructure" of the superimpositions in a development. Perhaps by this procedure we shall be able to reach more easily the conclusions that will impose themselves at the end of this prolonged exploration of the Stravinskyan realm.

Let us take as the first example one of the simplest phrases, in B major-minor, in which the five constituent notes are B–C sharp–E–F sharp, with D sharp being heard only in the suspensive ending. The phrase begins the *Cercles mystérieux des adolescents* (at No. 91 in the orchestral score).

I have placed the five members of phrases one under the other—that is to say, the two antecedents, the two consequents, and the conclusion. Below, I have placed the rhythmic pedal made up of the four notes of this theme: B–C sharp–E–F sharp, which are disposed over a wider separation of registers, the E–F sharp major second becoming a minor seventh, the C sharp–B second becoming a major ninth.

EXAMPLE I

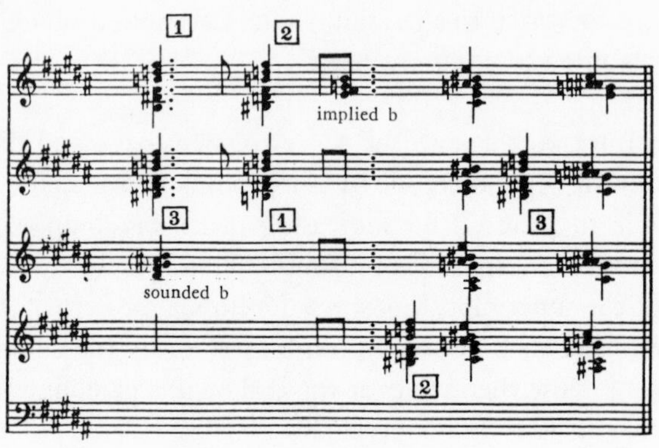

EXAMPLE Ia

We see that the antecedent I is built upon a rhythm of four quarter-notes plus two quarter-notes:

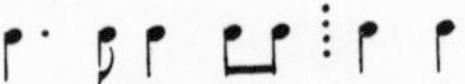

the total value of the first three notes—in separated values, dotted quarter, eighth, quarter—being formed by an embellishment of the dominant F sharp; the antecedent II is built in the same way, but between the two terminal quarters a fugitive F sharp is placed, the value of which is the unit—that is, the quarter, which gives four quarters plus three quarters. The consequent I is based upon the condensation of the antecedent I by the suppression of the initial embellishment and the transfer of the dominant F sharp to the tonic B, which gives us two quarters plus two quarters; the consequent II, parallel to the antecedent II, utilizes the same procedure in relation to the consequent I, the addition of an F sharp, but this time this note is situated before the two concluding quarters, and therefore is found transformed into an appoggiatura of the subdominant E; in values, we obtain two quarters plus three quarters. The conclusion takes up three quarters plus three quarters. We have, then, four phrase-members of unequal duration—6, 7, 4, 5, and a conclusion in which the duration echoes that of the first antecedent, with the difference of an internal division into four plus two and three plus three. Underneath that mobile structure, we have a fixed structure of four eighth-notes that will interfere harmonically and rhythmically with the first. In effect, the setting of the two antecedents corroborates that of the rhythmic pedal in being placed upon its strong beats—E–F sharp—whereas the setting of the two consequents contradicts that rhythmic pedal in that it coincides with its weak beats—C sharp–B; the conclusion returns to the strong beat and joins its own twice three quarters to the thrice two quarters of the rhythmic pedal.

This stability of rhythmic construction is reflected in the harmonic conception of the passage. Under the decorated F sharps of the two antecedents and under the escaped F sharp of the antecedent II and the F sharp appoggiatura of the consequent II, there is an appoggiatura'd major-minor chord composed of a chord in B minor at the upper octave and, at the lower octave, of a variable B chord formed by the third or the tonic raised by a half-tone; three solutions are presented, then: chord 1—B–D sharp–F sharp (raised third); chord 2—B sharp–D natural–F sharp (raised tonic); chord 3—B sharp–D sharp–F sharp (raised third and tonic). Antecedent I utilizes chords 1 and 2. Antecedent II utilizes chords 3 and 1 for the embellished dominant, chord 3 for the escaped one. Consequent II utilizes chord 2 for the appoggiatura. Let me demonstrate this play of symmetries clearly: antecedent II utilizes chord 3, not used again, and terminates with it symmetrically in relation to chord 1; this chord 1 is placed on the F sharp after the embellishment, symmetrically in relation to antecedent I, where it is found on the F sharp before the embellishment; finally, in consequent II, the F sharp appoggiatura utilizes chord 2, whereas antecedent II has utilized chord 3. This means that the order of the second hearing of chords 3 and 2 is in reverse with relation to their first passage 2 and 3, chord 1 being placed ahead each time and taking on greater importance from the fact of its position at both ends of the embellishment of the dominant F sharp, chords 2 and 3 being once on the dominant F sharp, another time on the appoggiatura or escaped F sharp, a note of less tonal importance.

Furthermore, the escaped B, the second eighth-note, common to all the groups, is harmonized with a minor subdominant chord, whereas the real note B, which begins the two consequents, is harmonized with a tonic major chord of the sixth degree.

The two final quarter-notes—E–C sharp—common to both groups are harmonized with chords of which the three top notes are identical, but of which the lower notes vary this way: the first has this motion in the bass—C sharp–E, with C sharp–E–G natural in the first chord, E–G natural in the second; the second has the immobile bass C sharp, but the interior voice-motion E–G natural with C sharp–E natural–G natural; the third has the bass-motion A sharp–C sharp, with A sharp–C sharp–G natural and C sharp–G natural; the fourth, the inverse bass-motion C sharp–A sharp, with C sharp–E–G natural and A sharp–C sharp. In this last chord, the A sharp of the upper octave is suppressed to give added value to the seventh A sharp–A natural. The bass-motions, then, are always different, but always by a minor third; furthermore, the chord on E is the same in antecedent I and consequent II, the chord on C sharp the same in antecedent II and consequent I, so that the order of these chords on second hearing is retrograde in relation to the first hearing.

At its conclusion, the melody makes heard the D sharp not employed earlier, while the bass accompanies it with a leading-note chord of the fourth on the A natural not used earlier in the bass.

On the consequent I, finally, there is a regular display of four notes—B–C sharp–E–F sharp in quarters, to which the consequent I adds D natural before the cadence on the chord in which D sharp plays the role of leading note.

Let me now take examples in which there are not only rational divisions of the unit, but also irrational divisions—by which I mean quintuplets, triplets, and all similarly deduced values. Let it be the following famous phrase, which begins the work:

EXAMPLE II

I do not think that this phrase became famous solely because it is expounded in the high range of the bassoon, with such an elongated attack on the C natural. Nor do I think that it owes its fame to its defective modal consonance (lacking F natural), which is, above all, very traditional—the notes of tension, the dominant E and subdominant D, are at a distance of a fourth on either side of the tonic, and the pauses all take place hierarchically on the mediant and the tonic A; the modal consonance, furthermore, is contradicted by a cadence with C sharp as mediant, with, already, the major-minor antinomy, and is then contradicted more energetically by that same cadence on C sharp with an amplified chromatic embellishment of the first simple embellishment, the cadential notes being doubled a fourth lower. I think that the very well-earned reputation of this phrase comes equally from its own rhythmic development, which is remarkable in many ways.

The phrase can be divided into four fragments of unequal length: I, III, II, IV, in decreasing order. Furthermore, the first two sections contain triplets, the last two none, the second having given birth on the G flat to an adjacent motive that makes use of nothing but triplets throughout the development of the Introduction.

Let me analyze fragment I. It is formed of four cells; the first is composed of two sums equal in value: quarter-note and quarter-note, the first remaining a unit, the second divided into four sixteenth-notes; the second cell is also composed of two sums equal in value: quarter-note and quarter-note, both of them divided into eighth-note triplets; the third cell is composed of three unitary values divided into two eighth-notes; thus it is the exact contrary of the second; furthermore, it is symmetrical in tension, given that it mounts on the fifth note to D, the subdominant, whereas the fifth note of the second cell descends to the dominant E; finally, the fourth cell includes four unitary values, the first being divided into a quintuplet of sixteenth-notes, the second and third being linked, the fourth being shortened by an anticipation of the succeeding cell. This gives the following schema:

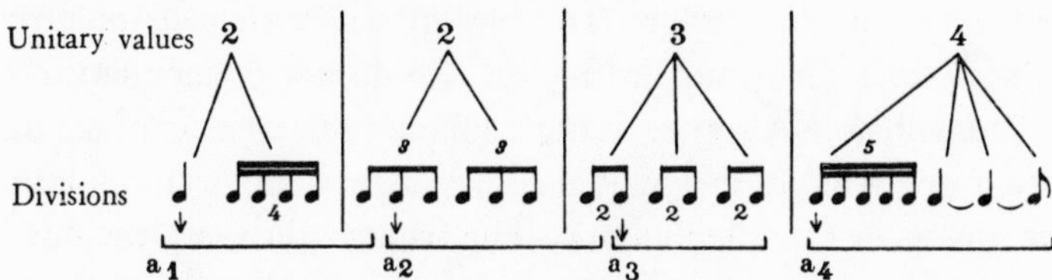

This permits us to conclude that the cell *a4* is in symmetric retrograde—in sound-time, that is—with respect to cell *a1*, they being constantly differentiated by the rhythmic precipitation in *a4* as well as by the number of unitary values. Furthermore, the cells *a2* and *a3* are inverse in sound-time and symmetrical in sound-space. We must notice the increasing number of unitary values corroborating these constructive symmetries and parallelisms. Additionally, a value or division of value found in one cell is not found in another. Finally, the attack on C natural, with which each cell begins—I have indicated them by arrows—is produced on a strong beat in *a1*, on a weak beat of the triplet in *a2*, on a weak part of the unitary value in *a3*, and again on a strong beat in *a4*. I ascertain again that the cadence on C sharp is produced in *a1* and *a4*, and that the decoration of that cadence is brought about in *a3* by means of a triplet, which also recalls the rhythm of *a2*.

Fragment II, as I have said, develops the triplet element and modulates, for we find B flat and G flat in it, notes foreign to the initial mode. It is made up of four unitary values prolonged by an anticipation (an eighth-note) in the preceding cell. It even develops the triplet element within the triplet:

Fragment III is a slightly varied restatement of fragment I, cell *a6* being a restatement of *a1* preceded by an anticipation (a triplet eighth-note) which recalls that of fragment II and is unequal to it. Cell *a7* is a textual restatement of fragment *a3*; cell *a8* is an abridged restatement of *a4*, with two unitary values rather than four; in this cell we do not count the three linked half-note A's, they being a simple prolongation of sound into a new motive that will also play a very important role in the course of the Introduction. The triplets, then, are excluded from this variation after fragment II, which is devoted to them. Thus one observes the laws of symmetry of fragment I, but simplified and in the extreme groups.

Fragment IV is an elided restatement *a9* of fragment *a3*—with only a single unitary value, but with the tension of the subdominant, which constitutes the phenomenon native to this fragment—followed by a reprise *a10* of fragment *a8*. Fragment IV is the exact termination of fragments I and III. One thus has as general structure: equilibrium of values (fragment I), breaking-up of values by dissociations (fragments II and III), conclusion by elided restatement (fragment IV).

An example will give us again an idea of the great rhythmic diversity deployed throughout the Introduction by Stravinsky. It is at No. 9 in the score (Example III).

The fragment in question is based on the four notes F–B flat–C–E flat doubled at the upper octave.

The phrase that I have called *a* is composed of two fragments; fragment I is divided into four cells repeated two by two in a slightly varied fashion.

Cell *a1* begins on the F common to the two phrases *a* and *b;* it is made up of two eighth-notes and a quintuplet of sixteenth-notes, or two unitary values; cell *a2* begins on the C a fourth lower and is made up of a quarter-note and a sextuplet of sixteenth-notes, thus also being two unitary values, making it a variation of cell *a1*; cell *a3* is an oscillation on the first quarter note, in triplet, with rhythmic precipitation on the F natural; it is also of two unitary values, the second being a quarter-note; cell *a4* is cell *a3* with the second quarter-note elided. One has, then, an oscillation from F to C natural, then a return to F; these are the two pivot-notes of this fragment; on the other hand, the cell *a3* is disposed symmetrically in relation to cells *a1* and *a2* in division of unitary values.

EXAMPLE III

Fragment II is a very slight variation of the first in the sense that, *a5* being identical to *a1*, *a6* shows this difference from *a2*: the first unitary value is divided into quintuplets, like the second of *a1* and *a5*. The undivided unitary value of *a3* is suppressed, being replaced by a trill in *a7*, and it further includes a termination on F natural which prolongs it by one unitary value—for which reason *a4* is suppressed in the restatement.

The phrase that I have called *b* is composed of two fragments. The beginning of I resembles that of *a*1 in that it moves by a fourth, but this fourth rises to B flat; then one has an accent on E flat, then a sudden conclusion with a quintuplet of thirty-second-notes, which return to F natural. Fragment II presents the prolongation by a quarter-note of this E flat and the conclusion prolonged by the transformation of the quintuplet of thirty-second-notes into four simple eighth-notes, with continuation on a quarter-note F. The accent here is thus placed on B flat and E flat.

The phrases *c* and *d* are grafted onto the added quarter-note of fragment *b*II and unite the characteristic registers of *a* and *b*. They also present, abridged, all the divisions used in the two principal phrases: binary divisions (thirty-second-notes), ternary divisions (sextuplets of thirty-second-notes), irrational divisions (quintuplets of thirty-second-notes). Finally, they corroborate the pivot-notes C natural and B flat, which give this superimposition its ambiguity.

I have dilated so much on the analysis of these few passages in the Introduction because such an experience is exceptional even with Stravinsky and because so great a refinement of periodic asymmetry and symmetry, such renewed variation of the rhythmic phenomenon by the use of irrational values, is scarcely to be encountered elsewhere in his work, certain passages of *Le Rossignol* aside. His chief technique, as we can see throughout *Le Sacre*, consists of rational division (2, 4, 8) or the rational multiplication of a unitary value. But we shall have to return to this Introduction, remarkable for its individually superimposed developments, for the complex structure that results and for the phenomenon of "*tuilage*" in the composition—that is, of the overlapping of developments.

Up to now I have been occupied only with themes constructed melodically, in a single dimension. With the next example (Example IV), I shall approach the study of a theme of which the structure may be doubled by contrapuntal ele-

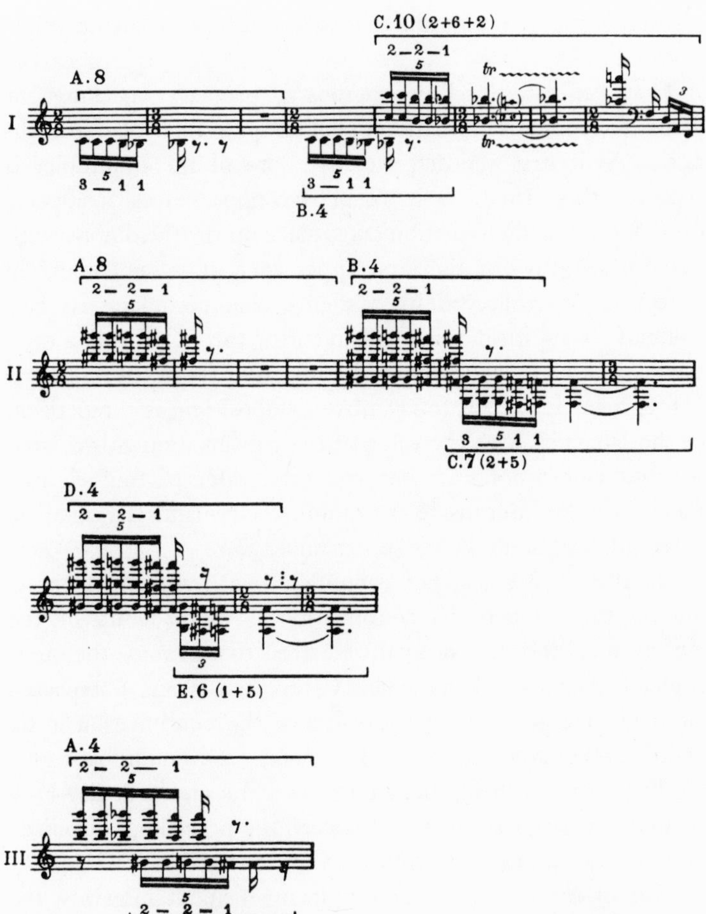

Example IV

ments, which, though very simple, still may modify its exterior aspect sufficiently to differentiate it from the precedents. This passage is taken from the *Danse sacrale*, No. 151 of the score. Here we find a chromatic sensibility curiously manifest in a very brief abridgement.

This theme, with an extremely short generating cell, makes three appearances during this development, each time with dissymmetries so noticeable that they can be examined profitably.

That generative cell is composed, properly speaking, of three descending chromatic notes in a quintuplet of sixteenth-notes. As it first appears, the first note of the quintuplet is repeated three times; in its other two appearances, it appears only once. The continuation takes place on the third note, with variable length—for this first appearance, it is very short: a sixteenth-note followed by a silence that completes its real value of six eighth-notes. That gives, for this initial cell, a total duration of eight eighth-notes. Let us call it fragment A.

Fragment B, which follows by juxtaposition, is a repetition of the same cell with the value of the continuation abbreviated by four eighth-notes, giving us a total value of four eighth-notes. The division inside the quintuplet remains the same: C three times, B natural once, B flat once.

Fragment C is placed contrapuntally over fragment B, entering on the value of its continuation; it is made up of ten eighth-notes and may be analyzed thus: first group—the quintuplet C–B natural–B flat, with C repeated twice, B repeated twice, B flat given once; the value of the continuation is six eighth-notes (a dotted, trilled half-note), continuing by a glissando to a third group beginning with the chord A flat–F–A natural—that is, the junction between the preceding chromaticism and the arpeggio to follow. That arpeggio is the transformation of the chromatic quintuplet in disjunct intervals; the rhythmic difference is that the five notes, consequent to the preceding quintuplet, are divided into two sixteenth-notes and a triplet of sixteenth-notes, expressive of a rhythmic slowing-down and a precipitation in relation to that quintuplet, the sixteenth-notes and the triplet of sixteenth-notes forming the exact embodiment of the values of five. Before leaving this period I, let us note that the fragment A is set forth in simple sounds in the middle register; that the canon between B and C is made at the upper octave and at a distance of two eighth-notes, that this response is in octaves, and that the disposition of the quintuplets is made in the following order:

$$\underbrace{3\ 1\ 1}_{5} \qquad \underbrace{3\ 1\ 1}_{5} \qquad \underbrace{2\ 2\ 1}_{5}$$

Period II is the reverse of the first, with a fourth fragment added.

Fragment A is the exact image of fragment A of period I—that is, it lasts eight eighth-notes and is made up of a quintuplet of sixteenth-notes and a value of six eight-notes. However, this quintuplet is disposed $\underbrace{2\ 2\ 1}_{5}$.

Fragment B similarly is the exact image of the fragment B of period I, lasting four eighth-notes, again with the difference that the quintuplet is disposed $\underbrace{2\ 2\ 1}_{5}$. It equally follows fragment A by juxtaposition.

Fragment C, in a like way, is contrapuntally superimposed at the quarter-note, but the value of the continuation is cut, lasting only five eighth-notes, and does not include the third symmetrical, conclusive group possessed by fragment C of period I. Let us notice, furthermore, that the exposition of fragment A is made in the upper register in octaves, then in double octaves, and that the response is in the middle register (with the upper octave), resulting in a crossing of registers, whereas in period I the registers were distinct. The disposition of the quintuplets is thus made in the order opposite to that of the first time: $\underbrace{2\ 2\ 1} \quad \underbrace{2\ 2\ 1} \quad \underbrace{3\ 1\ 1}$.

Fragments B and C are followed, again by juxtaposition, by the repetition of their canon, with the response elided, fragment D being identical to fragment B, fragment E presenting in lieu of the quintuplet an unrepeated triplet of sixteenth-notes, and the value of the continuation being the same as in C—five eighth-notes; consequently, the total value of this group is six eighth-notes.

Finally, section III is composed of cell A—a duration of four eight-notes, the quintuplet being divided into B repeated twice, B flat also twice, and A stated once, and cell B—a response in canon at the lower minor third, with the same division of the quintuplet, the continuation value being cut by one eighth-note; for the first time, the canon occurs at a distance of an eighth-note; that is to say, within the period of the quintuplet serving as its antecedent.

None of the three sections of this theme, however summary in appearance, has the same physiognomy as another, and each of them is based upon an extremely keen chromatic sensibility, of which it is possible to pick out another example in the same work. This (Example V) is the theme that joins the *Jeux des cités rivales* to the *Cortège du sage.*

I am giving the measures from No. 64 to No. 69 in the score. We have a lower embellishment of G sharp, sometimes at a distance of a minor second on G natural, sometimes at a distance of a major second on F sharp, the one doubled when the other is simple and vice versa. The cells vary in this manner:

1) 5 measures, that is, 4 plus 1 measures—embellishments: G natural twice, F sharp once;
2) 4 measures—embellishments: G natural once, F sharp twice;
3) 2 measures, by the elision of one of the embellishments and of the repetition of the other—F sharp once;
4) 3 measures, by elision of the repetition of one embellishment—F sharp once, G natural once;

In the *Cortège du sage:*

5) 4 measures—G natural twice, F sharp once;
6) 4 measures—G natural once, F sharp twice.

EXAMPLE V

From this point on, given the rhythmic superimpositions, the theme is congealed in the physiognomy of that cell to the end of the development. One should note the parallelism of cells 5 and 6 and the contrasting elision of the two central cells. What also differentiates this theme from its exposition in the *Jeux des cités rivales* is the constantly unequal duration of the cells, which decrease to two and increase to regain the stable formative value, four, in the *Cortège du sage*. Finally, I note that the order of the embellishments is always G natural–F sharp, this being modified only in cells 3 and 4, where it takes on the contrary order: F sharp twice, G natural once.

Thus one sees that the structure of this theme is based upon an extremely balanced fluctuation showing the same chromatic sensibility to be found in the theme—analyzed above—of the *Danse sacrale*, a sensibility of which the exact expression is to be found in the play of the rhythmic symmetries.

In my view, the most important thematic phenomenon in *Le Sacre* is the appearance of a rhythmic theme, properly speaking, that achieves real existence inside a moveless sound-verticalization.

The first example of which I take notice is to be found in *Les Augures printaniers*, at No. 13 in the score (Example VI).

The rhythmic theme is found to consist of accentuations during a regular procession of eighth-notes. The first appearance of these repeated chords lasts for eight measures and is developed two measures at a time. At the outset, we have an unaccented preparation of two measures. Then a cell A is subdivided into an accent on each weak beat of the rhythm (*a*1) in the first measure and a silence in the second (*a*2). Cell B is subdivided into an accent on the weak part of a strong beat in the first measure (*b*1) and an accent on the strong beat of the second measure (*b*2). The second cell B′ is in retrograde order with relation to the first: *b*2 *b*1 with the same characteristics.

This accentuated theme returns in elided form in the four measures leading up to No. 15. The unaccented preparation now lasts one measure, diminished by half. Cell A returns unchanged. Finally, cell B, which is doubled, is here deprived of one of its constituents, showing only *b*1.

The accentuated theme then flows by osmosis into the melodic theme, which is developed from No. 15 on, and to which it gives its beginning by means of cell A.

It then reappears in the median development, in the chords of superimposed fifths to be found from the beginning of the fourth measure after No. 16. It has cell A at first, then a new cell C, of which this is the sole appearance, and which consists of accentuation of the weak beat, never heard again, and finally of a restatement of A. This cell C, moreover, is one of the sources of the development of this median section, where one reencounters it on a rhythmic pedal on a sustained C.

At the restatement of the first development we have—from No. 18 to No. 19—an exact repetition of the rhythmic theme as given from No. 13 to No. 14.

From No. 14 on, the rhythmic theme sometimes passes from the melodic theme to the repeated chords of the accompaniment. And we find in the order analyzed in the example: melodically, A (*a*1 *a*1) modified by doubling B (*b*2) elided;

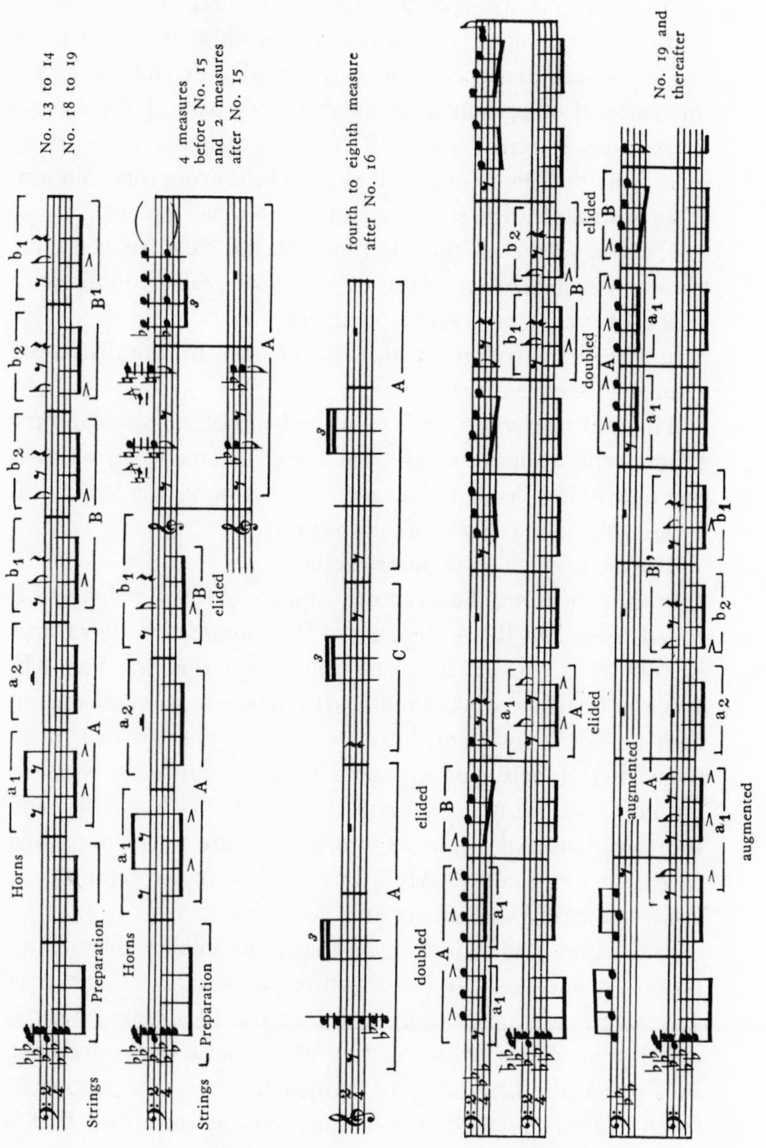
No. 13 to 14
No. 18 to 19
Horns
Strings
Preparation
a1
a2
A
b1
b2
B
B1
4 measures
before No. 15
and 2 measures
after No. 15
elided
fourth to eighth measure
after No. 16
C
doubled
No. 19 and
thereafter
augmented
B'

EXAMPLE VI

harmonically, A (*a1*) elided; three measures of unaccented transition; harmonically, B normal *b1 b2*; three measures and a half of unaccented transition; harmonically, A augmented by the addition of accentuation on the weak part of the second occurrence, B′ retrograde of B (*b2 b1*); melodically, A transformed by doubling (*a1 a1*), B elided (*b2*). From this point on, there is no accentuation to the end of this development.

The disposition of this rhythmic theme calls for some remarks on its general structure, in which we shall again discover effects of symmetrical correspondence.

In the first section of this theme—up to the harmonic change—we have the structure:

AB′ AB elided A, of two cells related by contrary effects—the disposition AB′ not being symmetrical, whereas the disposition ABA is so, and, furthermore, the second B appears elided in the second disposition.

The median cell is symmetrical ACA.

In the repetition, the structure appears: ABB′—*A doubled B elided* A elided—B—A augmented B′ *A doubled B elided*, that is, four cells divided into one and three: the first cell AB′ asymmetrical, the second and fourth presenting a symmetry in their outside constituents in relation to the third, which forms the center. I note, for my own personal curiosity, that the unfolding of the nonsymmetrical elements of the second and fourth cells (AAB′) is in a symmetry inverse to the unfolding of the first cell cell (AAB′), but perhaps this is pushing the consequences of such an organization too far.

Finally, one can remark again that in its totality this organization presents two parallel structures situated on either side of a symmetrical organization, and that the unaccented periods that I pointed out in the analysis are in increasing order from No. 19 on, the first being of six quarter-notes, the second of seven quarter-notes, the last of fourteen quarter-notes—that is to say, a little more than the sum of the first two.

I have chosen this accented theme as the first example be-

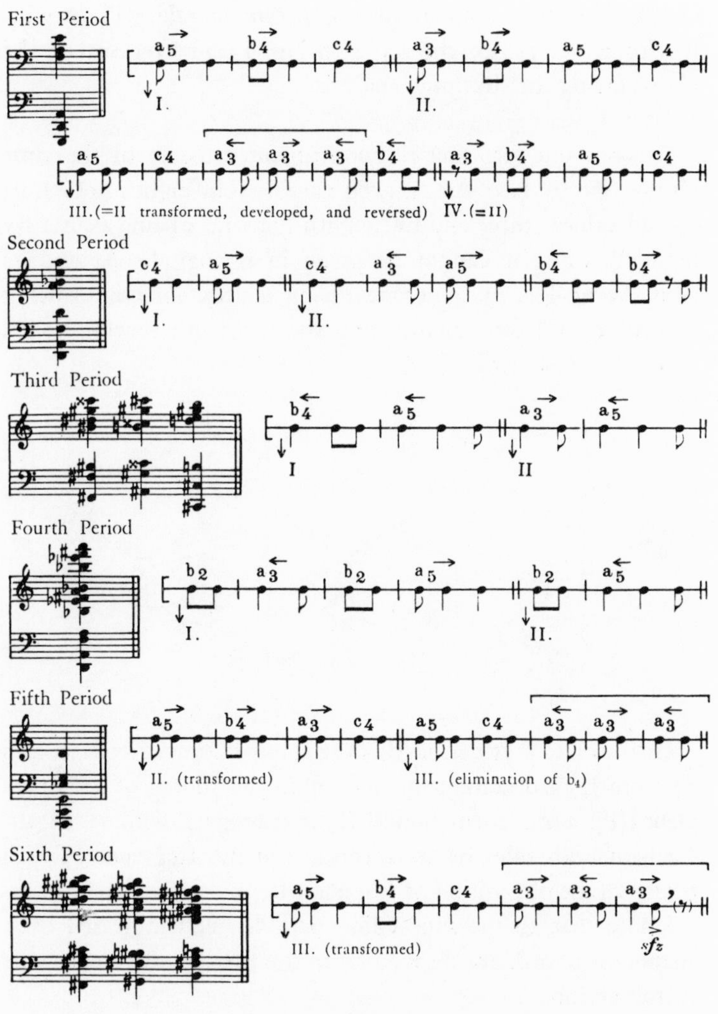

EXAMPLE VII

cause it is relatively simple and has the peculiarity of resting sometimes on a rhythm, sometimes on a melodic theme. But now I shall analyze a uniquely rhythmic theme having no accentuation, in which the sections are organized upon a single chord. The first couplet of the *Danse sacrale* will provide it—from No. 149 of the score to No. 154. I have placed the chord facing the rhythmic analysis.

At once one sees that the constituent cells are of the same family two by two, *b4 c4*, even values (four eighth-notes), *a3 a5* odd values (three and five eighth-notes), *c4* being neuter by nature because it cannot be given in retrograde, *b4* and *a3* being reversible, *a5* sometimes being neuter, sometimes being reversible, and thus conjugating the three other cells. I shall establish this schema:

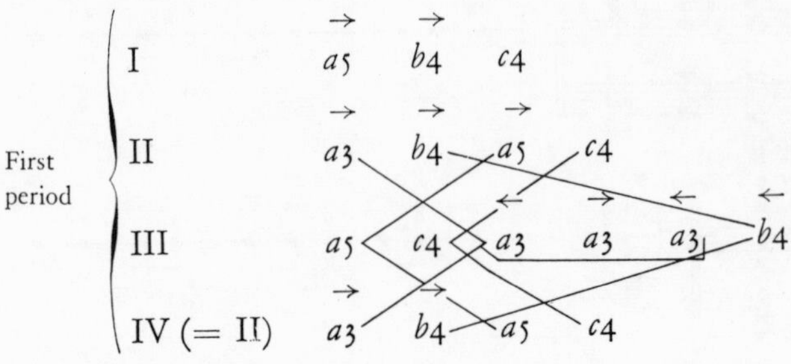

One notices that period II is the transposition of cells *a5* and *b4* from I, *a5* becoming neuter—with the adding of *a3*. Fragment III is a transformation of II (in diagonal), with $\overrightarrow{a3}$ lengthened on both sides by its reversal. Finally, fragment IV is a return to the disposition of fragment II.

I note that all the succeeding periods, each indicated by a change of chord, are derived from the first by extremely able workmanship.

The second period (No. 154 to No. 157), always based on a single chord that is always embellished, is made up of:

$$c4 \quad \overleftarrow{a5} \qquad = \text{I}$$
$$c4 \quad a3 \quad a5 \quad = \text{II}$$
$$\overleftarrow{b4} \quad \overrightarrow{b4}$$

that is to say, it reproduces fragments I (in retrograde) and II (in retrograde, with transformation of $a5$ and $a3$), rejecting the two cells $b4$ at the end, these forming a third fragment.

The third period, modulating—on three chords—is an eliminative period; it includes:

$$\overleftarrow{b4} \quad \overleftarrow{a5} = \mathrm{I}$$

$$\overrightarrow{a3} \quad \overleftarrow{a5} = \mathrm{II}$$

The first fragment reproduces fragment I of the first period, but with the elimination of $c4$; the second fragment similarly reproduces fragment II of the first period, but eliminating, this time, $b4$ and $c4$.

The fourth period, again based upon a chord, identical to that of the second period and identically embellished, is similarly a period of elimination and reduction; it includes:

$$b2 \quad \overleftarrow{a3} \quad b2 \quad \overleftarrow{a5} = \mathrm{II}$$

$$b2 \quad \overleftarrow{a5} \qquad\qquad = \mathrm{I}$$

The first fragment is fragment II of the first period with cells $b4$ and $c4$ transformed: $b2$, in fact, can be either the diminution of $c4$ or the elision of $b4$; it thus becomes a neuter cell. The second fragment is fragment I of the first period with compression of $b4$ and $c4$ transformed into $b2$.

What follows is regular elimination of seven successive eighth-notes, leading to a second section of the rhythmic development. This second section includes only two periods; it begins after an anacrusis of one eighth-note rest.

The fifth period, based on an unembellished chord, is formed this way:

$\overrightarrow{a5}\ \overrightarrow{b4}\ \overrightarrow{a3}\ c4$, the first fragment, which is fragment II with permutation of $a3$ and $a5$; $a5\ c4\ \underbrace{\overleftarrow{a3}\ \overrightarrow{a3}\ \overleftarrow{a3}}$, the second fragment, which is fragment III of the first period with the elimination of b_4.

The sixth period, on an embellished chord, includes $\overrightarrow{a_5}\ \overrightarrow{b_4}\ c_4$ $\underbrace{\overrightarrow{a_3}\ \overleftarrow{a_3}}\ \overrightarrow{a_3}$, which is fragment III of the first period with permutation of b_4.

We should note some particularities of that cell a_5, which can be neuter or reversible. In the first period of the exposition it is first in the forward direction, then neuter three times.

As for the periods in the development of the first section, in the second, the cell is twice in the forward direction; in the third, twice in retrograde; in the fourth, once in each direction. A balance is thus established between the forward and the retrograde cells. In the periods of the second section one returns to a predominance of the forward and neuter cells.

One can see what a richness of rhythmic variation, without alteration in the values of these cells, one can attain by simple permutation and by application of a procedure as simple as that of retrograde motion.

Having made so extensive an examination of linear rhythmic procedures in Stravinsky, one should try to discover how these procedures can furnish a structure of development, their entire justification.

In Stravinsky in general, the simplest rhythmic development—aside from the linear procedure extended throughout the orchestra—is that of the appearance of two rhythmic forces. That antagonism may put into play two simple rhythms or a simple rhythm and a rhythmic structure, or two rhythmic structures.

My first example will show the antagonism of a simple rhythm and a rhythmic structure (Example VIII—*Jeu du rapt*, No. 46).

The simple rhythm, which I shall call B, has at first a value of three eighth-notes (B3) and is repeated twice; then it diminishes, taking on a value of two eighth-notes (B2) and is repeated twice; it increases to six eighth-notes (B6) and is repeated twice; it diminishes to four quarter-notes (B4) and is repeated twice. Appearances of the same value then take place two by two. It is conveyed by a bass or a chord.

The rhythmic and melodic structure opposed to it is made up of five sequences.

The first, AI, is composed of two equal fragments of five eighth-notes, *a* and *b* (anacrusis and accent).

The second, AII, includes fragment *a* (anacrusis) elided by an eighth-note, fragment *b* (accent), fragment *b* augmented by an eighth-note (repetition of the accent), and fragment *c*, consisting of five eighth-notes (conclusion).

The third, AIII, is a variation and condensation of A; it is made up of four fragments of identical melodic purport; the value of six eighth-notes being divided unequally into twice three, thrice two, thrice two, twice three—that is, in a symmetrical cell.

The fourth, AIV, is formed of two equal cells, always of six eighth-notes divided into twice three.

The fifth, AV, is also formed of two equal cells of six eighth-notes, divided into thrice two.

AIV and AV are merely the separation of AIII by similar rhythm. From AIII on, then, the physiognomy of group A is motionless.

How is the development of these two structures one in relation to the other, to be organized? I note that they are imbricated one to the other, but by juxtaposition. That is to say that their periods depend upon one another reciprocally.

At the very beginning the rhythms B3 rule periods AI and AII. Then the groups B2 encompass group AIII, thus forming an asymmetry. Group AIV encloses two groups B2; group AV similarly encloses two groups B2, similarly forming two other symmetries. Finally, group A is eliminated, leaving only group B.

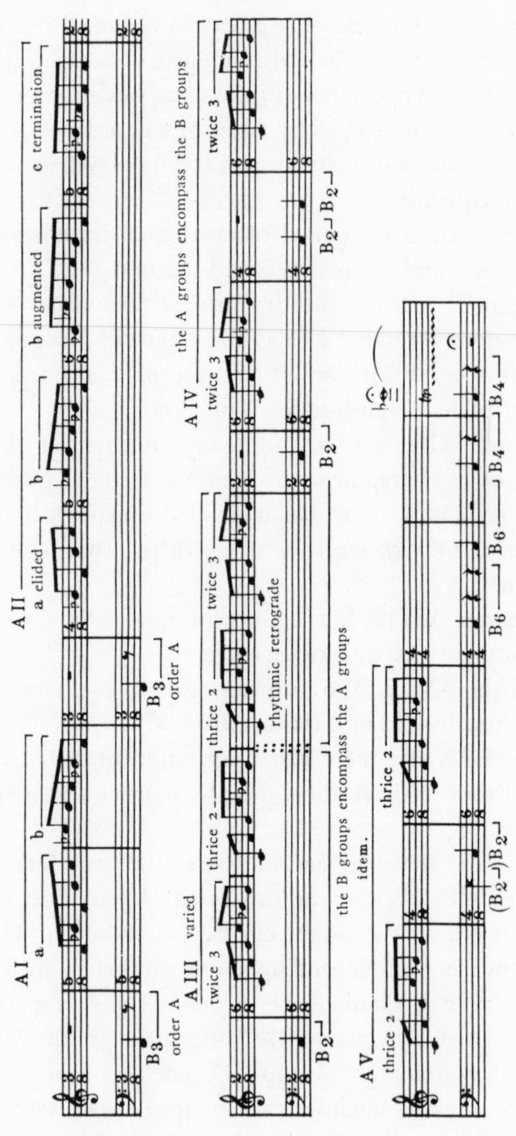

Example VIII

I note, then, that in the first part group A is mobile, B immobile, the disposition asymmetric; in the second part groups A and B are immobile and symmetric; in the third part group B is mobile.

There is, then, a reciprocal exchange of the mobility and immobility of a rhythm in the two groups, each group following a procedure inverse to that of the other.

I pass on to study the superimposition of a developing rhythm and a fixed rhythmic structure. It is found at No. 86 of the score (Example IX).

We find two constructive elements in this structure: a conjunct embellishment group on the dominant B flat; a counterpoint group with conjunct embellishment, also forming embellishment, this time disjunct and oscillating in the direction of dominant-tonic-dominant. In cell A, we find these two elements with the support of a rhythm nonreversible through the conjunct embellishment, produced sometimes on the half-beat, sometimes on the beat; a nonreversible rhythm—that is, a rhythm symmetrical in relation to its own center

for AI: or for AII:

with the support of a regular unfolding of quarter-notes for the disjunct embellishment, which does not descend from the B flat except to what might be called the second sensible degree (F flat) of the mode used throughout this whole passage. That given superimposition will have its own rhythmic development.

In cell B we have the conjunct embellishment element of B flat, which becomes an embellishment—always at the distance of a whole-tone—of the chord of the appoggiatura'd dominant placed on B flat. The rhythm is ordered by a symmetrical disposition of the values around a quarter-note tied to another quarter, odd values on one side (3 and 3), even values on the other (4 and 4). That order of values is displaced by accents in symmetrical parallelism:

In fact, the last half-note of a cell loses through an anticipation of the succeeding cell, a quarter-note thereafter joined to the first dotted quarter-note of that next cell. The disjunct embellished group in counterpoint already has a different rhythmic aspect from that of the conjunct embellishment, because instead of being divided into 4 plus 5 quarter-notes, it utilizes the opposite division, 5 plus 4, a division made apparent by the repetition of the rests:

One sees that there are two of these rests in each measure, the second two being halved in relation to the first two. In this disjunct embellishment, finally, the oscillation always moves to the tonic, which avoids cell A, as we have seen. This cell B then organizes the same elements as A, but rests upon a rhythmic pedal.

Finally, the true antinomy embellishment note, which we have seen established in differing forms in the two cells A and B, but always in an oscillating form, will be established here in an immobile form with two chords, the chief chord in uninterrupted duration each time that this embellishment is sounded in cell B. Nevertheless, this chord-embellishment in uninterrupted durations participates in the disjunct embellishment through its accentuations. It thus continues the two rhythmic divisions of cell B.

Thus, in the interior of a vast embellishment of the dominant B flat, and therefore of an immense static arrangement, the following hierarchy:

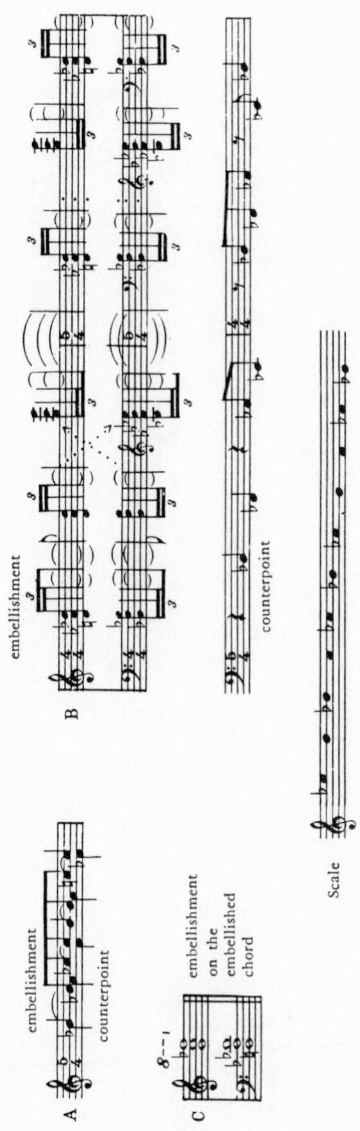
A
embellishment
counterpoint
B
embellishment
counterpoint
C
embellishment
on the
embellished
chord
Scale

Example IX

Chromatic theme—embellishment
A1
A2
A1
A1
Counterpoint
11 beats
1st Part
B Embellishment
Counterpoint
A1
A2
2nd Part
A1
C
B
C
A1
A2
A2

GROUP A: Rhythmically mobile	: Oscillation of the principal note of the embellishment;
GROUP B: Rhythmically immobile	: Oscillation of the chord or of the principal note to the embelished chord or to the embellishment;
GROUP C: Rhythmically immobile	: Fixity in the superimposition of the chief chord and the embellished chord.

Now we shall see how these groups react upon one another by their rhythmic characteristics. One can distinguish two sections of development in the fragment being studied, the first being preponderantly rhythmic in group A, the second establishing the supremacy of groups B and C.

In the first section, group A modulates rhythmically as follows:

11 beats	10 beats	5 beats	11 beats
A1 A2	A1 A1	Silence equal to A1	A1 A2

Here again one discovers Stravinsky's great care in establishing interferences with symmetries of placement. They are so evident by their numerical and musical (sound, silence) definition that there is no need to explicate them.

Group B is embryonic and has not yet taken on its real physiognomy; it is expounded only once in prefiguration and is so placed that it concludes at the same time as the silence of group A, the duration of which equals A1, leaving the reexposition A1 A2 exposed. The first four measures of its exposition, then, coincide with the last four of group A1, the four last being presented exposed. Finally, group C is absent.

In the second section, group B is stated once exposed, then renewed three times in superimposition with A. Group C this time is set forth and pursued in parallel to group B. As for group A, it makes a first appearance (A1) at the opening of the second group B. The third group B demands a second appearance of A1. The interval of silence between those two A1's, then, is four quarter-notes, a silence of which the duration is ruled by group B, inverse to what was produced in the first section. From this moment on, the two groups are superimposed in apparent independence. In reality, thirteen measures remain to be filled if one wishes to coincide with the ending of another group B. The possible solutions, then, are present in the following way: to find an equivalence for the two groups A1 (ten measures—Sound) and a silence of four quarter-notes, with an over-all duration of thirteen quarter-notes. Stravinsky chose the most balanced solution in the contrary direction, with two groups A2 (twelve measures—sound) and a silence of one quarter-note. Furthermore, he chose to place the silences in dissymmetical fashion, the silence included between the two groups A1 being included in its new form between the two groups A1 and the two groups A2. The result is the juxtaposition of the two A2's, and in the second section a decreasing order of silences of group A (nine, four, one, none).

Clearly, I have not attempted here to analyze the creative process as it really takes place; I have simply attempted an a posteriori analysis of the musical results proceeding from that creation.

To complete the analysis of this passage and add an element of curiosity (sometimes, perhaps, of coincidence) to it, we may look in detail at how the theme of the conjunct embellishment appears shortly before it assumes its own structure. At No. 83 in the score, we see it unfolding in the bass, where it then takes on exceptional value as a harmonic support:

EXAMPLE IXa

Furthermore, it is placed in relief by the following particularity: the upper part is composed of four-note chords moving regularly in eighth-notes. The sound-disposition, then, is compact in the upper and middle parts, which have short values, but is spaced out in long values in the bass. The double embellishment (distance of a half-tone, then of a tone) is then presented in a form reversing the counterpoint of the figure that it will present in its development and around the note A, a half-tone below the future B flat. It is stated in the rhythmic order:

whence a symmetry of odd values in relation to even values, a symmetry that we shall encounter later on in the form

or, again, in the form

This represents, I think, not a simple coincidence, but a desire to oppose odd and even values—or, if one wants to speak in a more "solfeggio" fashion, of normal and dotted values.

The movement of the eighth-notes (short values) later passes from the lowest part to the medium-bass in order to lead to the second prefiguration of cell A1, which is presented this time in its principal form: pitch, duration, and timbre. Again, a cut in which the movement of the eighth-notes occupies the whole gamut, with a return to the deepest register. This final interruption lasts eleven measures—that is, for the exact duration of the two cells A1 and A2 conjugated in the first complete presentation of group A. Perhaps this is only an accident, but let us congratulate ourselves that it is so happy. For it will be good to remark, as we advance in this study, that I have no wish to mention the arithmetic relationships of which we discover the more or less conscious existence, and which are, above all, very simple, as merely arithmetic relationships, a short-sighted procedure. I want to mention them as the most graspable manner of perceiving the balance of the structures brought to light. That having been done, I shall search for more complex structures and, above all, for the ways in which they can dominate the architecture of a musical whole.

I shall proceed this way: I shall look, one after the other, at the *Glorification de l'élue*, the *Danse de la terre*, the *Danse sacrale*, and, finally, the Introduction, the most exrtaordinary part of this entire composition, defying analysis by the multiple interferences through which it achieves its development.

The form of the *Glorification de l'éue* can roughly be said to be ternary: an exposition, a middle, and a reexposition—what in composition jargon is called song-form. In effect, it is a ternary form in which the differentiations differ completely from common usage. Here is why:

The first section makes use of an almost contrapuntal combination of three mobile rhythmic cells. I say "almost contrapuntal" because they fit into one another without contrapuntal superimposition, properly speaking. However, this rhythmic architecture occurs on horizontal planes despite any vertical aspects that it may assume when being heard.

The second section is based upon the vertical and antagonistic partitioning of two divisions (sound and rhythm), with each of them preponderating over the other during the section. I emphasize the idea of vertical juxtaposition and partitioning, which are the essential characteristics of the opposition between the first and the second, the two cells being equally mobile.

In the third section, finally, only one rhythmic cell is used, the first of the two others being suppressed, the second serving as an introduction and not being repeated. The horizontal-vertical difference, then, is done away with.

This establishes the following schema of rhythmic organization: horizontal, in opposition, three cells; vertical, juxtaposed, two cells; horizontal-vertical, one cell. Thus the rhythmic phenomenon imposes an architecture on this *Glorification de l'élue* above and beyond the sound-disposition, which remains static in all instances despite various distributions.

Now I must justify these conclusions by an analysis of the musical text itself.

The first section is composed of three sound-rhythm organizations, which I shall call *a, b, c* (Example X).

Cell *a* or *a'* is fixed, and at first includes five eighth-notes, the eighth-note being the unitary value, thus differentiating it from *b* and *c*, which have a quarter-note unitary value. This cell *a* I shall therefore call *a*5. The combination *aa'* makes seven eighth-notes. It can be preceded by an anacrusis *αx*, of variable duration, on a ternary base (6,9), when *a* is not even. We also shall find the cell *a* in diminution in an elided form, form *a*2. In that form, however, it plays no constructive role, properly speaking, being always the issue of group *b*.

Group *b* is composed (1) of a chromatic ascent on a chord rapidly increasing in speed by the alternate use of irrational groups and rational groups (triplet of eighth-notes, four sixteenth-notes, quintuplet and then sextuplet of sixteenth-notes, and finally thirty-second-notes), leading to the unitary value with a brief attack (thirty-second-note, dotted eighth-note, rest); (2) of an ascent by disjunct intervals (the two supports being found on two leaps of a major seventh) in repeated irrational values (triplets of eighth-notes). The original group *b* is composed of five quarter-notes; I shall call it *b*5. The group is transformed by elision into *b*4, each of the *b*4 groups being individualized by unlike elision of its components.

Group *c* is constituted of a repeated chord. This chord can be of full duration or divided into two strokes (two eighth-notes), but it always has the unitary value: a quarter-note. This group is in constant diminution, beginning as eleven quarter-notes (*c*11) in full-duration chords, then having seven quarter-notes on divided chords (*c*7), and finally showing by elision six quarter-notes and an eighth-note (*c*6½).

From the dynamic-sound point of view, one can recognize

Example X

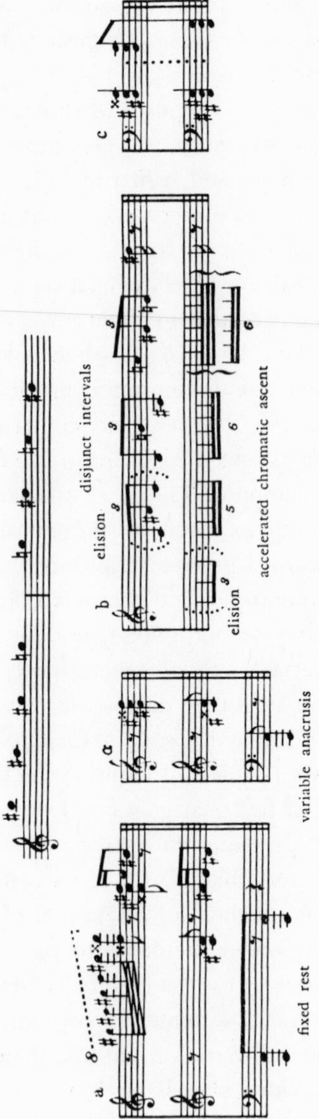
a
fixed rest
variable anacrusis
b
elision
disjunct intervals
elision
accelerated chromatic ascent
c

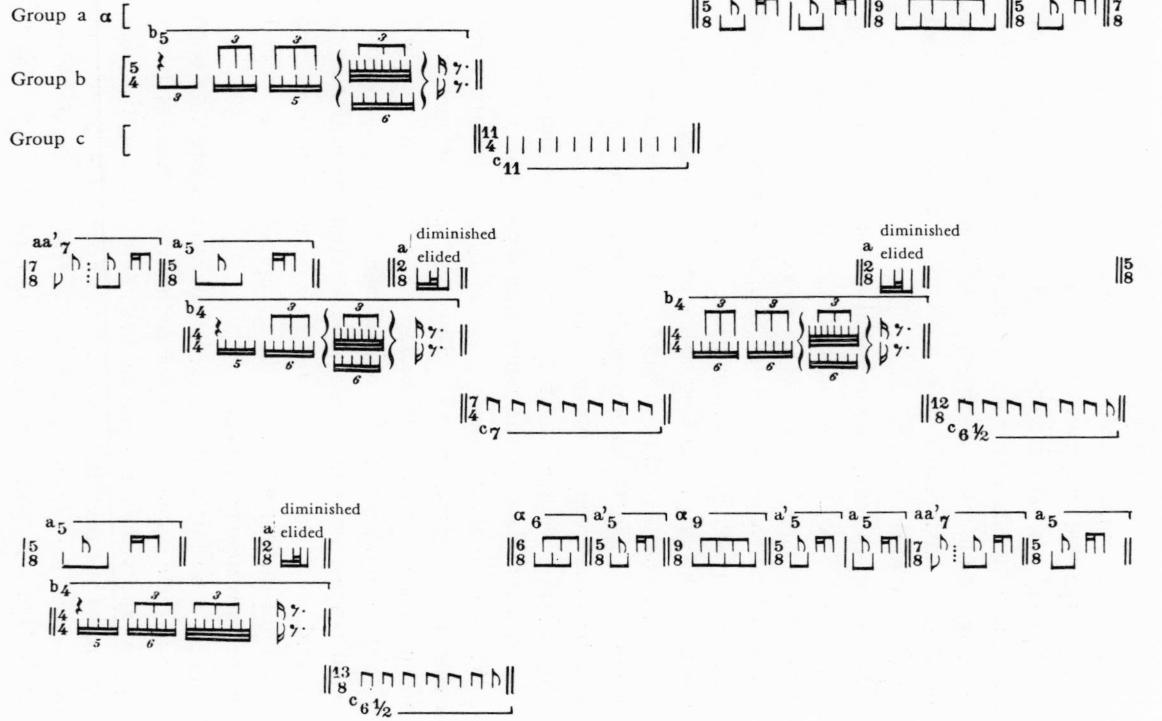
Group a α
Group b
Group c
diminished
elided
diminished
elided
diminished
elided

that the group *aα* is at the same time static (repeated anacrusis *α*) and dynamic (accent termination *a*); that group *b* is purely a dynamic, chromatic, and disjunct ascent on an accent; as for group *c*, it only is static. To establish an equilibrium of these differing characteristics, we have seen that, practically speaking, groups *b* and *c* cannot be dissociated, and that they form a bloc antagonistic to *a*, the static *c* always being tied immediately to the dynamic *b*.

To sum up, this first section includes three stages of development. The first consists of stating *bca*, some after others. The composition being *b*5 | *c*11 | *a*5 *a′*5 *α*9 *a*5 *aa′* 7 *a*5.

The second eighth-note of the final *a*5 leads to the second stage, which will give predominance to groups *b* and *c;* in effect, one has: *b*4 *c*7 linking on *b*4 *c*6½, then again, like an elided repetition, *a*5 linked to *b*4 *c*6½. There is, then, constructive alternation in the counterpoint of these rhythmic structures between group *a* on one side, groups *b* and *c* on the other. Finally, we must not forget the elision of diminished *a* (*a*2), which is placed at the conclusion of each group *b*.

Whereas the second stage is linked to the first, the third arrives by juxtaposition and consists only of development of group *a*, made as follows: *α*6 *a′*5 *α*9 *a′*5 *a*5 *aa′*7 *a*5. One sees that, in relation to the group of the first stage, it presents only tiny modifications, the transfer of a value *a*5 from the beginning to the middle of the ensemble by an anacrusis group *α*6, not used until this point; finally, the groups of anacrusis *α*6 and *α*9 are both appoggiatura'd.

There is no further necessity, I think, to call attention once again to these symmetries in the asymmetry or these asymmetries in the symmetry—which belong to the essential phenomena of the rhythmic construction of *Le Sacre.* So we can move on to the second section of the *Glorification de l'élue,* which begins at No. 11 in the score and marks, as I have said, the alternative partitioning of two vertical structures. These two structures, which appear together, we shall call A and B.

Example XI

Common to them is a decorated pedal on F natural, at a distance of a half-tone on either side of this F natural, with the difference, however—at least in the beginning of A—that this double embellishment is made in the opposite direction (F–E–G flat in structure A, F–G flat–E in structure B) and that in the resulting figure there is a certain reversal of the intervals employed, sometimes a major seventh, sometimes a half-tone. What may be called their melodic constituent, on the other hand, is directed, *grosso modo*, in the opposite direction: descending, B flat–A flat–G flat in structure A (the C being sometimes embellished, sometimes omitted, I shall not describe it as a chief note); rising, B flat–C–D flat in structure B. This double symmetry of groups around the dominant F and the tonic B thus defines the key of B-flat minor, the first and third sections resting chiefly on an altered dominant of C-sharp minor.

Structure A is broken up in a fixed anacrusis of three eighth-notes—which appears only three times—not using for its divisions of the unitary value anything except irrational values (triplet of eighth-notes, sextuplet and septuplet of sixteenth-notes), and in a mobile group with quarter-note unitary value, in which essential rhythm is furnished by triplets. The pedal on F is set forth in quarter-notes. Structure B is composed of chords accentuated on weak beats (I shall call them rational syncopations, whereas I shall call the syncopations of

A irrational); it too has the quarter-note unitary value. The pedal on F is set forth in eighth-notes.

This second section of the *Glorification de l'élue*, like the first, is broken up into three phases:

First phase: group A is set forth alone with a prefiguration of B; it is in constant augmentation. If we give as an index to A the number of unitary values that it contains, without taking into account the anacrusis already mentioned, we obtain this schema:

$$\underbrace{A3\ A4\ A6}_{\text{with anacrusis}} \ \mid B5 \mid \ \underbrace{A9}_{\text{without anacrusis}}$$

This phase is ended by elision of A, an elision of suspensive cadential character: A2. I notice, furthermore, that, very logically, it is the intrusion of group B that causes the anacrusis of A to be suppressed.

Second phase: group B is set forth alone by a constant oscillation of value on a fixed rhythmic pedal. This gives us B5 B6 B5 B6 B5.

Third phase: groups A and B alternate by partition, group A always having the suspensive cadential character. As analysis of this phase we obtain: B5 | A3 | B6 | A2 | B3 | A4; finally, an enlarged cadence terminates the entire section. The only element of juncture in the partition is the continuity of the rhythmic pedal of four eighth-notes on an embellishment of F during the alternation of the two groups. Finally, we shall notice that group B augments and then diminishes ($5 \nearrow 6 \searrow 3$), whereas group A observes the opposite motion ($3 \searrow 2 \nearrow 4$).

The third section returns to the first, harmonically and rhythmically. I have said already that it introduces the total suppression of *c* and the suppression of *b*, which figures only as a transition between the second section and the third. There remains then only the schema of *a* in a single construction on both sides, the restatement being textual: *a*5 *a'*5 *α*9 *a*5 *aa'*7 *a*5 | *α*6 *a'*5 *α*9 *a'*5 *a'*5 *aa'*7 *a'*5. We have already examined the details of this schema.

I believe that by means of this example I have demonstrated that the "form" is constituted at least as much by rhythmic structural characteristics of very great complexity as by harmonic relations of great simplicity.

The *Danse de la terre* is infinitely more complex, if not in its total architecture, at least in its periodic rhythmic structures. We shall have occasion to notice that some of these structures, with their semifixities and rapid alternations, recall the rhythmic structures of drums in black Africa. I even think that in this respect the *Danse de la terre* is one of the most remarkable sections of the entire score.

As is nearly always the case with Stravinsky, it is established harmonically on a distribution over large planes: here around a tonic, C.

First plane,	continuous: scale of whole-tones stretching from the augmented fourth to the third;
Second plane,	interrupted: the perfect chord of C major, with the addition of the appoggiatura F sharp, as well as its decoration at the distance of a tone; the perfect chord of D major;
Third plane,	continuous: a chord of fourths in which the attracting polarity is D (E flat–B flat–F–C), this polarity being disclosed increasingly as the development progresses.

The architecture of the piece is binary, and it acts upon these oppositions. The first section rests on a fixed rhythmic pedal and utilizes no superimposition of structures—unless we are to see one in a sporadic prefiguration of the principal rhythmic cell of the second section—but utilizes elements evolved by partition, with interdependence of its constituents. In the second section, the deep rhythmic pedal is expanded and acquires its own periodic fluctuations; the rhythmic cell, prefigured in the first part, organizes two parallel structures that are completely independent both of each other and of the transformed rhythmic pedal; at the end, the directing idea of the first section is recalled and superimposed. One understands at once the relationships established: fixity becomes mobile, the interdependent vertical structures become independent horizontal structures; the same intrusion on both sides of the element in opposition to the one that organizes their composition. The only characteristic common to the two sections—rhythmically, be it clearly understood—is the same "polydivision" of the unity (in eighth-notes, sixteenth-notes, and triplets of eighth-notes).

The first section is constituted by the fixed pedal that I shall call P3; it is set forth in a ternary measure that will give the whole piece its appearance, the real rhythms being others, as we shall see at once.

Example XII

Upon that rhythmic pedal are developed, by partition, three elements that I have differentiated; element A, which is the perfect chord of C major with the appoggiatura F sharp; element B, which is an arpeggio in septuplet and sextuplet of sixteenth-notes, preceded or succeeded by rests—in which, by elimination, nothing can remain but the rests; element A′, which is a decoration of the C chord in the form of a six-four chord that is itself embellished. The complete plan of this first section is established this way: preparation, which includes element B; first schema A; first schema A′ and B; second schema A; second schema A′ and B; third schema A.

Let us look at the A schemas. They are built upon a 2/4 rhythm that contrasts with the rhythmic pedal (3/4).

The first A schema is built this way:

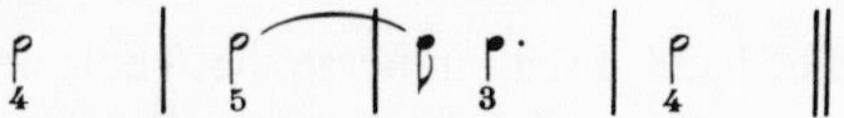

the values are counted in eighth-notes and do not take account of the more or less brief duration of the attack; the first schema is presented in the form:

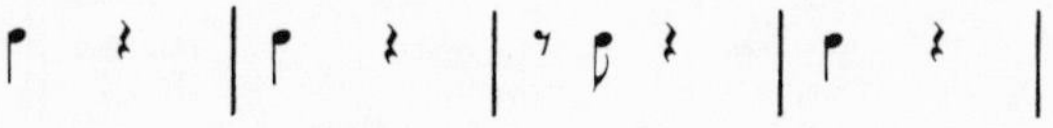

The second schema A:

Finally, the third schema A:

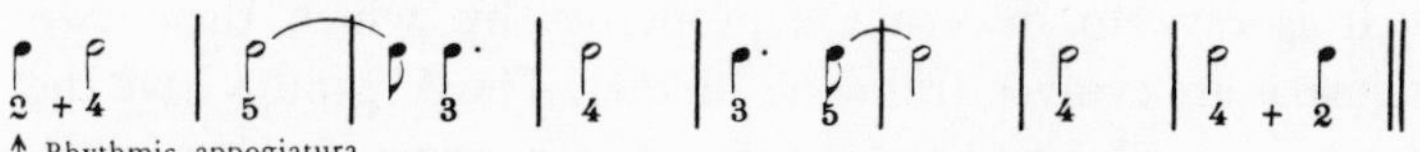

Some remarks must be made about these schemas. The first has the value 4 as its initial and concluding value; these two values 4, then, are symmetrical in relation to the central dissymmetry 5 3. The second schema is the retrograde of the first, with the final, concluding value 4 suppressed. The third schema is a combination of the first two schemas, with a rhythmic appoggiatura of 2 added to the initial value 4 and the addition of that appoggiatura'd cell in its retrograde order, this arrangement producing a symmetry resembling that which we saw in the first schema. (Notice that the first schema being in forward motion, the second being retrograde, the third is the neuter combination of the two; for one can say first schema forward, then second schema forward, or rather second schema retrograde; this being a natural consequence of the retrogradations.)

Schemas A′ and B are slightly more complex. I shall indicate the embellishments A′ by the figure of their unitary value in the order in which they appear for the first time (Example XII).

On the other hand, I shall indicate the whole arpeggio B and its rests by the addition of unitary values. It appears thus:

the first schema	A′	B	A′	B	A′	B	A′	B
	1 2 3 4 5	2	1	2	2 3	1	1	1
		←→ arpeggio and silence		←→ arpeggio and silence		←→ silence		←→ silence

the second schema	A′	B	A′	B	A′	B	A′	B
	1 2 3	1	2 4	1	2 4	4	2 4	3
		←→ silence	(=4 5 rhythmically)	←→ silence		←→ arpeggio and silence		←→ arpeggio and silence

It is easy to discern the properties by which these two schemas are evolved from one another. The A′ groups have the same total value and are eliminated in contrary fashion in the first and second schemas. In the first, one has the exposition 1 2 3 4 5, then the two eliminations: 1 2 3, 1; what is eliminated, then, is the final embellishments, two times two.

In the second schema, one has a varied exposition 1 2 3 2 4 (in which, rhythmically, this last 2 4 is equivalent to the 4 5 of the first schema); then the two eliminations 2 4, 2 4. What is eliminated, then, is the first three groups, one times three.

The B groups, which I shall call groups of interruption, follow first in the order B2 B2, B1 B1, then in the order B1 B1, B4 B3. This order, then, is asymmetrical in relation to the two equal B1 values, the B4 and B3 values being irregular in relation to B2 B2. (This irregularity comes simply from the rhythmic pedal P3, which imposes its period on A′ and B.) Furthermore, these B interruptions are produced in dissimilar ways in the first and second schemas; one can take account of them easily in the schemas as I have given them, by the addition of double bars and arrows, which facilitate comprehension of the groups. Extremely simple but extremely effective displacements result. I have spent considerable time over related cases, so that now it is unnecessary to return to them.

Nonetheless, it still will be good to remark on the placement of these two schemas in relation to one another and on the achievement of their balance. The first and second schemas A are equivalent in value to the third schema A and equal in duration to the first A′B schema (first A schema: three measures; second A schema: two measures; first A′B schema: five measures). The first A′B schema equals the second A′B schema in architectural value, the latter being equivalent in duration to the third A schema (six measures in both cases).

Thus the architectural values of these groups and their durations are balanced in contrary tension of equal strength, with disymmetrically varied dispositions that make this inception of the *Danse de la terre* an exceptional model that I shall indicate in this form:

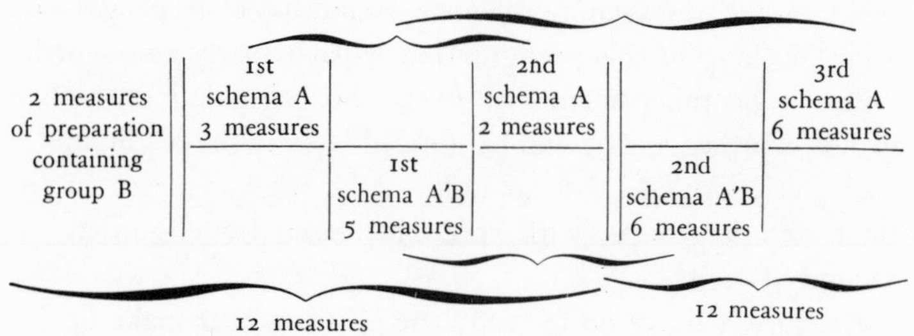

Onto the final values of the second schema A is grafted an element in triplets that will preponderate in the second section, which I shall call element *b;* I shall give its context in the study of that second section. Let me indicate it now as a jump of a descending fourth followed by repetition of the introductory note; it makes use of division into eighth-note triplets; let us apply to it as coefficient the number of unitary values—that is, of quarter-notes—that it employs:

EXAMPLE XIII

As the frequency of this cell's appearances, we obtain: *b*2; silence of 12; *b*2; silence of 7; *b*1; *silence of* 1; *b*2, *b*1; silence of 6; *b*1 *b*1; *silence of* 1; *b*1; silence of 1. The *b* groups increase, whereas the intervening silences diminish. That progression aside, nothing in this prefiguration is particularly noteworthy unless it be the presence of *b*1 at the beginning of each *b* group, a presence that will be noticed later at the beginning of each period ruled by *b*, or unless it be the symmetry of the final two *b* groups, with speed increased by elision in the second of them.

But now I move on to study the elements that make up the second section. I have said that the pedal of three sounds of the scale by tones on tonic C is fixed at first, but becomes mobile. In fact, it becomes a rhythmic development in three large periods. It will be useful to call the three tones F sharp, G sharp, B flat P3; the six tones of F sharp, G sharp, B flat C, D, E, Π6 (Example XIII); thus we have a first period composed of three different combinations: P3 P3 Π6, Π6 Π6, P3 Π6. The second period is a repetition of the first with permutation of its two final combinations—that is: P3 P3 Π6, P3 Π6, Π6 Π6. As we have seen, the development of this bass is very easily comprehensible and, in a way, rather regular.

The second element, resting on that scale by tones, is that interval of a fourth with repetition on the introductory note (E flat B flat) which I have already pointed out, varied from *b1* to *b3*; it is accompanied by what may be called an embellishment-cell *a*, the value of which is immobile: *a2*. It appears only twice under the form *a3*, which is its extension by *b*. Then, as a cadential group added to *a* and *b*, there is a neuter group *c:* the beats of its unitary values form a retrograde of the beats on the division values (notes on which I have placed arrows in the example), a retrograde parallel to the scale in tones. Its periods are extremely complex: an attempt to analyze them may appear to be arbitrary or even nonsensical.

However, I shall distinguish four orders of groups:

1. a fixed cadential group: *c;*
2. a fixed semicadential embellished group: *a2 b1*, *b1 a2*;
3. variable embellished groups without cadential tendency, but with the character of accentuation: *a3 b3*, *a2 b2*, *a2 b2 a2*, *a2 a2 b2*, resulting from the juncture of elements *a* and *b*, which have the same duration;
4. finally, variable groups of repetition—more exactly, of rhythmic prolongation or expectation; these are repetitions of *b*, *b1*, *b2*, *b3*.

Given this classification, which I consider justifiable, we obtain the number 5 for the periods *a–b–c*.

I:	*b1 b3 b2*	*a3 b3*	*a2 b1*, *a2 b1*
	(4th order)	(3rd order)	(2nd order)

II:	*b1* (4th order)	*b3 a3, a2 b2 a2* (3rd order)	*b3 b1 b2* (4th order)		
	b2 a2 (3rd order)	(*a2*) *b1, a2 b1, b1 a2* (2nd order)	*c* (1st order)		
III:	*b1 b3* (4th order)	*a2 b2 a2* (3rd order)	*b1 a2* (2nd order)	*c* (1st order)	
IV:	*b1 b2* (4th order)	*b2 a2* (3rd order)	*b1 b2* (4th order)	*b1 a2* (2nd order)	*c* (1st order)
V:	*b1 a2* (2nd order)	*b1 b2* (4th order)	*b1 a2* (2nd order)	(*a2*) *b2* (3rd order)	
	b1 b2, b2 b1 (4th order)	*c* (1st order)			

One thus perceives that the first four periods observe the same law, which is to tend toward the cadence after a variable repetition (I: 4th, 3rd, 2nd; II: 4th, 3rd; 4th, 3rd, 2nd, 1st; III: 4th, 3rd, 2nd, 1st; IV: 4th, 3rd; 4th, 2nd, 1st). Only the fifth period observes the contrary procedure (V: 2nd, 4th; 2nd, 3rd, 4th; 1st), which is to say that it tends from a semicadential order to a rhythmically expectant order so as to reject in isolation, with greater force, the cadential group that terminates it, and equally to supply a conclusion to all the other periods. Again one can verify the manner in which, according to the periods, the groups of like variable order are varied. I content myself with pointing out that both of them proceed by elimination of *a3* and *b3*; above all, that they proceed by short cells, with elimination of longer cells until one sees the third periodic element proceed partly in contrary fashion.

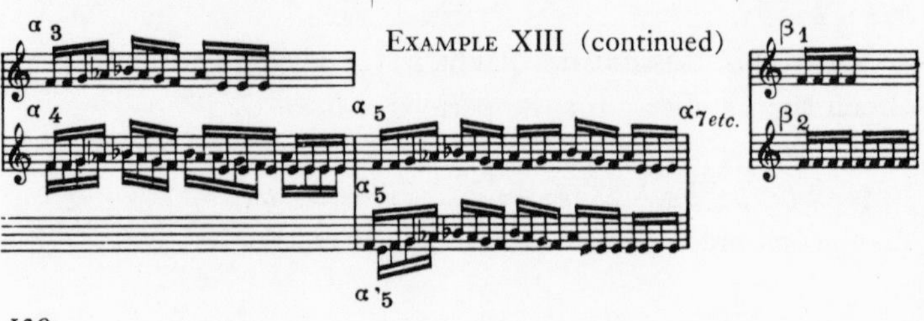

EXAMPLE XIII (continued)

The third constructive element that I shall analyze is an element parallel to the second in the sense that it makes use of cells α and β, the function of which is the same as that of the preceding *a* and *b;* α is a embellishment-cell, β a repeated-note cell. This third element has no neuter cadential group comparable to *c*. Let us notice further that the cell α is generally longer than cell *a*, whereas, on the contrary, β is shorter than *b*, a fact that dissolves their parallelism. The third element rests upon the second period of the second element, precisely on its first group of the third order, *b*3 *a*3, and takes on a similar form: $\beta 3\ \alpha 3$, so as later to assume its particular periodicity.

Cell β has three values—$\beta 1$, $\beta 2$, $\beta 3$, which create distinguishing points in the organization of groupings $\beta\alpha$. Thanks to those points, one discerns three periods:

$$\text{I} : \beta 3\ \alpha 3; \beta 2\ \alpha 4; \beta 1\ \alpha 3 — \beta 1\ \overbrace{\alpha 4\ \alpha 3}$$

$$\text{II} : \beta 2\ \alpha 4\ \alpha 5; \beta 1\ \alpha 5; \beta 3\ \alpha 3\ \alpha 3 — \beta 1\ \overbrace{\alpha 7}$$

$$\text{III} : \beta 2\ \alpha 3; \beta 1\ \alpha 4\ \alpha 3\ \alpha' 3\ \alpha' 7\ \alpha' 5\ \alpha 3$$

One sees that the first two periods include three $\beta\alpha$ groups, differentiated by $\beta 3$, $\beta 2$, $\beta 1$, then a concluding group $\beta\alpha$, differentiated by $\beta 1$, this final group being the same except for a slight variation ($\alpha 7$ instead of $\alpha 4\ \alpha 3$). The third period eliminates $\beta 3$, but the concluding group, beginning with $\beta 1$, is here greatly extended and forms the essence of this final period. Let us note, then, that as its conclusion this third element employs a procedure of aggrandizement, whereas we recall that the second element, in its fifth period, reverses the hierarchical order in the course of its presentation, a fact that isolates the conclusion.

In Example XIV I have shown schematically how the superimposition of these differing periodical structures is produced in the writing of the score—that is to say, the division into

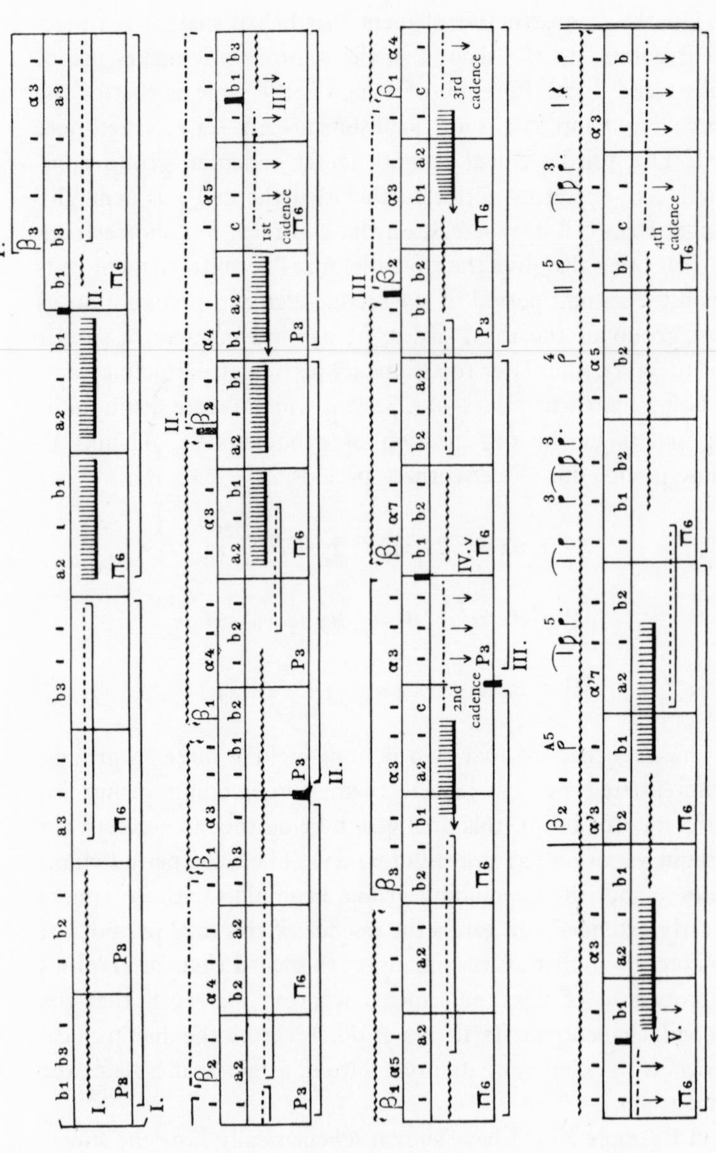

EXAMPLE XIV

measures in three times. In Example XV, furthermore, I indicate how the cadences are then produced from the progression of group *c*.

EXAMPLE XV

Finally, in order to complete the analysis of the *Danse de la terre*, we still must see in what way the elements of the first section appear at the end of the second and are superimposed in a concluding period derived by a very simple procedure from their first form.

Six measures before the end, we have, in effect, a restatement of groups A and B, which became familiar to us in the first section (see Example XII).

Group B is normal, being composed of an arpeggio followed by a silence, each on a unitary value; it serves to introduce the two A groups, just as it did at the outset of the first section. The fissionable group A follows:

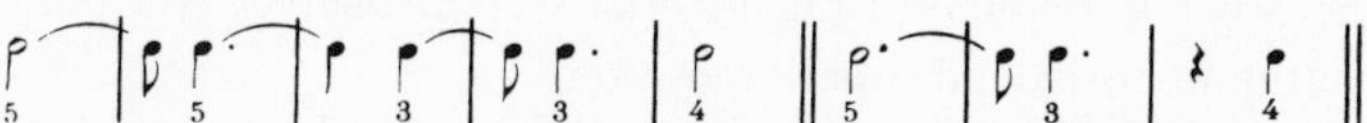

This final schema of A, then, is identical in its first phase to the first schema of the first section, with the difference that here the uneven values have been doubled and the even value, on the other hand, appears only once. Its second phase is the varied repetition of the second schema of the first section, the uneven values being inverted and the final—even—value coming on a syncopation.

I believe that in this way we have been able to examine the extreme complexity of the development of the *Danse de la terre*, in which—for the first time, it seems—structural oppositions were realized, from the rhythmic point of view, playing with horizontal independences and vertical independences upon monorhythmic or polyrhythmic organization of the sound-material. These oppositions will be met again, in still more definite form, throughout the *Danse sacrale*.

One is always bound to say of the *Danse sacrale*, that it is a rondo; doing so, one affirms only the strictest, most summary evidence. Perhaps I may be more curious and attempt to perceive the reasons for the organization in rondo. They are not summarized in simple, formal questions—of the most banal formalism—but put into play almost all of the rhythmic schemas that one has been able to discern here and there in *Le Sacre*, confronting one another here under the very ambiguous patronage of that rondo form (which, as one knows, is, with the variation form, the loosest of forms or, if one prefers, the least rigorous). Thus, one distinguishes two refrains, two couplets, and a coda to the refrain.

The refrains and the coda are monorhythmic—that is to say, a single rhythm governs what should strictly be called harmonic verticalization, not polyphony. The first couplet makes use of two rhythmic schemas, the one exteriorized vertically, the other horizontally. Finally, the second couplet is a polyrhythmic horizontal superimposition.

The second refrain, furthermore, is a textual reprise of the first, a half-tone lower. The schema of these two refrains is very simple to establish. It is composed of three elements (Example XVI).

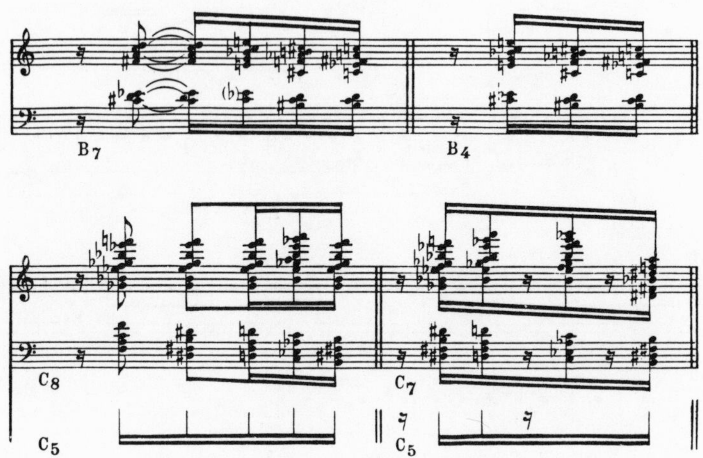

Example XVI

An element A formed of repeated chords serves as preparation for the element B, which is formed by the accent followed by its termination. Let me say that the elements A and B form a group Γ. A group C comes, through a chordal change, to balance group Γ; group C, formed of a preparation followed by an accent, is then transformed into preparation-accent-termination, with a fixed distribution of values: sixteenth-notes for the preparation, eighth-notes for the accents, sixteenth-notes for the termination (see Example XXII, that complete succession being analyzed in its transposition in the coda). One can dis-

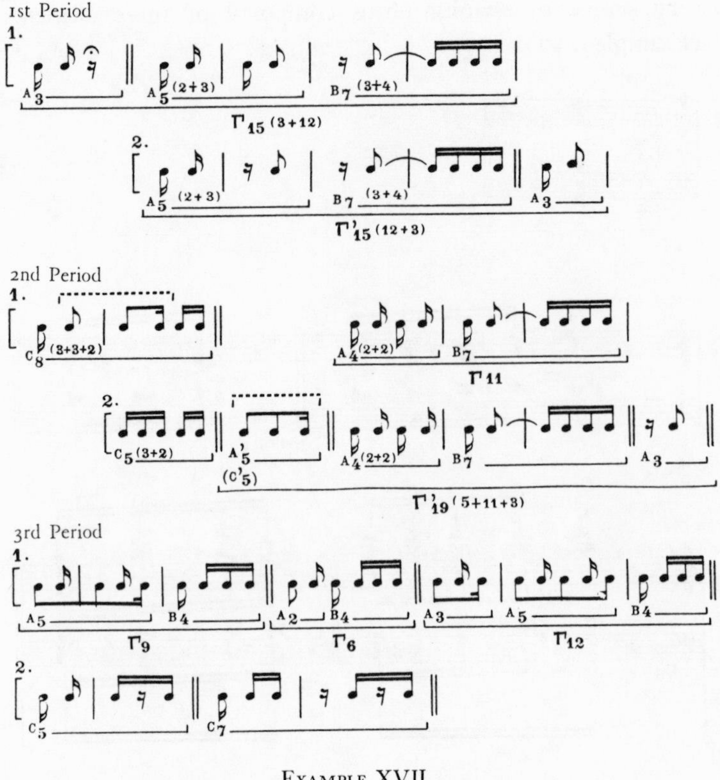

EXAMPLE XVII

I { 1 A3 A5 B7, A5 B7 A3, which gives:
Γ15 Γ'15
2 C8, A4 B7, C5, A'5 A4 B7 A3 : C8 Γ11 C5 Γ'19 }

II A5 B4, A2 B4, A3 A5 B4, C5, C7:
Γ9 Γ6 Γ12 C5 C7

cern two periods in the development of this rhythm (Example XVII).

It will be noticed that whereas A and C vary irregularly, B includes only two fixed values B7 and B4, the second coming as an elision of the first.

In the first period, one will note the symmetrical disposition A3 | $\underbrace{\text{A5 B7}}$, on the one hand, $\underbrace{\text{A5 B7}}$ | A3 on the other.

The second period utilizes A4, a contraction of the element A5 as it appeared in the first period; and a form A′5 derived from C8.

The third period introduces B4, a contraction of B7, as well as the variants C5 and C7, which will be used later in the terminal development.

The first couplet includes the vertical rhythmic theme that I analyzed at length in Example VII, supporting a horizontal thematic construction analyzed in Example IV. I shall not return to that development.

The second couplet is developed in three stages with their own period; they are superimposed by successive entries. This second couplet is divided in the middle by a short restatement of the refrain, constituted thus: A3 A5 B7 $\underbrace{\text{A2 B4}}$, that is, Γ15 Γ6. Thus it does not make use of group C, which, as we shall see, is the essential element of the coda.

The first section puts into play only two superimpositions (Example XVIII), a rhythmically varied pedal (P), and a subject-response group (S–R) at the interval of a fifth, admitting of slight chromatic differences. In S, the three notes 1, 2, 3 are separated by a tone C–B flat–A flat. In R (transposed), note 1 is lowered by a half-tone (C flat). In S′ (also transposed), the notes 2 and 3 are raised by a half-tone B natural–A natural.

But let me begin more logically with a rhythmic study of the pedal. The cell that engenders it lasts for five quarter-notes. It is based upon an alternation of eighth-notes and eighth-note triplets in the following order: two quarters, a triplet, two quarters, two triplets. One may also discern in this cell a sort of *Klangfarbenmelodie*, but in very rudimentary state, including

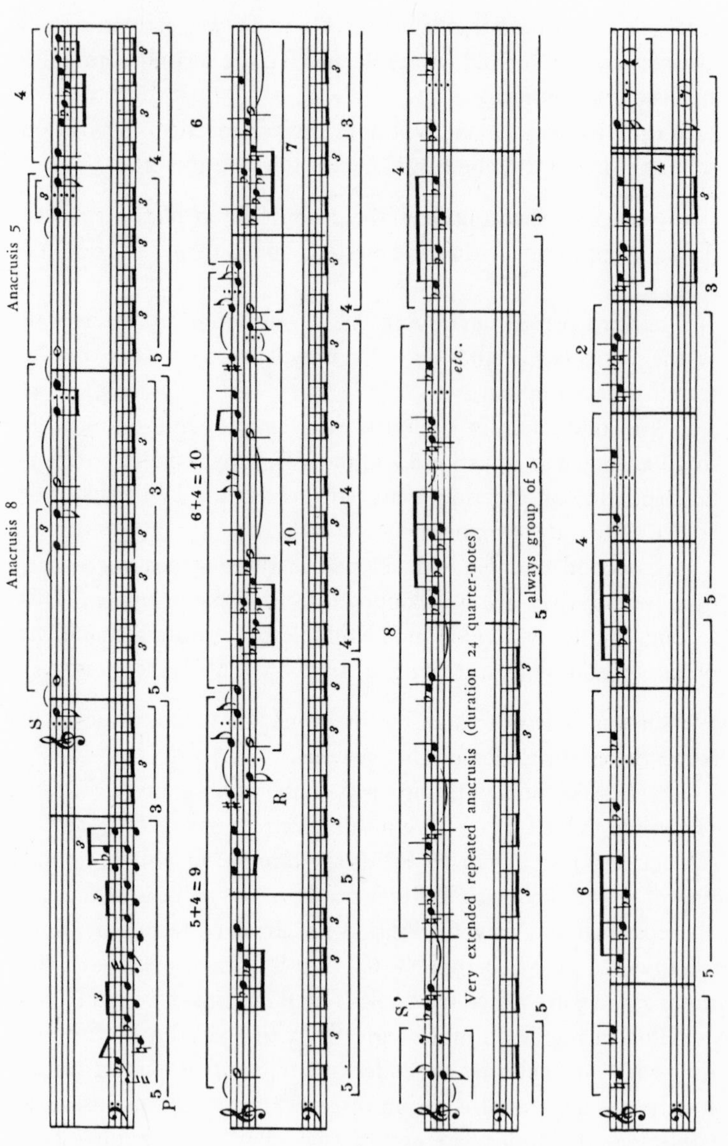

EXAMPLE XVIII

even such percussion instruments as the tam-tam and bass drum. That cell of five quarter-notes can be abridged to three or four by elision of its last or its last two unitary values. The elements that organize the development of that pedal move two cells by two cells, and succeed one another thus in the first section 5 3 5 3 5 4 5 5 4 4 4 3 5 5 5 5 5 3.

On the final quarter-note of the first 5 3 element, the subject S takes off on an anacrusis repeated twice, the first lasting eight quarter-notes, the second five. After that double anacrusis, the beginning of the subject (four quarter-notes) is unfolded; then, twice, the whole subject (nine quarter-notes and ten quarter-notes), and, finally, again, the beginning of the subject, also twice: the first lasting six quarter-notes, the second preceded by a long anacrusis of twenty-four quarter-notes and lasting four quarter-notes. Response R is produced at the end of the first subject S in its complete exposition; for the rest, it includes only the beginning of a complete restatement. The variation of the subject S′, finally, at the distance of a half-tone up, is placed at the end of the restatement, under the simplified anacrusis that precedes the final unfolding of subject S, properly speaking. It is eliminated irregularly in periods of which the duration, in quarter-notes, is 8, 4, 6, 4, 2.

Example XVIIIa

In the second section (Example XIX), there is added to these same elements of pedal and the subject-response couplet a harmonic element H that is rhythmically connected to the subject-response couplet, linked first to the varied subject S′,

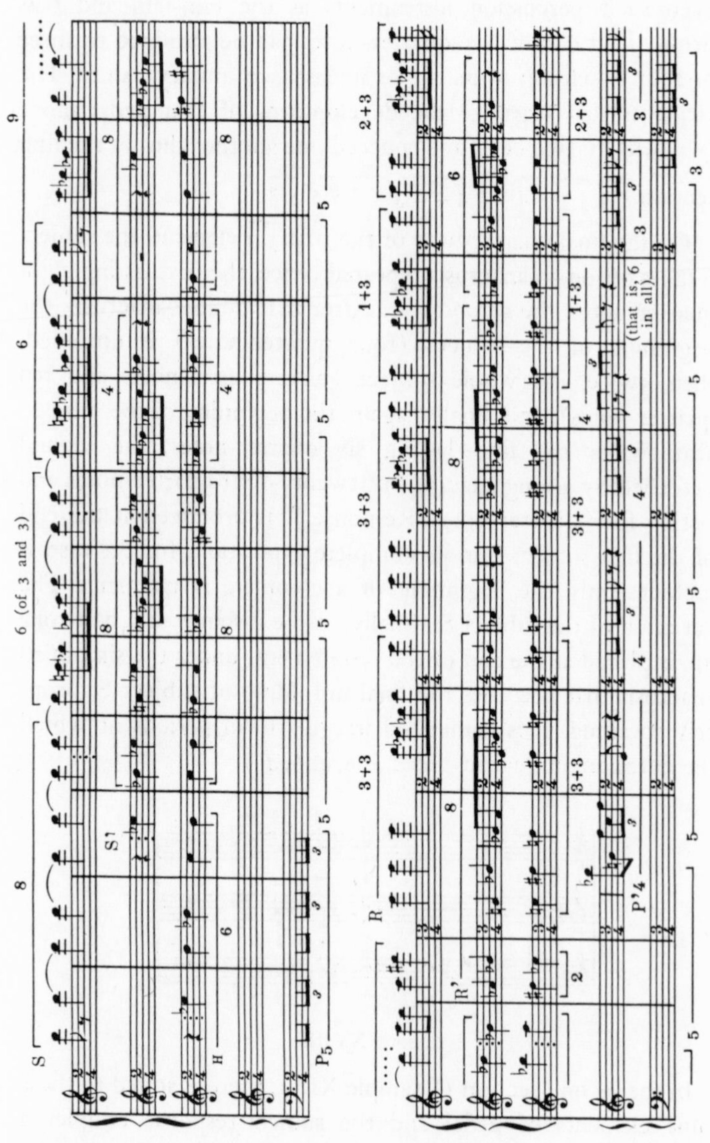

EXAMPLE XIX

then to the response R. Toward the conclusion of that second section, the pedal is doubled by a response P′ having its own period. Let me begin with the study of that pedal and its response. From rhythmic mobility it passes to a fixed cell of five quarter-notes repeated nine times and followed by a cell of three quarter-notes. Onto the final quarter-note of the sixth repetition is grafted the response P′, of four-quarter-note value, at first repeated twice, then superimposed in canon (constantly of value 4, which gives a total value of 6 for the two P′ cells), and finally two cells of three quarter-notes. The group S includes from the beginning an anacrusis of eight quarter-notes, then twice the beginning of the subject (six quarter-notes), and finally the entire subject cut in the middle by a syncopation (entire duration: nine quarter-notes).

Group S′ lasts eight quarter-notes; then, by elimination of the initial embellishments, decreases to half that duration—four quarter-notes; and finally returns to the duration of eight quarter-notes, still eliminating the initial embellishments, but replacing them with equivalent silences.

The subject-response couplet is developed thereafter in R and R′, R at the upper fourth of S, R′ at a fourth below S′, the periods of R′ being respectively of durations of eight quarter-notes, eight quarter-notes, six quarter-notes; the periods of R being three plus three quarter-notes, three plus three quarter-notes, one plus three quarter-notes, two plus three quarter-notes (the difference coming solely, one sees, from unequal repetitions of the first note).

The group H, harmonically sustained, follows, as I have said, the periods of S′—that is to say, eight quarter-notes, four quarter-notes, eight quarter-notes—preceded, before the entrance of S′ itself, by a group of six quarter-notes. Between the conclusion of S′ and the beginning of R, an interval of two quarter-notes defines an intermediate period equal to that in H, which then takes on the periodicity of R (that is: three plus three, three plus three, one plus three, two plus three quarter-notes). These, finally, are the schemas:

{S : 8 6 $\overbrace{6\ 9}$, 6 and 9 having a common note
{R : 6 6 4 5

{S′ : 8 4 8
{R′ : 8 8 6

P′ : 4 4 $\underbrace{\overbrace{44}}_{6}$ 3 3

I think that the asymmetric effects of balance organizing these various groups will be perceived without my describing them again.

The second couplet is followed by the coda, returning to the monorhythm of the refrains. This coda is in two sections. The first is based upon the preponderance of group Γ (AB), with two appearances of group C in its first, noncadential form. The second section is constructed on the single cadential group C, including fixed values, which I described above (see Example XXII). The first section of the coda has this schema:

I— $\underbrace{\text{A5 B4}}$ | $\underbrace{\text{A2 B4}}$; $\underbrace{\text{A5 B4}}$ $\underbrace{\text{A5 B4}}$ | $\underbrace{\text{A2 B4}}$; A5

being: Γ9 | Γ6; 2 Γ9 | Γ6; Γ5 elided;

II— $\underbrace{\text{A5 B4}}$ | C5 ; A5 | C5

being: Γ9 | C5 ; Γ5 elided | C5.
This period is expanded to the superior octave of the precedent.

III— $\underbrace{\text{A5 B4}}$ $\underbrace{\text{A5 B4}}$ $\underbrace{\text{A5 B4}}$ | $\underbrace{\text{A2 B4}}$

being: 3 Γ9 | Γ6.
Similarly, this period is expanded to the superior octave of the precedent.

One will note the position of the C5 cells isolated in the middle of that first section and preparing the development of the second section. Furthermore, one notices that this development is built uniquely on the alternation of Γ groups of fixed value, whence the cadential tendency that will specify C in its interior by the fixed distribution of its values.

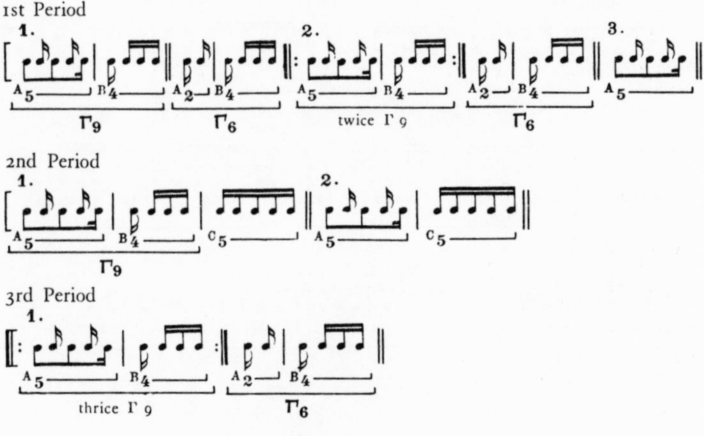

Example XX

Period I of this second section (Example XXI) is based on the alternation of C and C′ cells; being composed, by dissociation, entirely of deep C chords. One can distinguish three small subdivisions in this period I:

1. Alternation of C and C′—C5 C′5 C6
2. C alone—C′5 C′5 C′6 C′5 C′8
3. Alternation of C and C′—C5 C′6

One thus observes the fixity of durations of five and six sixteenth-notes and the unique appearance of a value of eight sixteenth-notes, at the end of the second subdivision, prefiguring Period II.

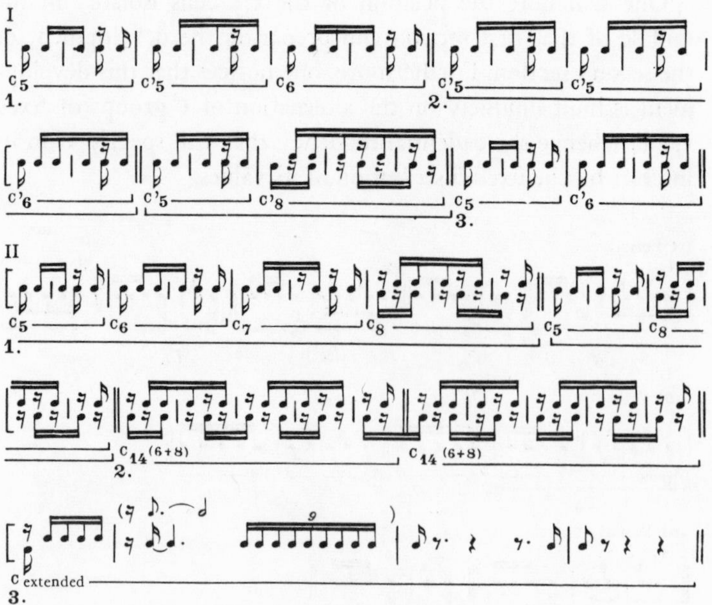

EXAMPLE XXI

EXAMPLE XXII

This period II is devoted to the rhythmic expansion of C, with the suppression of C′. Here too I distinguish three subdivisions, following the values of the expansions.

1.—C5 C6 C7 C8 | C5 C8

(This increases progressively from the minimum 5 to the maximum 8, then jumps directly from the minimum to the maximum.)

2.—C14 C14

(This is fixed upon an alternation 6–8.)

3.—which includes the four last measures of *Le Sacre:* the fixed values of C are abolished; furthermore, the expansion takes place not only in the rhythm, but also in the melodic figure that constitutes group C.

Let me point out that the bass achieves rhythmic independence with group C8, becoming a group of two repeated eighth-notes, an independence also prefigured in the very first C′8.

Thus this coda tends from the beginning toward the cadence, but then becomes only a large cadential group. I permit myself to emphasize the fact, very important in my view, of this fixed division of values within group C, a rhythmic phenomenon that gives the end of this coda its essential aspect: apparent motion dialectically linked to an understood immobility.

I must still speak of the Introduction, the most easily dissected and nevertheless the most secret mechanism. Beyond the extraordinary diversity of rhythm in the variation, beyond the utterly exceptional use of oppositions between rational and irrational values and the strait overlapping of long and very short values (this last procedure already familiar in Debussy), beyond the perfection of the organizing rhythmic structures—all elements of which I have demonstrated the importance in this essay—I believe that the Introduction to *Le Sacre* shows an exceedingly interesting architectural phenomenon: a sort of development by progressive recovery which is very difficult, if not impossible, to analyze on a succession of more or less contrasted levels like those in all the other developments of *Le Sacre.* But now I am generalizing prematurely, for one cannot fail to perceive that preoccupation in the dimension of the entire work. And it is precisely there, it seems to me, that we find the reasons that can explain the constant care for diverse thematic liaisons that have, so to speak, no internal structural rapport with the development under way. (Let me point out such a need with Berg, in the *Lyrische Suite* for example, expressed, at least in general, in a certainly more able way.)

I do not mean to analyze the Introduction in detail here; I should have to cite the entire musical text, and in its orchestral version, so great is its complexity. That would be to falsify such an undertaking absolutely rather than to carry it out summarily. I shall content myself, therefore, with as precise a description as possible of the architecture of the Introduction.

I think that one can single out four phases in this development without fear of contradiction.

First phase: (from the beginning of the score up to the measure after No. 3): an introductory phase in which one can mark the two principal organizing elements of the second phase.

Second phase: (1) Development of the first leading motif one measure after No. 3, up to No. 4; (2) development of the second leading motif (No. 4 to No. 6); (3) restatement of the first leading motif, followed by a cadence pursuant to the second (No. 6 to No. 7); (4) the two motifs alternated (No. 7 to No. 8); (5) presence, principally, of the second leading motif, the first being transformed by change of registers (No. 8 to No. 9).

Third phase: (1) appearance of a third leading motif (No. 9 to No. 10); (2) superimposition of these principal and secondary motifs (No. 10 to No. 12).

Fourth phase: restatement of the first phase simplified, all the secondary and principal motifs being repeated, followed by a demi-cadence and a preparation of the following section (No. 12 to No. 13).

Wanting to take the real characteristics of this Introduction into account, one must note the way in which all these subdivisions are linked and differentiated. I have showed in Example II how the first phrase for the bassoon gives birth to the second leading motif—in triplets—and how this motive, detached from it, rules the succeeding structures by complete suppression of the triplet. It will be good to generalize this point of view to show how a motif or several secondary motifs, once expounded, can take on their own period, detach themselves from the principal motif engendering them, and form the liaison between two subdivisions of a structure. For example, the second and third phases are not simply juxtaposed, but are joined by a motif that displays its own development during the final subdivision of the second phase and the first of the third phase; this motif does not make any caesura during the passage from the second phase to the third (Example XXIII). It comes

Example XXIII

to life in the third subdivision of the second phase and serves in a way as counterpoint to what I have called the first leading motif (No. 6 of the score). In the fourth subdivision, it is given in the deep octave (and passes from flute to bassoon—fourth, sixth, and seventh measures after No. 7). In the fifth subdivision, it assumes total independence with respect to the first leading motif and takes on great importance in view of its numerous rhythmic variations, an importance that it preserves under the exposition of the third leading motif (No. 8, then

No. 9 of the score) and throughout this exposition. Its transitional role between the second and third phases having been carried out, this motif appears no more in the second subdivision of the third phase, which is, as I have said, the superimposition of the three leading motifs. I should remark that Stravinsky himself has pointed out in his score the increasing importance of the secondary motif of which I have spoken when it appears in the second phase. In fact, in my third subdivision it is the first leading motif that is placed in relief by "*en dehors*" (No. 6 of the score). In our fourth subdivision, at the place of the change of register and instrument, this secondary motif is emphasized by "*très en dehors.*"

I think that this single example will sufficiently demonstrate the characteristics of the architecture that we are studying: that is to say that underneath a structure delimited in precise levels by principal motifs, secondary motifs are set out which soften and blur that structure by constant renewal and by their diversely varied ways of superimposing themselves upon the principal motifs. It is this double plan of development, double both in its function and in its modalities, which we may judge to be one of the most profitable lessons to retain from the Introduction to *Le Sacre*, without forgetting the individuality of the instrumentation, a manifestation of the intelligence animating that architecture.

And so I think that I have attempted, at least with reference to the rhythm, a reasonably complete labor of clarification. In passing, I have noted harmonic and melodic characteristics and have been able to take into account that if some of them tend toward a destruction of the tonal language, they are really the exceptions. All to the contrary, most of the characteristics are connected with extremely strong tendencies toward the tonic, the dominant, or the subdominant, as, for example, in the *Danse sacrale* and the *Danse de la terre*. When there are contrapuntal attempts, they are frankly feeble, and I refer back to the second couplet of that same *Danse sacrale* (Example XIX), in which the subject-response couplet appears extremely summary aside from the chromatic anomaly pointed out. When there are superimpositions of motifs, they are carried out in an extremely rigid fashion, each motif unrolling obstinately on the same intervals. In sum, there is no development properly speaking, but only varied repetition, no chemical reaction, but only physical mixing; we can allow ourselves to see in that difference a great lowering of level.

Shall I speak of the polytonality that has been noted so often in *Le Sacre*—to the point at which only it has been seen? That would be anachronistic, so clearly has polytonality been relegated to the museum of useless accessories, of exhausted masks. Fortunately, *Le Sacre* is devoid of those absurdities. At the most, it signals a polymodality taking off from the very notes of polarity. I have already cited the place in the *Danse de la terre* at which, there is grafted on a tonic C a whole-tone scale and a modal attraction following descending fourths (*E flat–B flat–F–C*); I pointed out (Example VIII) the fixity of a chord below the embellished chord. I can note again, in the Introduction to the second part, a unique modality on the tonic of D that plays over this ambiguity—the separation of notes of attraction and other notes, thus giving a character of alteration and passage. *Le Sacre* owes its harmonic physiognomy exactly to that hierarchy which is organized on notes of attraction. We could not be farther from polytonal gratuitousness.

Should I also speak of what has been called absence of melody in Stravinsky? Without striking a polemic attitude, but taking into account a melodic tradition inherited from Italy and Germany (and I mean to refer to Italians of the seventeenth and eighteenth centuries, Germans of the eighteenth and nineteenth), it has been established that Stravinsky lacks the "melodic gift." It remains to discover whether Stravinsky has not, rather, amplified and divulged a melodic construction that is derived from a certain kind of popular song. And perhaps it is against this precise point that one can place the misunderstanding about his "folkloric" themes (some degree of malice attaches to this qualificative word when it is used thus to indicate plagiarism and lack of invention). I have located Stravinsky's tendency toward vertical fixity of sound-material in a horizontal form as well. In the sense that the notes of a mode have been determined initially at a given height, the notes of the whole melodic structure do not depart from the scale thus established. As often he does not use all the notes of the mode or as, in the opposite case, the points of support preponderate, one immediately grasps the static aspect that such a melody assumes from the point of view of sound, and I think that this static aspect of the scale has caused that denunciation for a supposed "absence of melody." One also discerns the rapport with melodies on the defective modes of the music of Indochina, of Tibet, for example, or of black Africa and, closer at hand, of Stravinsky, with certain popular melodies of which the sound-reflection was already familiar, principally in Borodin and Mussorgsky. One is dealing, then, not with an absence of melody, but with a certain aspect of melody—one of an archaicizing tendency from the tonal point of view—which can only corroborate Stravinsky's definite favoring of an archaicizing tonal language by dint of grouping around primarily polarizing attractions. We can say "archaicizing" without excessive fear because the language of *Le Sacre*—and, even more, that of *Les Noces* or *Renard*—created, in relation to the evolution of the language with and after Wagner, what could geographically be called a tidal phenomenon, and that archaism doubtless permitted, as I have remarked, the most daring research into rhythmic structures.

I have come, finally, to believe that this work has, despite and thanks to its lacunae, as great a usefulness in musical evolution as, for example, *Pierrot lunaire*. For even though nothing can be retained of the structural means of *Le Sa-*

cre—no more can those of *Les Noces*—they being a survival, the rhythmic writing, on the other hand, still remains all but unexplored, at least for its internal consequences; no one can doubt that certain procedures more or less mechanized in a completely appliquéd fashion have passed into the contemporary language in the form of rhythmic coloration, just as they have been appliquéd to a summary coloring of tonalities with some intervals of anarchic tendency. Let me remark that few works in the course of musical history have been able to boast of such a privilege—not to have, forty years later, its potential of novelty exhausted. Let me say here that this novelty is on a single plane, that of rhythm; but even with that restriction, it represents a very enviable sum of invention and quality of discovery.

Perhaps in proportion to the conclusions that I have drawn from various analyses, I shall be accused of a certain tendency to exaggerate the arithmetic relationships, of not taking the unconscious into account. Must I repeat here that I have not attempted to uncover a creative process, but to take account of the result, the arithmetic rapports being the only tangible ones? I have been able to note all these structural characteristics because they are there, and to me it is of small importance whether they were placed there consciously or unconsciously or with what degree of acuity in the intelligence of the conception, or, again, with what interferences between the labor and the "genius." To establish such a genesis of *Le Sacre* would be of great speculative interest, but it would deviate completely from the single musical aim to which I wanted to limit myself.

Nevertheless, it is impossible not to examine one's conscience in the Stravinsky case with some anguish. How explain, after *Les Noces*, that accelerated exhaustion manifested in a sclerosis of all the realms: harmonic and melodic, in which one comes upon a faked academicism—even rhythmic, in which one sees a painful atrophy produced. Can one, then, speak of the reaction of one of these realms upon the other? In fact, one can determine, at the beginning of the twentieth century, a curious dissociation between the evolution of rhythm and that of sound-material: on the one hand, Schoenberg, Berg, Webern, points of departure for a new morphology and syntax, but related to a rhythmic survival (this is a very summary view of the members of the Vienna School, among whom there are irreducible differences); on the other hand, Stravinsky. At a half-way point there is Bartók alone. His sound-researches never fall into the Stravinsky ruts, but they are very far from attaining the Vienna level; his rhythmic researches are very far from equaling Stravinsky's, but still, thanks to their folkloric backgrounds, they are generally superior to those of the Viennese.

If, then, we consider the Stravinsky case, the lacunae in his writing have taken precedence over his rhythmic discoveries, have prevented them from culminating. There are lacunae of all sorts in the writing, both in the domain of the language and in that of development. Logically, Stravinsky could not rest content with a summary system warped by composite and anarchistic formulas. Rediscovering an already proved hierarchy colored with eclecticism—such was the immediate assuagement by hypnosis.

Furthermore, those reversals of prestidigitation—in which the object juggles the manipulator—are of little importance to us, given that a truly Stravinskyan domain existed earlier. Also, that period with which one had become diversely conscious of a new world—in a more or less episodic, more or less rational, fashion—should keep Stravinsky's name on the very first level; even when the tardy expansion by Schoenberg, Berg, and Webern has cruelly brought his errors to light and called him down from his unique-magus pedestal. Whether it be Stravinsky's or Schoenberg's, further, premature deifications are not my business. Who, unless frenetically thuriferous sectarians, would dream of returning to a less affective optic?

P.S.—I may be criticized for so unilateral an attitude with regard to rhythm or, at the least, the hypertrophied importance that I attribute to it may appear astonishing. In truth, it seems to me that the very problem of the language itself is much closer to solution since the adoption—more or less widespread—of the serial technique; from that point on, it is a question of re-establishing an equilibrium. Alongside all the musical disciplines, in fact, rhythm profits only from very summary notions that each one can locate in the usual solfeggios. Should one see this as only a didactic insufficiency? More validly, one can think that, since the end of the Renaissance, rhythm has not been considered a peer of the other musical components and that the best part of it has been left to intuition and good taste.

To find the most rational attitude toward rhythm in our occidental music, one must turn to Philippe de Vitry, Guillaume de Machault, and Guillaume Dufay. Their isorhythmic motets are decisive testimony to the constructive value of rhythmic structures in relation to the different sequences implied by the cadences. What better precedent to invoke for contemporary researches than that of this epoch in which music was thought to be not only an art but also a science: which avoided all sorts of convenient misunderstandings (despite the permanence of a no less convenient scholasticism)?

"Isorhythm," Guillaume de Van wrote in his preface to Dufay's works, "was the most refined expression of the musical ideal of the fourteenth century, the essence that only a small number could penetrate and which constituted the supreme testimony to the composer's ability . . . The restrictions imposed by the rigid dimensions of a plan that in advance determined the smallest details of the rhythmic structure did not at all limit the inspiration of the Cambresian, for his motets give the impression of free, spontaneous composition, whereas in fact the isorhythmic canon is observed strictly. It is the harmonious equilibrium between the melody and the rhythmic structure which distinguished Dufay's works from the entire fourteenth-century repertoire (Machault excepted)."

Thus one sees something that may seem unthinkable to many listeners, and even to many contemporary composers—that the rhythmic structure of those motets *preceded* the writing. There is not only a phenomenon of dissociation, but also a procedure contrary to that which we observe in the evolution of Occidental musical history from the seventeenth century on.

After that brilliant efflorescence, all but unknown in our time under that aspect still reserved entirely to specialists, one can see an attempt at rhythmic control in the pieces "*mesurées à l'antique*" of Claude Le Jeune and Mauduit. The preface to an edition of that period places its accent on the importance that the rhythmic structure should assume in relation to the "harmonic" context. "The ancients who dealt with music," it reads, "divided it into two parts: harmonic and rhythmic . . . The rhythmic was carried to such perfection by them that they produced marvelous effects . . . Afterwards, that rhythmic was so neglected that it has been lost altogether . . . Nobody was found to bring a remedy to it until Claudin Le Jeune, who is the first one emboldened to rescue that poor rhythmic from the tomb in which it has been lying for so long and to put it on a par with the harmonic."

This is not a question of discussing the grounds of that Greco-Latin lineage, but one of noticing, rather, that before the simplistic solution of the barred measure, men were preoccupied with coordinating in coherent fashion the rhythmic data of music as much as the harmonic and the contrapuntal.

Also, it is time to adhere to such a logic, which is indispensable if one wishes to remedy the lack of cohesion that I have discussed—in the course of this essay—between the evolution of polyphony itself and the rhythmic discovery. And I do not believe that I shall be contradicting myself or playing with paradox if I advance the notion that at the very outset we should release rhythm from the "spontaneous" direction that for too long has generously been attributed to it; that is to say, liberate rhythm from being, properly speaking, an expression of polyphony and move it up to the rank of a principal factor in the structure by recognizing that it can preexist polyphony —an idea that has as its aim nothing but linking still more closely, but much more subtly, polyphony to rhythm.

Eventually . . .

Donquixotism is, if one wishes, a form of redemption. Nevertheless, I do not at all share the pessimistic point of view of depressed solitaries which consists essentially in asserting—one does not know, furthermore, in view of what, unless it be of their flagrant cowardice or incapacity—that we are living through a frightening decadence. They are always pleasant, these death shrieks that are launched regularly and that, no less regularly, are seen contradicted in the nick of time by rudely contradictory events. All those predictions of an aborted Apocalypse are a burlesque spectacle for anyone lacking a mentality of permanent disaster: individual crises of lazy men who boast of their superiority as ignoramuses.

May I put forth as an ineffable pleasantry the reality of the statement that few epochs in musical life have been so exalting to live in?

At the very beginning, why not play the sniper for a few moments?

Most of our contemporaries would seem to be unaware of what happened in Vienna with Schoenberg, Berg, and Webern. That is why, even though it may become irksome, one still must describe, shorn of all prophetic legend and all admiring, exclamatory style, the real achievement of the three Viennese. The dodecaphonists find themselves involved in the present misunderstanding of this subject for a reason. Organizing *congresses*—those of specialists playing at initiate ceremonies for fearful beginners—falsely doctrinaire, absurdly conservative, they lord it in stupid repletion for the greater glory of the avant-garde. They have adopted the serial system, whether in the comfortable belief that nothing but vulgar ruse exists outside that orthodoxy or with the intention of erecting a salutary guardrail. This is an attitude that does not even have the advantage of being uncertain.

In another camp, the serial system is considered under some aspects that are not without flavor!

The deaf find in it nothing but artifice, decomposition, and decadence (see above . . .). A possible reaction might be a smile that certainly will have passed beyond commiseration.

The sentimental do not witness the implantation of chaos without terror, but in the legitimate anxiety not to allow the present situation to bypass them, they try to make use of chaos in order to oppose to it—and it is, let it be clearly understood, a symbol of our epoch—the classic vocabulary. Puffing from that sketchy exploit, they hold themselves freed of fear.

They are close to the libertarians or libertines who are not at all terrified, in principle, by all the technical research. They make those interesting acquisitions theirs, but, in the name of *liberty*, defend themselves from being *prisoners* of the system. They want *music* above everything, or at least what they proclaim to be music: they do not want to lose sight of *lyricism* (who will ever penetrate the mystery of the concepts covered by that vague word?). Their biggest preoccupation is of a rather encyclopedic order. They want to lock up all of history after monophony. They allow themselves the illusion of being vast and innumerable.

As for the generous, their reasonings take divergent paths. They try to persuade you that the serial discoveries are old, that all that was known in 1920. Now one should create the *new*, and in support of that brilliant theses, they cite to you fake-Gounods, pseudo-Chabriers, champions of clarity, elegance, and refinement, eminently *French* qualities. (They adore mixing Descartes and *haute couture*.) They are convinced adepts of the time machine. The fashion in which they explore is, furthermore, unspeakable.

Finally, there will be the indulgent, who consider dodecaphony a venereal disease, who consider that having had a turbulent youth is logical, almost well-mannered, and—why not?—glorious. But it becomes inexcusable if one relapses after the delay granted to madness has expired.

The dodecaphonists themselves at times acquiesce to some of these points of view. Otherwise they are plunged into their restricted manifestation of minorities in exile, exactly like some semisecret, gently illuminated, or moderately speculative association. Or, the second eventuality is that they can give themselves over, as a group or individually, to frenetic arithmetic masturbation. For in their necessitous speculation they have forgotten to go beyond the elementary stage of arithmetic. Do not ask them for anything more: they know how to count up to twelve and in multiples of twelve. Excellent spirits as apostles and disciples.

So dodecaphonists and independents labor under the ensign of *liberty*. Humor has it that the avant-garde glorifies the liberty of agreed-to discipline, whereas the conservatives favor anarchic freedom. The latter, in particular, consumed by disquiet over what they call the *multiplicity of techniques*—a pompous phrase in support of a notorious ineptitude. All that mediocrity still legislates for the majority; it is a survival that is breaking up. Nothing of it but anecdotes can endure.

What can we conclude? The unexpected: I, in turn, assert that any musician who has not experienced—I do not say understood, but, in all exactness, experienced—the necessity for the dodecaphonic language is USELESS. For his whole work is irrelevant to the needs of his epoch.

I hasten to give precise answers to the laggards who still assert that the series is a purely arbitrary, artificial creation by a master outside the moral code. It seems sufficiently evident that the epidemic of chromaticism after Wagner was notorious; Debussy will not contradict that. Thus the serial technique is nothing but the bringing to light of musical problems in ferment since 1910. It is not a decree; it is an authentication. A close analysis of Schoenberg's opus 23 allows us to take very precise account of the transition effected in what may be called ultrathematization—where thematic intervals become absolute intervals freed of the rhythmic figures, capable of assuming by themselves the writing and structure of the work, able to move from horizontal unfolding to vertical coagulation. (But who would dare to boast of such a study among those friends of amateurism?) One refuses systematically to see the series as a historic result because its detractors more willingly agree to consider it a daring postulate. The disdainful word "grammarian" is then brought into play; it is believed that the whole thing has been crushed peremptorily and definitively. That is simply to give proof once again of unconstrained routine. It will be useful to ask whether or not grammarians, obeying that eternally repeated formula about the glory of chance, appear after the works of genius. Without going as far back as the Middle Ages, we can suppose that—Rameau, isn't it? . . . But now I shall pose that ambivalent question about formalism to myself: up to what point can a theoretically coherent attitude harm or help a composer's activity?

Furthermore, the series was exploited in very different ways by Schoenberg, Berg, and Webern. Webern was the only one of them, in fact, who was conscious of a new sound-dimension, of the abolition of horizontal-vertical opposition, so that he saw in the series only a way of giving structure to the sound-space, in a way, to give it fiber. He reached that point, in the final analysis, by specious means that, in some transitional works, embarrass us. Nevertheless, that functional redistribution of intervals toward which he tended marks an extremely important moment in the history of the language.

Now, on the other hand, we realize that a certain rhythmic realm was scarcely suspected by the three Viennese: for them it was not related at all to the principles of serial writing itself. One should in this connection note a curious phenomenon of dissociation which was brought about at the beginning of this century. If we are reaching a period of balance and organization, there was, beginning about 1910, a phase of destructive researches that abolished the tonal world on the one hand and the regular metric on the other. Stravinsky evolved rhythm by entirely new structural principles based principally on the asymmetry, the independence, or the development of rhythmic cells; but he remained closed up, from the point of view of the language, in what might be called an impasse, but which I prefer to call a survival, and even an intensified survival, for those procedures of aggregation around very elementary magnetic poles conferred unexampled strength on laws of balance which had become frail. In *Le Sacre*, as in *Les Noces*, not to speak of other scores, this seems to be a matter of auditive coloration. In another way, serial evolution supplies a new methodology for giving structure to pitches. That view certainly is somewhat simplified, there being, on both sides, significant offsetting factors. Nonetheless, it remains true that the two levels of research—language, properly speaking, and rhythm—do not coincide.

Perhaps I ought also to note that this phenomenon of dissociation has been of powerful service to the evolution of both structural elements. In order to achieve rhythmic discoveries, Stravinsky undoubtedly felt a need for simpler, more malleable material on which to experiment with them; Webern more easily had time to develop the morphology because he did not occupy himself at all excessively with rhythmic structures. I leave the task of debating this question to amateurs of dialectic. What is indispensable now is a regrouping of all that research, for—with certain exceptions that I shall mention later—it has produced nothing new since those keys to contemporary music; the succeeding generation has stamped about grimacing after its predecessors, but not a single score can be considered even a feeble success. Always from lack of coherence: that dissociation having been pursued everywhere to some extent, and the Viennese activity having long been kept in the dark to the profit of an obsession with classicism or a residue of romanticism, both of them brackish solutions.

What remains for us to attempt after that? Is it not to assemble the bundle of possibilities elaborated by our predecessors and to demand of ourselves at least a minimum of constructive logic? In an epoch of transformation and organization, in which the problem of the language is posed with particular keenness, and in which, it seems, musical *grammar* will trickle along, we assume our responsibilities intransigently. What holds up our working with the sensibility, the palpable necessity of our epoch is not simulated cardiac hypertrophies.

In view of that intention, we must expand the means of a technique already discovered; that technique having been, up to now, a destructive object linked, for that very reason, to what it has wanted to destroy, our first determination will be to give it autonomy. And, furthermore to link rhythmic structures to serial structures by common organizations, which will also include the other characteristics of sound: intensity, mode of attack, timbre. Then to enlarge that morphology into a coalescent rhetoric.

I shall begin by explaining at once what I understand by writing with a series. Up to now, we have written the original series and then its twelve transpositions on the chromatic degrees, rising or descending. For each series, one has numbered the notes from 1 to 12, and the same for the reversals.

The series are linked together either by being placed in

Example I

similar regions—certain groups of notes presenting common horizontal, or even vertical, elements (that is to say, independent of the serial order)—or by pivot-notes—notes common (one or two generally, more rarely three) to the beginning of one series and the ending of another. This slightly empirical procedure puts in evidence a numeration, but not a figuration. To reach the latter, the simplest means is that of transposing the original series by following the succession of its own notes; having numbered that original series from 1 to 12, one applies that figuration to transpositions and reversals. Here, in all the series, E flat is numbered 1, D natural 2, etc.

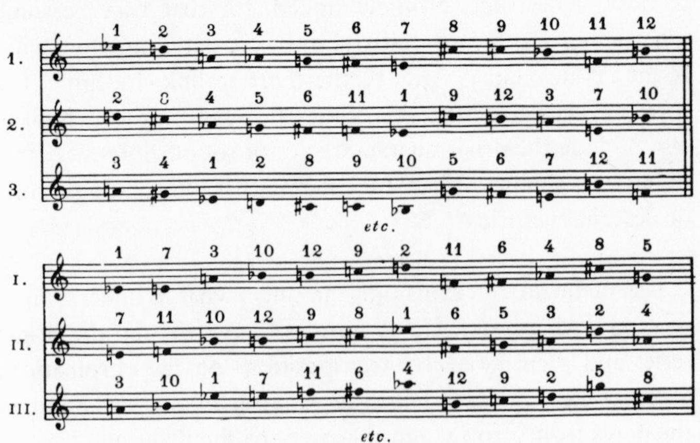

Example II

In that way one obtains a table of transpositions and reversals which is coherent because, thanks to a first permutation, it establishes the fixed limit of the permutations to be employed within a work. Thus one has defined in a network of possibilities the universe of that work. Furthermore, the fact of taking possession of that universe, of no concern until the moment when one chooses *its* series, is effectuated according to the schema of that series itself.

The purely mechanical drawing-up of tables of successive transpositions from half-tone to half-tone implies a certain passivity of the series in relation to the space of which it is going to be the principal regulator. This is something like a survival of the concept of modal or tonal transpositions, a latent preponderance of the horizontal, whereas in the present-day perspectives of which the serial discovery has been the cause of our consciousness, the *sound-figure*, the most general object offered to a composer's imagination, transcends the traditional opposition between notions of vertical and notions of horizontal.

1	2	3	4	5	6	7	8	9	10	11	12
2	8	4	5	6	11	1	9	12	3	7	10
3	4	1	2	8	9	10	5	6	7	12	11
4	5	2									
5	6	8		*etc.*							
6	11	9									
7	1	10									
8	9	5									
9	12	6					*Original series*				
10	3	7									
11	7	12									
12	10	11									

1	7	3	10	12	9	2	11	6	4	8	5
7	11	10	12	9	8	1	6	5	3	2	4
3	10	1	7	11	6	4	12	9	2	5	8
10	12	7									
12	9	11		*etc.*							
9	8	6									
2	1	4									
11	6	12									
6	5	9							*Retrograde series*		
4	3	2									
8	2	5									
5	4	8									

EXAMPLE III

These permutation tables can be generalized for any sound-space taken as material. That is why I like to speak of series of *n* intervals, these intervals not necessarily being multiples of a single unit—the half-tone in the case of a series of twelve tones. Just as in making use of the idea of irrational rhythm, so we can introduce the notion of nontempered sound-spaces. Let us imagine a series of *n* sounds included between any frequency whatever and another, higher frequency. The habit is to consider a series as limited between a given frequency and that frequency doubled—that is to say, the octave. I hope it is possible to create sound-structures no longer limited to the octave, but based on any interval whatever. The octave being linked to the modal or tonal phenomenon, we no longer have any reason to consider it privileged. Let us then imagine a series of *n* sounds in which no single sound is repeated either in its original frequency or in that frequency doubled. The following schema shows graphically how, while representing the transpositions by translations, it is possible to bring about all the series within a given band of frequencies. If, in fact, the obtained sounds pass the boundaries of that band of frequencies—as is the case here with the sound c″—one submits it to a translation equal to the difference of the extreme frequencies.

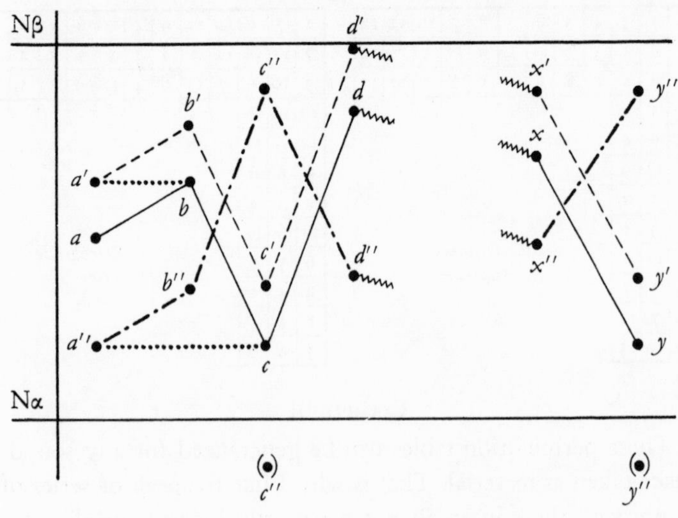

Example IV

(To some musicians this may seem hermetic; nevertheless, it is what they do ordinarily when transposing to the octave. Mathematicians call it the modulus.)

To obtain any tessitura whatever with the aid of this organization of the space, it will suffice to transpose an original sound by the defining interval or multiples of it.

If we want to push farther our investigation of the realm of serial structure, we can imagine homothetic series. By that I mean that in the intervals of the original series, the series will reproduce itself by—one might say—reduction. Let me give an example using the twelve-tone series already cited.

Example V

It is not impossible to conceive between sounds 8 and 5—the final tones of the original series in retrograde, forming a diminished fifth—a series of twelve quarter-tones, an exact diminution of that original series in retrograde. It is licit for each person to generalize this particular case and to see that no incompatibility need exist from then on between the microdistances and intervals equal to or wider than a half-tone. By giving small or large variations in pitch that coincidence of point of departure, one will have the means for controlling them.

One is correct in considering all these possibilities as pure mental exercise. For the time being, there is no question of displaying any such virtuosity in still-unrealizable works. Nevertheless, as we shall see later, the time will not be long in arriving when a certain credit will be given to speculations finding their base of support in new tablatures, whether for mechanical or electronic means.

How to link the series to one another is one of the most naïve problems, but apparently one of the most delicate in the serial technique. If, in fact, there is no general logic of succession, one comes upon the useless paradox of a hierarchical infrastructural organization, the superstructures being given over to indolent anarchy, the empiricism of which—not always sound currency, be it remembered—moves tentatively and provides some recipes. I have already mentioned pivot-notes: that means seems to me a little rudimentary and capricious. To make series neighbors in similar regions is infinitely more satisfactory because by that fact harmonic ambiguity plays a very great role; that, however, supposes series of remarkable properties and implies playing nearly always on the same properties.

It also seems to me much more diverse to expand the serial functions to include the very linking of series. In that way one will obtain functions of function, from the simplest linear case to the most complex derivations. Danger of a certain automatism in the writing will thus be avoided. In fact, I must deplore any comic belief in the absolute efficacy of arithmetic. It is not enough to steal names at random to be assured about genius. Seeking for a dialectic among morphology, syntax, and rhetoric supposes some difficulties less easily surmounted than elementary problems in combinatory analysis, as I shall explain later on.

I should not like to conclude this short study of the series without mentioning the importance of sound-registers, having spoken of—so to say—abstract serial intervals. What interferences are provoked between the series itself and the tessitura by the single fact that each of these components can be mobile or immobile in relation to the other? Let us imagine only the instabilities of a single series in relation to a constantly renewed tessitura, or the disequilibria of various series in relation to a completely congealed tessitura—extreme points in a play of sound-ambiguities which can also combine ambiguities of rhythm or intensity.

Unquestionably, it would be helpful to bring rhythm into consonance with the serial structure. How can this be achieved?

Paradoxically, the point of departure will be to release polyphony from rhythm. If I must give an example, I would cite the isorhythmic motets of Machault and Dufay. This is to show that I accord equal importance to rhythmic structures and serial structures. My aim will be to create a reservoir of possibles in this domain too.

The simplest case will consist of taking a series of values and having them undergo a number of permutations equal and parallel to that of the pitches, by giving each note of the original series a permanent duration. Referring to the graph of Example III, let us suppose, from 1 to 12, a series of chromatic values going to the thirty-second-note at the dotted quarter. Thus E flat, number 1, will correspond to a thirty-second-note; D natural, number 2, to a sixteenth-note, etc.

Making the table of durations, we shall have completely irregular series (see diagram, page 158). (Example VI.)

Then, in the course of the composition, we shall be able to desolidarize the rhythmic series from the pitch series that have engendered them and, above all, create a structural counterpoint between the pitches and the rhythms. Let us notice how, departing from a simple arithmetical rhythmic progression, multiple of a single unity, one rapidly reaches a complexity that is already remarkable; to point out all the resources of such a technique, it will suffice to mention the use of irrational values.

Having described this extreme case, in which the organization of the durations is equivalent to that of the pitches, I shall speak of organizations in which, to be sure, the rhythm has a serial structure, but one based exclusively on principles of rhythmic variation, independent of the structure of pitches. Then the structural counterpoints could evolve on parallel planes, if one may say it that way, but they would not be reversible as in the preceding case.

etc.

EXAMPLE VI

Let us take an example to illustrate this proposal. Let there be three rhythmic cells, I, II, and III; we shall obtain IV by the synthesis of I and II; V by the synthesis of I and III; VI by the synthesis of II and III; VII, finally, by the synthesis of I, II, and III.

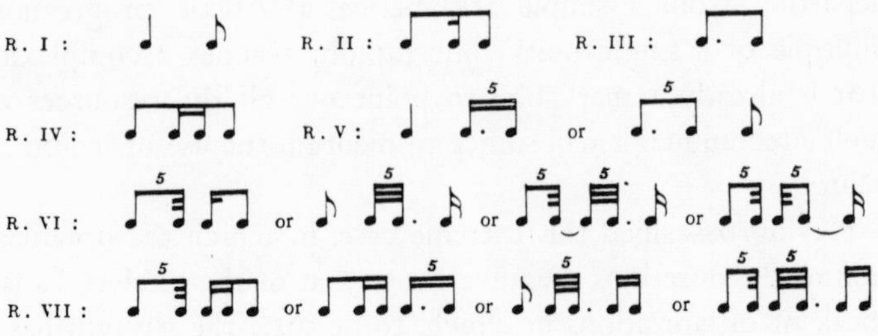

EXAMPLE VII

We now have a series of seven rhythmic cells, sometimes not reversible—that is, they are symmetrical in relation to their middle, sometimes reversible—that is, not symmetrical in relation to their middle. Cells I, III, V, VI, VII are reversible; II and IV are not.

To these cells we can apply a series of transmutations which I shall define thus:

1. Simple transmutations—that is, augmentation, diminution, regular or irregular (regular when the hierarchy of the initial cell is respected, irregular when the components of the cell are differently modified); irrational transformation (the unit of value being given, the new unit of value will be in an irrational relation—triplet, quintuplet, etc.—to the old); addition of a dot (augmentation by half of the value, and therefore being shaped on the value to be augmented, creating a new hierarchy depending from the first one), addition of dotting that can be simple, double, triple, etc.; amputation of components of the cell of an equal value (which would also suppress the primitive hierarchy of the cell).

2. The rhythm expressed in units of value, the different components of the cell being expressible in different units of value. The downbeat of the mother-cell is preserved or replaced by a silence.

3. The rhythm hollowed out. By this I mean to say that the values making up a cell are transformed by syncope in two possible ways, either by having silence occupy half of the value and the new value the other half, or by having the new value enclosed between two silences of equal duration. The exactly opposite possibility need not be excluded—that is to say, a silence could be enclosed between two values of the same duration.

4. The rhythm demultiplied—that is, rhythm engendering itself in the sense that within each value of the mother-cell that mother-cell itself will be reproduced homothetically.

5. Derived rhythm—that is, decomposition of the rhythm

by its beginning. This is a composition of expressed rhythm (No. 2) and demultiplied rhythm (No. 4), the expression of the rhythm in units of value being made according to a homothesis of the mother-cell.

6. The replacement of a value or of several values by a silence. In a nonreversible cell, this replacement could be brought about on the pivot-note or, again, on symmetrical notes; we reach a new symmetry of sound and silence. In a reversible cell, the parallel values would be replaced by a silence.

7. The same operation will be reproduced, but in contrary fashion; in a nonreversible cell, one will replace with silences the pivot-note and one of the symmetric notes, or just one of the symmetric notes; in that way, we shall obtain asymmetry of sound and silence. In a reversible cell, the opposed values will be replaced by silence.

Thus, for a rhythm as simple as rhythm I, I shall sketch this table of possibilities of transmutations that—it can be asserted—already offer a certain number of resources.

With rhythms VI or VII, it will be seen that the result may be very complex rhythmic cells such as:

Example VIIIa

I should mention that in some particular cases, these transformation project themselves one upon another. The first, sixth, and seventh forms of variation can react on the other four.

Furthermore, both symmetric and asymmetric extension are possible in a linear way on the basis of a single rhythm; that is to say that the reversible rhythms become nonreversible, then again reversible, etc., according to whether one adds to them all or part of their constituent values (the contrary happens

Example VIII

with nonreversible rhythms). These rhythmic graftings can be placed freely either among the values, in the mother-cell, or outside that cell.

I shall take as an example the case of cell II, which is nonreversible.

The first transformation (α) is achieved by placing the entire mother-cell between its first and second values, which gives a reversible rhythm; this result also can be obtained if one places the mother-cell between its own second and third values. (The added mother-cell is emphasized in the example by a note-flag.) One could just as well add only one or two of the values forming the mother-cell.

The second transformation (α') is achieved inversely by rendering the new rhythm nonreversible, but always by extension—that is, by adding all or part of the mother-cell.

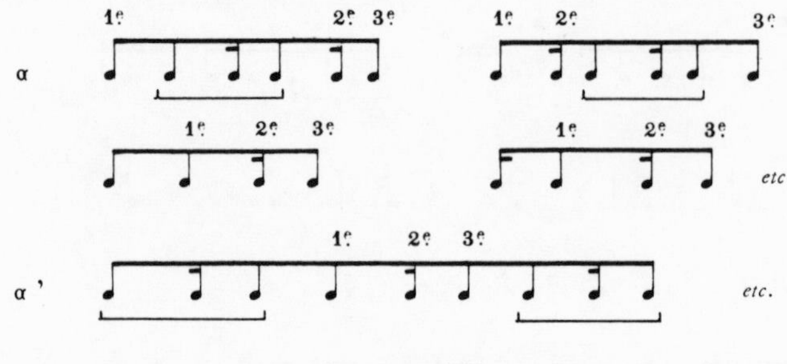

EXAMPLE IX

The possible transmutations of the initial cell are applicable to all of these extensions.

We thus obtain an equivalent of the serial transformations on a purely rhythmic level. And we can draw up a table of seven permutations applicable both to the cells themselves and to their mode of development. One can also have the two variations played together, and thus cause the rhythmic begetting and its mode of variation to interact. With regard to the concurrent or divergent series, we thus have established the store of possibilities toward which I wanted to move. A conception of composition is born which no longer feels the need to recollect the classic architectures, not even in order to destroy them. I believe that we are headed, without further restraint, toward a very real mode of being in which the autonomy will have nothing further to renounce.

I have mentioned silence as an integrating factor in rhythm.

One has a general tendency to remember only the *solfège* definition of music: *Music is the art of sounds.* Certainly! But cannot one attempt to realize, less simply perhaps, but in a livelier way, a close combination of those two antagonists: sound and silence? Without reference to many definitions that might be given to silence in music—silence of registers, silence of timbres, among others—let me consider it under the most elementary definition: absence of sound. Here too, Webern was the first to explore the possibilities of a dialectic of sound and silence. If we analyze, for instance, either the last movement of his Piano Variations or the second movement of his String Quartet, we shall find *silences* as integral parts of the rhythmic cells. That perhaps was Webern's only, but revolutionary, rhythmic discovery. If we pursue the consequences of such a conception of silence, we shall be able to vary it just as we can vary the values themselves and finally make them participate actively in the rhythmic life. This has led me to imagine what might be called a negative print of a rhythmic cell, in the sense that it would invert sounds and silences: everything that is value—that is, sound—becoming silence; all that is silence being transformed into value—that is, into sound.

Example X

Example X on page 163 shows a rhythmic structure arising from the same cells seen at two interdependent visual angles.

Furthermore, one can insert that cell, written duration by duration in silences, between different sequences depending from that same cell. This introduces a more complex notion of the function of silence as intervening amid rhythmic functions attached to sound.

In order to make this idea concrete, I again permit myself to give an extremely simple example. Taking up again the cell IV mentioned above, we can derive four variations from it:

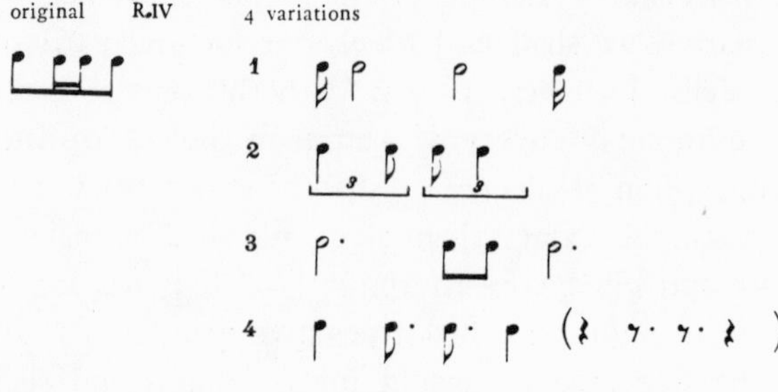

EXAMPLE XI

Now I write out, successively, the original and the first four variations, but instead of juxtaposing them, I separate them by the fourth variation, in which I have converted the durations into silences.

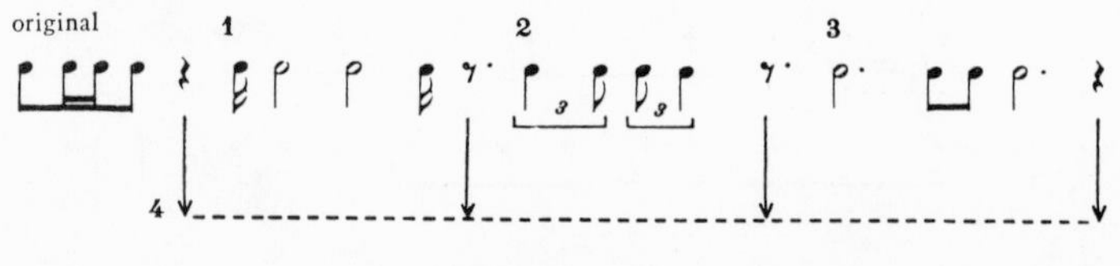

EXAMPLE XIa

On the basis of this rudimentary sample, one is in a position to imagine how these functions of silence could be conceived as integral parts of the rhythm.

Finally, I shall speak of a registration of durations, if it is possible to combine so eliptically two such constituents as pitch and duration. Given an enregistered sound, we are obliged, if we transpose, to increase its speed and, as a consequence, to shorten its duration; if we transpose it along the scale of the twelve half-tones, we obtain, inside the octave, twelve different durations, all of them having irrational relations among themselves; that is, relative to the sounds 1, 2, 3, 4 . . . 12, we shall have time units t_1, t_2, t_3, t_4 . . . t_{12}.

In order to embrace the entire register from bottom to top, I have been obliged to transpose these twelve sounds to six different speeds (that is, six octaves), which I have called:

$$4N, 2N, N, M, \frac{M}{2}, \frac{M}{4} \text{ (M being half of N).}$$

They indicate, then, a *tessitura* applicable to the twelve sounds.

Organizing the *tessitura*, the speeds imply respectively, what is more, a multiple of the smallest value t_1, t_2 . . . t_{12}, the speeds always crossing in geometric progression from the base 2 because, the octave having served as basis, the durations will diminish in inverse proportion.

Thus, corresponding to the speeds:

$$4N, 2N, N, M, \frac{M}{2}, \frac{M}{4}$$

we obtain a general table of tempos:

$$t, 2t, 4t, 8t, 16t, 32t,$$

applicable to the twelve units from t_1 to t_{12}. It is this, precisely, which I have called a register of durations. The sound 4 of speed 4N has a duration t_4; the sound 8 of speed M4 has a duration $16t_8$, etc.

But if we return separately to those durations which gave them birth, referring to the first example of rhythmic series that we examined, Example V, we shall obtain two parallel planes of serial structure. Not only shall we be able to employ different series, as I have already pointed out, but also we shall have the license to register duration as pitch and the one independently of the other. This, furthermore, will lead us to modify the sound—that is, to silence.

Let me take as our example the series:

1 6 3 4 10 11 5 12 7 9 2 8

for the pitches, and the series:

7 1 8 6 11 4 10 9 3 2 5 12

for the durations.

I shall register the pitches this way:

$$1.\frac{M}{2}—6.2N—3.4N—4.N—10.4N—11.\frac{M}{2}—5.M, \text{ etc.,}$$

and the durations:

$$2t_7—16t_1—32t_8—8t_6—2t_{11}—32t_4—4t_{10}, \text{ etc.}$$

If we combine the series of durations with the series of pitches, we shall obtain.

$$1.M2;2t_7—6.2N;16t_1—3.4N;32t_8—4.N;8t_6—\text{etc.}$$

The sound $1.\frac{M}{2}$ originally has a duration of $16t_1$. If we combine it with the shorter duration, $2t_7$, we shall be using it only partially. The sound 6.2N has an original duration of $2t_6$. If we combine it with the duration $16t_1$, after this sound it will have a silence corresponding to the difference: $16t_1—2t_6$.

Let us keep in view then that a structure is thus possible on the basis of the play of *tessituras*, pitch, and duration in an extremely supple way stretching from the complete remoteness of divergent *tessituras* to the brushing together of neighboring *tessituras*. I shall examine the means of achieving such a construction when I speak of the experience of *musique concrète*. There I shall indicate that it is even possible to prepare a score.

With regard to the question of rhythm, it has perhaps been noted that I have referred to two sorts of structures: the first in units of value, the second in rhythmic cells already organized and susceptible to variation.

Turning to the problem of the organization of pitches, in which I have considered only that of notes—equivalents of unitary value—it is possible to think of creating a kind of correspondence with the rhythmic cells and, by that means, of reaching the notion of complex sounds or of complexes of sounds.

There may be surprise at my labeling as "complexes of sounds" what usually are called "chords." Without speaking of the historic heritage to which the word "chord" is linked, I am not according any harmonic function, properly speaking, to such a vertical coagulation. I mean by it nothing more than the superimposition of frequencies as a sound-bloc.

Let me take the example of a series of twelve half-tones divided this way: three sounds, one sound, two sounds, four sounds, two sounds—or five *sonorities:*

EXAMPLE XII

If I apply to that series the principle of transposition which I defined above, I obtain five series of sonorities in which the sound-blocs are more or less complex; for in doing this, I multiply the constituents of each bloc, some by others. Thus, if one transposes a superimposition of three sounds by a superimposition of four sounds, one obtains, in principle, a superimposition of twelve sounds—4 times 3. But because of notes in common—here two, G natural and B flat—the new sound-bloc will have only ten tones.

Each of these superimpositions of frequencies is evidently susceptible to modification each time that it is reproduced, all the notes being novel as to *tessitura* and susceptible to permutations along a vertical line in relation to the intervals of definitions.

EXAMPLE XIII

EXAMPLE XIIIa

Furthermore, I can modify the color of that sonority by changing the attack—that is, the intensity—of one or more of its components:

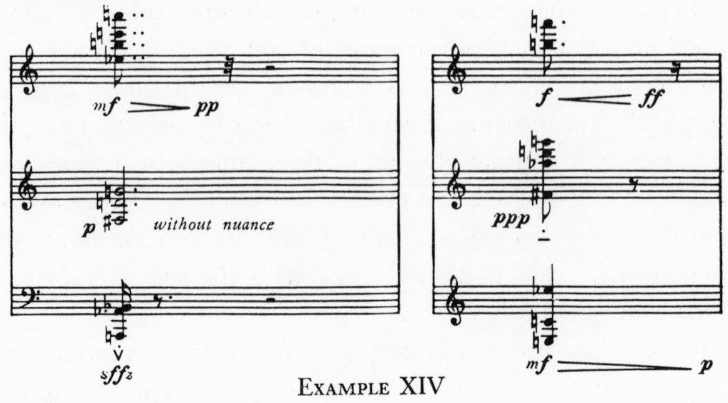

EXAMPLE XIV

Very evidently, the first bloc of Example XIII will not have the same sonority as the second bloc, although both blocs have been deduced from Example XII.

The extent of variants that one can apply to these complexes of sounds is, one realizes, huge and rich in possibilities, above all if one does not rule out the eventuality of nontempered realms and microdistances.

The sound-complex is more difficult to define, it being understood that it is not based on superimpositions of differing frequencies, but refers to the idea of a sound-body itself not emitting pure sounds—fundamental and natural harmonics—but harmonics not positioned in simple numerical relationships. In fact, one envisages a preponderant frequency superimposed on other frequencies of less intensity. At times—as happens, for example, with a gong—even the preponderating frequencies themselves vary during the evolution of the complex emitted by the sound-body. These complex sounds, if indicated on a tablature, are susceptible to serial use; it is convenient, then, to consider the series not so much as a control of variable pitches in relation to tessitura but as one of the controls of the permutations of sound-objects in some way fixed. I should cite apropos of this the prepared piano used by John Cage.

I have referred to concepts of attack and intensity as differentiating two complexes of sounds having the same constituents. In fact, I think that those functions should play a constructive role in the work, along with pitch, rhythm, and timbre, if one uses different timbres. I shall give an example of serial combinations of timbres. Here are eighteen instruments playing in seven symmetrical groups. They are, in the order of the scoring:

1. (3) Piccolo
Small clarinet
English horn
2. (2) Oboe
Bass clarinet

3. (2) Flute
Bassoon

4. (4) Small trumpet
Alto saxophone
Horn
Trombone

5. (2) First violin
First violoncello

6. (2) Second violin
Second violoncello

7. (3) First viola
Second viola
Doublebass

This symmetry of two outside groups of three instruments, of four median groups of two instruments, in relation to a middle group of four instruments (that is, two plus two) supplies the base upon which I shall establish mutations of groups among them. If one supposes that each group has determined serial and rhythmic functions, one sees that those functions will evolve through groups of the same patronymic numeral, but of variable composition.

Here are two of these mutations which will allow us to take account of the procedure of variation.

1.	(3)	Piccolo	Small clarinet
		English horn	English horn
		Second viola	First viola
2.	(2)	Flute	Horn
		First violoncello	First violoncello
3.	(2)	Small trumpet	Alto saxophone
		Second violoncello	Second violin
4.	(4)	Oboe	Oboe
		Alto saxophone	Bassoon
		Trombone	First violin
		First violin	Second violoncello
5.	(2)	Bass clarinet	Flute
		Second violin	Trombone

6.	(2)	Bassoon Horn	Bass clarinet Small trumpet
7.	(3)	Small clarinet First viola Doublebass	Piccolo Second viola Doublebass

Thus we obtain instrumental formations that play a very important role in the structure. It should be noted that these permutations are not arrived at automatically, but are selected for special qualities that they provide, that the point of departure for these researches and the aim that they propose is, above all, sound-*evidence*.

As for making attacks and intensities take part in the total organization of a musical structure, it suffices to separate them from the structures that presided over their elaboration, and thus to give them autonomy. As we have seen with durations, they can depend originally on the series of pitches or of rhythms or have their own independent domain from the outset.

One arrives now at tempos, which will justify equal care in giving them serial organization also. Just as with attacks, intensities, and timbres, such serial organizations are not likely to be less complex than those of pitches and durations; but one sees that they will be renewed less often, if one may speak so summarily. By this I mean that they govern, dominate, accentuate, or contradict large lines of architecture rather than participating in the immediate writing of a musical work.

I have separated the question of tempos from that of rhythm, properly speaking, because I consider these two aspects of musical time as essentially different. The first, rhythm, is related to a function of the unit of value, that unit which, for purposes of this study, it is possible to abstract from the tempo in which it figures. The second, tempo, is, above all, a *speed of development* of the musical text, essentially pragmatic. One sees, therefore, that tempo cannot vary every instant; as it would become confused with rhythm, given that it would create in the same way variations related to the unit of value itself. Furthermore, the important factor in the choice of different tempos is perhaps not rigorous metronomic exactness (which would be desirable here, just as in all music), but rather a hierarchy among their relationships—which will bring us back to establishing a relation of *speeds of development*, some in relation to others.

To be sure, I believe that this question of tempo and rhythm is much more free-flowing than that in the final analysis, for I also realize that a development will have cinematic or agogic qualities depending upon whether it is occuring in a fast or a slow tempo, and that, consequently, the rhythmic writing will be modified intrinsically even in relation to an unchanged unit of value.

These interferences of rhythmic stasis or dynamism with mobility or permanence of tempo can be brought into relation with those between serial structures and registers, already noted.

Perhaps there will be surprise that I still have not spoken of the composition of a work. But in everything that I have written about the discovery of a serial world, it must be very clear that I refuse to describe creation as the only way to make use of these initial structures; any assurance acquired that way would not satisfy me if it had the aspect of a reflex conditioned by the act of writing, an action with very little more importance than bookkeeping carefully observed or even minutely carried out. Composition could not take on the appearance of an elegant distributive economy, however ingenious, without condemning itself to inanity and gratuitousness.

Once we take off from the *données* that we have studied in detail, the unforeseeable arises. We have seen the free play left within these *données* and among them by all of these serial organizations, which seem rigid only to those who systematically remain ignorant of them or reject them—those prisoners of a somewhat secular routine and of conservative prejudice that wishes to preserve untouched the acquisitions of the past.

After this theoretical essay, which will appear to many as the glorification of intellectualism as against instinct, I shall finish. The unexpected, again: there is no creation except in the unforeseeable becoming necessity.

I do not want to pursue this study of present-day perspectives in music without mentioning the names of Olivier Messiaen and John Cage. They alone are the exceptions that I pointed out in the language's acquisitions after Webern, Stravinsky, Berg, and Schoenberg. The first through his discoveries in the rhythmic domain; the second by his prospecting among complex sounds, complexes of sounds, and also in the rhythmic domain.

To Olivier Messiaen we owe—in addition to the profound studies he made of plain chant, Hindu rhythm, and Stravinsky—the creation of a conscious technique of duration. The fact is unquestionably important, for aside from the inoperative mania, periodically recurrent, of wanting to reconstitute the Greek metric, one must go back to the fourteenth century to find a like preoccupation in Occidental music, whereas it was one of the constants of music in other civilizations (black Africa, India, the islands of Bali and Java).

To Messiaen we owe above all—among other acquisitions—the first idea of separating rhythmic writing from polyphonic writing. (An idea that can be found in an embryonic state in the numerous *Monoritmica* or *Hauptrhythmus* that occur in nearly all of Berg's works.) That was how he realized his first rhythmic canons, whether by augmentation or by diminution or again by dotting, the point of departure for a whole polyrhythmic technique. To him we owe the symmetric or asymmetric enlargements of rhythmic cells and the establishment of the difference between reversible and nonreversible rhythms.

To Messiaen, also, we owe the creation of modes of durations in which the rhythmic assumes a functional value; finally, we owe him the care in establishing a dialectic of duration through his researches into a hierarchy among the values (variable oppositions of shorter or longer values, even or odd), a dialectic that in itself furnishes a means of musical development when it is played upon structures of rhythmic neumes. We must also consider very important the research that he has pursued in creating modes of intensity and of attack paralleling rhythmic modes.

This succinct enumeration suffices to show how the serial rhythmic principles that I have set forth could not have been conceived without the disquietude and technique that Messiaen has transmitted to us.

As for John Cage, he has given us the proof that it is possible to create nontempered sound-spaces even using existing instruments. Thus, his use of the *prepared piano* is not merely an unexpected aspect of a piano-percussion in which the harmonic table is invaded by unexampled, metalizing vegetation. It is much more a questioning of the acoustic notions stabilized little by little in the course of the evolution of Occidental music, this prepared piano becoming an instrument able to give forth, through the intermediary of a workmanlike tablature, complexes of frequencies. John Cage thinks, in fact, that the instruments created for answering the needs of the tonal language do not respond to the new necessities of music, which reject the octave as a privileged interval as the point of departure of the different scales. In that way the desire to give each sound, from the beginning, a revealed individuality is affirmed. In a work of long duration, that individuality being an invariant, one reaches—through the fact of repetitions in time—an over-all and hierarchic neutrality in the scale of frequencies, which is to say a unique mode of multiple sounds covering the entire tessitura; then, perhaps, one tumbles into the trap that one has been trying to avoid. However, let us notice that if the tablatures were more numerous, the polarization would be much richer, given the reservoir of interactions that would be created among them. If, on the contrary, one gives each sound an absolutely neuter *a priori*—as is the case with serial material—the context brings up, at each occurrence of the same sound, a different individualization of that sound. That sort of reversibility of cause and effect is a phenomenon curious enough to be emphasized.

We also owe to John Cage the idea of complexes of sounds: for he has written works in which, instead of making use of pure sounds, he has employed chords devoid of any harmonic function, they being essentially kinds of sound-amalgams linked to timbres, durations, and intensities, each one of these characteristics being differentiable according to the diverse constituents of the amalgam.

I also want to point out Cage's way of conceiving the rhythmic structure, which he rests upon the idea of real time, placed in evidence by numerical relationships into which the personal coefficient does not enter; furthermore, a given number of units of measure gives birth to an equal number of units of development. In that way, one reaches an *a priori* numerical structure that John Cage calls "prismatic," but which I shall call crystallized structure.

More recently, he has been preoccupied with creating structural relationships among the diverse components of the sound, and for that he utilizes tables organizing each of them in parallel but autonomous scores.

The direction of John Cage's experiments is too near that of my own for me not to take note of it.

The experience of *musique concrète*, finally, seems to me indispensable in so far as it permits solution of the difficulties presented both by the creation of nontempered sounds and complex sounds and by the realization of rhythmic structures fractioning irrationals.

Up to now, the experience of *musique concrète* has above all evidenced a curiosity about and appetite for sound-objects, but it takes no great care with their organization. Could it have been otherwise with the very rudimentary means afforded by the procedures of recording on discs? It does not seem to. But with the more and more improved apparatuses constructed under the direction of Pierre Schaeffer, beginning in particular with recording on tape, it seems that results of very satisfying precision may be produced.

Thus it is that from the rhythmic point of view, given that the duration of sound recorded on tape is measured in length (the speed of unrolling being 77 centimeters per second), one can, by cutting the recorded tape and then by juxtaposing selected sounds a little in the manner of film sequences, realize rhythmic sequences unrealizable by performers.

If one writes:

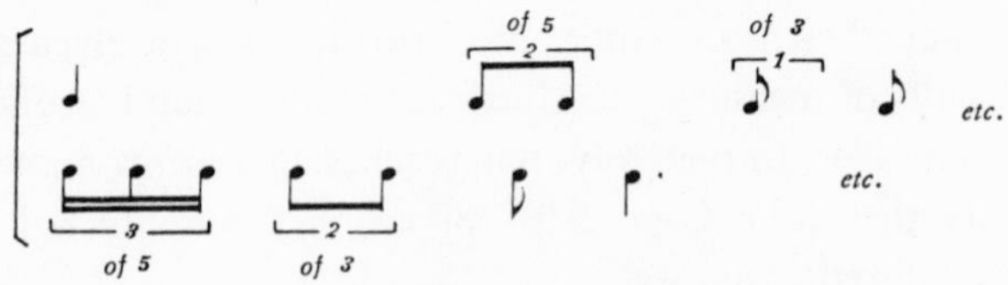

EXAMPLE XV

that is, if one wants to fraction some irrational groups, taking only two eighth-notes out of a quintuplet, one eighth-note from a triplet, etc., one is unable to do it in polyphonic writing, it being practically impossible to perform rhythms of that much difficulty when they have been superimposed.

Everything becomes simple on magnetic tape. Let me suppose that the quarter-note is recorded over 60 centimeters (which can be taken, among others, as a unit of value). The quintuplet quarter-note will be recorded over 24 centimeters, the quintupet sixteenth-note over 12 centimeters, the triplet eighth-note over 20 centimeters. Thus one would have this montage schema:

60 cm — 24 cm 24 cm — 20 cm — 30 cm.
12 cm 12 cm 12 cm — 20 cm 20 cm 20 cm — 30 cm — 90 cm.

Registration on tape also allows us to play with the curve of sound. Without lingering over reversal of sound or filters of frequencies, I can describe some serial permutations that can be brought to bear on a given sound.

Take a sound that I shall inscribe according to the axes of intensity and of time (Example XVI).

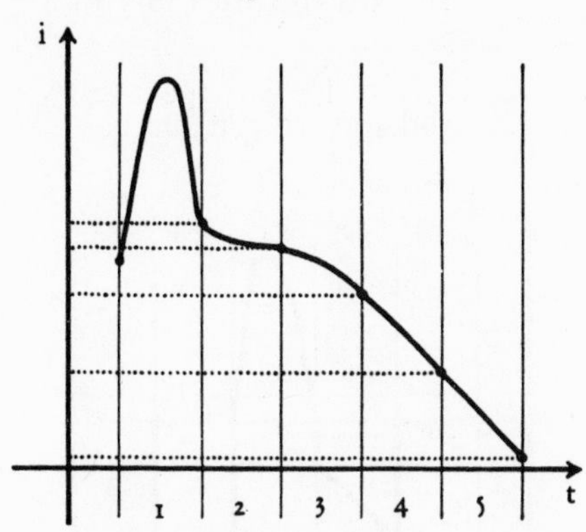

Example XVI

Let me divide it into five equal parts. (It is essential for me to concede that the number 5 is not arbitrary, but depends from other determining serial factors.) If one applies to this sound, so divided, a given series—say:

2 3 5 4 1

or again:

3 4 1 5 2,

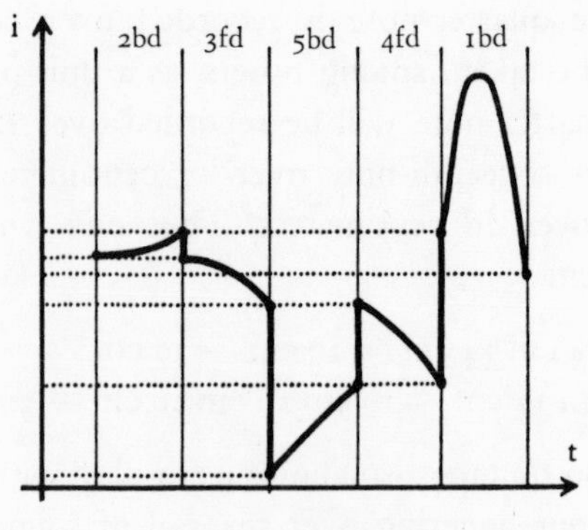

Example XVII

if one places these divisions sometimes forward (fd), sometimes backward (bd):

2bd 3fd 5bd 4fd 1 bd

or:

3bd 4bd 1fd 5bd 2bd,

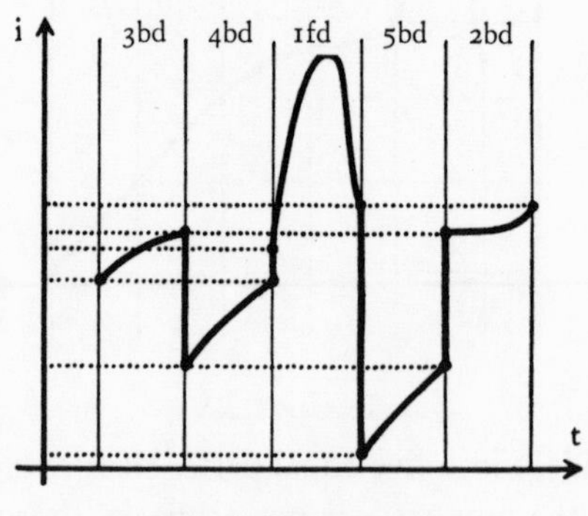

Example XVIIa

one obtains artificial curves that introduce a new dimension into the possibilities of variation.

Notation of the scores will be made in relation to the scale of lengths of recorded tape; with some conventions defining for each work the material used and the tablature corresponding to it, the placement on the page will be as legible as that of an ordinary score.

Who can deny that all the experiments of our epoch converge into an exceptionally rich reservoir of resources? To be sure, the exposition of them that I have given strongly invites my being accused of intellectualism.

Since the nineteenth century, the word "intellectual" has been the most outrageous epithet when aimed at a creator working in the so-called arts of expression. Thus one faces some confusions. The dodecaphonists in particular have been the objects of that accusation. But, contrary to what generally has been said about them—which has been nothing but hearsay—they mostly have had no intelligent comprehension of the musical phenomenon of our time. They have been satisfied to rest on bases acquired with destructive purposes by their predecessors; these they apply, in the manner of the later Schoenberg, to an antihistorical course. We are asked to take such a larval academicism as intellectualism, whereas it is merely the secretion of limited spirits short of expedients.

Sometimes, nonetheless, the confusions are other than anecdotal. The "intellectual artist" almost answers to this definition: he establishes *his* theory in a closed circuit, he strongly wants to convince others of the efficacy and availability of that theory; for that reason, making newness a sort of proof, he sets out to produce works that finally have no criterion other than that of proof by newness. If the creation is bad, there is a rush to treat him with contempt as a theoretician, clockmaker, etc. If the creation is good, there is an equal rush to assert that it is not the theoretician who should enlist agreement, that his theories are not very important, given that he has produced a beautiful work. To reach that glorification, they forget all relation of cause and effect, which, in the contempt case, they themselves placed in evidence.

But why should we be ashamed of our technique? I retort to the contrary and assert that the reproach of intellectualism is ill-founded because it starts from an erroneous understanding—when it is not stained with bad taste—of the interpenetrating role of sensibility and intelligence in all creation. Let us not forget that in music, expression is intrinsically linked to the language, to the very technique of the language. Music is perhaps of all phenomena the one least dissociable from all its means of expression in the sense that its own morphology is what in the first place gives an account of the perceptible evolution of the creator. Thus one sees that those reproaches of intellectualism are wrongheaded because the formal means supply the only possible communication. I am not being paradoxical when I say that the more complex the formal means are, the less they are perceived intellectually by the listener. Analysis, then, is impossible during the course of a performance; and even when one has analyzed a complex structure, experience shows that the best-constructed forms—and therefore the least visible forms—are recomposed as heard and again challenge the analytic intelligence by submerging it. One could mention many works thought of as simple in which one perceives—this time in a very intellectual way—the schematic character precisely because it is foreseeable.

These schemas, which content those who reject the sin of intellectualism, are culpable as much for their gratuitousness, their arbitrariness, as for their *a priori.* They can not lead to any consequence but sterility solidified outside the circuit. Even if they are pompously baptized *liberty*, even if they are justified in the name of lyric expression, nothing but their proneness to sclerotic tendencies is thus justified or baptized.

As a last recourse, however, there is protest in the name of the creative imagination. One must bow very low to minds with such fertile imagination. They are odd, for the rest, these protestants, in holding that faculty to be so fragile that it will not bear direction. In fact, I have already noted that it is not only fragile, but also very weak—whereas they proclaim it all-powerful; they fall, all unaware, upon all the caltrops of the worst commonplaces. On the contrary, I have the tendency to find that the imagination requires some of these springboards supplied by the formal means put at its disposal by a technique that dares to be called by its own name.

Thus we reach that unbearable question of formalism. The final residue of romanticism, it always conceives of theoretical research as a closed cycle not coinciding with creations, properly speaking, as I have already mentioned. Let us free ourselves of that obsolete legend: it cannot be thus, under pain of mortal asphyxia. A consciously organizing logic is not independent of the work to whose creation it contributes; it is linked to it in a reversible circuit, for what leads to the evolution of technique is the need to make precise what one wants to express; that technique reinforces the imagination, which then projects itself toward the unperceived; and thus, in a perpetual play of mirrors, creation is pursued; organization, living and lived, leaving possible all the acquisitions, enriching itself with each new experience, completing itself, even changing accentuation. I shall say more: it is by the glorification of rhetoric itself that music is justified. Otherwise it remains only laughable anecdote, noisy grandiloquence, or morose libertinage.

Should one break off? Once again, the unexpected: *The heart, an organ that takes the place of everything* . . . (Verlaine . . . 1865 . . . answering Barbey d'Aurevilly . . .)

". . . *Auprès et au loin*"

It seems that the present generation can now take leave of its predecessors; it has reached a self-definition sufficiently precise and explicit so that it need no longer accept sponsorship, need not suffer patronage. One knows the chief living forces of recent musical evolution; it would be superfluous to recall again the divergence of particularizing points of view which they manifest. It is our duty to discern the seeming aspect of these contradictions, to resolve them in a justified synthesis.

To make the point about this generation's acquisitions of assets will be to declare clearly its state of mind, its way of thinking music. One fact is sure: from the morphology of the language to the conception of the work, everything has been put to the question—not out of a more or less gratuitous will to make a revolution, which would be content to apply certain postulates without relation to their object, but out of a series of intuitions guided by a logic indispensable to their homogeneity.

In fact, it must be said that these researches are homogeneous despite the chaotic appearance that they sometimes take on. It seems that the great preoccupation has not been to overthrow an esthetic in the name of noisy principles, or to refine the morphology for hyperdelectation, or even to turn the language from its veritable affection for creating hiatuses of shock, but much rather to coordinate all the constituents of the language, or be it all the constituents of sound—after having become sharply aware that their analytic dissociation was a scientifically valid point of departure—in a unique system of references, taking into account the disparity of their perception. From that beginning, a new organization of the sound-world was created, of which I shall detail the principal characteristics; that organization demands a totally reshaped workmanship, both in the formal conception—the intellectual apprehension of the structures—and in the instrumental or electroacoustic realization, two aspects that in certain cases lead to reciprocal absorpion of the phenomena native to each; that such a conception of the work—morphology and rhetoric—should lead to overturning the domain of the "poetic" is not surprising; on the contrary, the meaning of the work has been modified to the point at which closed or open structures, the automatism in their play, or the free will introduced into them have created new dimensions, almost a new fashion of perceiving the musical work, of experiencing its necessity. The work no longer takes its place in a hierarchy that it corroborates or damages, but engenders its own hierarchy each time; above all, it no longer has any tendency toward a preexistent schema related to very precisely determined functions. Moving contrary to that course, the present-day work tends to be constituted of the possibilities of functions that, by certain characteristics, engender for it a universe of its own of which the schema is one of the manifestations.

It goes without saying that such a conception must wound the upholders of a tradition that is now devoid of life, they unfortunately having too great a tendency to take as natural, immutable laws their own habits of thought and their routines. However, to read some documents in the evolution of musical morphology is edifying: as the art of music, despite everything, must take into account certain "rules of play," the systems—those attempts at codification attempted very regularly from Guido d'Arezzo to Rameau and D'Alembert—

appear to have been as humanly "systematic" as possible until the habit of living with and for them gave them that divine aspect, any transgression of them being rejected as a veritable negation of their immanence. Ought not one to see, without paradox, in those accusations of "dogmatism" launched peevishly against a new system of references that is establishing itself with more and more assurance, only a manifestation of characters ferociously attached to an ancient system become dogma? The more so, it appears, since absolutely no further discussion is possible with certain contradictors, their articles of faith not allowing any possibility of discussion. I consider that the reproach of fanaticism made against the promoters of present-day music is the translation of that belief, held by a pack of crackpots, in a Truth forever revealed, the inevitable result of a misunderstanding that it would be a mistake to take seriously.

Be that as it may, certainly no musical system, neither in our Occidental civilization nor in the Asiatic or African civilizations, for example, is absolutely justified by natural laws. Arab theories and Chinese theories are as logical as the Pythagorean theories and are responsible for equally valid sound-worlds. What is more, we must recognize that every time a justification of that sort has been undertaken, a certain number of approximations has resulted, even to such a degree of approximation that one may harbor some doubt about the basis of such enterprises. Shouldn't we rather envisage a sort of law of the evolution of systems? One could define a system, in general, as an ensemble of procedures designed to engender maximum coherence in the management of sound-phenomena, the evolution of the procedures inside a system of references itself constituting the evolution of the system; when the need for it has ceased to be real, it decays and falls into desuetude. We might parody Valéry's famous mot: "We other systems, we know now that we are mortal."

To eliminate some prejudices about a Natural Order, to rethink acoustical notions on the basis of more recent experiences, to envisage the problems posed by electroacoustics and electronic techniques—that is the course demanded now; we are not unaware that we have not as yet reached unassailable coherence, indisputable clarity. Too many points remain obscure, too many desires are still unsatisfied, too many needs have not even been formulated. But it is impossible not to concede that the demands of present-day music are on a par with certain currents in contemporary mathematics and philosophy. Not that I wish to force coincidence among all the human activities of a given time, following a rigorous parallelism; the most superficial relationships that one might rush to put in evidence would not suffice to justify such a parallelism. It seems that one might, without fear of being gratuitous, dream of the theory of ensembles, of relativity, of the quantum theory, when one comes into contact with the sound-world defined by the serial principle; recourse to the *Gestalttheorie* or to phenomenology does not seem to me senseless either—to the contrary. I have no illusions about the reality of the correspondences that might be established, almost too easily, among music, mathematics, and philosophy; rather, I am prepared to notice that the three activities show similarity in the extension of their domains.

As to the *rapprochement* among the "arts," or, rather, between music and poetry, music and painting, the insolvency of the *Gesammtkunstwerk* has made everyone very circumspect, and each seems to want to work in his own domain without, what is more, occupying himself with any hypothetical solidarity. It seems, then, without returning to the romantic dreams of unity, that present-day thought wants to indicate more reciprocal confidence by taking the very general principle of structures as a basis; that concept at least has the merit of not denying liberty, of not installing any constraint.

If one wishes to emphasize the character of genuine necessity in the experiments of the young musicians, one must, at the outset, locate that activity. There is posed on this subject a terribly important—and very general—question: how is a tradition transmitted? The young composer, in fact, becomes conscious of his métier little by little through the métier of his predecessors, making their acquisitions his own, assimilating their powers; a phenomenon of osmosis is produced, accompanied by a reaction conducted in relation to that osmosis. Let me recall what Malraux said on this subject: "Painters and sculptors, whenever they are great, transform the works that they have inherited—modifying forms no matter what they are or what their nature"; and, later: "Whoever becomes a painter when faced not with the most beautiful woman, but with the most beautiful pictures, feels no less emotion upon becoming one; that which is born from art, like any other, carries within it the desire for permanence"; and, again: "The painter passes from a world of forms to another world of forms, the writer from a world of words to another world of words, in the same way that the musician passes from music to music."

How is that continuity of transmission possible? Through teaching, to begin with; then, when teaching has become ineffective—saturation reaches a degree at which the student feels the need to define for himself his own proper coordinates in relation to a tradition—one has recourse to analytic reading of scores. A young composer's métier thus depends on a heritage in the choice of which he intervenes more or less. Both transmissible and intransmissible heritages exist; distinction must be made between what history renders obsolete and what it metamorphoses, a situation constantly in flux, which explains certain of the relationships that we perceive between periods. It is a fact that a given moment in history recognizes itself more willingly in certain anterior moments, confers upon them privileges that can be abolished by the intervention of other privileges. Very exactly, this phenomenon can be called the harmonics of an epoch. But, taking this coefficient of the historic moment into account, one must mention a primordial personal coefficient; I might almost say that only it justifies analysis, becoming without analysis a sterile academic undertaking.

In truth, the spirit of analysis is a custom propagated with exciting swiftness in our day. Having been preceded by a generation made up in large part of meritorious illiterates, do we have a tendency to become a crop of technocrats? To reply to adversaries lacking any ambition but that of the mason or the prostitute, can we ourselves hold no objective but that of the engineer? The perspective is not at all happy, and one has too much tendency to let oneself be hypnotized by that gleam produced by the ambition to be rigorous; the inquisition is set up: one is tamed. If we could let ourselves imagine the joy of cutting a good or bad figure among the inquisitors, that would be the exact opposite of my proposal. I have no aim other than that of trying to place myself ever more precisely in relation to the predecessors to whom I am tributary. The analytic "accounting" is, in fact, not of itself valuable or gratuitous: a certain number of procedures is brought to light, procedures that "render an account" in the most plausible fashion, whether an account of the writing or of the structure of a given work. Nevertheless, if one gives oneself to an exegesis of that sort, it is not only for the empty satisfaction—a pleasure easy to reject—of knowing the "how" of the work, out of mere curiosity. The great works, happily, never yield up all of their mystery. If one takes care not to sink into a hopeless mood when faced with that mystery, which refuses to be clarified, one will divine painlessly from then on the movement of a mind launched on such a quest—a sort of act of faith in the transmission of the métier from generation to generation by this unique and irreplaceable means, even though then the second impossibility will arise: the work cannot be completely adequate for us. In fact, is any transmission of the métier truly possible? It is in that that a spirit of analysis cannot in itself be justifactory. Taken as a projection of itself over the works that preceded us, it will then maintain a modesty of relation without which one can only sink into academic pedantry, flounder in derisory rhetoric. I also abandon without regret the deceptive precariousness of a satisfactory precision and avow a relativity that rules out no analysis.

In this domain the search for a method implies difficulties that it is well to point out. At the very beginning, in relation to the idiom: it is completely ineffective to take account of a work by means of *a posteriori* investigation; it is equally ineffective to examine a work by imposing upon it a system of references to which it was anterior. The attempt to analyze a Bach piece in relation to a study of pitches and registers is just as vain as trying to compare a Webern structure literally to a Beethoven structure. The work, then, imposes the choice of the means with which to approach it: which by no means guarantees that in such a procedure one will inescapably overtake the composer's intuition. We need not busy ourselves about the mechanism that leads to the work, but rather with the work itself, which, once composed—by the mere fact that it has been achieved—casts into night all the preliminary procedures. The achievement implies abolition of what might have been: chance abolished, but without forgetting the element of chance which can intervene in that abolition. What absolute masterpiece could aim to remain outside that situation? That should not permit us to forget that evens did not coincide for the composer from the outset to give a "sound-phenomenon." Creation is in some part analytical. By accident, notebooks containing sketches by great musicians have been preserved for us, and in certain cases reading those manuscripts—in inks of various colors—can be very instructive. The sound "phenomenon"—which there may be too much tendency to believe indissociable—was often attained by successive approaches to a satisfactory state. Some examples of that are especially striking in Beethoven: the first sketch of the scherzo of his Ninth Symphony is marked "*Ende Langsam*," and one can still read below the notation of the theme: "*Fuge*." To speak once more of creation for which the material is selected in view of its possibilities, all foreseen, is to give proof of a determinist Utopia of curiously hybrid nature. The same is true of any harping on "English horn" melodies, sonatas with "specifically" pianistic or "specifically" violinistic themes; misunderstandings of that sort are very tenacious and reflect a very deeply rooted religious mentality; the composer is God and his clairvoyance embraces the entire work from the moment he decides to create it. Did not Arnold Schoenberg write, in *Style and Idea:*

> To understand the very nature of creation one must acknowledge that there was no light before the Lord said: "Let there be Light." And since there was not yet light, the Lord's omniscience embraced a vision of it which only His omnipotence could call forth. . . . In fact, the concept of creator and creation should be formed in harmony with the Divine Model; inspiration and perfection, will and accomplishment coincide spontaneously and simultaneously. In Divine Creation there were no details to be carried out later; "There was Light" at once and in its ultimate perfection. . . . Alas, it is one thing to envision in a creative instant of inspiration and it is another thing to materialize one's vision by painstakingly connecting details until they fuse into a kind of organism.

Taking into account the humor in that declaration, that nostalgia for the lost Paradise which was very characteristic of Schoenberg—he, the final representative of the romantic current—one encounters it in more or less anodyne forms with many "spontaneists," strange as that may seem. The "spontaneists" of the preceding generation were not, in fact, anything but the pale progeny of their romantic predecessors, with the difference that God had been metamorphosed into the Carnival King and that pasteboard had become the only material for their creation. Faced with that "divine" conception, which is not about to cede its privileges, having come to light insidiously among that very generation under the subtlest aspects, or which takes on "scientific" allure by catching up with the mystique of numbers, one can imagine a procedure leading to the creation of a work which would safeguard intuition—but not vision—and would be purified of this myth of "clairvoyance," but would not forget magic and divination. I shall try to set forth my own point of view precisely later on.

The study of sound "phenomena," if we return to it, does not, then, favor most of the concepts reducible to the method employed in describing them; for, at the other extremity of the creative process, to consider a work as an indissociable entity like a created world exactly parallels the composer's "vision"; a "small, portable cosmogony," it facilitates above all a superior dilettantism—of high category, it must be admitted—but a dilettantism that always considers phenomena from the outside, some considerations of luminous order being insufficient to satisfy our demands. Analysis should not deal with various "aspects" of the differently clarified phenomenon; it should, inside the work, approach the various constituents that concur in its realization. The meaning of that word "constituents," which can lead to nonsense, should be explained; one should not understand by "constituents" unilateral factors (rhythm, melody, harmony) being *joined together* in a monstrous, unreal addition; one should understand, rather, vectoral constituents which, in being added together vectorally, lead to a result of which the direction is different, though it is defined by the constituents. That these "constituents" exist, even though in rough state, cannot be denied if we examine popular music. In fact, there are rhythmic schemes—based on a determined meter —which can engender a category of dances (gigue, saraband, tarantella, to cite only examples closest to a western European), rhythmic schemes which, at a given moment, really did preexist these dances; this clearly results from the more or less clarified position of a musical "genre" in relation to history. Nonetheless, it remains true that each of these dances, if taken individually, constitutes a unique case, an indissociable "phenomenon"; but then it seems that study of the perception of the work is being confused with the work itself. Even though perception of the work may not be as total as one wants to suppose, it is believable that the only time that one perceives a musical "phenomenon" as an inseparable entity is upon first hearing it—I would gladly say at the first hearings, above all if they are spaced out. After that exceptional instance, memory plays an important role, whence the power of analysis, memory permitting comparison of various phases of the sound "phenomenon" and more or less close-up examination of their parity or disparity. I do not assert that this power of analysis extends throughout the duration of the work; rather, it will be sporadic, and the fluctuations of its acuity will be a function of the listener and of the work listened to. It appears, then, that from the point of view of perception or from the angle of creation, the sound-"phenomenon" cannot so easily be reduced to a whole; on the contrary, it seems that the abstraction practiced on rhythm or melody in a score, for example, is not solely a theoretical operation and that the leaps made from one plane to another during the hearing of a work—with more or less virtuosity according to individual musical education—may even most often be the concrete way in which the listener perceives the music. The vocabulary of amateurs who take into account the hearing of a work is explicit in that regard: they grasp this or that component, here "the harmony," there "the rhythm"; very rarely do they perceive the whole—a rare occurrence lightly called "a state of grace" as related not only to the whole formal conception of the work heard but also to the realization of each of its instants.

If analysis from the inside is valid insofar as it is justified by the genesis of the work and by some characteristics of perception, one should take those two factors into account, for otherwise one risks loss of balance. Also, when I see account taken of certain sorts of music, dodecaphonic or not, by means of a numerology with no ambition but to give examples, I think of this as a surviving variety of a venerable aberration, an entire academic tradition preserved under a refabricated face. It suffices to establish a gauge of the work to be studied—always an easy definition because it is essentially an abstract operation—a gauge of pitches, or of rhythms, as deduced on the basis of some details of the numbers, usually very simple. Even suppose it valid: as applied to the work, it gives equations or balance in a form resulting from its inception. It remains to attribute those laws of balance triumphantly to the measure-gauge chosen; were one to employ another, just as arbitrary, one would reencounter exactly the same laws under other visual aspects, which does not explain the phenomena of structural balances that are the real character of the work. One will merely have cloaked one's indigence in garrulous tautology.

If we are to avoid that reef, we must practice analysis in such a way that the work will appear not as a distributive balance sheet, but in relation to deduced structures. And if, for that purpose, one has need of numbers and letters, that is a last resort in the sense that it risks—with the advantage of practical ease in designation—the peril of taking these sign symbols to be the object of the study. An ambiguity that must be unmasked at any cost because it provides the solid base of all the confusions; it is in its name that a certain style of admiration—and of limitation—tends to occur. The consequences of which one can have an intuition are really perceived through study of the morphological structures, to begin with; then one enlarges that first plane to encompass the whole structure; then, studying the mode of the begetting of these various planes of the structure, their interrelationships—that is, in gradually generalizing step by step—one may come to describe what, properly speaking, makes up the course of the work.

To reach that objective requires a certain element of creative spirit. I can see that the drawbacks in the analytical essay, in the exegesis of this or that work, are owing to a profound lack of invention, to a notorious indigence of imagination. That is why, moving on from the same predecessor elements, it is possible either to create a "mannerism" or come up with a new sheaf of discoveries.

I shall try to make such discoveries clear in a sufficiently succinct way so that there will be no need for technical explanations that could interest few people. I am not sorry, furthermore, thus to avoid the reproach of technocratic esotericism which gives a feeling of superiority to adversaries proud of their ignorance. On my provisory balance sheet, I shall separate the various "constituents" of a work in view of the warnings already given. Nevertheless, let me say, before specializing in the various domains, that the primordial need felt was to consider the series not as an ultratheme forever linked to pitches, but as a generating function of all aspects of the work. The series, then, is not attached to any privileged figure; it can introduce hierarchy among complex elements if it takes account of the specific characters and properties of those elements. Otherwise it is merely gratuitous, a meticulous way of playing heads or tails.

The series of pitches may be conceived in several different ways. It is urgent to make clear that the serial phenomenon is not constituted of the successive unfolding of the elements that it puts into relation. The series is not an order of succession, but is truly a hierarchy—which can be independent of that order of succession. It is in that sense that harmonic regions—making use of the same interrelationships of intervals—are capable, for example, within a certain number of transpositions, of grouping the series in families. It is in that sense too that the notions of horizontal and vertical find their ins and outs confused in a principle of distribution. It is always by virtue of that hierarchy that all the notes of a series can be taken as beginning notes without diminishing the organizing power. In the final analysis, every way of conceiving the series depends on a musical phenomenon sufficient to justify it; necessary and sufficient as a condition, it excludes the need for other conditions while having the possibility of accommodating itself to their demands. Thus, one sees a definition of "free" and of "rigorous" style appear which has a proper definition in relation to the admitted forms; it appears in the course of musical evolution as most representative of these two aspects. It is certain that all musical thought feels the need either to invent freely by constant renewing the sense of that invention or to elaborate, on the basis of one or several generating ideas, a development based exclusively upon them, and that in a more or less strict way. Thus one had come to define a "rigorous" style perfectly by the various canonic forms, some of them very difficult to handle because the vertical harmonic control forbids a large number of accidental conjunctions; thus, too, a "rigorous" form evolved in fugue, the perfect expression of a certain writing, and up to Bach proving adequate for the musical thought of those who used it. (I must point out in the very interior of the fugue alternations between passages of free writing and passages of canonic writing.) *Das musikalisches Opfer*, the "Canonic Variations" for organ, and *Die Kunst der Fuge* are the most nearly complete and most successful manifestations of that state of mind, the outcome of centuries of experimentation: by that very fact they brought to a close the evolution of that manner of thinking music. Since Bach, every attempt at a "rigorous" style has been a return to the canonic forms and to fugue, with all the anachronism that such a return implies. This phenomenon usually has been produced in a composer's mature works: Mozart and Beethoven felt the fascination of the rigorous style when reading Bach and Handel. In Beethoven's case in particular, that encounter was not without wounds, not without violent shocks—for harmonic relationships are not always easily accommodated to intervals contrapuntally employed; that "rigorous" music—the purest expression of a style, of a writing—thus becomes eminently "dramatic" music. (In fact, it is noticeable that the works of Beethoven's last period, in which that constraint does not make itself felt to such a degree—for example, the "Diabelli" Variations or the variations in opus 111—provoke a much less violent shock.) What gives Beethoven's fugues their exceptional character, what makes them unique, unequaled creations, is precisely that perilous confrontation of differing orders of rigor, which can only enter into conflict; at the frontiers of the possible, they bear witness to the hiatus that was being accentuated between forms that remained the symbol of the rigorous style and a harmonic way of thinking that was emancipating itself with increased violence. When the drama of that hiatus is felt in as piercing a way as it was by Beethoven, it results in the fugue of opus 106 and the *Grosse Fugue*, among others. But when the fugue is no longer the symbol of that rigorous style, to be obeyed mechanically, the result is Mendelssohn—and even Schumann was never at his best in that order of ideas. (There is Brahms, isn't there? . . . and Franck . . .) An academic tradition was perpetuated, one of its last incarnations being the fugue of *Le Tombeau de Couperin*, which nevertheless was new in intention, for with Ravel that "recourse" to the rigorous form is wholly within quotation marks, a citation, well named a "tomb." Neoclassicism was born; it would not always have that humor and that lightness in evoking a style already achieved.

Because its invention depends from its morphology, the "free" style is always adequate to the evolution of musical morphology. That is why we note in this realm the abundance of formal schemes that are altered from one epoch to another, or are transformed, or disappear altogether. Some phenomena are above all tied to an epoch, to the characteristics of an epoch; nevertheless, one could say that the "variation," under different names, has remained a constant in the "free" style, being a jack of all trades able to accommodate itself very easily to morphological evolution.

Clearly, no sharp frontier separates the "rigorous" style from the "free"; the "passacaglia" sufficiently proves the validity of coexistence of these two tendencies in musical creation. Nonetheless, it is true that these two domains are increasingly difficult to combine without catastrophe. That the rigorous canonic forms as well as the passacaglia and the variation reappear with the Viennese is not accidental: they constitute that sort of common terrain upon which ambiguity can develop rapidly and evoke the possible novelty, the divergence, between strict and free invention.

In what way can the series express that divergence? One would have to introduce a notion of the field of action and of punctual encounters. A field would leave free will the possibility of manifesting itself within limits large enough not to be at all constricting; a punctual encounter, on the contrary, will be the only solution to be envisaged at a given moment. Now I shall describe some means of deducing the consequences of a basic series. I shall not forget that a series in action in a work takes into account, whether separately or all at one time, the succession and the simultaneity of the absolute intervals and the registers.

(*a*) Let me begin by considering the series only under the aspect of its absolute intervals; that will give us the system of transposition already inaugurated by the Viennese, in which in turn each degree of the series engenders a series parallel to the basic series, restored each time to the interior of the interval produced by the extreme sounds of that basic series: thus one has a hierarchy variable by either development or superimposition—depending on rhythmic values or structures of groupings—and which also can be varied in register—that is, by the concrete extension attributed to an abstract intervallic value.

(*b*) If the structures of groupings intervene in the basic series and have particulars linked to it, one will have a very different product, which to some degree will be a harmonic product, but by its nature resembling little of what one usually understands by the word "harmonic": the functions of relation will not be external to the chords used, but will properly belong to the constitution of those chords. In reality, there is great ambiguity in the use of these chords, which are "sound-blocs" that can become objects, "ones"—timbre and intensity then becoming an integrating aspect of the association; that is why one feels the need for the creation of a hyperinstrument of which the sounds will in themselves be a function of the work. This approaches the current preoccupations of electronic music, in which that aim is envisaged through the use of pure sinusoidal sounds; nevertheless, in most cases up to the present, a superimposition of sinusoidal sounds very rarely produces a timbre that seems to be one; rather, one obtains refined harmonic effects. It will be useful to analyze under what conditions—with electronic sinusoidal sounds, with that hyperinstrument, or with conjugations of existent instruments—the ear really can perceive a resulting timbre and not a simple addition. I must point out that Webern in his last works—in particular, the first movement of the Second Cantata, opus 31, is very remarkable in this regard—was much preoccupied with this question. (I also point out that at certain moments in his works—the fifth movement of the same Cantata, opus 31—notions of harmony and counterpoint become, curiously, a function of time, harmony having come to be nothing but the simultaneous manifestation of elements revealed successively in the counterpoint. It is possible to have, in the process of putting these same elements into play, progressive *rapprochement* to the point of simultaneity, in the time of the succession of their use—*rapprochement* of their entries, in short, an idea of harmonic stretto to be found, for example, in the B-flat minor fugue of Book Two of *Das wohltemperirte Clavier*, in the coda; a fugue-subject in parallel sixths in stretto, with the reversal of the subject in parallel thirds. This comparison is meant to be no more than indicative, as the thought diverges completely in choice of means, and even in the conception of successive time becoming simultaneous time.) This simultaneous time incorporated into the basic series will give derived series differing totally among themselves, it being understood that when a sound-bloc is transposed from another sound-bloc, it forms a third sound-bloc, a product of the other two blocs. The densities of the constantly varying blocs, which may consist of from one to ten or eleven notes, introduce in the interior of the series a notion of variability intervening in its constituent elements; they are not reducible to a unity among themselves. It is from that point on that, rhythmic values intervening, one can develop these sound-blocs horizontally. But because their transposition does not have, above all, a developmental function, the direction of the development will be absolutely free; and in addition to the notion of variable density—density within a simultaneous time or according to a time of succession—one will have installed a dimension not oriented to development or, with more reason, to superimposition. One sees how imagination, invention, is safeguarded by such birth-giving procedures; a writing thus constituted acquires great suppleness from the fact of two variables existing on two different levels: density, being an obligatory function of the engenderment, and orientation, not depending upon anything but free will or phenomena not identifiable with it—the rhythmic structure, among others, among the most important.

(*c*) If the interval is linked to a duration, and if one has that duration intervene in the order of succession of the deduced series, one has a form of engenderment which is much stricter than the three others, for the pitches are ineluctably linked to a duration from the beginning; but then the richness of combinations is just as great, the order of succession being modified at each deduction; thus one has different groupings horizontally and vertically in which one can vary the unit of duration, the relation of the order of succession to the duration being a function relative to a unit common to all the durations used. In this form of engenderment, then, time itself is the only condition necessary, and it is sufficient for the creation of a hierarchy, and that under an absolute form not susceptible to variation (the order of succession) and under a variable relative form (duration, unit of duration). Here again we shall have respected that duality which I have defined as a principle of all musical action—free will possible inside a coherent system. Gratuitousness is necessarily absent.

(*d*) Finally, serial transposition may be conceived by making it necessarily depend upon the registers. Said otherwise, one gives the initial series given and unique pitches; one will base the transpositions of defined, unique intervals on these pitches of the same nature. For a transposition of the series, there will then be only one possible way to use the frequencies; no confusion can occur with the other transpositions; from then on, the order of succession is no longer indispensable for distinguishing one from another, and one may respect it or not without diminishing the clarity of the musical functions. The register established for the basic series is evidently susceptible to variations; thus all the forms deduced from it by transposition will be modified. We shall discover the same duality found in the other methods already described for engendering a sound-universe on the principle of a basic source. A duality that we shall try to establish in the act of composition; to preserve it seems to me the indispensable guarantee for a living creation. Perhaps we shall discover still other methods for engendering a sound-universe; nonetheless, it seems to me that each of the four I have described places in relief the characteristics native to pitch and time, primordial to each work, in themselves capable of giving birth to a sound-universe, whereas intensity and timbre, though they certainly have an important function, are impotent to assume such responsibilities.

Time itself can participate from the beginning in the series of pitches, as we have seen. But that unique point of view is far from being the only one that can be adopted to preserve the coherence essential to a musical work. The organization of duration is also conceivable as heterogeneous in the organization of the pitches; and I insist here on the fact that each organization should be supple enough—that is, susceptible at each instant—so as not to lead to absurdities or simply to incompatibilities. (Certain "*accelerandi*" on silences set one to dreaming in that order of more-than-abstract ideas . . .) That these organizations may enter into more or less violent conflict is, on the contrary, highly desirable for the life of the work, and it is in these conflicts or relaxations that a musical form may arise owing nothing to the "architecture" about which there has always been talk in connection with music, and with good reason, moreover. (Goethe accurately said that architecture is frozen music. And in our time architecture so tends to alter its points of view that Goethe's phrase will still preserve a valid meaning . . .) The "cadential ogive," whose disappearance Wilhelm Furtwängler deplored, is in fact linked to a given syntax; once that syntax has changed, that architecture-become-sound will no longer give us reason for its preservation, and truth will then be, rather, a lived form in time itself—and not in time brought back again to a notion of temporal space comparable to visual space, with memory playing the role of the eye capable of a certain angle of vision—with what that notion includes of the fundamentally irreversible. Debussy's last works testify to a singular premonition in this domain; it is not unusual to see scores like *Jeux* accused of lack of "form"; that pointillism seen in them, or that lack of inspiration—it has been said that the very late Debussy lacks inspiration, and the statement has been shored up on absurd supporting evidence related to matrimonial matters or accusations of determined, artificial modernism owing to his meeting with Stravinsky (the fear of being "bypassed" by a man younger than himself! but with no consideration given to simple emulation of creative faculties)—in short, in my view that absence of "form" resulted, on the contrary, from a radically new conception of total structure linked to a material in constant evolution, it no longer being feasible to insert ideas of symmetry incompatible with such evolution. One must go through an entire work in order to become aware of its form; that form no longer is architecturized, but is *woven;* said otherwise, there is no distributive hierarchy in the organization of "sections" (statics: themes; dynamics: developments), but there are successive distributions in the course of which the various constituting elements assume larger or smaller functional importance. One understands that such a sense of form can only run counter to auditory habits shaped through contact with three centuries of "architectural" music. (I emphasize in passing that those same habits related to form create obstacles to hearing the music of the Middle Ages and the Renaissance much more than does the fact that its morphology now appears singularly restricted.)

To return to the organization of duration—whose relations to those of the organization of pitches led to my digression—various solutions, generally parallel to those which I described above apropos of pitches, are available. It is evident that the idea of register in tessituras corresponds to one of register in durations, in the sense that the smallest unit to which these durations are related (whole or fractionally, furthermore) is susceptible to variation, a fact that creates a veritable transposition of time (which will be felt logarithmically: the small multiples of the variable unit will have noticeably neighboring durations, whereas the larger multiples can undergo enormous variations). That idea of register having been acquired, if one creates a correspondence of the idea of the rhythmic cell to that of the sound-bloc—a comparison that is not at all gratuitous, the rhythmic cell being in relation to time exactly what the sound-bloc is in relation to pitch, i.e., suscepible to the same variations from the horizontal to the vertical, the successive being able to become simultaneous progressively or not, partially or not at all—it then is optional to recognize the forms of serial organization according to the absolute intervals of time, according to the rhythmic cells, according to the unfolding—coincidence with the organization of the pitches—or, finally, according to the registers of time.

It goes without saying that my reason for not describing those modes of engenderment is to avoid launching upon a description that would become tedious, given that I have already done that work with regard to pitches, thus making the process with regard to durations easy to imagine. But one should not forget—and this remains in the forefront of my preoccupations—that a desire to organize durations along the same lines as tessituras is purely gratuitous. That is why I shall maintain that these organizations should be isomorphic, but are never at any moment identifiable among themselves. If one employs a certain number of durations at every instant, the result will be an impression of equilibrium beyond all attraction, all weightiness, an effect that may be sought for certain special cases, but which it would be insupportable to understand as a general principle of all rhythmic structure.

Let me note that the phenomenon of composition itself is not a question of putting all the means into play at each instant. The misunderstanding that lies in wait for us, and which we should mistrust terribly, is that of confusing composition and organization. A coherent system is indeed preliminary to all composition; I do not want to say that such a system should be developed to its final consequences from that moment on; I believe it rich in possibilities that can be discovered only as one advances in the work. But the reservoir of possibilities offered by such a system should not be simply expounded and thus considered as satisfying the demands of composition. It seems, in fact, that out of "religious" respect for the magical puissance of the number and out of a desire for "objective" work depending on a criterion much less vacillating than the composer's free will, and out of some considerations, furthermore, about a contemplative method of listening, one transfers the cares of composition to organizations. That is to say that the interferences provoked among them (they being very subtle, very refined, and at times more or less foreseen) will suffice to justify a complete structure by simple addition. One realizes the amount of naïveté in that idea. In reality, that preoccupation with giving the composer's role to the organizations and their interferences results from that erroneous belief that the series is a whole linked to all its possibilities, no one of which can be isolated without compromising a species of equation of total balance. That absurd notion, once accepted, can have the most unlikely consequences, such as total gratuitousness in the temporality of the work. If, in fact, we allow the organizations to act, their encounters—if one has attained a certain number of organizations governing a certain number of elements—can be produced by the thousands; one cannot say that one has ever used them all during a work, for one would pass beyond the point of saturation from the single point of view of the time required for hearing it. Thus the work is kept within the bounds of a sort of probable fragment among many other fragments; and what is thought "objective" and exempt from all the composer's hazards is, in the final analysis, nothing but the least certain and least willed of possibilities.

Let us rather see the work as a series of refusals in the midst of so many possibilities; one must make a choice, and it is there that we encounter the difficulty so well sidestepped by the expressed desire for "objectivity." Such choosing is precisely what constitutes the work, being renewed at each instant of composing; the act of composition will never be identical with the juxtaposition of the confrontations established in an immense statistic. Let us preserve that inalienable liberty—the constantly hoped-for happiness of an irrational dimension.

"To the farthest reach of the fertile country"

(PAUL KLEE)

Faced with the world of electronic music, the composer is put out of countenance by unforeseen obstacles in a realm that he nonetheless judges to be the only one acceptable if he desires to make use of thinking with consequences that pass beyond instrumental means. It would be pointless to speak of the setbacks that he may encounter on coming into contact with the apparatus in a studio: those difficulties can be surmounted if he knows how, little by little, to tame the new universe in which he intends to express himself. The real abyss of the encounter with electronic means is dug by the overthrow of the whole sound-conception to which the composer has been habituated by education and experience; the result is a complete reversal of all the limitations that formerly had been imposed upon him—more than a reversal, a sort of negative of what had been positive: all that had been limited becomes unlimited, all that he had thought of as "imponderable" must suddenly be measured with precision. For the rest, precision in turn becomes mythical after having been lived with intimately for a long time: the more one wants to reduce error, the less it allows itself to be circumscribed. One is remote from the enchantment that one had been prepared to discover, the enchantment within the power of a composer finally liberated from all the fetters accumulated during residual centuries!

In the two extreme cases to be envisaged, the two courses are radically different; a natural sound-body produces sounds of which the essential defining qualities are: timbre, more or less modifiable; *tessitura*, wide or limited; a certain dynamic scale; and, finally, sound-duration of which one is or is not master. Making use of a natural sound-body, one immediately takes account of the possibilities that it furnishes, as well as of a certain "inertia" that imprisons the performer inside its limitations when he himself is not a prisoner of his bodily capacities. Thus one has need of a given ensemble of sound-bodies, each furnishing a different group of possibilities; those possibilities are already latent in the sound-body before one dreams of using it, are there within very precise and supposedly known limitations. In the electronic domain, as is very evident, one is dealing from the outset with a nonlimitation of possibilties in timbre, *tessitura*, intensity, duration: an undifferentiated universe from which one can evoke—because it itself creates the various characteristics of the sound—a work coherent not only because of its internal structure, but also because of the constitution of its sound-material, properly speaking.

Rarely in the history of music could one have been witness to a more radical revolution, for one must understand that the musician finds himself facing an unprecedented situation, the creation of sound itself—not the choice of sound-material for its decorative effect or for its clarity: that would be banal. In effect, one must transpose into another realm the problems of orchestration or instrumentation as they have been understood up to now; at stake now is nothing less than the choice of material in view of the qualities of intrinsic structure that it englobes. The composer at the same time becomes the performer, given that the performance, the realization, takes on capital importance. In a certain sense, the musician becomes a painter: he plays a direct role in the quality of his realization.

Well, even if a real coming-together has resulted, one cannot assert that there has been a coincidence of attempted adjustments of one to the other. Much to the contrary, it seems that as a result of this contact, musical thought gushes forth in still unformulated questions, whereas the technician must solve a certain number of unusual problems in order to "realize." I spoke earlier of the veritable reversal of the limitations imposed upon the creator: one of the most manifest aspects of that reversal is the fact that the musician is placed face to face for the first time with the notion of the continuous. It is worth noting that this continuity is provoked not only in relation to pitches, but also in relation to durations, to dynamics, and, above all—the most disconcerting phenomenon—in relation to timbre. Never before was it so clearly understood that pitch, duration, and dynamics are linked irreducibly both in the sound-organization and in the very production of sounds. The continuity of the projection in space is a last obstacle linked to "interpretation"; unlike the earlier reversal, here the limitations are found to be inescapable; the lure of the "objective" work is dissipated rapidly because one cannot avoid the psychic reactions of an audience subjected to music coming from loudspeakers, and which therefore no longer has the leisure to link a gesture to a sound; the spatial distribution no longer is a *mise en scène* of more or less spectacular visible effects, but has become a structural necessity. Nonetheless, the notion of stereophony, so vulgarized by the cinema in various forms of sound-light, has been absorbed by these showy pretexts, so that confusion reigns in this domain and the best intentions are discouraged by anecdotal appearances of similar utilizations. When the interpreter has disappeared, is the concert hall necessary? Isn't it tied irrevocably to instruments? Should we appeal to new modes of hearing or should we think unforgivingly of uniting a visual double to an "artificial" music? There we touch upon the exterior influence of the interpreter on human communication; but that disposition of the interpreter also brings consequences that react inside the conception of the work. Everything of which the machine is capable is at the same time much and very little in comparison with an interpreter's powers—measurable precision as against imprecision impossible to notate absolutely (with regard to tempo, particularly, this matter is primordial in respect to the interpreter's relations to it and the machine's); one is tempted to say that the extreme measurable precision is only a restricted efficacy in proportion to an imprecision going beyond all the limitations of notation. Above all, it is this incompressible margin of error which interests me more than the fact of a definitive realization not subject to the fantasy, the daily inspiration, of a human being.

Will that liberty with regard to the sound-material, so desired by the composer, outdistance him? Will it come to do away with the poetic potential of the work? Will one ever be able to imagine a synthesis in which the contradictions of the two sound-universes can be put into play by an extension of perceptible structures? Will we spare ourselves nostalgia and the avatars of a new "total art"?

The first demand that the composer addresses to the electronic means is that they allow him to attain the realm of the absolute in the intervals: he wants everything possible. At the very time when temperament and the twelve equal half-tones were permitted to pass from unorganized chromaticism to the series, they seemed to lose all necessity. One had already felt the need for intervals narrower than the half-tone, for making use of narrower and narrower divisions going from the quarter-tone to the third-tone and even the sixth-tone. However, experimentation with the microintervals has produced no works of great interest; they take refuge in hyperchromaticism without really modifying the basic disposition of the intervals—that is, in a very extended modality. In the most recent experiments, this renovation reveals incomparably greater importance; no longer hyperchromaticism—tempered or not—but a sound-universe specific to each work, given the characteristic intervals that it uses; the interval, the basic unit, plays no part—in principle. In fact, the electronic experience shows that this notion of the absolute interval is fictitious and that the discriminative power of the ear largely depends either precisely upon a basic unit or upon the extent of the register in which the intervals are comprehended. This is to avow that the ideas of continuity and discontinuity become precarious and that one cannot dream at all of applying them mechanically.

In fact, to choose any basic unit whatever—other than the half-tone—is to conceive a sort of temperament native to the work; all the intervals will be understood as functions of this basic temperament, which, in the final analysis, will modify the direction of hearing. Again because our ear, at least at present, has an invincible tendency to relate intervals thus understood to *falsified* intervals depending upon chromatic temperament. Nevertheless, if one develops the structural consequences resulting from such a choice of departure point, the melodic influence, the harmonic climate of these arbitrarily tempered universes is undeniable. I must point out that these temperaments can take place inside the octave—that is to say, without at all modifying the definition of the register to which we have become accustomed with the twelve half-tones; but it is permissible to act so that the interval of renewal of the register will be other than the octave, so much so that the registers of a sound will seem completely divergent. To evoke the difference between these two systems, I should gladly take as a point of comparison the difference between a flat surface and a curved surface.

I said earlier that the ear's discriminative power depends equally on the extension of the register within which these intervals are comprehended. By that I mean that a microinterval is not sensibly perceived except in a restricted tessitura. One has already made this observation apropos of duration, when noting that when two long values are played in succession, differing among themselves by a small amount of duration, one is practically incapable of discerning which is the longer of the two. In the same way, let me take a relatively wide interval like the twelfth (octave plus fifth); it is certain that between this true twelfth and that same interval augmented by a sixth-tone, the ear—at first encounter—will have some difficulty in establishing a precise difference, whereas the modification of a whole-tone by a sixth-tone will be perceived more or less immediately. Thus there is a power of accommodation in the ear, just as one says that there is such a power in the eye. Within a restricted field, the use of microintervals playing an enlarging role, the ear acquires—momentarily—a sensibility that it cannot preserve over a wider stretch, in which it reestablishes a scale of appreciation in proportion to the intervals used. I mention this fact in relation to medium pitch, it being clearly understood that these capacities diminish toward the extremely high and the extremely low. As for harmonic appreciation, it is still more delicate because the ear's separating power must intervene in relation to a simultaneity of sound-phenomena rather than, as in the preceding case, in a succession of them, where memory plays a very important part. Study of various musics of the Far East and Near East always accentuates, what is more, the nonharmonic character that differentiates them from Occidental polyphony; this is what explains their greater richness, the greater complexity of the intervals they employ (especially Hindu music, the rhythmic complexity of which has had the same origin).

One must, then, resign oneself to having to accept less simple ideas than that of a "continuum" that will free the composer from all fetters, and to consider that use of this famous "continuum" implies servitudes to the ear—that is, to a certain extent, a dialectic, virtual or real, between the notion of temperament (on no matter what basic interval) and the size of the tessitura utilized. In place, then, of a free space upon which neither powers of appreciation nor possibilities of transformation are exercised, in place of that theoretical, immalleable space, a greater ambition of electronic music will be to create a multidimensional space eminently taking account of the ear's faculties for accommodation, a multiple dimension which, furthermore, can be expressed happily through a real multiplicity of dimensions in stereophonic space; but I shall approach this question later. For the moment, I simply pose the question of a synthesis of the electronic and instrumental universes solely from the point of view of sound-pitches; it seems to me improbable that if such a synthesis is to be manifested (the question of its necessity is another matter), it could be achieved without recourse to that notion of multidimensional space. A multiple dimension, successive or simultaneous, with the same basic principle or different principles. Thus it is that if a structure is made on large intervals—that is, in a wide tessitura, with a basic unit like the half-tone—a respondent structure will be built on microintervals in a restricted *tessitura*, whether with a very small basic unit or in irregular intervals defined by a series; for this example, one imagines the possibilities of various thresholds between temperament and nontemperament, between microcosm and macrocosm. Electronic music alone being capable of proceeding to the *limit* of these transformations, the instruments—normal or with a sort of tablature—will be the fixed stages of an evolution in which continuity will be assured precisely through the electronic domain. Let me consider this point of view as, above all, a project, a working hypothesis freed of all contradictions by experiences not yet brought about, certain utopias that one cannot fail to pursue.

Up to now, one has accented the possibilities offered the composer working with magnetic tape of utilizing whatever duration pleases him, or even an ensemble of durations unperformable by interpreters—given that his whole task is to record on the length of tape corresponding to that duration. This facility camouflages three traps: perception of these durations, definition of the tempo, continuity of a formless tempo placed at the composer's disposition. I shall note that the first of them is not nearly so important as the second, which poses the redoubtable problem of shunned relationships between the interpreter and the creator: nothing is *indicated;* everything must be *realized.* (Could one say that what essentially defines an interpretation is the "tempo," as it determines different phases inside the work itself, and that the transitory accelerandos and ritardandos appear as fictional, virtual ideas, beyond all precise control despite the luxuriant use of irrational values?) As for the principle of formless tempo, it forces us to reflect upon the fact that the arithmetic and logarithmic scales are, at the limit, susceptible of becoming a real continuity. But where does that limit lie?

Let me return to the first objection that the new concrete manner of cutting up time raises—the danger that it may not be perceived by the listener, that it exceeds criteria regarding the smallest value perceptible. I just mentioned irrational values; their use does not arise from a certain notated "rubato," but from a meeting of variations on the unitary value and variations on the duration, properly speaking. That meeting can give rise to fractionings of irrational values, to irrational values fractioned inside irrational values of another degree! . . . In short, in order to realize them instrumentally—without, for all that, losing from view the pulsation of the basic unit of value—one would have to be able to realize almost simultaneously three mental operations while deducing one from another—the supposedly acquired unitary pulsation, the meter, the irrational value of a superior degree, the irrational value or its fractioning depending upon it. Strictly, if one were to conduct these operations one by one in unfolding the music, carefully study of the text could lead the interpreter to realize such durations; but the operation of simultaneous deduction is practically impossible. It will be more useful to appeal to a notion of changing tempo, which renders certain otherwise unperformable passages readable. I have described this difficulty of the rhythmic microcosm to help myself in pursuing my analysis in the electronic realm. Should one conclude that working with tape will tend merely to solve problems of transmission elegantly for us? To what end? it will be asked; if one must appeal to a mechanical circuit outside man, he is powerless to perceive what he cannot perform. This specious reasoning sometimes takes on the colors of good faith, which does not prevent its being believed in as an intransgressible natural law. Furthermore, that the ear cannot perceive subtleties that the hand cannot perform has not been proved; at least, if the ear does not perceive them exactly, it registers them; that almost suffices for me. But electronic music is not, and should not be, reduced to this role of a robot carrying out inhuman tasks; on tape, it cannot be a simple transcription of unrealizable values; that is possible, but does not go beyond a facility that one concedes. It will be better to rethink musical time and its organization. How? By means of lengths, directly.

That implies recourse to a series of unitary values comprised between extremes whose relation is from the simple to the double. Starting from there, I shall use a registration of the durations, if I may be permitted to ally the two nouns elliptically. This means, in my understanding, the generalization in time of an idea that up to now has been reserved wholly for pitches—applying to the series of unitary values modifications that will allow it to cover all the eventualities of time which the composer will need. The principal difference from music for instruments will reside in the will to base it not on a unique pulsation, a single unit of value, but on a series of unitary values. Thus we shall have a new conception of rhythm to which to appeal, a conception in which the only anterior reference will be the double unit of value—normal value, and dotted (in the relation of two to three), which one already finds in some folkloric music. Definitively, we shall be dealing with a registration of durations depending on a mobile unitary value. As we have seen in connection with pitches, it is clear from then on that the notion of continuity and discontinuity cannot be dissociated in practice.

The second trap inherent in a concept of duration as measured out by lengths on a tape: the definition of the "tempo." If, in electronic music, one does not conceive as valid the simple carrying forward of abstract values to which we are accustomed, one is disoriented by the absence of "tempo" in the traditional sense of that word. What does one habitually think of as being called "tempo"? This has certainly been one of the worst-defined characteristics of music despite the fact that it has evoked the most numerous commentaries. In any case, this is not a question of a certain "volume-flow" of notes as one speaks of a river's "volume-flow." Certain rapid movements may encompass a feeble density of unfolding; certain slow movements, on the contrary, may contain a great density—despite which they are sensed as typically slow or fast. What intervenes evidently is the frequency of harmonic changes or the more or less ornamental quality of the unfolding of the sound-pitches; what also intervenes is what is called the agogic of the development. In instrumental music, thanks to acquired habit, these questions are not exaggeratedly embarrassing when one wants to give them a satisfactory answer; furthermore, an entire reservoir of indications exists which can guide the interpreter as to the direction to give to the durations, and if there is one idea to which not much attention is ever given in instrumental music it is the duration iself—in absolute time—of a sound-value; on the contrary, what is always thrown into relief is the relativity of various tempos among themselves or the permanence of certain unfolding speeds. One relies on the rhythmic pulsation—more or less complex—as felt bodily or mentally; all the landmarks are noted in relation to that internal pulsation. But in making a montage on tape, one takes into account, before anything else, the absolute gauged duration of a sound-value; no psychological indication is possible; everything will depend on precise measurement. One must confront oneself, that is, with an absence of pulsation, an absence of "tempo" properly speaking. The most general notion that can be substituted for the definition of instrumental "tempo" is that of a registration enlarged to the general plan of the composition. I described earlier what I mean by a registration of durations; we must be able to extend that phenomenon to an ensemble of durations, which will then give a direction to ensembles not oriented in the beginning; the meeting of these two variable registrations will give rise to networks of variable "lengths" (on tape, an absolute tempo is thus transcribed), a "length" itself changing meaning as it is included in one or another of these networks. Thus, it is to a "discontinuous" conception that electronic music must have resourse in such a superior order as "tempo," whereas instrumental music appears to appeal more and more to continuity, with variable tempos in which transitories (accelerando, ritardando) take on increased importance from the fact that they intervene structurally. The two sound-worlds possess in common a certain definition of duration, but they are equally capable of opposed notions that differentiate them profoundly and give them their original physiognomies. *Grosso modo*, I shall sum up the two contradictory aspects: in one case, immobile "tempo," but with values susceptible to almost infinitesimal variations; in the other, excessively mobile "tempo," but with values unable to pass beyond a certain limit of subtlety in variations. In view of a synthesis, the similar organization of a registration of time, whether manifested directly upon the unit of value or, in superior degree, upon the "tempo" itself. I may perhaps be thought obsessed by the idea of uniting instrumental music and electronic music by the facts of their contradictions or singularities; but I repeat that it does not seem to me reasonable to suppose that one of the two sound-universes will supplant the other, and to conceive a simple "progress" from one to the other appears to me futile and inconsequential.

Before completing this glance at durations, let me stop for another look at the principle of indeterminate tempo, to which the use of tape-montage liberates us by giving us every facility for succumbing in the face of such an obstacle. I have looked at the way in which the organization of the tempo implies networks of "lengths"; but I have not spoken of the possible subtlety of these networks. The limit of precision which one can readily achieve on tape is in principle one millimeter—in a carefully done montage; on a tape moving seventy-six centimeters per second, this represents a duration of one seven-hundred-sixtieth of a second. That precision doubtless goes beyond the ear's discriminiative power if it were being asked to deal with two widely separated values of that order of size, whatever the duration of the two values, properly speaking. There are optimum conditions for hearing rhythmic structures which for practical purposes prohibit the use of unrestricted continuity of any sort. Fechner's law with regard to pitches holds that the sensation corresponds to the logarithm of the excitation; and in fact one has already noticed that the classical rhythmic takes account of that law as transposed into the domain of time: the different values are established on a logarithmic scale from the simple to the double (from the sixty-fourth-note to the double whole-note) or from the simple to the triple (dotted values in the ternary division). But the same arithmetic difference can be considerable or negligible according to the specific case; if the relationships of that difference to the values themselves are very small, the difference itself will be hard to perceive (a whole-note and a whole-note augmented by a sixty-fourth note). (I have already referred to this phenomenon above when saying that in practice the ear is incapable of differentiating between two very long values that differ by a very short duration.) If those same relationships are very big, the difference is considerable; one can no longer speak only of neighboring values (a sixty-fourth-note and a thirty-second-note). Whether one is dealing with simultaneous values or successive values, one must—differently, to be sure—take this phenomenon into account. The logarithmic scales and the arithmetic scales of durations can be made use of in the same way as microintervals in relation to big intervals; an arithmetic scale will be perceived more easily in closely related sizes of values, even in a rather weak progression, whereas a logarithmic scale will be conceived as covering a more differentiated space-time. Here again we encounter what, in relation to pitches, I called the ear's "accommodation." That this use determines the rhythmic life of the electronic work is certain, and just as we have seen a multidimensional space-pitch, so we can seek an equally multidimensional space-time; which again leads me to my idea of synthesis, electronic music being capable of going to the *limit* of these rhythmic transformations and the principles of such writing being applicable, statically, to instrumental music.

I do not think it necessary to tarry long over the dynamic, which does not undergo notable modifications or pose specific new problems; for a long time, intensities on instruments have been applied in continuous curves (crescendo and decrescendo). The only novelty brought about in this domain, on the contrary, will be great precision in the use of a discontinuous scale of intensities. Nothing is more difficult for an interpreter than to adapt himself to the necessities of contemporary musical thought and to be freed, if need be, from the intensity of an emotional power (heritage of the nineteenth century)—to pass, said otherwise, from the "nuance" to the dynamic itself; that is, to establish a certain number of degrees of intensity which are to be rigorously respected each time that the indication appears in the score. For an instrumentalist to gauge truly the dynamics that he employs is almost impossible, and the indication "forte" rarely receives an unchanging interpretation: the interpretation will depend upon the context, the attack, certain psychological factors, the very characteristics of the instrument itself. The more reason why one should not be deceived; in an instrumental work, the scales of intensity—modified by the attacks—will bring about a delicate zone in the interpretation, so that when writing, one must take into account rather a "psychological" notation than a real one.

On the other hand, under the control of the apparatuses, one may gauge such dynamic scales with all the desirable precision; but another question is posed. To tell the truth, a scale of dynamics is absolutely valid only for a small sound-zone; one therefore must modify it along the curve of audibility if one wishes to give the same acoustic effect throughout an entire extension. The measure of a sound-level, then, is not an absolute notion, but an entirely relative value that will be modified in turn by the timbre.

One will be content with pointing out the interferences between real intensities and "psychological" intensities, these interferences playing their roles in opposite senses in the instrumental and electronic realms; if one adds the conditions of listening, nothing is more relative than a dynamic scale, and it does not, properly speaking, pose any new problem. Despite all the precautions taken to assimilate it to the sound-constituents—whence the delicate zone that constantly surrounds them—intensity preferentially requires a necessary superstructure endowed with demonstrative powers rather than relative organizational strength—at least if it does not participate in the elaboration of timbre, which I must now examine.

Among all the characteristics put into play in composition, I have saved timbre for last for two reasons: to begin with, timbre combines, within the sound-phenomenon, the three dimensions that I have already discussed—pitch, duration, intensity; then, it is with timbre that the greatest divergences—I could say the fundamental antinomy—between the natural sound-body and the electronic processus are manifested. That not only because the composer must select his material, but also because he must acquire other reflexes with regard to a "continuum" of timbre, certainly the most disconcerting notion that he is required to face for the first time in the history of music.

The instrument makers, in fact, have always tended to create families of characteristic timbres according to the sound-body used, the way of making that sound-body vibrate, and the way of maintaining the sound thus obtained. For several millennia, instruments have varied but little, at least in their principles: strings rubbed, plucked, or struck; wind-instruments using a bevel, a reed, an embouchure; wood, metal, and skin have furnished the essential parts of the percussion, whether of definite or indefinite pitch. Three large families themselves divided into three groups—with them one covers the largest part of the "natural" sounds. The employment of *Klangfarbenmelodie* in the orchestra, or that of the series of timbres—by instrumental groups—has modified the meaning that one can give to sound-combinations by placing the accent on the acoustic side of these combinations rather than on orchestration properly speaking. Like intensity, orchestration no longer is that solely decorative power which it often became in the nineteenth century; it acquires a structural power hitherto unknown; it is no longer an "investiture," but the sound-phenomenon in its total manifestation. Even thus conceived, the use of the orchestral timbres, even when it softens, dilutes the frontiers between the various groups, takes well-defined families of timbres into account—timbres, I hasten to recall, that are the results not only of the superimposition of various harmonics but also, at least as much, of transitory registers, of attack, of the appearance or disappearance of certain harmonics in proportion to their intensities.

In electronic music, we must "constitute" each sound that we mean to use. This is not a question of copying natural sounds—some of them being excessively complex, that synthesis is in practice impossible; furthermore, the very idea of creating an "*ersatz*" natural sound-universe is dubious: it will have neither the quality of the natural nor the specific characteristics that one has the right to expect from it. This is the sandbank upon which nearly all the specialists have run aground: hybrid, asexual, the electronic instruments have not been capable of posing the real problem of the timbre in this "artificial" realm.

The procedures for achieving a real sound-complex are various: either one starts with pure sinusoidal sounds and then superimposes them in conditions adequate to the formation of a single complex or, on the other hand, one starts with the sum of the frequencies included between this and that frequency-limit and then purifies that "noise" until it becomes a true sound. I shall not expound again here the various experiments that have been made with sound-complexes; I shall speak from the more general point of view of the experimental procedure with respect to obtaining an effective result in the composition of sounds. The first question that comes to mind is this: can one abstract natural harmonic relationships or should one rely upon arbitrary relationships dependent solely upon the composer's will? Using exclusively one method or the other, one runs the risk of obtaining either pseudo-natural sounds or harmonic complexes lacking the homogeneity of a *single* sound. A guided empiricism appears for the moment to be the most certain means for achieving results satisfactory to the ear—an empiricism based on the interferences between a system of acoustic relationships and a conjugation of the harmonic relationships. Beginning with a result thus obtained, perhaps one should work from there on the "sound-object" thus created. I do not mean by "sound-object" the alluring knickknack that one has wanted to make of a reality susceptible to more ambitious possibilities; but just as, when one is composing, development consists of work on particularizing complexes elaborated on the basis of certain consequences deduced from a simpler, more general principle, so the working of the "sound-objects" thus formed will consist of subjecting them to a superior echelon of transformations parallel to those which contributed to their formation. Thus one will not lack tributary suspension of a basic organizing principle, but will be in a position to conceive a ramified development constantly grafting its transformations onto preceding transformations; and one will be freed from the obsessions of a unilateral organizing principle tending to much too ascetic impoverishment of the sound-means. It seems to me that the "sound-object" as I understand it can contribute to lessening the disarray felt by a composer faced with a universe of absolutely undifferentiated timbres, and that it effectively corroborates in the morphology what the composer brings about in the work's rhetoric. I must specify that, in order to make good use of this labor of composing with "sound-objects," one must enlarge the idea of series to include the interaction of the first temporal unfolding on differences of organization intervening among these objects—or inside a single family of objects deduced from one another. But here I add that I am dealing with working hypotheses that nonetheless are based upon experiments which, whether failures or successes, helped me to formulate them. May I, finally, advance the idea that the control will become confining and detrimental if it does not give the sound-phenomenon its chance, and that these new ideas are, precisely, supple enough to invite the unforeseen to take part?

If I wished to pursue thoroughly my investigation into what concerns the "continuum" surrounding the composer on all sides, I should again have to examine, and more completely, the idea of continuous real space, in which the sound-ensembles will be projected. As long as the instrument is a fixed source, stereophonic projection is easily accommodated to dynamic relief; without it, one does not escape the reef of a pseudo-instrument, given that the ear takes its guidelines in relation to a single loudspeaker, a fixed source. But at the beginning of this essay I mentioned the psychical reflexes of an audience obliged to assimilate a music not related to any visual fact, without the gestures of a performer to render it present.

That leads me to some reflections on the esthetic design of electronic music. At the beginning of the electronic experience, the schemes were very grandiose and very naïve: liberty, precision, boundlessness were going to reach the composer as gifts of a truly modern civilization; music was going to live and breathe in the twentieth century. But the liberty that the composer has desired so much swamps him; he is obliged to dam it lest the gratuity of the experience waylay him; the more he seeks that precision, the more it withdraws before him and shows itself practically unattainable, the epsilon of error being irreducible; the boundless and the bounded vacillate and interchange. Continuity and discontinuity are ideas holding such a charge of ambiguity that one is obliged to have recourse to their internal contradictions if one is to achieve a positive result in surmounting them.

Thus I refuse to believe in the "progress" of instrumental music to electronic music; there is simply displacement of the fields of action. What will attract us most? To confront—I repeat, in conclusion—the two sound-universes in multidimensional constructions: an investigation that doubtless will lead us, force us, as in the title that Paul Klee chose for one of his pictures, *to the farthest reach of the fertile country* . . .

Directions in Recent Music

If, thinking of the musical language, we glance back along the road traveled, what is clear is that we now find ourselves in a period of balance and organization; it was preceded by a period of destructive experiments that abolished the tonal world and regular metric. Furthermore that period produced a curious phenomenon of dissociation in musical evolution.

On one side, Stravinsky influenced the evolution of rhythm through entirely new structural principles based on asymmetry, the independence and even the development of rhythmic cells: from the point of view of language, however, Stravinsky remained caught in what might be called an impasse (because one knows that it led to an impasse), but which I prefer to call a survival, even an intensified survival, in which procedures of aggregation around very elementary polarities could give the vocabulary unprecedented force.

On another side, in Vienna at the same time, a new language was patiently formed, in several steps; in the beginning, dissolution of the tonal attractions (a procedure contrary to Stravinsky's), then functional ultrathematization, which could only lead to the discovery of the series; then the series exploited in differing ways by Schoenberg, Berg, and Webern. In reality, Webern was the only one of them who was conscious of a new sound-dimension, of the abolition of the horizontal-vertical opposition, so as not to see the series as only a method of giving structure to the sound-space, of giving it fiber, and he reached that realization, in the final analysis, by specious means that trouble us in certain of his transitional works. For he reached that degree of invention by working with regular canonic forms, seeking to use the series as a contrapuntal means with harmonic control. Later, he occupied himself with a functional distribution of intervals which marks, I believe, an extremely important moment in the history of the language. On the other hand, the rhythmic domain is not at all in rapport with the serial language.

Perhaps I should remark that this phenomenon of dissociation was useful to both elements of the language. In order to make his rhythmic discoveries, Stravinsky needed a simpler, more malleable material on which to try them. In the same way, Webern had time to occupy himself with a morphology, properly speaking, because he did not devote himself excessively to rhythmic structures.

Certainly that statement is a little too schematic to be entirely exact. That is why, as a counterbalance, I much want to travel a less familiar road and begin by playing truant with the work of Varèse, an isolated freebooter whose conception of music very fortunately has never replaced orthodoxy. That music, one must realize, is occupied essentially with the sound-phenomenon for its own sake; one imagines its composer as constantly preoccupied with the efficaciousness of chords becoming objects; the function of the chords is no longer traditionally harmonic; it appears as a value of the sound-body, calculated as a function of the natural harmonics, of inferior resonances, and of various tensions essential to the vitality of that sound-body. Whence the remarkable phenomena of intensity to be noted in Varèse's *oeuvre*. One perceives clearly the rejection of what can in the pejorative sense of the term be called the expressive nuances (a constraint inherited from a certain *fin-de-siècle* conception of romanticism); here intensity plays the role of a tensor; above all, it is a necessity for the optimum rendering of an aggregation of notes. A role infinitely more evolved, for instead of remaining on a solely affective plane, it participates in the harmonic structure, from which it can be detached only by completely destroying the equilibrium of music so written. These two remarks—abolition of the traditional function of chords, taken for their intrinsic sound-quality, participation of intensity in the structure—can, I believe, be linked to Varèse's great preoccupation: acoustics.

Considering the acoustic phenomenon as primordial among the sound-relations, Varèse applied himself to discovering a way in which he could govern a musical construction. This work led him to a point at which he was utilizing—for a unique experience—only percussion instruments (*Ionisation*).

With Varèse, finally, I note—to point it out only now—the profound rejection of temperament, which he called *the wire for cutting the octave*. In fact, one knows that temperament is the most artificial thing imaginable and that it was adopted in the eighteenth century for comfort. If temperament allowed Occidental music its amplitude of scope, which it is impossible to forget, one nevertheless must insist that it is a purely Occidental phenomenon and that there never has been any question of temperament in other civilizations, just as there never has been a question of not conceiving basic intervals besides the half-tone. For Varèse, given his acoustic attitude toward musical structure, temperament was manifest nonsense. He even spoke of nonoctavic scales reproducing themselves according to a *spiral* principle so as to be clearer, a principle by which the transpositions of sound-scales would not be organized on the octave, but on various intervallic functions.

In the next generation, an American musician, John Cage, was led to think that if one must avoid the clichés of the old tonal language with such care, the responsibility lay in great part with our instruments, which had been formed for the needs of that tonal language. He therefore, like Varèse, turned to the percussion, a world of sounds of nondefined pitch, in which only rhythm is an architectonic element strong enough to allow valid, nonimprovised construction. This is, of course, not to mention the relations of timbre and acoustics existing among the different categories of instruments used (skin, wood, or metal).

Opposite that music unwilling to occupy itself with sound-relations considered from the point of view of tessitura was situated Webern's work, in which the chief preoccupation, on the contrary, was to discover a new structure of pitches. Certainly the most important phenomenon of our epoch, the threshold of contemporary music, in the sense that Webern rethought the very idea of polyphonic music on the basis of the principles of serial writing (a writing that he discovered through his works by the primordial role that he gave the interval, properly speaking, and even the isolated sound). Throughout all his compositions, one senses the effort to reduce the articulation of the discourse as much as possible to serial *functions* alone. For him, the purity and rigor of the experience had to be preserved above all. More and more, Webern enlarged the field of his musical possibilities without in any way losing his furious intransigence. That led on to the irruption into the acquired sensibility of the first rudiments of a musical mentality irreducible to the fundamental schemas of the preceding sound-universe. It strongly seems that here we are dealing with a break comparable to that between monody and polyphony—that is to say, a radically new conception of usable sound-space. Because melody remains the fundamental element in the very interior of polyphony, one may say that with the serial system as Webern conceived it, the polyphonic element itself is what becomes the basic element, with the result that this way of thinking transcends notions of vertical and horizontal. The significance of Webern's work, its historic *raison d'être*, independent of its indisputable intrinsic worth, is thus that of introducing a new mode of musical *being*.

That thought, however, lacked a certain rigor for achievement. Webern was preoccupied with the structure of pitches

—an eminently Occidental problem, but the rhythmic questions did not engage him to an equal degree—nor did phenomena of intensity, although intensity plays a certain structural role in his writing.

More recently, Olivier Messiaen concretized these needs, which are dispersed almost everywhere through valid contemporary music, and gave us a *Mode de Valeurs et d'Intensités*, in which the idea of an organized universe—modally, in this precise instance—is applied not only to the *tessituras* but equally to durations (that is, the rhythmic organization of musical time), to intensities (that is, the amplitude of the sounds), and to attacks (the initial profile of the sound). With Varèse, let me recall, intensity played a structural role in the name of acoustic preoccupation; here intensity, in the same way as duration and pitch, is organized as a function of composition itself; that is to say that, beyond acoustics, properly speaking, the intention is to integrate all the sound-*données* in a formal research.

The point still to be discovered remains that of the nontempered sound-universes. Why, in fact, consider sacred a decision that rendered immense services but now has lost its *raison d'être* because the tonal organization that had demanded that normalization has been practically destroyed? Certainly, the instrumental factor is not one of the least causes now delaying the development of musical thought based upon nontempered intervals and making use of ideas of complex notes or sound-complexes. All the acoustic approximations accumulated little by little during the evolution of Western music should disappear, no longer being necessary; but how resolve, at this moment, the problem posed by the production of the sounds?

John Cage's prepared piano furnished an artificial, embryonic, but nonetheless plausible solution. In any case, the prepared piano has the immense merit of having rendered concrete the sound-universes that we must provisionally renounce, given the difficulty of realizing them. Thus treated, the piano becomes an instrument capable of producing, by means of an artificial tablature, complexes of frequencies. An artisanal tablature, for in order to prepare the piano, one places between the strings, at certain determinable points of their length, such different materials as metal, wood, and rubber, materials that modify the four characteristics of the sound produced by the vibrating string: duration, amplitude, frequency, and timbre. If one recalls that over a large section of the keyboard three strings respond to a single key, if one imagines the various modifying materials at different determinable points on each of these three strings, one can get an idea of the variety and complexity of the sounds thus obtained. From then on, the way is indicated toward a future evolution of music in which the instruments will be able to serve, thanks to tablatures becoming more and more nearly perfect, in the creation of a new sound-world that has need of them and demands them.

If, after that incursion into a domain where Webern did not penetrate, we return to his work, we shall find there an extraordinary preoccupation with timbres and with a renovation of their use. The sound-clarity of which I spoke above is not neglected on this level. The orchestration does not have a merely decorative virtue, but forms part of the structure itself; it remains a particularly effective means of relation and synthesis among pitches, durations, and intensities. So much so that with Webern we can no longer speak of an evolved orchestra, but must discover newly indispensable orchestral functions.

Now one can understand the degree to which it is urgent to bring together all the experiments, to generalize the discoveries made, to enlarge the means of a technique already found, that technique, *grosso modo*, having up to the present had a destructive object above all—and, for that reason—its being linked to that which it wished to destroy—we still must give it its autonomy. To link the rhythmic structures to the serial structures by means of common organization, including not only duration, but also timbre and intensity. One imagines the confounding amplitude of the discoveries to be made with constructive means of investigation. The evolution of musical thought is called upon to rush onward after Webern, the serial principle being capable of justifying the entire sound-organization, from the tiniest constituent to the whole structure.

This serial thought can, finally, escape from the number twelve, within which it has remained confined for a long time, and with reason: it was precisely the twelve tones—that is, chromaticism—which permitted the passage from the weaker and weaker tonal structure to the serial structure. Definitively, what has the greatest importance is not the twelve tones, but, much more, the serial conception—that is, the notion of a sound-universe, proper to each work, founded on an undifferentiated phenomenon up to the moment when the series is selected, then becoming unique and essential. The permutations thus defined, thanks to the first permutation, can be generalized to any sound-space whatever given as material. That is why we should talk about series formed of nontempered intervals, even based on definitions of frequencies, on an indeterminate number of intervals defined otherwise than by the octave. (Here again we come into contact with Varèse.) No longer does any incompatibility exist among microdistances, nontempered intervals, and the familiar twelve half-notes.

It is the same when one turns to rhythms; I can imagine not only whole divisions of the unit but also irreducible fractional divisions employed generally within a basic unit. If we want to fraction these basic units—as we are obliged to when we come to superimposing series of units and series of values, which renders all performance practically impossible and graphic writing-out of the score unrealizable, an exception being made of the bringing forward of a given scale of the unit and its various fractions—if, then, we want to introduce a notion of total freedom of the rhythm, what can we do but address ourselves to the machine?

We are at the edge of an unheard-of sound-world rich in possibilities and still practically unexplored. One only begins to discern the consequences implied by the existence of such a universe. Let me note (I neither find this excessively fortuitous nor am I astonished that musicians in various countries who are interested in these experiments should be connected by a certain community of opinion) the happy coincidence supervening in the evolution of musical thought: that thought is found to have need of certain means of realization exactly at the moment when electro-acoustic techniques for supplying them are available. In reality, there are two sound-producing means: the natural sounding-body and the electronic means—that is artificial production. Midway, the electro-acoustic transformation of a sound furnished by a natural sounding-body. In the two extreme cases, the procedures envisaged are radically different: the sounding-body produces sounds of which the essential definition is timbre, duration, *tessitura*, and the limits within which intensity can be varied; if one uses a natural sounding-body, one must at once take account of the possibilities that it furnishes, the only modifications possible being in the intensity and the variations in attack and termination of the sound; therefore, one has need of a certain ensemble of sounding-bodies, each having a different group of characteristics. Those characteristics are virtual in the sounding-body itself, within very precise and recognized limits. If one envisages the realm of electronics, it is very clear that at the beginning one is dealing with nonlimitation of possibilities in timbre, *tessitura*, intensity, and duration; thus one creates the characteristics of a sound, characteristics depending on the general structure; this sound is reversibly linked to the work, whereas the work is linked to the sound. Entry into the domain of sound itself, into the interior of sound, opening-out of serial perspectives that already have proposed a particular universe for each work, and from the single point of view of the series of frequencies.

Rarely in the history of music could one have witnessed so radical a revolution—the musician come face to face with an unprecedented situation, the choice of sound-material; not merely a choice of materials in view of decorative effect or clarity—a banal translation of questions of orchestration or instrumentation—but rather the choice of material because of intrinsic structural qualities that it includes. The composer becoming performer in a realm in which the performances, the realization, takes on increased importance and he thus, like a painter, takes direct part in the quality of realization.

Moreover, the questions of tempered and nontempered scales, notions of vertical or horizontal no longer have any meaning: one comes to the sound-figure, the most general object offered to a composer's imagination; the sound-figure—or even, with the new techniques, the sound-object. If one extends the idea of series, in fact, to the interaction of the first temporal unfolding, to the differences in organization intervening among these objects, if that notion of series is ramified to include even the modifications that can be brought to these sound-objects, one finally will have constituted a universe of works free of all constraint foreign to that which is not specifically themselves. An abrupt transformation, if one thinks that formerly music was an ensemble of codified possibilities applicable in an undifferentiated way to each work.

These formulations, however, still are premature; we are only on the way to realizing such a music. Important researches into the intrinsic qualities of sound remain to be undertaken; apparatuses perfected, manageable, essential to the composing of such works still have not been built. Nevertheless, these views are not so utopian that they can be ignored; it is even probable that the increasing interest aroused by the epiphany of an unprecedented, unheard-of sound-world will only hasten the solutions. Let us wish, modestly, to be the first artisans.

III

SOME ÉCLATS

Present-day Encounters with Berg[1]

In Paris, a showing of masterpieces from the Vienna museums has brought us a fortnight of Austrian music which must be placed in the forefront of current interest. Its organizers were not, in fact, content to turn to such classics as Haydn, Mozart, Schubert, and Mahler: an important role was reserved for Alban Berg, of whose works we have been able to hear three vocal excerpts from *Wozzeck*, the Violin Concerto, the *Kammerkonzert* for piano, violin, and wind instruments, and, finally, the *Lyrische Suite*. I shall not discuss the interpretations of these works, it sufficing to mention that the Vegh Quartet played the *Lyrische Suite* and Désormière conducted the orchestral works and the *Kammerkonzert*. My purpose is not to criticize the concerts, but rather to reflect a little upon the exceptional case of Berg.

Be reassured! I shall not talk about ludicity, authenticity, reactivation, or the other clichés that have become current on this subject; I shall approach the problem in a much less "*philosophaillonne*" manner, and shall try to sharpen my critical intelligence as much as possible so as to locate Berg clearly and without complaisance.

What is more, Berg is now recognized by musicians of all stripes as a great genius, even as the excuse and miracle of the

[1] This essay, first published in 1948, was written apropos of a fortnight of Austrian music heard in Paris, the Quinzaine de Musique autrichienne. —TRANS.

EXAMPLE I—*Lyrische Suite*, III

EXAMPLE II—*Lyrische Suite*, III

dodecaphonic technique. These judgments derive from an evident misunderstanding. Exactly what these dear musicians find most reassuring in Berg is exactly what I admit the least: his romanticism and, it must be said, his attachment to tradition. They wish to assure us, for one thing—and this by means of arguments that are more or less convincing—that Berg's role as the transition between tonal music and dodecaphonic music was indispensable, that it was essential to consolidate the new values gradually and break with the old ones. Others discover in this conflict the apex of a psychological distress that gives his work all its dramatic direction and all its humanity. Still others, encumbering themselves with fewer explanations, find in it simply heart and music.

Poor Berg! To have aroused that sort of commentary on the part of fervent disciples, passionate admirers, or pontiffs of the moment who granted him admission as an *enfant terrible* into a confraternity whose members, what is more, were very sick!

In reality, Berg is only the final point in a post-Wagnerian genealogy that gave birth both to the lovable—in all the horripilating senses of that word—Viennese waltz and the Italian veristic bombast. René Leibowitz, despite his licensed admiration, clearly feels the pinch of the shoe at this particularly sensitive place on his austere skin. He wrote, at the end of an article about Stravinsky: "I do not know which German critic once said when speaking of Alban Berg that if he had not been a pupil of Schoenberg, he would have written Viennese operettas or, if driven to it, operas like Puccini's. Let us admit it. But here is the point: Alban Berg was the Alban Berg that he chose to be—that is, precisely a pupil of Schoenberg, with everything implied by that, the composer, not of operettas or of operas '*a là Puccini*,' but the composer of *Wozzeck* and of the *Lyrische Suite*." [2] That comment to prove, as it was intended to do in *Les Temps modernes*, that existence creates essence, that one chooses and then involves oneself.

[2] *Les Temps modernes*, April 1946.

All that is very well; but nonetheless the problem is posed in all its irritating acidity. One senses in Berg an amalgam of the most ill-assorted things, one in which bazaar exoticism takes a place alongside the tango in the cantata *Der Wein.* Perhaps it will be thought that I am given to exaggeration: I shall try firmly to disillusion the reader by citing precise examples. Here we have, in the *Lyrische Suite,* the *trio estatico,* which, with its exacerbated sentimentality, seems to me related to the most vulgar veristic bombast in Italian opera. It is evident that those reiterations of two notes, supported by accents (measures 74, 92), those spun-out sounds *crescendo molto* (measures 74–5), those simultaneous ascents, those bundles of chords (measures 76–7–8), those jumps of octaves by thirds (measures 91–2) go back to the bad taste of the romantic effusion carried to paroxysm. It may be replied that a real difference, nevertheless, is established between the fabricators of patented lyricism and Berg—by such fine points as that found in measure 76, where the ascent is rhythmically diversified, with the first violin in septuplets of sixteenth-notes, the second violin in quintuplets of eight-notes, the viola in eighth-notes, the cello in triplets of quarter-notes—none of these values coinciding within a measure; or where the habitually parallel, chromatico-diatonic scales here have a dependence of figures in each instrument, the first violin opposing its whole-tones to the predominant thirds of the second violin, etc. All that is well and good! Without that superiority, in fact, Alban Berg would not be Alban Berg; that is not enough.

Following, is an example of the Viennese waltz. No need for comment. I call attention only to the fact that the music-hall aspect is again accentuated by the orchestration of the phrase confided to the flute and the saxophone. Similarly, I could cite the waltz that disfigures the first movement of the *Kammerkonzert.* Alas! Berg did wrong in sacrificing to secret *amours* an energy capable of aiming higher.

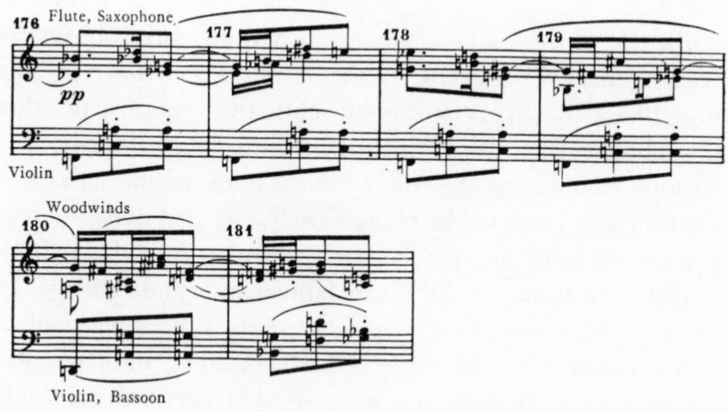

EXAMPLE III—Violin Concerto, I

If up to this point I have insisted only upon the flaws, that is because the *Lyrische Suite*, *Kammerkonzert*, and Violin Concerto include such really extraordinary moments that I bear badly the variations of quality in the musical material. Let us blame that on Berg's temperament, that final hothouse flowering of postromanticism, with all the avatars that it implies.

But I want to make two other points. The first concerns what Leibowitz has called the operatic gestures in *Wozzeck*—that is, the military march, the polka, and other inventions of that sort. It will not do to put the blame on Stravinsky and the *Histoire du soldat;* but when Berg includes a military march in *Wozzeck*, appeal is made to his prodigious ingeniousness so that it can be found remarkable and be deemed necessary within what is pompously called an operatic gesture. What ridiculous purposelessness in thus torturing the intelligence! Operatic gesture excuses nothing. Nor do I intend to exempt the *Histoire du soldat* from anathema any more than the military march in *Wozzeck*: both of them bear the yoke of a certain eclectic esthetic that never has produced good results. To attach more importance to it than it merits is unwise.

Grave in another sense seems to me the error that Berg made

at the end of the Violin Concerto by writing variations on the Bach chorale "*Es ist genug!*" I am aware that here too I shall be tossed knockdown arguments by subtle theoreticians: (1) that this chorale is perfectly integrated into Berg's text by the tri-tone common to the four terminal notes of the series and the four first notes of the chorale itself; (2) that dodecaphony permits it, being so rich in possibility that it includes both tonality and atonality. All that is ratiocination and verbiage! In the exposition of the chorale, where Berg's serial harmonization alternates with Bach's tonal harmonization, an unacceptable hiatus results from the hybridization between the tonal system at its most solidly established and the dodecaphonic system. I do not reject the principle of serial harmonization of a Bach chorale because of the supposed real harmony that was found enclosed in a melody. But it was necessary to choose one or another of these solutions, not to use them together; the materials being of different natures, the construction can only prove unjustified and not solid. Hearing it makes this cruelly clear. For the rest, I believe that the dodecaphonic language has more imperious necessities than domesticating a Bach chorale.

I ask myself—while feeling passing regrets—why I am so intransigent with regard to Berg. I think that my rigidity is owing in part to present-day instances of this blurring which reveal it as the usage of a veritable Moloch. The discovery of Berg has become the point of departure for a very confusing return to Wagner. Why such ease? That position must be condemned unremittingly; we are not here to attach ourselves to Wagner again by way of Berg. Considered as a transition, Berg was possible decades ago—while still living alongside Webern. Today, new forms of sensibility have become embodied which cannot be rejected, from Debussy to Webern. Returns to Wagner are flagrant anachronisms and facile solutions to be discarded at once.

I have allowed myself to criticize Berg because I place him

far above all the Gribouilles who believe and call themselves dodecaphonists, and whom we feel loath to shake by the hand—even to celebrate their eulogies—above that putrid class which constitutes the most noticeable part of the "Parisian" musical world!

Trajectories: Ravel, Stravinsky, Schoenberg

Ravel's *Trois Poèmes de Stéphane Mallarmé;* Stravinsky's *Three Japanese Lyrics;* finally, Schoenberg's *Pierrot lunaire*—these three works, thus placed side by side, permit me to examine closely the mythology of renewal which has crystallized around *Pierrot lunaire*, a mythology trailing the aroma of an old scandal. And one may ask if it was not simply a misunderstanding very widely diffused in the period after World War I which has given Schoenberg—and this composition in particular—that prestigious mystery, the privilege of being a musician more "damned" than others. Absent from all the concert programs, surrounded by a cohort of rather fanatic disciples—another manifestation of "damnation"—Schoenberg has benefited from a legend of which it will be necessary to disembarrass him if we are to be able to see him in proper perspective as an ex-prophet amid the smashed drums and other just as factitious accessories with which he has been surrounded in profusion.

It is already significant that in 1913—one year after the composition of *Pierrot lunaire*—two composers, Ravel and Stravinsky, belonging to different generations and finding themselves at completely different stages of their dissimilar evolutions, but driven by a curiosity in common, should have had an equally false view with regard to Schoenberg: the works avowedly showing his influence were, by the one, the *Trois Poèmes de Stéphane Mallarmé* and, by the other, the *Three*

Japanese Lyrics, both of which bear witness to that optical illusion. The legend had begun.

What in reality links these three works is the choice of instrumental form.

With Ravel: voice, piano, quartet, two flutes, two clarinets.

With Stravinsky: voice, piano, quartet, piccolo, flute, clarinet, bass clarinet.

With Schoenberg: *Sprechstimme,* piano, violin or viola, cello, flute or piccolo, clarinet, bass clarinet.

The parallelism of these *nomenclatures* (I emphasize the word "nomenclatures" because the comparison cannot be made on any other basis) puts into relief the superficial resemblance of the scores, and thus allows us to understand how much Schoenberg's influence could be felt in the second degree. In fact, it was during a stay in Berlin in December 1912 that Stravinsky encountered Schoenberg and heard *Pierrot lunaire.* As André Schaeffner made clear, Ravel was inspired by the idea that Stravinsky verbally gave him of that work. The imagination, operating through a like mechanism with the two composers, took the place of actual study of the score, which was not engraved until 1914.

Even if the shock that Ravel received from Schoenberg had not been so external, he could have absorbed it only in a completely illusory manner. By 1913, he already had behind him a large part of his discoveries, all of which were of the tonal order. We should not forget the "false-academician" side of Ravel's complaisances; those discoveries, of the harmonic order, go back to a complexity of writing—unresolved appoggiaturas, anticipations, pedal tones or chords—in extremely simple linkages based for the most part on steps of thirds or of common tones (I excuse myself for this "harmony class" language, indispensable in this sort of situation). Ravel was too old to be able to emerge from this framework, a fact that I do not mean to hold against him, but which we must understand clearly. We have an infallibly precise indication in the fact that he would take refuge—with, however, a technique of writing which the French "innovators" of 1920 certainly lacked—in superficial and false discoveries, polytonality, among other camouflages and subtleties, Fountain of Youth waters much adulterated by a sound-organization striken by impotence to renew itself and logically leading to its own destruction. I think in particular of certain passages in the Sonata for Violin and Cello, of *L'Enfant et les sortilèges*, in which the ruse is so obviously naïve that the two staves are written with different key-signatures.

Schoenberg's whole effort in *Pierrot lunaire*, however, consisted in the use of constant chromaticism to break apart the tonality; it led to the path of rational use of the half-tone, later synthesized by the use of the dodecaphonic series.

With the *Trois Poèmes de Stéphane Mallarmé*, then, we have an extremely striking example of the misunderstanding so long pursued in relation to Schoenberg—that misunderstanding contained in the surf raised within a still-coherent tonal system by a shock coming from the fracturing of that system. The effects turn out to be of a purely "auditive" order; I do not apply the term as an attack against the supposed "hedonist," who, in the event, would be Ravel—that is where the whole difference from Stravinsky is located—but in the sense that the influence of *Pierrot lunaire* will be translated by intervals, instrumental dispositions, sound-effects, all of them transposed into the already formed Ravelian language, attached to it with great precision. Let us say that Ravel would never have pushed this far the harmonic refinement, the balance of the sound-dosage; but one always discovers this in the declining continuity of an evolution approaching impossibility, given the "out-of-register" quality and the destructive element in these new acquisitions. We shall find these kinds of refinements again only in the *Chansons madécasses*, which date from 1925—and over which it is not impossible that *Pierrot lunaire* again presides, as their first performance in Paris occurred in

1922, when it spread tumult and confusion. Apart from that second effort, Ravel renounced this dangerous game, which led him inescapably toward self-annihilation. That was why, as I said above, he turned toward precarious discoveries that belong, badly rather than well, to the already existing order, but do not fundamentally destroy its coherence.

In that connection, it will be useful to liquidate some constantly repeated insipidities about Ravel as a contrapuntalist, for the Schoenbergian influence was not felt in that direction at all. Even in Ravel's final works, there is only a melodico-harmonic complex that can, I think, be traced very clearly back to Gounod and Fauré; which does not at all exclude certain "*contre-chants*" whose very name defines their feeble contrapuntal value well enough. Touching again upon the fugue in *Le Tombeau de Couperin* or that in the Sonata for Violin and Cello, the polyphonic writing takes on a coagulated aspect running contrary to the idea of counterpoint. After Franck, furthermore, a very curious conception of counterpoint was formed in which two parts almost always were in imitation or in canon in a slightly showy way, arising from a compact, tutelary, rather dictatorial harmonic mass; let us recall only the celebrated finale of the Sonata for Piano and Violin. With Ravel these concepts are refined, but they are nonetheless underlying, and one must wait for Webern for a clear affirmation of an essentially contrapuntal writing—Schoenberg being the point of departure for that happy result, but only the point of departure, as he himself had too many attachments to the nineteenth century to be able to disembarrass himself radically of an endangered heritage.

I must still note that even in the use of the instrumental ensemble, the influence of *Pierrot lunaire* resides above all in the nomenclature. For whereas Schoenberg's use of various elements—which he *chose*—proceeded from a need to express himself contrapuntally, that is, by individualization of each instrumental component, Ravel made use of a like formation—in some degree imposed—as a restricted orchestral apparatus.

It seems that this was owing precisely to that poverty in the contrapuntal writing—and that Ravel utilized the various instruments as a facing for the timbre. There again, I am not attacking a "hedonistic" conception; I merely consider that writing for an "orchestra of soloists" to have been the logical result of the Ravelian evolution. To tell the truth, there is only a difference of degree between *Daphnis* and Mallarmé songs, which is less surprising than it may at first appear. More crudely, I should say that the difference is quantitative. In the Mallarmé songs, one again encounters that apparatus of sound-presentation, more studied than ever, which proceeds from doublings, superimpositions, sound-effects that have nothing to do with *Pierrot lunaire*, but result from a certain "mechanics" of orchestration—the refined outcome of classic orchestration.

What I have just said about that work has not, above all, been intended to contest its very great beauty; however, I believe that it can be considered as a sort of extreme circle, mysterious enough in the fact that it can lead only to its own negation—a success condemned to remain forever turned back upon itself. Devoid of consequences, because contradictory, this was a trial from which Ravel did not emerge intact.

If we cannot doubt at all Ravel's good faith in his encounter with *Pierrot lunaire*, a key word lights up Stravinsky's reaction; when he heard *Pierrot lunaire* at Berlin in 1912, he found its poetic dated, which seems to me perfectly justified, but which completely falsified his perspective, unless a wholly erroneous perspective drove him to pronounce the judgment. Apropos of his *Japanese Lyrics*, it is interesting to note that Stravinsky wrote them while he was working on *Le Sacre du printemps*, from which, it is scarcely necessary to mention, they differ in both orchestral dimension and length. It was the beginning of a series of works which includes *Pribaoutki*, and

Berceuses du chat . . ., and of which the fulfillment is the very famous *Histoire du soldat;* the instrumental compositions were to be extremely reduced, the extension of the works—or of the numbers constituting them—generally very short. Consequently, one might think that the encounter with Schoenberg was particularly striking, if not fecund, for Stravinsky. That would be a completely superficial judgment.

From the beginning, in fact, Stravinsky had profoundly mistrusted the esthetic implied by *Pierrot lunaire;* that prevented him from seeing its solution to the problem of the language—a solution that furthermore proved transitory. Having rejected its poetic, he rejected the technique as its cause, without investigating farther; there, precisely, can be located the beginning of a setback that had to result once use had been made of the various artifices by which that terrible lack of language attempted to camouflage itself. And as we are in 1913, why not try to see elements of that rejection in *Le Sacre* itself? I think—despite the indestructible admiration I feel for that work—that *Le Sacre* was the germ of the "Stravinsky impossibility." Although we find in it a revolutionary concept of rhythm, in which the three Viennese were wanting, certain Webern pieces aside, a rhythm-development handled rudely but very clearly, in a way full of undeniable consequences; on the other hand, nothing in it permits even the foreseeing of a sensibility about the transformation of the vocabulary. That is why, I fear, *Le Sacre* entered musical manners so swiftly; without destroying the constituted language, it merely brought it another surcharge. I would even say—at the risk of seeming paradoxical—that *Le Sacre* represents the unique effort to control the tonal language by its utmost enlargement, or rather by the hypertrophy of its functions. A language must less destructive than Debussy's, in which the chromatic relationships and tonal functions are of a much more ambiguous essence and a much greater complexity.

Can I explain clearly without citing technical details that

would be much too tedious? In Paul Collaer's *Stravinsky*, I find a terminology that is easily understandable. Collaer explains that for Stravinsky "harmony was established with the aim of creating tensions," that therefore "dissonances are attracted toward consonances." In the gratuitous and perilous apriorism that was to ensue resides the whole irreducibility to Schoenberg. Collaer, in fact, continues: "Resulting from that profound reason, which *cannot be changed, it being the very basis of music*,[1] he [Stravinsky] built a harmonic language of which the reason is the same as that of the current harmonic language, but of which the use is singularly more powerful, more efficacious . . . The note D will no longer be the tonic of the key of D major or D minor, nor the dominant of the key of G or the seventh of E flat. It is D *tout court*. . . . The D, which I have selected as an example, will constitute a pole of attraction for all the other notes." I do not think that I have ever come upon a clearer or more crushing explanation of Stravinsky's language than Paul Collaer's definition of the "polar notes." It is certain that in the amplified tonal-modal language this "polarization" of a note restored considerable strength to the idea of tonic—a sort of hyperdegree—a strength that it had lost rapidly after Wagner, a strength that it had possessed to this degree only at the inception of the tonal language. That polarized idiom, inordinately emphasized (I should be tempted to call it gross) was the final bristling reaction of the tonal order, which could not survive it; it was a kind of "exorcism by ruse."

I spoke above of the irreducibility of that reaction to that of Schoenberg. This is why Stravinsky's mistrust of the poetic of *Pierrot lunaire* can be explained equally on the basis of the very conception of the musical language, although it is very difficult to determine which of the two reactions led to the other. Be that as it may, and to return to the *Japanese Lyrics*, *Pierrot lunaire* signifies in a manner more apparent than real a person-

[1] Italics mine. —P.B.

ality on the verge of bankruptcy. In fact, there is not the least variation of language, except that imposed by the instrumental form, between *Le Sacre* and the *Three Japanese Lyrics.* The leaps of a major seventh or a minor ninth, the wide intervals, the broken lines, the irreducible chords are also used in the symphonic work in the "polarly" incorporated manner described by Paul Collaer. There again we find the idea of "false counterpoint" utilized in the Introduction to *Le Sacre,* in which—I shall speak of this later—we can also see the principle of the writing for soloists. What exactly is this "false counterpoint"? Essentially, it consists of a superimposition of pedal-lines, independent above all in rhythm, the ensemble of which is ruled by a tonal relationship resulting from the different constituents disposed analytically. One sees immediately what that idea may include of mechanics, even of the anticontrapuntal, as it is to absorb the essential function of counterpoint, namely the dynamism of the sound-relationships. Such a superimposition, in fact, is eminently static, in the sense that it coagulates the space-sound into a series of unvarying stages—for I do not call real variation the ornamental variation that intervenes—and in the sense that it annuls the entire logic of the development. Here we reach a phenomenon of capital importance: although it is still badly discerned in Stravinsky—and, above all, is wrongly carried out—here we do find for the first time a notion of sound-agogic which Webern clarified in the most conscious way, thus putting us in his debt. Here I only want to mention—I shall speak of it again apropos of Webern—this phenomenon of dynamic in the registration. But Stravinsky limits himself to a relatively simplistic superimposition, one that is above all arbitrary.

It remains, I believe, to settle that quarrel about "hedonism"—I used the word for lack of a more justifiable qualificative—mentioned in connection with Ravel. I have spoken of the Ravelian reaction to Schoenberg's discoveries as purely "auditive," because of the degree to which their passage into Ravel's work was effected through appropriate translation. With Stravinsky—and not exclusively under the influence of *Pierrot lunaire*, as one finds similar usages in *Le Sacre du printemps*—the morphologies in common with Schoenberg's *oeuvre* proceed from a hedonism which, though not to be condemned (moralizing inquisition is the worst of matters), was at least perfectly sterile. By "hedonism" I intend to indicate exactly the nonfunctional role, the exclusively decorative side, of these morphologies. The irreducible aggregations, for instance, resulting from polarization around a chord-key, clearly lend that chord a tension that it did not originally have, but as aggregations they are the merest purely individual creations, autonomous, having no force as a coherent vocabulary. In that surcharging of an existent language, some augurs have wanted to see this extension around classified morphologies as one of Stravinsky's essential qualities—objectivity; and our wise men have wanted to bring about a confrontation with the subjective Schoenberg. These are very dubious ideas for dealing with the results of a technique of language. In any case, it is certain that the sort of objectivity which consists of taking the sound-effect—why not say the sound-effort?—into consideration for its own sake (an objectivity that others might call hedonism) could not show Stravinsky a path to fecund discovery. To the degree that he left behind him works that had exhausted a certain number of provisional sound-combinations, he found himself driven to palliate that exhaustion by equally provisional solutions, no longer having at his disposition a language coherently constituted: solutions that became more and more schematic, arbitrary, stereotyped, until they were no longer solutions at all, but only "tics" that the ear came to foretell, but by which it was more and more irritated. I think in particular of the automatic use of the major-minor third, of diminished or augmented octaves, of displaced basses: one came to the obligatory regime of the avoided note, of the poor disposition, of the defective cadence—for example, the Choral of *Histoire du soldat*, a regime as disastrous as that of the flattest of the academicisms. Starting from hedonism, one reaches the worst of the uglinesses: oh, dialectic of opposites!

As for the instrumental apparatus, can one say that it is necessarily tied to that hedonistic conception of the language? That fact is so evident that there seems no need to insist upon it. Let me, however, note the difference from Ravel. Just as Ravel follows his own logic by treating the instrumental ensemble for the Mallarmé songs as a little orchestra (furthermore, had he not written that way in his Introduction and Allegro for harp, flute, clarinet, and string quartet?), so Stravinsky in the *Japanese Lyrics* refines conceptions that one finds earlier in the Introduction of *Le Sacre*. These differ from the Ravelian writing in the desire to individualize each constituent element. A desire related only in externals to Schoenberg's similar wish. In fact, by a phenomenon parallel to that which led Stravinsky to seek the sound-combination for its own sake, not functionally, the instrumentation is chosen primordially for the physical aspect that it presents. I recognize that this last remark may be found rather specious. For, finally, should one not select one instrumental combination rather than another because it "will render" acoustically better, and for that reason alone? Certainly it would be foolish to deny that, since that principle is implicit in all orchestration, even Monteverdi's. I do want to say more precisely that Stravinsky's instrumentation is not a direct function of the musical text: it is selected for its own sake; I should add that later on the instrument will become tyrannical, that it will often have the air of dominating, of denying the text. That is clearly not true of *Le Sacre*—in which the opening phrase for bassoon, among others, remains a noted discovery—or of the *Japanese Lyrics*. The instrumental "tic," nevertheless (again described by his admirers as objectivity), will become noticeable in *Pribaoutki* and, above all, in *Histoire du soldat*. Furthermore, the notion of "false counterpoint," which I spoke of earlier, is not irrelevant to the misunderstanding that weighs upon Stravinsky's "little formations" or, in general, upon the use that he makes of solo instruments (as in the Introduction of *Le Sacre*). These superimpositions, the mechanical and sometimes arbitrary processes on which I have remarked, seem in fact to call logically for an individualization of instruments; but because of their arbitrary essence they rule an instrumentation no less arbitrary, as little justifiable as through an "end in itself" of that superimposition, of that exchange of registers. To give an example that is enormous to the verge of the absurd: a given passage played on the piano may disappoint us by its poverty, whereas when it is heard in the orchestra, the able arrangement of various dispositions may hold all our attention. This does not prevent me from justly noting the extreme assurance of the instrumental combinations, their perfect balance in the use of tessituras, most of them previously unused, and their acoustic discoveries, to which we have not always been accustomed by Schoenberg or even by Webern, for whom the idea of timbre is almost abstract, and who never cared at all about the physical conditions of sound-emission.

I have approached the Stravinsky case through that negative reaction which he underwent when faced by the poetic of *Pierrot lunaire*. Personally—and I insist upon this point—I think that in effect he took full revenge in this domain. I find no comparison more striking than that with Mussorgsky and Wagner. Without fear of error, it can be said that Wagner caused the language to evolve in an infinitely more active way than Mussorgsky did, but nevertheless, Mussorgsky's poetic, almost paralleling Debussy's, overthrows for us all the bombastic romanticism in which the man at Bayreuth was so agitated: *Boris* is infinitely dearer to us than *Tristan*, and seems to me more consistently current. Thus, in relation to Schoenberg, Stravinsky, while making use of a vocabulary of no utility, of a morphology devoid of result, of a practically valueless syntax, seems to me to furnish a poetic of overwhelming beauty. Therefore *Le Sacre* could destroy the notion of "concert music," therefore the three *Haï-Kaï*, in their elliptical concision, reflect a still-unknown sensibility. I do not re-encounter this impression until I listen to Webern, especially to the works that he composed in the years from 1909 to 1913. That sensibility of Stravinsky's turns short, whereas with Webern . . . The mystery of that evolution—analyses of a language or a technique can demonstrate, but they never succeed in explaining completely. One takes the material aspect of a score into account, but is powerless before the poetic to which it is the key. That is why Stravinsky's *Japanese Lyrics* retrospectively take on for us the enchantment and anguish of an essential impossibility.

By studying works by Ravel and Stravinsky, we have in a way obtained a negative of *Pierrot lunaire;* but in order to perceive its nature better, we shall have to approach it less indirectly. The first question to be elucidated is that of the place, privileged or not, that these melodramas hold in the continuity of Schoenberg's *oeuvre. Pierrot lunaire* did not announce a new stage in the sense of a *revelation-work.* It would be useless to demonstrate again the progression of Schoenberg's morphological discoveries, which in my view began only with the Three Pieces, opus 11, for piano and in certain pages of the scherzo of the Second Quartet, in F sharp, opus 10. In fact, I consider earlier works—*Verklärte Nacht,* the First Quartet, in D minor, the *Kammersymphonie*, opus 9, and the larger part of the Second Quartet, opus 10—as purely documentary pieces, the necessity of which—language research justified at that exact time—is no longer felt today (and perhaps that proposition could be enlarged to include all of Schoenberg's works; but we shall see that later on). Transitory works, I should say very passé if I wanted to provoke a rather easy scandal: the umbilical cord to Wagner-Brahms had not yet been cut; it never would be cut completely. (A slow oscillation between the first and second of those predecessors even was the most remarkable characteristic of that long career.) With the *Hängenden Gärten* (of Stefan George), opus 15, and particularly with the Pieces for Orchestra, opus 16, we already have reached a more advanced searching, which later passes through *Erwartung* and reaches *Herzgewächse*, a work that might be called the dress rehearsal for *Pierrot lunaire*. That brief song—for voice, celesta, harmonium (which, despite everything remains a truly horrible instrument, used one knows not why), and harp—sums up all the principles of writing which we shall find, practically unchanged, in the next work. What at once strikes one in that writing is its "savant" aspect. Let me say, in less good-natured language, its contrapuntal construction. It is there that one must locate in great part the novelty of *Pierrot lunaire*. The counterpoint, furthermore, is taken up here in its most traditional form, almost its most scholastic. As is well known, the eighth piece—*Nacht*—is a rigorous passacaglia and the eighteenth—*Nacht Mondfleck*—is a double canon; I should never finish were I to mention all the more or less strict imitations that are the basis of the score. Curiously, such a respectful attitude toward counterpoint is found also in the manner in which Beethoven approached it in his final works; let me recall the Fugue of opus 106, "*con alcune licenze*": an attitude amply justified by the difficulty of combining a very evolved harmonic style with dynamic principles, certainly, but again perceived as resulting from a technique of writing much anterior to that evolution. It seems to me, in that respect, extremely convincing that the violent development of counterpoint in Beehoven's last works (most especially the fugue of Opus 106 and the *Grosse Fuge*) had been such a danger to the tonal system that those works had to be kept completely isolated for a century (for I do not count Wagner among the contrapuntalists any more than I do

Brahms, despite the care given to the writing of interior voices, a care that did not arise from a contrapuntal need but rather from the necessity of filling the sound-space between the upper voice and the bass). Nor was it reserved to Schoenberg to make the essential discovery in this domain—that is, the need to deduce a work's structure from contrapuntal functions, and from them only: Webern, in a series of resounding works—I think of the Symphony for Chamber Orchestra, the Quartet for clarinet, tenor saxophone, violin, and piano, the Concerto for nine instruments, the Variations for piano, and the String Quartet—would implant that audacious conception, which goes back to Beethoven's rough answer and justifies it, in a way, *a posteriori.* For it must be stated clearly that Schoenberg's contrapuntal constructions are formal rather than intrinsic, and that the tenor of his language is not inseparable from its structuration: this seems to me the gravest charge that can be made against *Pierrot lunaire*—the lack of profound coherence and "uterine" relation between the language and the architecture. Just as the most irrefutable proof of Ravel's attachment to the tonal system lies in watching him, after the Mallarmé songs, adopt the false solutions of polytonality, so in support of the preceding assertion I can follow Schoenberg's evolution after *Pierrot lunaire.* When, after seven years of silence, Schoenberg composed the Five Pieces for piano, opus 23, and the Serenad, opus 24, the serial technique virtually had been discovered; although rudimentary, it is implicit everywhere, for it appears through the dodge of a sort of *ultrathematization.* But what do I see in these works? A march, a minuet, a waltz . . . ; the Suite for piano, opus 25, includes a prelude, a gavotte, a musette, an intermezzo, a minuet, a gigue; similarly, the Wind Quintet is composed of the four movements of the Beethovian sonata. That simple enumeration permits me to assert that Schoenberg was employing the nascent serial technique to enclose preclassic and classic forms in the elaboration of a world ruled by functions antagonistic to those very forms; the articulation of an architecture not flowing entirely from serial functions, the hiatus between the structural edifice of the work and the determination of its material is clear. Let me say this more simply: the novelty of the language has changed nothing in the manner of thinking anterior to that language—a malaise that will be accentuated later, as it alone can take account of without justifying—an attempt to reconstitute the tonal language inside the dodecaphonic system: witness the *Ode to Napoleon,* in which the weakness of thought and the indigence of realization are completely exemplary. It will be objected strongly that the preclassic and classic forms used by Schoenberg in opus 26 and the Third and Fourth quartets are not imitations, but are revivifications through a greater complexity; clearly, I do not take Schoenberg for a backward *Kapellmeister* whose richness of imagination was limited to the work of a conscientious copyist or a badly civilized librarian. It nonetheless remains true that these preclassic and classic forms are the most nearly perfect *misunderstanding* to be discerned in contemporary music, a misunderstanding that in a general way seems to me to annihilate the import of Schoenberg's *oeuvre*—that *oeuvre* was pulled in opposite directions by antinomic conceptions: the result was sometimes catastrophic.

If, in fact, I want to go farther with my inquiry into Schoenberg's language, I shall necessarily recognize that the adoption of the dodecaphonic writing—I insist upon the word *writing* and what it may represent, in this case, of incompleteness—did not change the basic principles of the tonal language. I refer to ideas of melody, harmony, and counterpoint envisaged as separate functions, ideas valid in the language of the eighteenth and nineteenth centuries, although the superiority of Bach, for example, or of the late Beethoven, resides precisely in the intimate unification of those three aspects of the tonal system. That adoption even allowed survival of some notorious debasements, among which I gladly would cite accompanied melody, which Schoenberg never renounced (see the opening of his Fourth Quartet), and which, transposed into serial writing, led to results that threw doubt upon the utility of its survival. Again because of that misappreciation of the serial functions, properly speaking, Schoenberg was led to preserve that idea of *principal part* and *secondary part*, derived from the remains of which I spoke above, and which Webern always refused to admit. To sum up, from the point of view of the writing, what was changed except the formal aspect of the manner of writing? I know perfectly well the full importance of that "change," without which the valid music of the years since 1909 would not have existed; but I must emphasize—in opposition to the unilateral exegetes and out of simple honesty, in order to attempt clarification of the musical situation of our times—what there may be of the extremely incomplete and even of the reactionary in Schoenberg's thought and *oeuvre*. For another aspect of that *misunderstanding* appears in the rhythmic, which is only the classic rhythmic recovered—it too with a complexity of which the guile, rendered so visible by certain naïvetés unhappily used, has misfired.

I found in Paul Collaer's *Stravinsky*, in relation to explication of the harmonic language of *Le Sacre*, a comical enough *a priori;* I find one of the same sort in René Leibowitz's *Schönberg*, which accounts for the rhythmic lack manifest in all the works of the three Viennese, the Webern exceptions aside. "I must say," René Leibowitz writes, "that the authentic polyphonic tradition does not admit *the idea of rhythm in itself* [Leibowitz's italics]. Rhythm is nothing but an element *born spontaneously* [my italics—P.B.] at the same time as the horizontal and vertical sound-figures, being precisely the element that articulates the unfolding of those figures, the element without which any sound-discourse would not be conceivable." That definition is eminently close to the one that the alchemists called phlogistic in explaining combustion. I pass over some rather absurd phrases concerning Stravinsky's rhythm, about which I have already demonstrated the extreme novelty in the construction by variable cells, themselves generators of a structure—close to African or Hindu rhythms—at the same time as the embryonic side of that novelty (but would Stravinsky's language authorize greater complexity?), and I come upon this key conclusion: "Thus it is quite impossible to study rhythm outside the melodic, harmonic, and contrapuntal formulas in which it is incarnated." Thus I become aware of how rhythm is dismissed by that short view of the problems it raises: Schoenberg's whole adventure will consist of taking up again the classic idea of division of a large value into equal sections and of varying the rhythmic props within those equal sections or of giving preponderance of accent to one of them—that is, by obeying that decayed law of the opposition of strong beats and weak beats, for to make use of it as a disguise is to obey it. The conception of the basic regular meter—bringing with it periodicity of feet or even their uniqueness—as the larger common denominator of the rhythm should cede place, in view of the greater complexity of the writing, to that fecund concept of the smaller common multiple, a rational generalization of Stravinsky's discoveries. By having futilely employed gauche camouflagings of the Greek metric, Schoenberg again weakened the coherence of his language, just as Stravinsky, impotent to solve the problem of the writing, was unable to press his rhythmic investigations farther.

Clearly, this has taken me far from *Pierrot lunaire* itself, but I wanted by this means to show that the work does not occupy an exceptional position in Schoenberg's evolution and that the myth of the renewal which crystallized around it could as well have been crystallized around the Pieces for Orchestra, opus 16, or *Erwartung*, for example. Perhaps what alone earned this work its preponderant position was its small chamber ensemble. That leads me very naturally to speak of the instrumental make-up of *Pierrot lunaire*. In regard to Ravel and Stravinsky, we have already seen that with Schoenberg this form of instrumental writing grew out of contrapuntal writing, that he *chose* it, whereas the other two *adopted* it. This is the place to note a reversibility of instrumentation and the text that invokes it; writing contrapuntally to a text demands individualization of each line by individualization of the instruments, and vice versa. We have noted with Stravinsky, under seemingly like aspects, the irreversibility of these two ideas. I do not mean to advance this assertion without proof: in fact, it is extremely important that the *Japanese Lyrics* were written throughout for the same number of instruments—like *Pribaoutki*, for the case of *Histoire du soldat* is very different for many reasons—as were, furthermore, the *Poèmes de Stéphane Mallarmé*, whereas in *Pierrot lunaire* the disposition of instruments is different for each piece. I am not referring to the alternation of the flute, clarinet, and violin with, respectively, the piccolo, bass clarinet, and viola, an alternation that seems to me to respond to ease of performance. I place the accent clearly upon the variation of instrumental group from one poem to another. But that is so well known (the famous flute solo in the seventh piece, for example) that to dwell on it more would be extremely boring. I shall make only this remark: the use of the piano is sometimes visibly derived from the Brahmsian conception of chamber music with piano, a use that from the point of view of sound is not always satisfactory.

I have not yet touched upon *Sprechstimme*. I note at once that its discovery did not date from *Pierrot lunaire*, for Schoenberg had refined the technique in the opera completed shortly before, *Die glückliche Hand*. Here we are in the presence of one of the most valid means of vocal expression which has ever been used to terminate that boring discussion, which lasted for two centuries, about the relative primacy of pure singing as a recognized convention and of singing reproducing the inflections of the spoken language as faithfully as possible:

antinomy of Italian opera and French opera, of Wagner and Debussy, not to mention the problem of recitative after Monteverdi. That incorporation of the spoken language into the sung language is the only solution envisageable, it seems to me, for certain especially difficult enigmas involved in the superimposition of poem and music. That solution is presented with great precision of writing, for in several pieces imitations occur between the spoken voice and the instruments. What is more, I note that lack of precision—or, if one prefers, the presence of illusory minutiae—in the writing renders the writing for the reciter in the *Ode to Napoleon* relatively arbitrary.

In this regard, it remains to be noted how Berg made able use of this procedure in *Wozzeck;* but equally—and I can hit upon no reason unless it be intransigence explicable by an extreme desire for purity and a rejection of all dramatic element—I observe that Webern made no use of this procedure in such important vocal works as his cantatas, *Das Augenlicht,* opus 26, and the two Cantatas, opus 29 and opus 31, or in the earlier collection of songs.

What is certain is that the primordial characteristics of *Pierrot lunaire* were the rupture of tonal functions, the short durations of the pieces, their individualized instrumentation, and, finally, *Sprechstimme.* But all that novelty was thrown out of balance by the rhythmic lack—which I have already explained—and also, I think, by the esthetic that was released in *Pierrot lunaire,* Schoenberg having participated with all his sensibility in the German postromanticism of the nineteenth century. For Debussy to be able to write the first measures of *L'Après-midi d'un faune* required extraordinary energy, but thanks to his having become aware of a new poetic direction, all of Wagner's heavy heritage was liquidated; Debussy was truly great in knowing how to profit by the discoveries of the Wagnerian language and how to repudiate its esthetic. Schoenberg certainly drove the morphological discovery farther, but he never had enough strength to disengage himself from that sensibility inherited too directly from Wagner and Brahms. That is why Schoenberg's *oeuvre*—and *Pierrot lunaire* in particular—seems to me to stumble so quickly into a closed world in no way corresponding to a present-day dialectic of poetic expression.

But I am obliged to recognize the sound-influence and indisputable efficacity of the "climate" of that work despite the distance that separates us from the esthetic—at once postromantic and expressionistic—which presided over its elaboration. The true immediate emotion seems to me to result from the use of *Sprechstimme;* in conformity with the first destination of the work (it was commissioned from Schoenberg by an actress, Albertine Zehme), if one frankly gives the diction of the text its full value without, for that reason, neglecting the perfect justice of the spoken intervals, the possibility results of being at ease in the tempo indicated and in a tessitura that at first glance may seem difficult or even inaccessible. One has a sensation of the natural: when the instrumental ensemble takes preponderance, the voice, located on a different (acoustic) level, does not have to struggle violently in the same (musical) domain.

Whatever the transitional nature of this work—both on the level of the language and on that of the esthetic that it implies—it is nonetheless true that one finds oneself in the presence of a musical fact that is uniquely successful. It seems to me, however—among the multiple varieties of illumination created by the formal transparence and the sound-equilibrium created by the divergent hierarchies—that the pieces with humorous intention and certain excessively "dramatic" pieces are not the best; my preference goes toward the pieces in "half-tint," in which expressiveness is achieved through musical means of perhaps greater suppleness.

That "unique" character, finally, justifies the privileged—and as if symbolic—role that has been conferred upon *Pierrot lunaire* in the evolution of musical writing, although its language is not, to sum up, so very different from that of the works surrounding it.

Can one find it easy to form such an opinion from a vantage point forty years later? It will be more equitable to consider the problems in the perspective of 1912. Nevertheless, objective reasons have inclined me to enter such a strict judgment of Schoenberg's *oeuvre;* I hope that I have set them forth clearly enough. That his oeuvre was utilitarian rather than useful is a fact that I am ready to recognize and profit by. The renovation of writing which *Pierrot lunaire* implied at that time remains immense in relation to what creators contemporary with it were able to propose, even in all good faith and to their own peril, as with the Ravel of the Mallarmé songs. That its teaching was not accepted profitably by the Frenchmen of 1920 is evident and disastrous; I quote this phrase of Paul Landormy as representative of the then state of mind: "In all that, little to be taken by the French except encouragement to daring." The stupidity of taking that position has become excessively glaring; I do not believe that it was provoked by consideration of the lacunae in Schoenberg's technique, which most of those personages, whose chief virtue was not consciousness within their métier, would have had difficulty in perceiving. But Debussy, Ravel, and Stravinsky already had brought forth a new manner of *being*—musically speaking—which, above all for sheep of that stripe, rendered impossible any contract with the Schoenbergian sensibility; and when one knows how the esthetes of the period became discouraged quickly and often, one sees that it was inevitable that in the face of a work that had to be approached with extreme discernment, great patience, and perfect technical awareness, the general reaction should have been a stampede excused principally in the name of ethnic considerations. Stupidity already had replaced very inconsistent good will. For a long time, everyone was to turn to the emaciated picturesqueness of Satie or the craftiness of Stravinsky—how much simpler and more restful that was! As for the "clear French genius," it was more than ever omnipotent in the material: a between-two-wars phase sickening in its nullity, some few exceptions aside. The next generation understood no better the importance of an *oeuvre* that always recapitulated, or came close to recapitulating, *Pierrot lunaire*. The legend of Schoenberg the "damned" musician was seriously implanted, and that condemnation to absence was comforting.

We refuse to corroborate that mythology any longer, even by omission. Because of the absence of a total phenomenon, I cannot—in Stravinsky any more than in Schoenberg—recognize a "prophet"—a religion, under whatever standard it may raise, always being a proof of indigence. It is better to note the play of balance which can be established between the two composers as a result of their symmetrical lacks, hypertrophied and leading to more or less the same result: the partial atrophy of their *oeuvres*. The sharpest impression I get upon hearing Ravel's Mallarmé songs, Stravinsky's *Japanese Lyrics*, and Schoenberg's *Pierrot lunaire* is an identical sensation of miscarriage on three very different trajectories: *oeuvres* incapable of solving the problems of that epoch or even of envisaging them completely; with regard to each of them, I have set forth sufficiently the sometimes contradictory reasons for their failures. Could it have been otherwise? I do not mean to institute a trial. In any case, I shall remark that these three works—allowing a small margin of time after them—marked a zenith in the evolution of each of the three musicians. For, in three different ways, they tried to practice a sort of neoclassicism: Ravel on the bases of the tonal language in its coherent acceptance; Stravinsky on the same bases, but so arbitrarily that he was forced into gratuitousness; Schoenberg having discovered the coherent dodecaphonic language. This will give us, respectively, *Le Tombeau de Couperin*, the Octuor for wind instruments, and the Suite for Piano, opus 25. That a certain scale of value is established in this parallelism is of no interest, and these works acquire no prestige from the variable degrees of their uselessness, their defaults being reflected in equally insupportable ways: affectation with Ravel, formal stiffness with Schoenberg, purposeless mechanism with Stravinsky.

In terminating this essay, I shall try to throw some light on the documentary side of *Pierrot lunaire* and the Schoenbergian *oeuvre* in general. In fact, it is undeniable that Webern's soaring flight required that springboard; but, in truth, Webern's Five Movements for String Quartet, opus 9, dating from 1909, already showed him taking a position more virulent than that of his master's works of the same era, a position that in a sense would lead to their annihilation. Will that prove to have been Schoenberg's only justification? It almost seems so. But does one, in saying that, have the air of wanting to push the paradox into absurdity? And yet . . .

Let us therefore give a pious thought to the famous pelican! That will reassure a goodly number of healthy spirits, and in all likelihood will not disquiet the others at all.

A NOTE ON SPRECHGESANG

As soon as one speaks of *Pierrot lunaire* or approaches its interpretation, the controversies inevitably revolve around the *Sprechgesang*. To tell the truth, Schoenberg's own texts on this subject (the note to *Die glückliche Hand* and the preface to *Pierrot lunaire*) are not very clear; the divinations of these oracles by excessive disciples, far from bringing light, have only created an inextricable confusion of so-called traditions inherited from the *Meister*.

The dedicatee of the work, as André Schaeffner recalls,[2] was not a *chanteuse*, but a *diseuse;* she recited melodramas—in the original sense of the word—against a musical background (such as those of Richard Strauss). Furthermore, in the Schoenberg correspondence already published, a letter (No. 125) addressed to Jemnitz supplies the following specifications: "I should tell you at once, and categorically: *Pierrot lunaire is not to be* sung! . . . If you were to have it sung, you would completely destroy the work and everyone would be correct in saying: one does not write that way for singing!" The interpreter with whom Schoenberg appears to have been most satisfied (according to direct private evidence that could not be more reliable) was Erika Wagner-Stiedry: he often asked her to take part in performances of *Pierrot lunaire;* and it was again she whom he chose to take part in a recording of the work made in the United States in 1941. A hearing of that recording gives us direct information about that style of declamation, not at all unlike that of Sarah Bernhardt, which today may be found terribly *démodé.* In any case, the intonations are very approximate (except for the rare sung notes, which are impeccably accurate); and the perpetual glissando from one note to another rapidly becomes irritating. Furthermore, the nerve-end expressionism of the voice deprives the parodistics of all humorous tint and throughout the work keeps up an exaggeratedly tense atmosphere that contradicts the nature of the instrumental interpretation.

We see, therefore, that it is not easy to form an exact idea of *Sprechgesang* even from an authentic document of it.

In fact, the notation indicates precise intervals, the notes being marked with a little cross. One piece (the seventeenth—*Parodie*) even presents a strict canon of the voice, the

[2] In his *Arnold Schönberg: Pierrot lunaire.* Schaeffner's text, the original poem by Albert Giraud, and its translation into German by Otto Erich Hartleben are included, with the present note, with the recording made by Pierre Boulez. —ED.

viola, and the clarinet, later with the flute, then again with the clarinet. Under those conditions, one accepts the notion of approximate intervals badly: why make use of so detailed—so rigorous—a writing if one is to be asked to be satisfied with a bastardized solution?

Leonard Stein, who was Schoenberg's assistant at Los Angeles, has furnished me with some interesting details. He assisted in the preparation of the *Ode to Napoleon;* also, working with the reciter, he prepared the first performance of it with the composer. He assured me that Schoenberg was infinitely more interested in *expression* than in the *intervals* (it is true that the notation of the *Ode to Napoleon* is very simple as compared with that of *Pierrot lunaire*); wanting to show the interpreter how to speak the text, he himself recited various passages, deviating considerably from his notation. Leonard Stein also confirmed to me that the deviations from the musical text in Erika Wagner-Stiedry's performance did not disturb Schoenberg at all.

If the exact intervals are not insisted upon, what interpretation can one give to the enigma of the Preface: "In singing, the pitch of the sound is maintained fixedly, where in *Sprechgesang* one leaves the pitch by a descent or a rise"? Meanwhile, it puts the performer on guard against both a "singing" manner of speaking and a realistic and natural speech . . .

Perhaps the mystery of that Preface lies in an error of analysis which Schoenberg made with regard to the relations between the spoken voice and the sung voice. For a given person, the sung *tessitura* is more extended and higher than the spoken *tessitura*, which is more restricted and tends toward lower pitches; on the other hand, many individuals who share a very similar sung *tessitura* will be susceptible to very different spoken *tessituras;* above all, this is true of women. This problem of *tessitura* is not posed practically in *Pierrot lunaire*, the more regrettable because the work is both too high and too low.

Finally, although the spoken voice in fact does not rest upon the sound, it does not behave as Schoenberg thought: the spoken voice leaves the sound because of the brevity of emission; if one wishes, the purely spoken voice is a kind of percussion of very brief resonance, whence the complete impossibility of producing *spoken* sound, properly speaking, over a long duration. (When actors, for example, have to hold a sound, they make simultaneous use of the resonance of the vocal apparatus and of song in whatever *tessitura* is coextensive with their speech.) And I say nothing of whispering, that "white sound" without definite pitch!

I have merely sketched the numerous difficulties to be encountered along the ill-defined road separating *speaking* from *singing*. Schoenberg had the great merit of attacking this fundamental problem, but the analysis that he made of the vocal phenomenon, given the contradictions that he forgot to resolve, leaves us facing insoluble problems . . . In that direction, as André Schaeffner has suggested, the theater of the Far East can offer precious enlightenment because it provides solutions, at once *stylistic* and *technical*, which Europe still has not discovered.

Schoenberg Is Dead [1]

To take a stand regarding Schoenberg?

To do so is urgently necessary, certainly; it is nonetheless an elusive problem, defying wisdom, perhaps a search without satisfactory result.

It would be vain to deny it: the Schoenberg "case" is irritating, above all because of its freight of flagrant incompatibilities.

Paradoxically, the essential experience is premature in the very direction in which it lacks ambition. That proposition could easily be turned around to say that it manifests the most demanding ambition where the most outdated symptoms appear. In that major ambiguity resides a misunderstanding full of discomfort over the origin of more or less conscious, more or less violent reticences, which one resents in a work of which, despite everything, one feels the necessity.

For with Schoenberg we attend one of the most important revolutions that has ever affected the musical language. The material, properly speaking, certainly does not change: the twelve half-tones. But the structural organization is altered: from tonal organization we pass to serial organization. How did the idea of the series materialize? At what exact moment in Schoenberg's *oeuvre* did it occur? From what deductions did it result? It seems that by following that genesis, we shall come very close to uncovering certain irreducible divergences.

Let me say, before anything else, that Schoenberg's discov-

[1] The present translation differs considerably—most notably in its greater length—from the version of this essay which appeared in *Score* (London) for May 1952. —TRANS.

eries were essentially morphological. That evolutive progression started from the post-Wagnerian vocabulary and reached "suspension" of the tonal language. One can detect very well defined tendencies even in *Verklärte Nacht*; the First Quartet, opus 7; and the *Kammersymphonie*; but it is only in certain passages in the scherzo and the finale of the Second Quartet, opus 10, that one can watch a true attempt at revolution. All the works just mentioned therefore are, in a way, preparations; I believe that today we may be allowed to regard them chiefly from a documentary point of view.

Suspension of the tonal system is achieved effectively in the Three Pieces for Piano, opus 11. Thereafter, the experiments become more and more penetratingly acute and lead to the renowned *Pierrot lunaire*. I note three remarkable phenomena in the writing of these scores: the principle of constantly efficacious variation, or nonrepetition; the preponderance of "anarchic" intervals—presenting the greatest tension relative to the tonal world—and progressive elimination of the octave, the tonal world par excellence; and a manifest attempt to construct contrapuntally.

These three characteristics already diverge, if they do not contradict. In fact, the principle, of variation can be accommodated only badly with rigorous (read: scholastic) contrapuntal writing. One observes a sharp internal contradiction in the exact canons in particular, where the consequent textually reproduces the antecedent—both the sound-figures and the rhythmic figures. When, on the other hand, these canons are produced at the octave, extreme antagonism ensues between a succession of horizontal elements ruled by a principle of abstaining from tonality and vertical control placing the strongest tonal constituent in sharp relief.

Nevertheless, a discipline is outlined which will prove very fecund; let us keep in mind very particularly the possibility, still only embryonic, of a series of intervals passing from the horizontal plane to the vertical and vice versa—the separation of the notes of a thematic cell from the rhythmic figure that has given it birth, with that cell thus becoming a series of absolute intervals (using that term in its mathematical significance).

Let me revert to the use of the intervals that I have called "anarchic." In Schoenberg's works of that period we often encounter fourths followed by diminished fifths, major sixths preceding major thirds, and all the reversals and interpolations that one can bring to bear upon those two patterns. Here I observe a preponderance of intervals if the unfolding is horizontal, or of chords if it is coagulated vertically, which are least native to the classic harmony based upon superimposed thirds. On the other hand, I note the great abundance of wide intervals, resulting in a stretching of the register, and thus giving the absolute pitch of each sound an importance never before dreamed for it.

Such an employment of sound-material provoked some estheticizing explanations that have since been used as an indictment or, at best, as a benevolent defense speech, which has not, however, included any general formulation. Schoenberg himself expounded on this subject in a way that permits us to speak of expressionism: "In the formal elaboration of my first works in the new style, I was guided above all by very strong expressive licences in particular and in general, but also, and not least, by a feeling for the form and logic inherited from the tradition and well developed by application and consciousness."

That citation obviates the need for any gloss, and one can only agree to that first trajectory, in which Schoenberg's manner of musical thinking manifests an interdependence of balance and experiments considered entirely from the formal point of view. To sum up, esthetic, poetic, and technique are in phase, if I may again be permitted a mathematical comparison, a flaw that one can pick out in each of these realms (I deliberately abstain from any consideration of the intrinsic value of post-Wagnerian expressionism.)

It even seems that in the sequences of Schoenberg's creations that began with the Serenade, opus 24, he found himself outridden by his own discovery; the no man's land of rigor can be located in the Five Pieces for piano, opus 23.

The last point of equilibrium, opus 23 clearly is the inauguration of serial writing, into which the fifth piece—a waltz—introduces us: each of us may be permitted to meditate on that very "expressionistic" meeting of the first dodecaphonic composition with a type-product of German romanticism ("Prepare oneself for it by serious immobilities," Satie might have said).

And there we are, in the presence of a new organization of the sound-world. A still-rudimentary organization that will be codified with the Suite for Piano, opus 25, and the Wind Quintet, opus 26, and will attain conscious schematization in the Variations for Orchestra, opus 31.

That exploration of the dodecaphonic realm may be bitterly held against Schoenberg, for it went off in the wrong direction so persistently that it would be hard to find an equally mistaken perspective in the entire history of music.

I do not make this assertion gratuitously. Why?

I do not forget that establishment of the series came, with Schoenberg, from ultrathematization in which, as I said above, thematic intervals could be considered absolute intervals released from all rhythmic or expressive obligation. (The third piece of opus 23, developing on a succession of five notes, is particularly significant in this respect.)

It behooves me to acknowledge that this ultrathematization remains the underlying idea of the *series*, which is only its purified outcome. In Schoenberg's serial works, furthermore, the confusion between theme and series is explicit enough to show his impotence to foresee the sound-world that the series demands. Dodecaphonism, then, consists of only a rigorous law for controlling chromatic writing; playing only the role of regulating instrument, the serial phenomenon itself was not, so to speak, perceived by Schoenberg.

What, then, was his ambition, once the chromatic synthesis had been established through the series, or in other words, once this coefficient of security had been adopted? To construct works of the same essence as that of those in the sound-universe he had just left behind, works in which the new technique of writing should "prove its worth." But could that new technique produce convincing results if one did not take the trouble to explore the specifically serial domain in the structures? And I understand the word "structure" as extending from the generation of the constituent elements to the total architecture of a work. In short, a logic of engendering between the serial forms, properly speaking, and the derived structures was generally absent from Schoenberg's preoccupations.

And there, it seems, you have what led to the decrepitude of the larger part of his serial *oeuvre*. The preclassic or classic forms ruling most of the architectures have no historic link to the dodecaphonic discovery; thus an inadmissible hiatus is produced between infrastructures related to the tonal phenomenon and a language in which one again perceives the laws of organization summarily. Not only does the proposed project run aground—such a language was not consolidated by such architectures—but also the opposite happens, which is to say that those architectures annihilate the possibilities of organization inherent in the new language. The two worlds are incompatible, and Schoenberg had attempted to justify one by the other.

One cannot call that procedure valid, and it produced results that could have been anticipated: the worst sort of misunderstanding. A warped "romantico-classicism" in which the good intentions are not the least unattractive element. One certainly gave no great credit to the serial organization by not allowing it its own modes of development, but substituting other, apparently surer ones. A reactionary attitude that left the door ajar for all the more or less disgraceful holdovers.

The persistence of accompanied melody, for example; of counterpoint based upon a principal part and secondary parts (*Hauptstimme* and *Nebenstimme*). We are in the presence of a very unhappy heritage owed to scarcely defensible scleroses of a certain bastard language adopted by romanticism. Nor is it only in the limited conceptions, but equally in the writing itself, that I see reminiscences of a dead world. Under Schoenberg's pen, in fact, there abounded—not without producing irritation—the clichés of redoubtably stereotyped writing representing, there too, the most ostentatious and obsolete romanticism. I refer to those constant anticipations, with expressive leaning on the key note; I mean those false appoggiaturas; or, again, those formulas of arpeggios, of devices, of repetitions, which sound terribly hollow and deserve to be called what they are: "Secondary parts." Finally, I indicate the morose, disagreeable use of a derisively poor—call it ugly—rhythmic, in which tricks varying the classic rhythmic are disconcerting in their credulity and ineffectuality.

How could we, without weakness, relate ourselves to an *oeuvre* manifesting such contradictions? If only it manifested them within a rigorous technique, the only safeguard! But what are we to think of Schoenberg's American period, during which the greatest disarray and most deplorable demagnetization appeared? How could we, unless with a supplementary—and superfluous—measure, judge such lack of comprehension and cohesion, that reevaluation of polarizing functions, even of tonal functions? Rigorous writing was abandoned in those works. In them we see appearing again the octave intervals, the false cadences, the exact canons at the octave. Such an attitude attests to maximum incoherence—a paroxysm in the absurdity of Schoenberg's incompatibilities. Ought one not to have pressed forward to a new methodology of the musical language instead of trying to reconstitute the old one? So monstrous an uncomprehending deviation leaves us perplexed: in the Schoenberg "case" a ruinous "catastrophe" occurred which doubtless will remain cautionary.

Could it have been otherwise? To answer in the negative now would be naïvely arrogant. Nevertheless, it is possible to see why Schoenberg's serial music was destined to defeat. In the first place, his exploration of the serial domain had been carried on unilaterally: it was lacking on the rhythmic level, even on that of sound, properly speaking—the intensities and attacks. Who ever seriously dreamed of reproaching him for that? On the credit side, I put down his very remarkable preoccupation, in timbres, with *Klangfarbenmelodie*, which could lead by generalization to the series of timbres. But the essential cause of his failure resides in his profound misunderstanding of serial FUNCTIONS as such, functions engendered by the very principle of series—without which they remain more embryonic than effective. Here I mean to say that Schoenberg employed the series as a smaller common denominator to assure the semantic unity of the work, but that he organized the language elements thus obtained by a preexisting rhetoric, not a serial one. I believe we can assert that it is there that the troubling lack of clarity of a work without real unity becomes manifest.

Schoenberg's failure to grasp the serial domain as a whole has caused enough dissaffectations and prudent flights to make full description of it unnecessary.

No hilarious demonism, but rather the most ordinary common sense, leads me to declare that since the Viennese discovery, every composer outside the serial experiments has been *useless*. Nor can that assertion be answered in the name of a pretended freedom (which could not mean that every composer would be useful in the opposite direction), for that liberty has a strange look of being a surviving servitude. If the Schoenberg failure happened, disregarding it will not aid us in finding a valid solution for the problem that the epiphany of a contemporary language has posed.

At the very beginning, perhaps one should dissociate the serial phenonemon from Schoenberg's *oeuvre*. The two have been confused with obvious glee, often with poorly dissimulated bad faith. It is easy to forget that a certain Webern also labored; to be sure, one never hears this discussed any more (so dense are the screens of mediocrity!). Perhaps we can say that the series is a logically historical consequence, or—depending upon what one wishes—a historically logical one. Perhaps, like that certain Webern, one could pursue the sound-EVIDENCE by trying to derive the structure from the material. Perhaps one could enlarge the serial domain with intervals other than the half-tone: microdistances, irregular intervals, complex sounds. Perhaps one could generalize the serial principle to the four sound-constituents: pitch, duration, intensity and attack, timbre. Perhaps . . . perhaps . . . one could demand from a composer some imagination, a certain dosage of asceticism, even a little intelligence, and, finally, a sensibility that will not be toppled by the least breeze.

We must keep ourselves from considering Schoenberg as a sort of Moses who died in view of the Promised Land after having brought down the Tables of the Law from a Sinai that some people obstinately want to confuse with Walhalla. (During that time, the dance before the Golden Calf was in full swing.) We certainly owe him *Pierrot lunaire* . . ., and some other very enviable works. This will not give offense to the environing mediocrity that wants, very speciously, to limit the ravages to "Central Europe."

Nonetheless, it has become indispensable to demolish a misunderstanding that is full of ambiguity and contradictions: it is time to neutralize the setback. That rectification will be accomplished not by any gratuitous bragging, much less by any sanctimonious fatuity, but by rigor free of weakness and compromise. Therefore I do not hesitate to write, not out of any desire to provoke a stupid scandal, but equally without bashful hypocrisy and pointless melancholy:

SCHOENBERG IS DEAD.

Incipit

As for Webern, the epiphany can be pinpointed by wiping clean the face of ignorance, the privilege of a discrete but effective curse. Although he seems to be the sharpest criterion of contemporary music, his *oeuvre* carries with it risks that it is difficult—or impossible—to conceal.

On the road to communication, that *oeuvre* has met with two bristling obstacles. The first is paradoxical, being its technical perfection; the second is more banal, being the novelty of the transmissible message. As a result, the reproach, a very gratuitous defensive reflex of exacerbated cerebralism: the eternal trial always lost by those who attempt it, but which is always essayed nonetheless.

One is only beginning to perceive the novelty of the perspectives that Webern's *oeuvre* has opened out in the realm of contemporary music—to perceive it with a certain stupefaction, given the work accomplished. That *oeuvre* has become THE THRESHOLD despite all the confusion with respect to what was too quickly called "Schoenberg and his two disciples."

Whence Webern's privileged position among the three Viennese?

Whereas Schoenberg and Berg allied themselves to the decadence of the great German romantic stream and terminated it with works like *Pierrot lunaire* and *Wozzeck* in the most luxuriantly flamboyant style, Webern—by way of Debussy, one could say—reacted in the direction of rehabilitating the power of sound and against all inherited rhetoric.

In fact, only Debussy can be compared to Webern as having

a like tendency to destroy the idea of preexisting formal organization for a work, a like recourse to the beauty of sound for its own sake, a like elliptical pulverization of the language. And though one could assert that in a certain sense—oh, Mallarmé—Webern was obsessed with formal purity to the point of silence, he carried that obsession to a degree of tension which music had not previously known.

Again, one could reproach Webern for an excess of scholasticism: a reproach that would be justified if precisely that scholasticism had not been the means for investigating newly discovered domains. One should note a lack of ambition in the sense in which that word has generally been understood: no large works or important formations or big forms; but that lack of ambition was his most ascetic courage. And even if one thinks that his cerebralism excluded all sensibility, it will be good to see that his sensibility was so abruptly new that its appearance ran all the risks of appearing cerebral.

As I have mentioned Webern's silence, let me add that there lies one of the most irritating scandals of his work. One of the most difficult truths to make clear is that music is not merely "the art of sound," that it could be defined much better as a counterpoint of sound and silence. The only, but unique, innovation that Webern brought to the field of rhythm, that conception in which sound is linked to silence in a precise organization for an exhaustive efficacy of the auditive power. The sound-tension is enriched by real breathing, comparable only to what Mallarmé brought to the poem.

In the presence of a magnetic field of such attraction, faced with so sharp a poetic force, it is difficult to see any but the immediate consequences. The confrontation with Webern is an exalting danger, even in the sense that it can be a dangerous exaltation. He was the third person of the Viennese Trinity; may we nonetheless keep ourselves from assimilating him to the famous tongues of fire: comprehension is never that surreptitiously swift.

I have said that Webern is the threshold: let us have the clairvoyance to consider him as such. Let us accept that antinomy of power destroyed and impossibilities abolished. Henceforth we shall cover his face, for he is not at all required to give himself up to hypnosis. Nevertheless, music is not ready to immerse that face in oblivion.

Of a Conjunction —in Three Bursts

I

There is the present, certainly. But of what good is that curiosity on the surface of the brain? The flexibility of that word "conjunction" permits, moreover, cultivation of some rhetorical flowers or the knotting of a pretty bouquet of thorns. Thus, one could maintain one's ease so as to fall upon minds that make reflection a métier.

They enclose activities in watertight hierarchies, an occupation for discharged soldiers; a semblance of cataclysm is produced, and there they are, struck stupefied, resenting as an injury that attempt upon their conception of the anthill. All pretexts are permissible for stigmatizing the one transfixed! His age—youth or senility; his faculties—too much adaptation, too much isolation; his close companions and their malignant or destructive influences. In short, nose distended, one sniffs old, stale odors, for these throbbing sorceries give evidence, in those who practice them, of a furious frenzy to seethe themselves in the cauldron of inhibition.

But here is where the contingent of the saved comes forward: their ferocious smile of serene derision stigmatizes an amiable fellow crushing their marbles and their ivories. Their nostrils dilate less as the result of painful, virtuous rage—which would be reasonable—than out of a kind of irrepressible nausea provoked by the stranger's sweat. The delicacy of their sense of smell is excusable: they are in a perpetual nervous pregnancy, although they never have children.

Faced with one conjunction, one encounters the other, the mediocrity of this one balancing the level of that one. Let us admit that it is necessary to bear the present.

II

A generation defines itself in relation to its parents. It seems that no more significant choice could have been made than the selection of Stravinsky and Webern as the two landmarks that have given most of the musicians of my generation the opportunity for a sort of practical geodesy . . . That conjunction displays a currency that is all the greater because one is present at this hour at a certain *rapprochement* of the "points of view," giving hope for an appeased synthesis.

Narcotic rather than appeased, it will be said in jest. And why that rage for synthesis? Need one reconcile his ancestors? If so, is that out of a desire for comfort, a nostalgia for unity, or simple inadvertence? Will you be your own *dupe?* Question marks of that sort are simulacra of harpoons. Nevertheless, questions, giving you shadows is a matter of indifference.

III

Subalterns love to conceive the universe in simple terms of a very precise political and military geography. Like Henri Michaux's "Plume," they have not "followed the affair" and they "go back to sleep."

For anyone who "follows the affair," on the other hand, to "go back to sleep" is not permissible: Stravinsky exactly illustrates the case for vigilant insomnia; one should salute him as exceptional in the circumstance and in the implication.

The circumstance? A completely unprecedented posthumous meeting. An obscure monk on one side, Webern operating in silence, indifferent, without any scandal; most often, he writes a music that—literally—has no time to cause any collective irritation, its generally slender sound-constitution not being one of those which provoke throats, driving them to belching and abuse; one can permit oneself to deal with him "high-handedly," "with contempt"—impasse, decadence, dust, brevity, lack of "body." On the other side, the magician-meteor, the brilliant laic, glory and scandal of the Ballets Russes, presenting his creations in the glare of the most famous theater; this Stravinsky, each of whose "awaited" works inevitably unlooses fabulous frenzies; everyone feels disobliging if he has not formulated his opinion on the *latest* work, the *latest* manner (reflexes comparable to those of fashion journalists—which explains why both exegeses and polemics are so afflicted with nullity).

After his encounter with the dead man, the living man reflects and is inflected; by acting that way, he pulverizes the mythology that has accumulated filthily in the folds of subaltern brains; the implication does not develop without wounds. One reacts, bitterly or happily; the evil—confusion between profound backwash and simple shock-waves; each one proposes his horoscope, his solution, his malice: a strange congress of astrologues, as strange as the meeting that provoked it.

Because up to now oracles have not had anything to do with musical creation, I limit myself to this observation: there, where so many stammerers have gone on lisping and pontificating, prating and prejudging, simpering and haggling, thundering, menacing, mocking, and torpedoing, Stravinsky has, simply, ACTED.

IV

ITEMS FOR A MUSICAL ENCYCLOPEDIA

Chord

The chord is an idea attached essentially to the harmonic development of music. It is a superimposition of sounds having a logic among themselves, in their own structure, and a logic of evolution in what is called degrees of consonance and dissonance. The chords habitually employed are based on a system of thirds related to the natural resonance of sounding bodies, as Rameau demonstrated. In the classic tonal world, chords have a function depending from the tonal hierarchy; but a chord is a generalizable entity, whether by inversion or by transposition. More recently, the chord having lost its structural function little by little, it has become a sound-aggregate selected for its own sake, for its potential of internal tension or relaxation according to what registers it occupies and what intervals it puts into play. Its structural function thus is discovered to have been both diminished and sharpened, which tends to prove that the properly harmonic era of occidental European music has ended.

Chromaticism

The word is derived from the Greek word *chromos*, color; it was applied to one of the three classifications of Greek scales. The Greeks considered chromatic modifications to be purely expressive effects that altered the coloration of the mode. In our time, chromaticism is the employment of half-tones within the interior of the notes of a diatonic scale. One can distinguish *chromatic passing notes,* which do not alter the principal tonality, and *modulating chromatic notes,* used to bring about modulations from the principal tonality, from neighboring tonalities to the most remote tonalities. By introducing all the chromatic intermediates into a diatonic gamut, one obtains the gamut called chromatic, which is outside all tonality (it includes the twelve half-tones within an octave).

Chromaticism is indicated by accidentals called sharps or flats according to whether they raise or lower a diatonic note by a half-tone. Double accidentals also exist—double-sharps and double-flats, which raise or lower a diatonic note by two halt-tones. A natural sign is used in a diatonic gamut in which there is a key-signature; it raises or lowers the note that it precedes, depending upon whether that note was formerly sharped or flatted. In general, one uses sharps in ascending movement, flats in a way that the writing of chromaticism, especially in contemporary music, has not precisely clarified. Formerly, the general rule was that an accidental remained valid throughout the measure; today, some composers use it as affecting only the note that it precedes. Still others, basing their usage on the fact of equal temperament, have invented systems of notation in which chromatic notes have special signs and different names (one of these is the *Obukhov notation*). None of these notations has been consecrated by usage; none of them has proved sufficiently practical to be capable of replacing the traditional system still in effect. The use of quarter-tones, sixth-tones, twelfth-tones, etc., has posed problems of writing still more difficult to solve, each composer having used a personal notation (Hába, Vischnegradsky).

Chromaticism was known in Greek music, as it is in all the Oriental musics; one may even speak of hyperchromaticism, as the intervals undergo modifications narrower than a half-tone.

It did not exist in plain chant; it is not found in systematic form in European music until about 1550, with Adrian Willaert (*circa* 1480–1562) and his pupil Cipriano de Rore (1516–1565). In medieval polyphony, however, chromatic intervals were used in cadences and to establish neighboring tonalities.

Gesualdo da Venosa (1560–1614) was one of the first musicians to make methodic use of chromaticism; he often opposed passages of great chromatic daring to diatonic periods that served to place them in sharper contrast. Later, the chromatic genre is encountered frequently in fugue subjects; one finds many examples in Sweelinck and Frescobaldi. Bach himself used it often, and *Die Kunst der Fuge* contains the famous theme made from the name B.A.C.H. (in German notation, B flat, A, C, B natural), which was used later by several composers, including Schumann and Liszt. In Bach's choral works—and before him one should cite Dido's famous lament in Purcell's *Dido and Aeneas*—chromaticism is more specially reserved for expressing the sorrowful and the tragic; it has a dramatic character. I should point out that equal temperament, which consists of equalizing the twelve half-tones of the chromatic scale, was adopted in the eighteenth century and that *Das wohltemperirte Clavier* was its most eminent manifesto. Temperament had been in dispute since the sixteenth century (Gramatteus, Galilei); as early as the fourteenth century the chromatic scale had been the subject of discussions by theoreticians, among them Marchetto da Padua. In France, Rameau and D'Alembert provided scientific and esthetic justification for the tempered chromatic scale. In the classic period, chromaticism was not very commonly employed; one finds it chiefly as a passing element in roulades, cadenzas, and other virtuosic passages; nevertheless, some of Mozart's mature works include very daring chromatic modulations. It is in Beethoven's "third period" that one begins to find chromatic relations that are more and more operative; one need cite only the subject of the *Grosse Fuge,* in which Beethoven showed himself to be a particularly audacious precursor. After him, Wagner utilized chromaticism abundantly; his concept of unending melody was, in a harmonic sense, essentially based on chromatic relationships in which tonality is more and more dissolved; he composed long passages (*Tristan und Isolde*) that mark the inception of the present chromatic era, and in which one could find a defined tonality only by very indirect analysis. Even though the idea of chromaticism is not linked formally to the use of the twelve tones, one finds in Debussy unresolved chords, free progressions based upon very refined chromatic relationships despite an apparent diatonicism; whether in the use of the whole-tone scale or chords made up of many superimposed thirds, or chords in fourths, everything contributed to giving to Debussy's *oeuvre* extended chromatic relations that escaped totally from the frame of classic tonality. On the other hand, the succession to Wagner, taken up by Mahler and Schoenberg, led to an integral chromaticism born from "expressionist" necessities; an anarchizing chromaticism having further deteriorated tonal relationships, the writing called atonal was soon reached. Schoenberg was the first to establish the twelve-tone technique, its basis the use of a system of relationships among the twelve sounds of the tempered chromatic scale; this is called a series. The era of diatonicism, properly speaking, seems to have been terminated; it would appear that every contemporary work must necessarily make use of chromaticism. Recently the idea of chromaticism has been extended to sound-constituents other than pitch. The chromatic schema has been applied to duration and intensity. Olivier Messiaen, in his *Mode de valeurs et d'intensités* for piano (1949), makes use of a chromatic mode of duration extending from the thirty-second-note to the dotted quarter-note by passing through all the intermediate values obtained by the successive addition of thirty-second-notes. Thus he obtained twelve values, among which the thirty-second-note may be considered the chromatic interval. Clearly, one can engender any series of durations whatever by starting from a given unit taken as the chromatic element. As for intensities, Messiaen, in that same piece, scaled them from *ppp* to *fff*. One sees, then, on the basis of this example, that the idea of chromaticism, enlarged to encompass the other sound-constituents, does not depend on chromaticism of pitches (of the half-tones themselves in the system of tempered half-tones, that is to say, and of the multiple twelve that must be reached to complete the octave), but on no matter what smallest common multiple that will serve as a basis for determining an arithmetic or logarithmic scale. That scale, furthermore, will not necessarily be octavic. With electronic or electroacoustic means, the idea of chromaticism or, more generally, of the discontinuous scale, tends to disappear in favor of a total continuum valid for all four of the sound-constituents: pitch (that goes without saying), duration, intensity, and timbre. The evolution of the sound-universe now tends to become a dialectic between the notion of expanded chromaticism and that of absolute continuum.

Concrete (Music)

Since the beginning of *musique concrète*, concrete music, it has been the beneficiary of a curiosity that sometimes has been justified. The purely technical interest that it aroused then has diminished little by little for very precise reasons, and now one can be certain that its role is of no importance, that the works it evoked are not considerable. Nothing more legitimate than the need felt for an "artificial" sound-universe (in contract to the "natural" instrumental sound-universe): it is not for having undertaken that search that one can blame concrete music.

The electroacoustic means that present-day techniques place at our disposition must be integrated into a generalized musical vocabulary. Meanwhile, the word *concrete* reveals how it was misled and the gross way in which the problem was envisaged; it was aimed at defining a material manipulation of sonority, that sonority itself not responding to any definition or being subject to any restriction. The question of the material, though primordial in such an adventure, was not taken care of there, where it was supplied by a sort of poetic display that prolonged the surrealistic practice of collage—painting or words. Beyond the fact that that poetic denuded of choice has aged, the absence of direction in the determination of the sound-material fatally brings on an anarchy prejudicious to the composition, however pleasant it may be. The musical material, if it is to lend itself to composition, must be sufficiently malleable, susceptible to transformations, capable of giving birth to a dialectic and supporting it.

In rejecting or, more exactly, ignoring that primordial activity, we "concrete musicians" were condemned to nonbeing. Add the grievance of producing sounds that, technically speaking, are execrable from the point of view of quality alone. That lack of directing thought resulted in total insolvency of the exploration that had to be made very rigorously in the bosom of the new electroacoustic domain. Apparatuses in constant confusion, an agreeable nonchalance made the concrete-music studio a flea market of sounds; the bric-a-brac, alas! revealed no hidden treasures. Rather than leading to a real acoustic classification, it was limited to the sampling of stock reserves given such fantastic names as "*son épais*," "*son éolien*," and other bagatelles of distorted humor. From those repertoire-ized sounds one could, with a little leisure, construct a small Dupuytren museum of inanity. As for the "works," they have nothing but those quotation marks to carry them to posterity; bare to the bone of all intention of composition, they are limited to not very ingenious or varied montages constantly using the same effects, with locomotive and electricity playing the star parts: nothing, absolutely nothing, resulted from that almost incoherent method. The work of wide-eyed dilettantes, concrete music, even on the terrain of the "gadget," could not compete with the fabricators of "sound-effects" for the film industry. If, then, it is not interesting from either the point of view of sound or that of composition, one is justified in demanding to know what aims or utility it may have. Once the first moment of curiosity passed, its star faded terribly. Happily, the composers who have attacked the problems of electronic music have a different scope. And if that domain does become important one day, it will be thanks to the efforts of the Cologne and Milan studios, not to the derisory, outdated magic of the amateurs, as miserable as they are needy, who operate under the tattered flag of concrete music.

Counterpoint

The word is derived from the Latin expression *punctum contra punctum:* point against point or note against note.

This signifies a combination of a given line and another line that has been created in relation to it, obtained by means of an ensemble of given relationships. Counterpoint is an Occidental phenomenon—by which I mean that the evolution of music in polyphonic directions is a cultural phenomenon exclusive to European Occidental civilization. In the various musical civilizations that preceded it, even those which rested on solid theoretical bases, one can discover no veritable polyphony, whatever some musicologists may say: one never observes that idea of responsibility which is the principal characteristic of counterpoint in the Occident. In so-called exotic musics, one observes heterophony, antiphony, and all the forms of superimposition resulting from simultaneous temporal relationships, but not *responsible* ones. The idea of counterpoint is applied to lines that can be developed from a principal given line, called *cantus firmus;* on the basis of the *cantus firmus*, thanks to certain intervallic relationships, one can establish diverse melodic lines having unique relations to that principal line. Therefore, a contrapuntal line, though vertically controlled, has all its importance horizontally. That is why one usually says that contrapuntal music is written horizontally. The study of the vertical relationships is more particularly the object of harmony, whereas counterpoint places the accent on various combinations that can be made between several melodies, horizontally, without the loss of their individualities as such (in the Academy, professors call that preoccupation *voice-leading*). Doubling a line at the unison or the octave clearly does not partake of counterpoint, as the new line thus obtained does not differ from the other. The contrapuntal line usually observes three motions in relation to the *cantus firmus:* (1) *contrary* motion, when the *cantus firmus* and the counterpoint move in different directions; (2) *parallel* motion, when the *cantus firmus* and the counterpoint move in exactly parallel direction at a given interval of distance; (3) *oblique* motion, when the *cantus firmus* remains immobile while the counterpoint moves in a given direction. It is evident that no music can be called either strictly contrapuntal or strictly harmonic: all music necessarily depends on both horizontal and vertical characteristics. When the preponderance is more especially manifest in one direction than in the other, one then says that the music is harmonic or that it is contrapuntal. As music evolved, these two tendencies interpenetrated more and more, giving birth to a species of free style having numerous steps between pure homophony and pure polyphony. In the first case, *homophonic* music, one can cite the typical example of accompanied melody; in the second case, *polyphonic* music, one can cite strict canonic writing. As a result of the considerable loss of rhythmic sense in Europe (after the Middle Ages), the evolution of counterpoint has not often been studied except in its melodic aspect or, to say it more generally, under the aspect of pitches. Rhythm is one of the most characteristic and decisive elements in that evolution: voice-leading does not lead to the real independence of voices unless one is careful to diversify the rhythmic characteristics as much as the melodic characteristics; doing just that, furthermore, was what gave strength to the *Ars nova*, among others.

The history of counterpoint divides into several periods: (1) the birth of organum (Leoninus, Perotinus Magnus); (2) the *Ars antiqua* and *Ars nova;* (3) the Renaissance and the *Golden Age* of counterpoint; (4) the *baroque* and *classic* periods; (5) the contemporary evolution. That classification lends some aid in analyzing the evolution of the writing, but one must not forget the many crossings that can occur among various historical currents and forms of creative thought.

1. The oldest type of counterpoint is *organum:* it was for two voices at first, based upon the fourth and fifth as consonant intervals in addition to the unison and the octave. The evolution of *organum* tended toward a greater independence for the upper voice in relation to the *cantus firmus.* The School of Notre Dame became celebrated for the beauty and supple-

ness of its counterpoints; it lay at the root of all the future development of music. One generally places at about 1200 the transformation of double *organum* (for two voices) into triple *organum* (for three voices); occasionally one even finds quadruple *organum.* In that later period one rarely counts the sixth among the used intervals, whereas the third, contrary to some assertions, is employed rather freely except in final cadences, which are always on a chord with the octave and an empty fifth.

2. The *Ars antiqua* was occupied chiefly with establishing various strict forms of composition, of which the *motet* and the *conduct* now appear most striking. The discovery of canon with the famous *Sumer is icumen in* probably belongs to that time, although the point is argued by some musicologists. Most of the works are for three voices, but one also encounters motets for two voices, more rarely for four. The *Ars nova* is one of the most brilliant periods of the polyphonic movement: a very rapid evolution occurred thanks to the discovery of proportional notation; that era is associated with the names of great theoreticians like Philippe de Vitry and with the name of one of the greatest of all composers, Guillaume de Machaut. Now we find greater rhythmic and melodic differentiation of voices; the developments become more varied and supple, thanks to greater melodic subtlety and a rhythmic flexibility that remains astonishing in more than one way. The vertical result of contrapuntal combinations also becomes richer through a larger use of perfect chords; the establishment of "conclusive clausulae" also assures a sort of initiation of harmonic foundation in the developments. One begins to find some uses of imitation of one voice by another. The music of Machaut reveals complexity, subtlety, and refinement that are remarkable; it shows a total mastery as much in the domain of melodic counterpoint as in that of rhythmic counterpoint; that music marks a date of first importance in the evolution of European music.

3. These tendencies were to develop farther in the following century, with the logical employment of imitation as a chief means for linking different contrapuntal lines through remarkable sound-figures. After Dunstable and Dufay, imitation was exploited more and more elaborately by Ockeghem, Obrecht, and Josquin des Prés. The structure of the canon was codified, and one finds the most stupefying examples of it among Ockeghem's works. But excessive complexity leads to disastrous scholasticism; that is why many musicians of that epoch are now forgotten. The end of the sixteenth century was to lead the practice of counterpoint to unequalled virtuosity, so much so that one often refers to it as the *Golden Age* of that discipline. An evolution had led composers to lavish greater and greater care on the harmonic aspect of note-encounters, to articulate clearly at once, by means of cadences, the various sections of the musical discourse, to differentiate better between the notes forming a chord and passing notes or delayed notes. These vertical preoccupations would more and more diminish the rhythmic subtlety of the older masters, which would have had other causes such as intelligbility of the sung text and mensuration *à l'antique*. The great names of that *Golden Age* were Orlandus Lassus, Palestrina, and Victoria.

4. During the succeeding period, deep changes occurred which were to carry music to a more harmonic specificity; the counterpoint of that period is known as *harmonic* or *tonal* counterpoint. The tonal organization had become preponderant, and the establishment of the major and minor tonalities began to destroy all conception of purely linear counterpoint. The homophonic style consolidated these tonal acquisitions. At the crossroads we find the name of Monteverdi. Music then was tending to cross the contrapuntal conception and the harmonic conception. One can say of Johann Sebastian Bach that he summed up the whole evolution of writing from the seventeenth century; in him one finds the closest liaison between the two types of writing, in a concord that could not be

achieved so easily after him; scholastic counterpoint still is taught with examples taken mostly from his work. He left us a contrapuntal *summa* in which we find summed up all the technique of that writing which can be acquired. That *summa* includes *Die Kunst der Fuge*, *Das musikalisches Opfer*, the "Goldberg" Variations (for harpsichord), and the Variations on "*Von Himmel Hoch*" (for organ). In those four works one finds all the forms of free and strict counterpoint from imitation to the strict canon.

5. After Bach, the situation altered rapidly; the balance was upset in favor of harmony, which explains why, a few exceptions aside, we find no great examples of counterpoint in Beethoven's first works. Under Bach's influence, Mozart made a sort of return to severe forms of counterpoint near the end of his life. One of the best-known examples is the finale of his "Jupiter" Symphony, which can be looked upon as one of the most striking models of virtuosity in the handling of strict contrapuntal forms. Nevertheless, in most of Mozart's fugues, that use of the purely contrapuntal style carries a certain amount of archaicism, which would tend to prove that writing so conceived remained linked to a definite style in history as well as in esthetic. With Beethoven, the divergence between counterpoint and harmony became accentuated, and one can see his final works as a violent conflict between vertical control of the results of superimpositions and the intervallic demands of melodic lines. Beethoven's nature led him to resolve the conflict between these two aspects of the writing dramatically; he found solutions whose audacity remained unequaled until the beginning of the twentieth century; as characteristic examples, one can cite the fugue that terminates the Piano Sonata, opus 106, and the *Grosse Fuge*.

The entire romantic period seemed not at all interested in purely contrapuntal writing, and in instances where it was not a matter of writing strictly in chords, one nonetheless can detect more painstaking writing of what in harmony is called "middle voices." Thus one finds in Wagner and Brahms a sort of false counterpoint, despite certain spectacular superimpositions such as the one always cited from *Die Meistersinger*. Paradoxically, it was to be from those very composers that the true renaissance of counterpoint would flow, a renaissance that neither Debussy nor Ravel seems to have foreseen.

Let me set aside certain attempted returns to counterpoint as formalistic as they were erroneous, symbolized by the abundant attempts at linear writing between 1914 and 1940, which were based more or less on a kind of renaissance and "return" to older schools: all those essays were of a grievous poverty, and at the same time resulted from a completely false historical point of view. Those composers, who practiced a species of free counterpoint in an extended tonality, of a summary diatonicism, failed; they did away with the idea of *responsibility* of one note to another, the idea at the basis of the whole flowering development of polyphony. Their efforts led to a sort of libertinism in writing of which the sadness was equaled only by the poverty.

The true contemporary revolution had to rise from a much more serious attitude in confronting the problems of writing. I want to make clear that this attitude emerged from profound necessities of expression, not from an *a priori* esthetic attitude devoid of all necessity. Necessity, in fact, was what guided the evolution of what is called the School of Vienna, an evolution that has led to the revivification of certain writing procedures that had more or less fallen into desuetude. Let us remember that the series includes the four classic contrapuntal forms—that is, *original*, *inversion*, *retrograde*, and *retrograde inversion;* the two last forms, however, were employed very rarely in tonal or modal counterpoint. That concept of the series had been derived from strict canonic writing, because the sound-figures thus engendered were completely identical to a like uterine schema. Let me say that this use of strict forms of counterpoint is an essential ambiguity that has allowed movement from the tonal world to the nontonal world; one will make a serious mistake if one attributes an exaggerated importance in the creative thinking of the Viennese to that use of canonic forms for their own sake; nonetheless, it is a trap into which some dodecaphonic composers have fallen who have been unable to see that the strict contrapuntal forms were only a transitional stage. The result has been a rather amusing confusion that has contaminated even musicologists. That is why nowadays one cannot mention the *Ars nova* without having certain musicologists condemn the "excesses" of that period, confusing them with those of contemporary dodecaphonists; it is not trite to see certain present-day polemics as interfering with judgments of a past period, above all when complete confusion and total lack of discernment are the basis of such interferences. It even seems that now the evolution of music is entering—after the two chief phases that were monody and then polyphony (from counterpoint to harmony)—into a third phase, a kind of "polyphony of polyphonies"—that is, appealing to a *distribution* rather than a simple superimposition of intervals. *Grosso modo*, one could say that music now has a new dimension. The evolution of the rhythmic language, properly speaking, favors that polyphonic idea, and it even appears that the problems have not been put with as much acuity as now since the Middle Ages, in all the domains. There you have the only justified comparison between the contemporary period and the *Ars nova*.

The teaching of counterpoint has followed the evolution of that sort of writing: the theoretical writings of the thirteenth and fourteenth centuries are very detailed on this point; a somewhat later writing gives many practical examples, a fact that makes it very valuable to consult: it is the *Fundamentum organisandi* of Conrad Paumann (1452). The teaching of counterpoint was to become more and more methodical; Zarlino describes the types of counterpoint in his *Istitutioni armoniche* (1558). But a great work in codifying the teaching of counterpoint upon a *cantus firmus* appeared much later; it was the famous *Gradus ad Parnassum* of Johann Joseph Fux; that work exercised authority for a long time, and the teaching of school counterpoint still derives, closely or remotely, from its expositions; none of the numerous academic treatises of the nineteenth century could equal it. The teaching of counterpoint as practiced now consists of deducing various types of melodic counterpoints from a *cantus firmus*. Counterpoint is practiced principally for two, three, and four voices; at the outside, one writes for five, six, seven, or eight voices. Such realizations present an increasing number of difficulties, and the rules become less and less strict: therefore they have smaller interest for the discipline of the writing, properly speaking. The *cantus firmus* can be located in the bass, in the upper part, or in one of the interior parts. There are five forms of counterpoint in relation to the *cantus firmus*, which always proceeds in whole-notes and consists of from eight to fourteen notes: (1) *note against note*—that is, in whole-notes; (2) *two notes against one*—that is, in half-notes; (3) *four notes against one*—that is, in quarter-notes; (4) *in syncopation*—that is, in whole-notes displaced a half-measure in relation to those of the *cantus firmus;* (5) *florid counterpoint*, or a kind of combining of the four preceding species. On the basis of these five forms, one then learns to write mixtures of three and more voices in which each voice is in a different form—at least, if not all of them are in florid counterpoint.

After these exercises, one practices the various canons on all the diatonic intervals. Later, one practices *invertible counterpoint*, which consists of establishing a line whose relation to the *cantus firmus* can be modified by inversion in relation to a given interval; that interval usually is the octave, more rarely is the twelfth, still more rarely is some other interval. Invertible counterpoint at the octave is usually practiced up to four voices. In the inversions at other intervals than the octave, or with a large number of voices, this becomes an exercise whose musical interest is disproportionately exceeded by its difficulty. Finally one practices the technique of the double chorus. The rules of writing are very strict: passing-notes on the beat are forbidden: one may use only one harmonic scheme per measure (that is, analysis of a conterpoint must not reveal more than one chord per measure); finally, use of the fourth and the sixth is strictly forbidden. The cadences must be made on the octave or the fifth, in some cases on the third, except in invertible counterpoint. Other rules concern the relations among intervals ruling the various parallel, contrary, or oblique motions; it would take too long to expound on them in detail here. As for rhythm, we have seen that counterpoint uses only multiples of two; recently, some professors have used ternary rhythms—that is, three or six notes per measure. There is, in fact, no reason not to adopt these ternary meters: in Bach, for example, one encounters them at least as often as binary meters. After the exercises in strict counterpoint, one may practice free counterpoint in order to make one's writing supple. In it, the writing has rules that are much less rigid, and one is not obliged to use a *cantus firmus*. Then the study of counterpoint is pursued through the practice of the *varied chorale* and *figured chorale*, and, finally, through study of *fugue*, in which the student puts all his acquired knowledge into practice. Generally, one does not study counterpoint until after having studied harmony; that is the order adopted by the Conservatoire National de Paris. At the Schola Cantorum, Vincent d'Indy sanctioned the opposite order, wanting thus to follow the historic evolution of the musical language. His example does not seem to have been much followed; nor does the "historic" method seem the best for acquiring a technique of writing. It would nonetheless be desirable that in present-day teaching of counterpoint a greater part be given to pre-Bach composers; for most professors, music began with Bach. Timid excursions into the Renaissance have been made, but no teaching has been seriously based upon the evolution of counterpoint from *organum* to the classic age; knowledge of the texts themselves is, furthermore, very limited because of the rarety and costliness of the editions thus far published. Neither Hindemith's treatise nor Schoenberg's is important in the teaching of counterpoint. As to the only dodecaphonic treatise that has been written, it is so ridiculously academic that its usefulness is illusory. The teaching of counterpoint still awaits a methodology truly of our epoch.

Series

The word "series" appeared for the first time in the writings of Viennese theoreticians describing Schoenberg's first works employing an unchanged sequence of twelve tones throughout a determined work. Schoenberg's own definition is this: "*Komposition mit swölf nur aufeinander bezogene Tönen*" (literally, composition with twelve tones unrelated except among themselves). The first, rudimentary use of a series is found in the fifth piece of Schoenberg's opus 23 (*Walzer*), which utilizes the twelve tones in unchanging order in varied placements. With his succeeding works—the Serenade, opus 24, and more especially the Suite for Piano, opus 25, that use was to be generalized and to find its definitive form gradually. Before the adoption of the series of twelve tones, properly speaking, we note in Schoenberg (third piece of opus 23) the preponderance granted to a succession of sounds—in some ways a unique musical figure—charged through its development and transformations with the whole organization of a piece. The appearance of the series in Schoenberg is thus linked to a thematic phenomenon; for him, the series is an "ultrathematization"; to the end of his life, he conceived the series as assuming a role equivalent to that of a theme in tonal music.

With Webern, on the contrary, the series suddenly took on the aspect of a function of intervals giving its basic structure to the piece itself; that definition was finally to prevail in later developments. By the Viennese School, generally speaking, the series is considered as a basic unifying principle linked to the classic forms of counterpoint. We find the original series, its inversion, its retrograde, and the retrograde of the inversion, or four modes of engendering; furthermore, these four types are applied to the twelve half-tones, which *in toto* gives forty-eight basic forms. Through the single fact of transposition on the chromatic intervals one sees that for the Viennese the series was conceptually a horizontal phenomenon susceptible to translation to all the degrees of a scale—the chromatic scale, as it happened. Webern's works have proved that it is better to envisage the series as a hierarchical function engendering permutations and manifested through a distribution of intervals independent of horizontal or vertical functions. Also, the Viennese School considered the series exclusively on the level of pitches—and among the pitches, exclusively those in the tempered chromatic universe. Discoveries that followed those of the School of Vienna have proved that envisaging the series from that single point of view easily provokes distortions in its use, because the sound-constituents (acoustically speaking) are not felt to be related to the same organization as the pitch is. The principle then had to be generalized for all characteristics of the sound-phenomenon—that is, the theoretical principle of the series had to be unified and universalized. One knows that the characteristics of sound include, in order of preponderances, pitch, duration, intensity, and timbre. The action of the series has now been extended to those four constituents by application to them of numbered relations characterizing the interval of frequency as well as that of duration, the interval of dynamic as well as that of timbre. I gladly simplify this discussion by not speaking of meshed relations of, for example, pitch and timbre, intensity and duration, etc., as those characteristics naturally are functions of one another and give birth to related phenomena through the reactions that they have to one another; nevertheless, in the large sense, the problem is posed. At the beginning of that serial generalization, the desire was to use, within a work, the same hierarchy for the four constituents, but that could lead to total absurdity, because it did not consider the fact that that these phenomena should be organized by different criteria and that numbers do not suffice to give deep unity to the different characteristics of sound and to integrate them into a general structure.

Thus, having generalized the principle of the series, one has been led to give it, for each of the sound-constituents, a specific form in which the number twelve no longer plays a leading role: the series has become a polyvalent way of thinking and not a mere technique of vocabulary. Today, serial thinking tends to emphasize that the series should not merely give birth to the vocabulary itself but should also extend the structure of the work; that is a total reaction against classical thought, which felt form as being, practically, a preexisting thing, as was the general morphology. Here there are no preconceived scales—that is, a general structure into which to insert a particular thought. On the contrary, the composer's thought, utilizing a determined methodology, creates the objects of which he has need and the form necessary for organizing them each time that his thought must be expressed. Classic tonal thought was founded on a universe defined by gravitation and attraction; serial thought is founded on a universe in perpetual expansion.

Bartók,

BÉLA, HUNGARIAN COMPOSER

(NAGY SZENT MIKLÓS, MARCH 25, 1881—
NEW YORK, SEPTEMBER 26, 1945)

He was born on March 25, 1881, at Nagy Szent Miklós, a small Hungarian provincial town. His family, proud of his gifts, easily agreed to his preparing for a musical career. He studied first at Bratislava, then at Budapest. In the latter city, at the Royal Academy, he studied piano with István Thomán, through whom he received the direct Liszt tradition. In composition, he was a pupil of Hans Koessler and little by little discovered all the music of the German tradition, from the classics to Wagner, Brahms, and Strauss. His encounter with the works of Debussy in 1905 was perhaps the most memorable experience of his life as a composer.

Beginning in 1907, he taught piano at the Royal Academy in Budapest, succeeding his teacher, Thomán. Until the 1914 war, he composed a great deal, principally: Second Suite for Orchestra (1907), Two Portraits (1908), Two Images (1910), all for orchestra; First String Quartet (1907); Bagatelles (1908), Four Dirges (1910), and *Allegro barbaro* (1911) for piano. The opera *Duke Bluebeard's Castle* (1911) was refused by the Budapest Opera and not performed until seven years later. The libretto had been written by Béla Balázs, who also furnished Bartók with the scenario of the ballet *The Wooden Prince.*

The Miraculous Mandarin, a pantomime written on a Melchior Lengyel text in 1910, marked a very important development in Bartók's writing, one already adumbrated by the *Allegro barbaro*. His first explorations into his country's folklore showed him the way to a specifically "Hungarian" music. In fact, he also was inspired by Romanian and Bulgarian songs. The Second String Quartet and the Piano Études, composed at the same time (1917–18), bear traces of related efforts to amalgamate popular tradition and composed music.

Bartók's researches became even more accentuated and marked the culminating point of his invention. During that period, he kept up very close contacts with the Viennese composers, thanks to Universal Edition, their common publisher; Bartók took an especially lively interest in the road being taken by Schoenberg. The result in his own works was extreme chromatic tension. The two sonatas for piano and violin date from 1921–22, the Dance Suite from 1923; the Sonata and *Out of Doors*, both for piano, are from 1926, as is the First Piano Concerto. The third and fourth string quartets were composed successively, in 1927 and 1928. They were followed by the *Cantata profana* (1930) and the Second Piano Concerto (1931).

Three works of great maturity, in which Bartók attained a remarkable degree of balance, followed in 1934–7. These were the Fifth String Quartet (1935), the Music for Strings, Percussion, and Celesta (1936), and the Sonata for Two Pianos and Percussion (1937). He also produced *Mikrokosmos*, a didactic collection stretching from elementary instruction to virtuosic difficulties.

Bartók then made a courageous stand against Nazism. He forbade his publisher to furnish proof of his "Aryan" descent; he refused to be included on the musical program that Goebbels organized in a frame of manifestations against "Jewish and degenerate art" and "cultural Bolshevism." Finally, when the Hungary of Horthy made a pact with Hitler, Bartók went into exile. The first performance of his Violin Concerto (1938) took place in Amsterdam. That work marked a decline in Bartók's thought, which thereafter produced works of less value—except, perhaps, for the Sixth String Quartet (1940). Among the principal works of that period, we can cite: *Contrasts*, for clarinet, violin, and piano (1938), Divertissement for strings (1939), Concerto for Orchestra (1943), Sonata for Unaccompanied Violin (1944). The Viola Concerto and Third Piano Concerto were completed after his death by his pupil Tibor Serly. Despite commissions from Koussevitzky and Menuhin, Bartók led a painful life in the United States: isolated, victim of a rapidly advancing illness, under material conditions close to want, he sank rapidly; he died in New York on September 26, 1945, and the League of Composers paid for his funeral.

To those who knew him, Bartók left the memory of a self-effacing, modest man whose conversation was neutral and without brilliance. That amenity concealed an impassioned intransigence that he demonstrated during several polemics on the subject of folklore, and which he pushed to the point of exile at the time of his protest against Nazism. In physique, he was slight, small; his face, with its extremely fine features, was animated by the directness and naïveté of a very blue gaze. An excellent pianist, he gave many concerts in the large cities of Europe and the United States; some recordings made at various stages of his career have been preserved.

Bartók's first works showed both traces of all the classic and romantic influences and denoted a dogged determination to create a truly Hungarian music. He could not be satisfied with a certain rhapsodic Gypsy color, the entirely exterior picturesqueness of which failed to reflect the true music of a people. In that, he set himself apart violently from Liszt and his imitators. Armed with recording apparatus as essential baggage, he set out to explore even the provinces most difficult to reach.

Periodically throughout his life, Bartók went out in search

of authentic documents, either to rest from his composing labors or perhaps to refresh his inspiration. Those excursions were justified by an impressive number of melodies collected and notated from the recordings with a fineness of ear and a rhythmic finesse that must arouse admiration. He notated the folkloric music without at all squeezing it into the framework of academic rhythms and scales. Thus he left us fundamental works on the musical folklore of Hungary, Romania, and Slovakia. His last excursion, in 1935, was devoted to the Arabs of Biskra and the Anatolian Turks.

Bartók the composer profited in the highest degree from Bartók the folklorist. A partisan of conventional nationalism in the face of the Hapsburg domination (in his symphonic poem *Kossuth* [1903], he parodied the Austrian anthem—that is, Haydn!), he satisfied a need for authenticity by searching out new materials and unprecedented techniques, which profoundly disturbed his esthetic and forced him to solve the problem of Hungarian music in a way that went beyond simple provincial exoticism. But, while we note the persevering influence of that Central European musical folklore, we must observe that Bartók's work is marked by deep-seated instability, which might even be called disparity, in its various constituents. He underwent the influences of all his contemporaries, and despite his powerful personality, sometimes assimilated them very superficially.

At the zenith of his work stand out the six string quartets, the Sonata for Two Pianos and Percussion, the Music for Strings, Percussion, and Celesta, and the two sonatas for violin and piano. Those seem to be the real heart of Bartók's creation.

On the whole, the six string quartets mark his evolution most precisely. Taking off from a kind of synthesis of the late Beethoven and the mature Debussy—a very odd synthesis—Bartók arrived at a phase of very specially chromatic experiments not far from Berg and Schoenberg; from there he went into a completely personal style that is a species of balance-point between popular music and composed music, between diatonicism and chromaticism. The Music for Strings, Percussion, and Celesta is a great instrumental success: two string orchestras answer one another and stand in opposition to a third group made up of piano or celestra, harp, xylophone, timpani, and percussion. The first-movement fugue is unquestionably the most beautiful and most characteristic example of Bartók's refined writing. In it, one finds a profusion of narrow intervals overlapping and crossing in the context of a constant chromaticism; the predominance of rigorous or free contrapuntal writing is affirmed in developments built on canonic imitations; the rhythm, finally, is in constant fluctuation, an alternation of even or uneven meters depending upon the dotted unit, a rhythm that also is often contrapuntal.

As for instrumentation, Bartók always wrote admirably for the piano, his preferred instrument, and for strings. He often made effective use of the celesta and the xylophone, the former for coloring arpeggios of divided-string trills, the second for exaggerating and draining dry the percussive side of the piano. Handling the strings, he knew how to make use of all the effects appropriate to those instruments, such as the *col legno*, the pizzicato struck on the frets, play on the bridge and the frets, and he knew admirably how to proportion a mixture of these diverse sonorities. The bow discovered a new freshness, even an aggressiveness of attack, which made it forget the romantic conception. The piano is used above all for its percussive, hammering value, more rarely for trilling effects like those of a Hungarian cymbalom, and still more rarely for resonances or to sing a melody. From the point of view of pianistic writing, the first movement of the Sonata for Two Pianos and Percussion is, with Stravinsky's *Les Noces*, one of the important testimonials of that generation.

Bartók, furthermore, devoted no less than three concertos to the piano, whereas he composed only one violin concerto. From the three piano concertos, the first two stand out clearly as strong, though not capital, works, the third of them being of only small value; the Violin Concerto cannot be placed among his first-rank works. On the other hand, the two sonatas for violin and piano, composed simultaneously, stand among the most attractive works that the composer ever wrote.

They mark a point of extreme tension in his search and conceal a savage violence that is found throughout Bartók's best pages. The equilibrium between the two instruments, so difficult to achieve, is maintained here by ingenious artifices and, above all, by the writing, which takes the specific nature of each of them into account so well that neither of them is "masked" at any essential moment.

Bartók wrote three stage works: an opera, *Duke Bluebeard's Castle;* a ballet, *The Wooden Prince;* and a pantomime, *The Miraculous Mandarin. Duke Bluebeard's Castle* was, with the *Cantata profana*, the composer's only significant venture into the realm of vocal music. He did not write much for the voice outside of popular transcriptions in a minor mode. As for *The Miraculous Mandarin,* it is his most brilliant work for orchestra, although it is less shaped for popularity than the Concerto for Orchestra. However, the stage inspired him little, and after *The Miraculous Mandarin* he composed no other theatrical work. It must be added that the response to his works from opera directors never encouraged him to continue in that field.

At the two boundaries of his production, *Two Portraits* and *Two Images* at one side, at the other the *Divertimento* and the Concerto for Orchestra mark the limitations of Bartók: those compositions are far from being good, though for very different reasons.

The first works are, like the *Two Portraits* and the *Two Images*, still too disparate to have the unity of an experienced style. The last works, on the contrary, display a smoothing-down and contain too many clichés of writing and construction.

Bartók occupies a very particular place in contemporary music. In the general view, he is, after Stravinsky, the only avant-garde musician to have been accepted completely. On the other hand, his recourse to the spirit of folklore has been a decisive argument in the hands of musical "nationalists": Bartók is seen as the only representative of human music as against the abstract and unfeeling experimenters of the School of Vienna and Stravinsky's cosmopolitan intellectualism. After the Second World War, in truth, his music won great popularity, and he has had numerous imitators who have created a certain factitious activism in their writing, inspired completely by the exterior of Bartók's real pulsation. After having long been ignored, he became the ensign name of the "reasonable" avant-garde, the one that did not lose contact with the public.

A certain dosage of misunderstanding inheres in that unusual situation of a musician, dying in want and penury, who is promoted posthumously to the first rank of "comprehensible" composers. For in the end Bartók found such receptive listeners only some years after his death, and it should be remarked that the pieces most applauded often are the least good, the ones most closely approaching Gypsy-Liszt, of doubtful taste; his best products are loved in their weaker aspects—with references to the fiddler and the neoclassic. His work triumphs now through its ambiguity, then. Ambiguity that will surely bring him insults during future evaluation, when his listeners will have experienced a recoil. Undeniably, Bartók belongs among the "five great" of contemporary music, with Stravinsky, Webern, Schoenberg, and Berg. However, his work has not the profound unity and novelty of Webern's, the rigor and acuity of Schoenberg's, the complexity of Berg's, or the vigorous, controlled dynamism of Stravinsky's. His language lacks interior coherence; that language came to weaken an imagination fertile in short-term inventions. As for his utilization of folklore in that directly assimilated form, even in its very valuable authenticity it is only a residue of the nationalistic thrusts of the nineteenth century, which extended from Russia to Spain. Folklore simply extended and made supple Bartók's rhythmic conceptions, while at the same time it singularly narrowed the horizon of his language. What is foreseeable is that his name will live in the limited, purified ensemble of his chamber music: string quartets, sonatas for violin and piano, Sonato for Two Pianos and Percussion, Music for Strings, Percussion, and Celesta. Whether in a brutal violence animating a "sound-material in fusion" or in a calm sweetness, aureoled in a crinkling, changeable halo, Bartók is incomparable in the successes in which his poetic genius allowed him the grace of effective realization.

Of the older world, the contradictions of which he could not surmount, he was very possibly the final representative gifted with spontaneity; generous to the point of prodigality, artful at the risk of naïveté, pathetic and unarmed.

Berg,

ALBAN, AUSTRIAN COMPOSER
(VIENNA, FEBRUARY 9, 1885—
DECEMBER 24, 1935)

Of a family of the Viennese *haute bourgeoisie,* he was born at Vienna on February 9, 1885; as a child he already showed a special disposition toward music; during his adolescence, he long hesitated between poetry and composition. His family vigorously encouraged him to cultivate his natural dispositions; while pursuing his secondary studies, he therefore wrote a large number of *Lieder,* the manuscripts of which were discovered after his death. His elder brother took the initiative of showing those youthful attempts to Arnold Schoenberg; the meeting that ensued was a determining factor in the youth's evolution. From 1904—that is, from the age of nineteen—to 1910, Berg took regular lessons with Schoenberg. Furthermore, the relation between master and student rapidly became a profound friendship; it is demonstrated in the dedications that Berg made to Schoenberg (Three Pieces for Orchestra, opus 6, Chamber Concerto, *Lulu*).

Schoenberg's teaching covered all the musical disciplines: harmony, counterpoint, analysis, orchestration, and composition, properly speaking, including the study of forms. Berg then composed his first works: *Sieben Frühe Lieder;* Piano Sonata, opus 1 (1907–8); *Vier Lieder,* opus 2 (1908–9); String Quartet, opus 3 (1909). They already show total mastery both in the realm of composition and on the instrumental or vocal level; from that time on, Berg knew the resources of his métier and the way to exploit it within the limits of a rational inspiration. At that time, he met Webern, another Schoenberg disciple, with whom he also became linked in a very great and lasting friendship.

In 1911, he married the singer Hélène Nahowski, who played a very large role in his life and sometimes even gave him suggestions for the arrangement of his work. He then undertook various jobs of transcription and arrangement in order to earn a living. From 1915 to 1918, he served in the army; because of his deficient health, he was assigned an administrative position that left him free time for pursuing his personal work. The *Peter Altenberg Lieder*, opus 4, on picture-postcard texts, were composed in 1911 and 1912; the work was performed for the first time during a concert that Schoenberg presented in 1913 and stirred up a demonstration that had to be stopped by the police (works by Webern and Schoenberg were also on the program).

The Three Orchestral Pieces, Prelude, Round, March, opus 6, were completed in 1914; this was Berg's first confrontation with composition for large orchestra alone. In 1914, having attended a performance of *Woyzeck*, he decided to compose an opera. The posthumous fragments of the drama by Georg Büchner (1813–37) having been given no dramatic coherence by their author, Berg's first task was to concentrate the dramatic text so as to eliminate subsidiary scenes. That arduous work, begun in 1915, was completed in 1917; then he set himself to composing the music, which was written entirely in 1919.

In that year Berg took an active role in the Verein für musikalische Privataufführungen (Society for Private Musical Performances), for which he prepared a prospectus that is interesting in several ways. Among others, it allows us to approach his conceptions of the relation between the musical work and the public. It was in the framework of this Society that he presented his Four Pieces for Clarinet and Piano, opus 5.

In 1921, having completed the orchestral score of *Wozzeck*, Berg sent the piano-vocal score, which he himself had prepared, to various opera houses in Germany and Austria, none of which offered to produce the work. The orchestra conductor Hermann Scherchen then (summer 1923) suggested that he make a concert version of several extracts from the opera; although Berg was little inclined to sacrifice the structure of his opera, so minutely arranged and profoundly carried out, he arranged a small cycle in which Marie is the central personage. These three fragments include the Military March and Lullaby of Act I; the Bible-reading that opens the third act; the big interlude that precedes the final scene; and that scene itself. The performance of these three fragments, conducted by Hermann Scherchen at Frankfurt on June 11, 1924, at once brought Berg a certain fame. The conductor Erich Kleiber was among the enthusiasts, and at his urging, the Berlin Staatsoper decided to produce the opera. The first performance occurred on December 14, 1923, after a long, minute labor of rehearsal which assured a performance of high quality. It was one of the greatest events in the German musical world of that period; it stirred up arguments that reached unexampled violence. The principal press criticisms were collected by Berg's publisher, Universal Edition, Vienna; they reveal a real indecency worthy of the insanities still produced by certain critics: bolshevism, degenerate art, barbarism, chaos were the words used most often by critics as surly as they were incompetent.

Despite that blaze of fury, *Wozzeck* found defenders and passionate admirers; the opera was produced very quickly by all the principal houses of the world and in all the important German towns: Vienna, Düsseldorf, Amsterdam, Cologne, Rotterdam, Darmstadt, Philadelphia, Frankfurt, Leipzig, Zurich, Brussels, London, New York. By the end of 1936, *Wozzeck* had been performed sixty-six times in twenty-nine different cities; Berg personally attended many of the *premières* in Germany and Switzerland.

The Library of Congress at Washington acquired the manuscript of the orchestral score in 1934; it is dedicated to Alma Mahler, widow of Gustav Mahler, who was closely associated with Berg. The success of *Wozzeck* was limited to the Anglo-Saxon countries; not until 1955 did La Scala, Milan, deign to mount this masterwork; as for the Paris Opéra, it still has not entered that competition,[1] and that it has been possible to see *Wozzeck* in Paris has been thanks to two foreign troupes—that of the Vienna Opera in 1952, that of the Hamburg Opera in 1955.

After *Wozzeck*, Berg turned back to chamber music, composing two of his masterpieces: the Chamber Concerto (*Kammerkonzert*), which was written between 1923 and 1925, and the *Lyrische Suite* for string quartet, the completion of which occured during 1925–6.

The *Kammerkonzert* juxtaposes two solo instruments—piano and violin—and a group of thirteen wind instruments. Dedicated to Schoenberg on his fiftieth birthday, it has thematic material based on the names of the three friends Arnold Schoenberg (D–E flat–C–B–B flat–E–G), Anton Webern (A–E–B flat–E), and Alban Berg (A–B flat–A–B flat–E–G), which are thus grouped in the motto placed at the beginning of the piece. On that occasion, Berg wrote a long open letter to Schoenberg in which he analyzed the structure of the *Kammerkonzert* and the underlying thoughts in the work. Among Berg's writings, this is one that most clearly reveals his working methods and the aims that he was pursuing during that period of his life. The entire work displays a

[1] *Wozzeck* was finally staged at the Paris Opéra in November 1963, under the direction of Pierre Boulez.—ED.

mystical obsession with the number 3: under the motto, one finds this proverb: "*Alle gute Dinge . . .*" which is equivalent to our "*Jamais deux sans trois*" [Never two without three]. However, Berg's humor never lost control of that rather primary mystique.

Except for *Wozzeck*, the *Lyrische Suite* is the most popular of Berg's compositions, and in any case was the one that contributed most to establishing his world-wide fame. It was in the *Lyrische Suite* that for the first time he used the *Zwölfton System*—that is, the dodecaphonic technique formulated by Schoenberg in 1924. In it, one can discern a determination to oppose that strict technique (based upon a series) and a free, uncodified chromatic organization. The work is for string quartet and is in six movements, the dramatic character of which is implied in their superscriptions. I cite as particularly revealing of Berg's esthetic *Allegretto gioviale*, *Andante amoroso*, *Allegro misterioso* (*Trio estatico*), *Adagio appassionato*, *Presto delirando* (*tenebroso*), *Largo desolato*. Here one sees an interplay of more and more rapid movements (allegretto, allegro, presto) and slower and slower movements (andante, adagio, largo); in another sense, the work, which begins in joy, ends in despair after paroxysmic movements of very great violence in the *Presto*. As purely instrumental writing, the *Lyrische Suite* is one of the greatest masterworks; nowhere else have the sonorities of a string quartet been exploited with so much genius. From that point of view, the *Allegro misterioso* is perhaps the most striking section, and the sonority of the *tenebroso* is incomparable.

Berg then felt the need to compose another opera. After having wavered a long time among several projects (the most important of which was a vague project to collaborate with Gerhart Hauptmann), he decided upon twin dramas by Frank Wedekind—*Erdgeist* and *Die Büchse der Pandora*. Berg joined them together, profoundly modifying them in the process, under the title *Lulu;* work on it was to occupy him until his death. He completed the music, but could not finish the orchestration of more than the first two acts.

Up to now, no one has succeeded in orchestrating the third act; no complete performance of *Lulu* has ever been mounted. The completed fragments were presented for the first time at Zurich in 1937; they were given again only in 1949 at the Venice Biennale, that time as staged. *Lulu* is wholly dodecaphonic and differs fundamentally from *Wozzeck* in structure. The role of Lulu, assigned to a coloratura, is extraordinarily difficult. However, Wedekind's text being infinitely inferior to Büchner's, it blunted the dramatic power of Berg's music. It is to be feared that this opera, too clearly stamped with the "expressionist" esthetic of 1920, will become dated rather than marking a date.

While working on the composition of that extended work, Berg twice interrupted himself to compose other pieces that interpreters requested as vehicles for their virtuosity. The first was the cantata *Der Wein*, composed at the request of the singer Ruzena Herzlinger in the spring of 1927. It is a large concert aria for soprano and orchestra which is marginal to *Lulu:* it shows the same characteristics, uses the same techniques, has the identical orchestral sonority. The text consists of three poems by Baudelaire translated into German by Stefan George. Berg wrote a vocal line equally adaptable to the German and the French (although, to tell the truth, French prosody is not consistently respected). The second of these compositions was the Concerto for Violin and Orchestra, ordered by the violonist Louis Krasner. It was composed very swiftly, if one considers the average length of time which Berg required to produce a work. It carries the dedication "To the memory of an angel," and was presented as a funereal homage in memory of Manon Gropius, daughter of Alma Mahler and the architect Walter Gropius, who had died at the age of eighteen. The Concerto was Berg's last work. Completed on

August 11, 1935, it was played for the first time on April 15, 1936, after his death, during a festival of the International Society for Contemporary Music at Barcelona. That performance, which was to have been conducted by Anton Webern, finally was taken charge of by Hermann Scherchen. In this piece, Berg attempted to reconcile series and tonality. For that reason, he employed a tone-row in which major and minor thirds follow one another, thus engendering a sort of ambiguity and oscillation between the relative tonalities of G minor and B-flat major. Its four movements succeed one another, linked together two by two, the final movement consisting of variations on the chorale "*Es ist genug*"*:* Berg alternated his own serial harmony with that employed by Bach in the cantata *O Ewigkeit du Donnerwort.*

Berg was forced to interrupt his activity because of an abscess of uncertain origin which considerably weakened his body, obliging him to cancel his engagements from September 1935 on. In November, however, he left the country to return to Vienna and busy himself with the *Lulu Symphony*—which, on the model of the three *Wozzeck* fragments, he had taken from his second opera during the summer of 1934; the first performance of the symphony was given at the end of that year in Berlin, Erich Kleiber conducting. The Viennese performance took place on December 11, 1935; despite his illness. Berg was able to follow the rehearsals and attend the concert. That was the last time that he could hear his own music and the only time he heard the orchestra of *Lulu.*

The fatigue brought on by that effort aggravated the condition of Berg's health. Leukemia appeared and was not ameliorated by a blood transfusion. He bore the illness calmly and not without humor. For some days it was possible to believe that he could be saved, but on December 22 his condition worsened. He died on Christmas Eve 1935 in the hospital to which it had been necessary to remove him.

At that time, only his closest friends fully realized the quality of the musician just lost. Nazism having practically forbidden all "degenerate" music, Berg's compositions underwent a ten-year eclipse. It was only about 1945 that they emerged from the silence into which they had been plunged, but then they quickly acquired such universal renown that *Wozzeck* is now taken to be the archetype of contemporary opera.

According to Berg's friends and the testimony of his life, he was a man of exceptional allure. Tall, with an aristocratic face, he was seen as one of the refined representatives of the Vienna *haute bourgeoisie*. Surviving portraits of him reveal undeniable affability. The dominant trait of his character was fidelity in friendship; he always displayed passionate deference to Schoenberg, who had been able to awaken his compositional gifts and expand them in the most convincing way. His relations with Webern were very consistent from the period of their common apprenticeship to his death; although their esthetics had few points in common, it is curious to note how high their reciprocal esteem remained. Very happy in his home life, Berg led a retired existence consecrated above all to his work as a composer. He had numerous pupils, having taught composition from 1919 on. His pupils looked upon him not only as a professor, but also as a true friend devoted to leading them in the search for their own personalities.

I should stop here briefly to discuss Berg's talent as a polemicist. He wrote, in fact, some brilliant articles to which one must refer if one wishes to understand their author's very attractive personality. These articles are sometimes analyses, sometimes virulent polemics conducted with sarcastic humor, sometimes explications, justifications, or data concerning his own works. In particular, he wrote a reply "Against Hans Pfitzner" that remains the model of a pamphlet against sickly academicism. At the time of the *Kammerkonzert*, he sent Schoenberg an analysis in which one can verify the solid classical formation that produced his mastery.

It has been said of Berg's *oeuvre* that it is one immense opera; and it is true that as a whole one can put the accent upon his eminently dramatic—one could say paroxysmal—character. However, that postromantic tendency was counterbalanced by a desire to push form to such a degree of complexity that it is impossible to think of advancing farther along that route. If one studies Berg's evolution, it is difficult to separate his dramatic work from his instrumental work: both show the same tragic tendencies, the same formal care. It has also been said that if Schoenberg in some manner represented the center of the Viennese trio and Webern always drove toward the most radical solutions—those most turned toward the future—Berg by taste and temperament was devoted to a sort of liaison with the past.

Certainly, Berg's *oeuvre* was, from beginning to end, marked by the postromantic tradition; in particular, he felt the influence of Mahler and of Schoenberg's youthful works. Berg remained strongly tied to the Austrian trend in music—we can even say to its Viennese expression. Furthermore, one finds in him an obsession with citation, both of musical texts (the first measures of *Tristan*, popular songs) and of a determined form of orchestra (the orchestra of Schoenberg's *Kammersymphonie* for one of the principal scenes of *Wozzeck*). Finally, in writing variations on a Bach chorale, he attempted a synthesis of the tonal and nontonal worlds through a very ingenious subterfuge, that of making the first four notes of the chorale coincide with the last four of the series upon which the Violin Concerto is constructed.

For all these reasons, it seems, Berg has now won a popularity incomparably larger than Webern's, and has even eclipsed Schoenberg's fame. In many musical circles completely refractory to the Vienna School in general, and above all to the theoretical thinking animating it, Berg has been looked upon as the only genius sufficiently "a musician" to create "music" on the basis of principles that are the least "musical"; whence the noted preeminence of freedom over rigor, of genius over scholasticism—all discoveries, one understands, that are very pleasant to those observers who distinguish badly the mechanisms, as much psychological as technical, of so complex a body of work. In short, this composer has been made a hostage to the uses of right-thinking people who at times amuse themselves by romping with the avant-garde and then return reassured from those incursions into remote lands. However, despite the public ear, young musicians have not turned particularly toward Berg when they have become aware of all the works of the three Viennese musicians. To them, Webern has seemed to possess powerful stylistic qualities, whereas Berg has been charged with an esthetic burden too anomalous for them to be able to depart from it to easy creation of their own working instrument. Some composers of the preceding generation (Dallapiccola in particular) felt Berg's influence strongly, but in a completely superficial way, in which expressionism was reduced to small change in order to justify an unbreakable attachment to traditional references. A curious fact: Berg's profound personality (and by that I mean his genius in establishing formal relations highly individualized in their complexity) has had no spiritual descendants. Perhaps stylistic searching is too sharp in our time for us to be able to absorb now that proliferation of relations that kept the privilege, with Berg, of being exercised upon an already existing language. But before drawing definite conclusions, we must analyze Berg's advance throughout his compositional career to see how he came to prefer and select certain solutions rather than others.

Grosso modo, we can for convenience separate Berg's works into three groups related to three periods of his existence: (1) a period of preparation, extending from the Piano Sonata, opus 1, to the Pieces for Orchestra, opus 6, and covering the years

1907–14; (2) a period of realization that includes his three gratest masterpieces: *Wozzeck*, the *Kammerkonzert*, and the *Lyrische Suite* (1917–26); (3) a period of experiment (1928–35), marking Berg's encounter with the serial system and the hesitations that he felt about embarking upon such a definite stage. This last is the period of *Lulu*, the cantata *Der Wein*, and the Violin Concerto. The second period seems to me by far the most important in the domain of creation, and the most successful; it is there that we must look, it appears, for a certain essence of the art of composition as Berg wished to understand and practice it.

In the Piano Sonata, opus 1, and up to the *Peter Altenberg Lieder*, opus 4, Berg progressively dissolved the constants of the tonal language. The Sonata still was written in B minor, but the Quartet, opus 3, already escapes the laws of tonality completely. In the Sonata, in which the influence of Schoenberg's *Kammersymphonie* is evident, one finds a sense of cyclical construction strongly anchored in the thematic discourse, which is used in a completely functional manner. All the themes, all the important developments, give proof of extremely urgent care for both unity and variation. The Quartet, opus 3, marks a deepening of these preoccupations; completely outside of tonal functions, its harmony is linked much more closely to the intervallic idea. From the perspective of pursuit of the developments, the working of motives here is infinitely more subtle than in the first two works; finally, in its expression, this Quartet is not far from the *Lyrische Suite* of fifteen years later. Certain forms of instrumental writing already bear so strongly the imprint of Berg that one will rediscover them, not greatly altered, in the later work. Whereas the Sonata was in a single movement, the Quartet is in two movements opposed to one another both in character and in tempo; we still are far, it seems, from both the multiplicity and the complexity of the *Lyrische Suite*. It is noticeable that in this period too

Berg made his only essay with "small form," *Lieder* apart. Whereas at the time Schoenberg's great preoccupation was precisely that "small form" (Little Pieces, opus 19, and, later, *Pierrot lunaire*) and Webern found in it throughout his life the most adequate means of expression, I believe that Berg never felt completely at ease in that realm: the experience of the Pieces for Clarinet and Piano was never repeated. For the rest, they do not display a true conception of "small form," being rather a reduction, a condensation, of a larger formal type.

The Pieces for Orchestra, opus 6, with the *Peter Altenburg Lieder*, opus 4, signaled Berg's first contact with large orchestra. Just as in his writing, so in the manner of his instrumentation, one encounters an irrepressible tendency to complexity. His orchestra is not one of those which can be called "clear"; it has reference rather to a Wagner-Mahler tradition from which Strauss is absent. In the Pieces, opus 5, the sound-density reaches saturation by the accumulation and superimposition of all the categories of timbre. In this case, it is not a matter of illusory density caused by simple doublings, but an accumulation of real parts, at times moving along with some misunderstanding of the arrangements attributed to the different instrumental groups.

Performance turns out to be very difficult if one wishes to avoid an opacity that weakens the discourse by its heaviness, by the unmanageability of its dynamics, and by a bad division between principal and secondary motives. In these pieces, Berg created an orchestral sonority that foreshadowed the one he would deploy some years later in *Wozzeck;* the third piece is characteristic in that respect. With these pieces ends the period that I have called preparatory, in which we see Berg becoming conscious of his personal needs and of the historical context in which he was placed, a consciousness that completed his break with the tonal world and consolidated his means for creating a hierarchy outside tonality by an adequate use of thematic material. That first evolution came about without bruises; it was with complete naturalness that Berg found himself ready, by his work and his evolution, to compose his principal masterpieces.

Wozzeck, the *Kammerkonzert*, and the *Lyrische Suite* are capital data in the evolution of Berg and in the history of music. These works are properties of first importance in the domains to which they belong—the opera, the chamber group, the string quartet. Here again one encounters the same formal preoccupations, almost the same manias—for example, the use of symmetrical forms in which one section is the exact retrograde of the other. I noted that in order to compose *Wozzeck*, Berg had first to give Büchner's fragments a definitive form; he reduced the number of scenes from twenty-six to fifteen and gave them a dramatic schema certainly more traditional than Büchner would have tried, to judge from his two completed works. This schema can be described as follows: (*a*) *exposition*, the first five scenes, making up Act I; (*b*) *peripety*, which includes the five scenes constituting the second act; (*c*) *catastrophe*, with the five final scenes grouped in Act III. To recapitulate the plot, we can say that it tells the story of a poor soldier, Wozzeck: his superiors abuse his naïveté; his mistress, Marie, deceives him; he kills her and commits suicide. The formal armature that Berg gave this text was to serve him in establishing the architecture of his music firmly. One discovers a certain parallelism between Acts I and III, which enclose the longer and more important Act II; thus one arrives at a sort of A–B–A schema. Furthermore, Act II uses forms more rigorous than the free forms utilized in Acts I and III. Each act, finally, concludes with a cadence on the same chord—with, however, modifications in its disposition.

The five scenes of Act I are composed this way: a Suite, a Rhapsody, a Military March, followed by a Lullaby, a Passacaglia, and a Rondo. These five scenes can be described as character pieces (*Charakterstücke*), each one of them portraying the relations of the chief protagonist, Wozzeck, with other personages of the drama as they appear. The five scenes of Act II make up five movements of a symphony: sonata movement, fantasy and fugue, largo, scherzo, rondo with introduction. The five final scenes, in Act III, can be considered as *inventions:* first scene, invention on a theme; second scene, invention on a tone (this is the renowned scene of the murder of Marie, with a B repeated constantly, until the entire orchestra has become nothing but the monstrous prolongation of that single note; the effect is considerable); third scene, invention on a rhythm; fourth scene, invention on a chord (in which one finds, related to the drowning of Wozzeck, a highly successful effect of sonorous engulfment), followed by an invention on a tonality (orchestral interlude in D minor); fifth scene, invention on a regular progression of eighth-notes (which ends the opera in a sort of musical indifference, comparable to the indifference of the children in the drama to the death of the two chief protagonists).

In view of that presentation, one might think that Berg had returned to the older form of opera in separate numbers as it was practiced before Wagner; in reality, his genius was to resolve the antinomy between a closed conception and that of the continuous musical drama as Wagner left it. *Wozzeck* thus sums up the opera as such—and perhaps therefore has ended the history of that form: after such a work, it really means that the musical spectacle must seek other means of expression. From the thematic point of view, the leitmotiv here plays a role very different from its role in Wagner; it truly serves to elaborate the forms, and thus integrates the dramatic thought and the musical thought in the most satisfying and adequate way possible. If it is impossible in a brief résumé to set forth the numerous utilizations of this procedure—the motive subjected to multiple variations, which gives the fifteen scenes of

Wozzeck the strongest possible coherence—I nevertheless must emphasize that use of musical forms in the opera because Berg attached extreme importance to it. He wrote an article on that subject in which he defended his conception with aggressive violence against his detractors. "It is allowed me to believe," he wrote, "that all the musical forms to be met with in the course of the work have succeeded. I can demonstrate in the most thorough and persuasive manner their appropriateness and the reason they are there. If anyone wants to be convinced, let him address himself to me. I shall give him the information very willingly." In another text, also apropos of *Wozzeck*, Berg also said: "Each scene, each musical entr'acte, then, must be seen has having its own musical visage and be identifiable, a coherent and clearly outlined autonomy. That imperious demand has as a consequence the so-much discussed use of old or new musical forms customarily used only in *pure music*. Only they could guarantee the pregnancy and distinctness of the various pieces." He added, and this is not the least important of his declarations: "Whatever acquaintance may be made with the multiplicity of musical forms contained in this opera, with the rigor and logic with which they were elaborated, with the combinatory direction that was worked into even their smallest details from the rising of the curtain to its final falling, not a single person in the audience will be able to distinguish the special place of these various *fugues* and *inventions*, *suites* and *sonatas*, *variations* and *passacaglia*, as attention is not absorbed by anything but the idea of the opera, transcendent to the individual destiny of Wozzeck. I believe that in this I have succeeded."

Thus we see Berg pursuing efficacity—in this case dramatic—by the most erudite formal elaboration; we shall encounter that same tendency integrally—in purely instrumental form—in the *Kammerkonzert* and the *Lyrische Suite*. Let me again point out in *Wozzeck* the reiterated employment of the voice in *Sprechstimme* (or *Sprechgesang*) as Schoenberg already had used it, especially in his opera *Die glückliche Hand* and in *Pierrot lunaire*. That utilization of the voice formed part of Berg's attitude toward general vocal problems: he not only tried to utilize it in the sole form of *bel canto,* but also introduced "rhythmic declamation," which safeguards all the prerogatives of an absolute musical "structuration," something that could not be done with recitative. On another side, such a use facilitates comprehension of the text and considerably enriches the theatrical resources of the voice, which can pass through all the stages from *pure speaking* to *pure singing*. In an article on the subject, furthermore, Berg spoke, not without humor, of *bel parlare*.

The *Kammerkonzert* is placed under the sign of a "ternary order of events." This is perhaps the most rigorous work that Berg ever composed. It is made up of three movements: (1) *thema scherzoso con variazioni;* (2) *adagio*, (3) *rondo ritmico con introduzione* (cadenza). It also uses three instrumental families: (1) keyboard instrument: piano, (2) stringed instrument: violin, (3) wind instrument: the ensemble of the instrumental formation. The first movement is assigned to the piano and the wind ensemble; the second to the violin and the wind ensemble; the third to the piano, the violin, and the wind ensemble; this last movement is preceded by a cadenza for the two solo instruments. In his formal conception, properly speaking, one sees Berg progressively approaching the serial technique, in the sense that in the first movement he makes large play with the four contrapuntal forms of a theme as the basis of the development in the first four variations, the fifth returning to the original theme (these forms are the original, the inversion, the retrograde, and the inversion of the retrograde). In the same way, the melodic phrase for the violin, in the second movement is made up of four forms of a series; this movement, furthermore, is wholly retrograde from its middle on. Finally, the third movement is the combination—with rhythmic modifications and modifications of registers—of the music of the first two movements; that combination is carried out in three different ways. A detailed analysis would lead us to a conception of form based wholly on a ternary character at the same time as it makes appeal to general serial structures even though the vocabulary is not entirely linked to a series. In this work, then, serial forms speaks of a more far-reaching elaboration than usual of the thematic material itself, which furthermore was selected for the purpose.

In the *Lyrische Suite,* Berg employs for the first time a strict twelve-tone technique. He applies it, what is more, to exactly half of the work so as to oppose it to a "free" making in the other half. It goes without saying that the sections, serial or not, are closely woven in the course of a movement, and that in the general framework of the composition, the movements, serial or not, correspond and form completely concerted symmetries. I already have pointed out the dramatic progression and the lacing of tempos of which the ensemble of movements gives proof. Once again, the *Lyrische Suite* makes use of well-established schemas: the first movement is a sonata; the second a rondo; the third a scherzo; the fourth a *Lied;* the fifth a double scherzo; the sixth a rhapsody. From the serial point of view, I single out the *Allegro misterioso* as the most successful movement; it includes, in fact, a use of the permutations of the series which creates a sort of harmonic stasis inside perpetual movement; furthermore, as concerns the instrumentation, the use of the various ways of playing with the bow and in pizzicato, which alternate in a functional way, creates a sonority that is essentially shifting and constantly differentiated. The thematic relations from one movement to another are extremely subtle and form an uninterrupted chain from beginning to end of the quartet; this is, furthermore, one of the most original aspects of Berg, the constant preoccupation with a thematic chain followed throughout the work.

The *Lyrische Suite* certainly marks one of the most important dates in the history of the string quartet; everything contributes to making this work a privileged monument: the abundance and diversity of its inspiration, the certainty and mastery of its form, the completeness and perfection of its instrumental realization all concur in the synthesis that Berg was seeking when composing the work. He had reached a point of extremely rare balance which he would not maintain in his succeeding works.

With *Lulu*, Berg did not succeed in finding again the exceptional conjunction so happily arrived at for *Wozzeck*. The text cannot be compared in poetic tenor or dramatic force to Büchner's. The music displays something of Wedekind's gross esthetic; it is not free of bad taste, far from it. The use of fixed forms, which had served Berg so well in *Wozzeck*, here seems veneered on. However, it entered well into the composer's intention to accentuate the synthesis of separate numbers and continuous drama. All the musical episodes of the opera are derived from a single row of twelve tones related to the character of Lulu; other series are drawn from that original series to form thematic figures related to various other personages and certain dramatic actions. Alwa, Doctor Schön, the Gräfin Geschwitz are thus bodied forth by derived series. It also happens that the instrumental color suffices to characterize certain of the protagonists; the athlete in particular always is signified by alternations of the white keys and black keys of the piano. (I should also note the first important use of the vibraphone in the orchestra.) As in *Wozzeck*, here again we find, as a result of theatrical necessity, real stage musics; but where in *Wozzeck* they were military marches and waltzes, the action here calls for modern dances, among others a tango and an English waltz. On this basis alone, one is tempted to make a comparison with Stravinsky's *Histoire du soldat*, in which a like stylization of popular dances operates: with Stravinsky, the humor perhaps is more incisive and more virulent, making evident the derisory side of such stylization; with Berg; the writing is so complex that the parody often becomes tacky. Also, the most "expressive" passages in the opera denote a clear degeneration from the quality to which Berg has habituated us. It is easy to discern in the musical text an undeniable turgidity or, at other junctures, a slightly insipid preciosity. In *Lulu*, the vocal part is still more elaborate than in *Wozzeck;* all the resources of the voice are utilized; Berg here is very meticulous in the notation of effects stretching from speaking to singing, and this in the extreme senses. Certain fragments are played without music; in others, the coloratura deploys a quasi-traditional virtuosity. Recitative also makes its reappearance, whereas one finds only a few measures of it in *Wozzeck*. As to the use of forms, here it is linked to the characters of the protagonists and not, more simply, to the organization of the scenes; thus a form is led to circulate throughout the work: the sonata form and the rondo form are related to the existence and evolution of the two principal male characters. That is certainly Berg's most interesting innovation in this opera; here one encounters again his profound need to conceive vast, ramified ensembles.

After one has spoken of *Lulu*, not much remains to be said of the cantata *Der Wein*. This work, furthermore, is not in Berg's best vein and bears the stigmata of bad taste and preciosity. Here again one finds a tango, in the most direct connection with *Lulu*. Furthermore, the poems that Berg used are not among Baudelaire's best. The employment of the series does not seem to have placed him at his ease, and he tries to rediscover tonal possibilities that the serial technique does not at all need.

Berg's last work, the Violin Concerto, displays that same will toward "conciliation"; however, it is more successful than the other works of that period. Perhaps it was the exceptionally happy choice of the series used, perhaps it was also a sort of spontaneous inspiration—for we know that the Concerto was composed in a very short time, an exceptional occurrence with Berg. As always, the form very visibly displays preoccupations with symmetry: the first part contains two movements, *Andante* and *Allegretto*, movements of which the tempos are neighbors in a half-scale. The second part also contains two movements, *Allegro* and *Adagio*, which, on the contrary, mark the two extreme tempos of a stretched-out scale. Furthermore, they are disposed in contrary directions, two by two; otherwise said, the tempos may be viewed as shaping a sort of arch. Berg again indulged his penchant for citation here, as in the second movement one hears a popular song and the fourth movement consists of variations on a chorale harmonized by Bach. In that fourth movement we find in the showiest way Berg's anguish between the tonal world, which he aspired to preserve, and the serial world, which he foresaw as a necessity. Unhappily, the relations between the two universes, however ingeniously managed they may be, are never convincing; and the legend that has grown up around this work (it was his final composition, and the chorale chosen is a farewell to the world) cannot, despite everything, soften us sufficiently to justify, as a matter of style, that attempt at synthesis. Let me say that this was perhaps the most spectacular of Berg's dramatic gestures. The tonality of the Concerto oscillates between the two relative keys of G minor and B-flat major; this return to a vague, diluted tonality is more successful here, it is well to recognize, than in the works in which Schoenberg used the same procedure—the *Ode to Napoleon*, for instance.

From a study of Berg's *oeuvre* one can easily deduce that he was one of the most significant composers of his era. Through the profound organic complexity that he folds into his creations, through the intense dramatic power that he breathed into them, he succeeded in giving a form its greatest significant force. The technical means that he employed—in *Wozzeck*, for example—to describe extremely strained situations made use of the most rigorous techniques. One may cite in particular the second-act fugue that so well depicts the desultory conversation between Wozzeck and the two other protagonists. I have, furthermore, pointed out Berg's need for citation, whether of a musical text or of a form or orchestra, a popular song, etc. This need not only put in relief what one has called a dramatic gesture; on the contrary, it also brings to light, the "discrepancy" that existed in Berg's mind between a composed music and a sort of musical stereotype; in this, he came close to one aspect of Stravinsky. The stage musics found abundantly in *Wozzeck* and *Lulu* should be understood as stereotypes integrated *en bloc*, organically, to the musical developments. Thus we find ourselves in the presence of an idea that has more or less intrinsic value according to the musical text and according to the esthetic quality with which it is hoped to charge it and the emotive, anecdotal power with which it can be endowed. We are in the presence of a poetic art that attempts to establish relationships of composite style. Comparing Webern and Berg in their poetic equivalents, one might say that Webern's search can be identified reasonably with that of Mallarmé in the *Sonnets*, whereas Berg's would be close to the spirit of Lautréamont. That is precisely why Berg's influence now has proved less decisive than Webern's despite the much greater immediate impact of his music. We can believe that when the stylistic of our epoch has become more assured, the influence of Berg may be felt in a more profitable fashion. It would be useless, in any case, to see in Berg only a hero rent by his contradictions or not to consider him as more than the end result of romanticism, one whose example will now be useless. On the contrary, by transposing the contradictions that are the key to his work outside the phenomena that gave them birth, one can take a most profitable esthetic lesson from Berg. His *oeuvre* still guards intact all its potential for influence; that is what contributes to giving it an irreplaceable value in the musical domain of our epoch.

Debussy,

CLAUDE (ACHILLE), FRENCH COMPOSER
(SAINT-GERMAIN-EN-LAYE, AUGUST 22, 1862—PARIS, MARCH 25, 1918)

He came from a family of *petits-bourgeois;* nothing destined him for music. His brothers and sister, with whom he maintained very little contact throughout his life, had no artistic gifts. With him, on the contrary, such gifts were manifested early. Various anecdotes are told of Debussy's first encounters with music; the best-known of them describes the child playing on an old piano military marches that he had heard in the street . . . His parents intended him to be a sailor. A stay at Cannes, his first encounter with the sea, remained engraved upon his memory for a long time; at Cannes, too, he took his first piano lessons, with one Cerutti. A little later, Mme Mauté de Fleurville, a pupil of Chopin (and Verlaine's mother-in-law), heard him playing the piano and was struck by his talent. She gave him lessons that were the real start of his musical apprenticeship. She inculcated in him a love for the piano like the one Chopin had transmitted to her, and it may have been in memory of that decisive initiation that Debussy, near the end of his life, composed the *Études pour piano* dedicated to the memory of Chopin. Mme Mauté de Fleurville helped her pupil's progress enough so that in 1873 he was able to enter the Paris Conservatoire in Lavignac's solfeggio class and then, two years later, in 1875 (he was thirteen), Marmontel's piano class. At the Conservatoire, solfeggio always has been studied with great care, as a sort of introduction to writing, properly speaking: it forms the ear in the best possible fashion. Lavignac appears to have been marvelously understanding with his pupil; himself still a young professor at that time, he willingly took an interest in Debussy's notions about the teaching of a discipline that his pupil sometimes thought faultily taught. Stronger in musical dictation than in theory, Debussy obtained a first prize in solfeggio in 1876. His lessons with Marmontel were more stormy: the professor, considerably older, could not understand his pupil's neglect of the exercises for the pleasure of sight-reading. He did not, however, fail to perceive the exceptional qualities of this extraordinary student, for one day he remarked to Ernest Guiraud: "That devil Debussy doesn't love the piano at all, but he loves music very much"; Guiraud was to play a determining role in Debussy's future studies. Debussy made small progress with the piano, although in 1877 he won a second prize in piano, which was granted more to the musician than to the virtuoso. He remained content with that, and all his life remembered the pleasures and displeasures of that period in Marmontel's class. It is said that he did not play Beethoven well, but felt much more at his ease in *Das wohltemperirte Clavier*, Schumann's sonatas, and pieces by Chopin; he had a touch of captivating charm. In class, he had a habit of preluding with arpeggios or chords of a "baroquism" that greatly astonished his professor; on the day when Debussy was awarded the Prix de Rome, Marmontel recalled him to Massenet and Delibes in these terms: "Ah! the rascal! He amused himself in my class with Chopin's harmonies! I'm much afraid that he didn't find them salty enough . . ." One cannot say that Debussy had found inspiration for them with his professor of harmony, Émile Durand: Maurice Emmanuel, in his study of *Pelléas et Mélisande*, describes that personage as not loving music, his profession, or his students. Debussy preserved a not very agreeable memory of his teaching, in which automaticism disputed with tastelessness. The "*chants donnés*" were a special horror to him; as for the *marches—"rosalies"* in student jargon—they were the pedagogue's mania, and Debussy rebelled against that stupid form of vulgarity. He won no prizes in harmony, leaving that honor to better disciples. In the long run, however, relations between professor and pupil improved, for the young Debussy dedicated to his master a Trio for piano, violin, and violoncello, with this agreeable enough inscription: "Lots of notes accompanied with lots of friendship." During his time at the Conservatoire, he aroused durable animosities, the most notorious of them in Camille Bellaigue, his happy rival in the piano class, who would become the most vicious of his detractors some years later. In 1879, Marmontel recommended Debussy to a woman of the world, Mme Nadejda Filaretovna von Meck, who was looking for a pianist to read new scores with her: she was smitten with Tchaikovsky, whom she adored without ever approaching him in person. In the abundant correspondence that she carried on with her favorite composer, one finds some references to the young "Bussy," as she called him. Thanks to his encounter with her, Debussy came into contact with European cosmopolitan life; he traveled through Europe, stopping in Florence, Venice, Vienna, and Moscow. Through Mme von Meck, he met Wagner in Venice, and in Vienna heard *Tristan* for the first time; thus he emerged from his very narrow Paris milieu. After so brilliant a summer, returning to the Conservatoire was not at all pleasant. In 1880, in Auguste-Ernest Bazille's class, Debussy carried off the first prize in accompaniment, which was awarded as much to knowledge as to ability. One can measure the way in which the young musician's natural gifts were developing: to be able to play a figured bass at sight, improvise an accompaniment to a song, reduce an orchestral score, transpose any piece of music whatever—all that certainly contained more of interest than mediocre exercises in harmony. When undertaking the study of composition, Debussy preferred Ernest Guiraud's class. However, Massenet, professor of the other composition class, more famous than ever, was the veritable man of the day (we are in 1880). Debussy's attitude toward Massenet was always a little distant. But he was on excellent terms with Guiraud as both teacher and man. Maurice Emmanuel recounts in detail some Debussy-Guiraud conversations that show how often the prevision of a genius is in advance of its achievements; he already was giving voice to points of view about the lyric theater which later would lead to *Pelléas*. Debussy spent the following summer with Mme von Meck. According to her children, he spent three successive summers in their family; there has been much discussion of the importance of these sojourns to his evolution as a composer and of the contacts that he may have made with music in the Muscovite milieu. Some writers make much of Gypsy songs that Debussy may have heard in the city's cabarets; others believe that his discovery of Mussorgsky and *Boris Godunov* dates from this period. Debussy's relation to Russian music was studied at length by André Schaeffner, who has dealt with that subject definitively. Russian influence upon him was exercised in a very capricious way, and his trips, whatever may have been the preeminence of Gypsies or of Mussorgsky, considerably enlarged his familiar horizon as a composer—a point of departure for the interest shown throughout his life in Russian art, an interest that revived when Diaghilev took his operatic and ballet troupes to France. His encounter with the Vasniers unquestionably was a capital event for his general and musical culture: Vasnier was a cultivated architect, a great amateur of the art of his time; thanks to him, Debussy came to know the poetry and painting worth considering. For Mme Vasnier, with whom he was more or less in love, he composed numerous songs and thus acquired a truly exceptional *vocal* knowledge. (He met Mme Vasnier in Mme Moreau-Sainti's singing course, for which he served as accompanist. He was also coach of the Chorale Concordia, the president of which was Gounod, who at once took an interest in him and proclaimed him a genius to anyone who would listen.) The Vasniers had a villa at Ville-d'Avray, to which Debussy went with pleasure, finding in that milieu the refinement and independence that he had lacked up to then. From that period date the first Debussy songs that we know, written for high soprano (Mme Vasnier). We have a first version of the *Fêtes galantes* (on poems by Verlaine); the celebrated *Mandoline* was composed at this time. Vasnier strongly encouraged him to prepare himself for the Prix de Rome, at that time the key to any musical career. Debussy won it in 1884 with *L'Enfant prodigue*, a cantata that reveals his dramatic and lyric gifts no less than it shows the strong influence of Lalo and Massenet. A surprising anecdote reveals the tacit—or, rather, the inevitable—influence of Massenet on the works of this young man, whose aggressive independence was notorious. According to Louis Laloy, Debussy showed Guiraud a score for Théodore de Banville's *Diane au bois*. Guiraud then warned him: "You must keep that for later or you'll never get the Prix de Rome." So Debussy ably seasoned his cantata with Massenet to please the members of the Institut, among whom, furthermore, Gounod's voice was preponderant. Later, in a page of *Monsieur Croche, anti-dilettante*, Debussy recorded with melancholy his impressions on the day when he was declared winner of the competition: " 'You've won a prize,' someone said, tapping me on the shoulder. Whether you believe it or not, I can nonetheless assert that all my joy collapsed! I saw clearly the boredoms, the irritations that the smallest official title fatally brings. What was more, I felt that I was no longer free . . ." He found the stay in Rome a veritable torture. Decidedly, the *hors classe* winners of the Prix de Rome did not appreciate their stay at the Villa Medici (are the numerous anecdotes about Berlioz's stay there remembered?). In his correspondence with Vasnier, Debussy abundantly slandered the Villa Medici. Lodged in a chamber known as the "Etruscan Tomb," he was bored and longed for the brilliant milieu of his Parisian haunts. His fellow pensioners—

musicians, painters, or sculptors—generally only repelled him. He found them gross, uncultured, not interested in anything that mattered to him. He often threatened to resign, finding his life in Rome completely "abominable," and saying that he was unable to do any work and that his inventive faculties were on the way to annihilation; in short, he could not bear so much ennui. However, he worked at the required "*envois*"; he began a symphonic ode entitled *Zuleïma*, after Heine's *Almanzor;* he turned back to *Diane au bois*, which he had begun in Paris; finally he composed *Printemps*. The Institut was by no means enchanted with these three *envois*: the reports of the Académie des Beaux-Arts show little tenderness toward the young musician. Apropos of *Zuleïma*: "Monsieur Debussy seems tormented by a desire to create the bizarre, the incomprehensible, the unperformable." As for *Printemps*, they denounced "this vague impressionism, which is extremely dangerous . . . in works of art." It truly seems that this was the first time that the term "impressionism" was used in connection with Debussy's music; the term was then much in vogue because the painters thus ticketed had become famous through scandal.

The three scores all had the same destiny, and we know them only by hearsay. Of *Zuleïma*, Debussy said laconically: "It calls Verdi and Meyerbeer to mind too much"; *Diane au bois* did not satisfy him at all, and he gave up completing it. Of *Printemps* one knows a symphonic version published much later, the orchestration of which is not by Debussy. The original score was conceived for chorus and orchestra, but all that remains of it is a choral version with piano accompainment. It never has been established clearly if it was on his own that Debussy gave up the task of orchestration before presenting the score to the members of the Institut. Finally, the only completed work dating from his Roman period is *La Damoiselle élue;* this *envoi* was to have been performed during the meeting organized by the Institut for a hearing of the young composer's works, but when it was decided to perform only *La Damoiselle élue*, and not *Printemps* too, Debussy, disgusted by that arbitrary selection, withdrew both works, so that the first audition did not take place until much later. *La Damoiselle élue* was composed in 1887–8, but was played for the first time only in 1893, at the Société Nationale. This work marked Debussy's meeting—and more generally that of the French symbolist milieu—with the English Pre-Raphaelites; in fact, it used a lyric poem "after Dante Gabriel Rossetti"—*The Blessed Damozel* in a French translation by Gabriel Sarrazin. The score leans strongly toward the "decadent" aspect of Pre-Raphaelite esthetics; the music is a little white and at moments of a very insipid preciosity. In its best passages it foreshadows what will be found in *Le Martyre de Saint-Sébastien* on a much higher plane and with a much richer and more developed musicality. Another work that Debussy composed during this period became known only after his death—a Fantaisie for piano and orchestra. The Société Nationale was to have given its first performance on April 21, 1890, but Debussy withdrew the score at the last moment—we do not know for what reason—and the work was not performed. Did he, perhaps, find it too academic? Its symphonic technique and thematic work seem to have obeyed too strictly the imperatives of "large" concert music as it was then conceived, particularly in Vincent d'Indy's entourage.

Having returned to Paris at the beginning of 1887, Debussy there completed or even composed his *envois* from Rome. He rediscovered the atmosphere that pleased him, and at once felt more at ease. We know little about the first years of his post-Roman Paris existence: he always showed so much discretion on this subject that it has never been possible to solve the mystery. According to fragmentary statements from various sources—they do not always agree—we know that he began a *Chimène* to a libretto by Catulle Mendès, a work that did not satisfy him a little later; in any case, he gave up the idea of having it performed. In 1887, he met Mallarmé and frequented his apartment in the rue de Rome, then renowned among the young intellectuals for its "Tuesdays." Many writers went there, but Debussy seems to have been one of the few musicians who approached Mallarmé. One knows that the poet, like all the symbolists, cherished a veritable cult for Wagner. Debussy did not break that rule: for some years he was one of the fervent admirers of the Bayreuth master, considering him the greatest musician of his time. In 1888, he made a first trip to Bayreuth; he returned there in 1889, hearing with great emotion *Parsifal*, *Tristan*, and *Die Meistersinger*. It is possible that in 1887 he also called upon Brahms, whom he might have met during a visit to Vienna, and with whom he may have had the honor of dining and of going to hear *Carmen*. The pilgrimages to Bayreuth left more memories than the supposed visit with Brahms; that would not be astonishing. Debussy's discovery of *Boris Godunov* is placed in 1889, when his friend Jules de Brayer lent him a copy of the score. This was, it seems, the original version, as the opera had not yet undergone the recasting by Rimsky-Korsakov. These encounters show Debussy in formation: although one cannot pick out immediate, precise traces of these influences, one supposes that they were deep, as is testified to by the products of his next years.

In 1888, Debussy published six *ariettes*, the future *Ariettes oubliées* (a title tinged with irony if one considers the indifference with which their first performance was greeted). In 1890 appeared the *Cinq Poèmes de Baudelaire*, also for voice and piano. This is the work in which Wagner's influence shows most clearly: the *Ariettes oubliées* surely are "more Debussyan" than the *Cinq Poèmes de Baudelaire*. Perhaps Verlaine's text constrained the musician less than Baudelaire's sumptuous poems. In *Le Jet d'eau* one can even detect Russian influence—not at all Mussorgsky, but Borodin. The *Cinq Poèmes* is one of Debussy's capital works even if only in that it served him as exorcism; delivered from a ponderous influence, he would thereafter be able to direct himself toward other horizons, which he would have been unable to do without having "liquidated" the Wagnerian heritage. The Exposition Universelle of 1889 revealed the Javanese theater to Debussy. Both its scenic esthetic and its musical sonorities gave him one of the most enduring shocks, echoes of which are found in his correspondence much later. Perhaps it was thanks to this Far Eastern theater that Debussy could detach himself from the Wagnerian grasp; it was not without irony that he noted: "The Annamites showed the embryo of an opera in which the tetralogical formula can be recognized. Only there are more gods and less décors. A small, ill-tempered clarinet conducts the emotion. A tam-tam organizes the terror . . . and that is all. No special theater, no hidden orchestra. Nothing but an instinctive need for art which is ingenious in finding satisfaction . . ." The shock of that tradition, codified differently than that of the Occident, but just as powerfully, undoubtedly was going to precipitate a rupture between the new music and traditional European elements. One may ask oneself if such an impression of freedom was not aroused by ignorance of the strict conventions of Asiatic music. Certainly its sound-scales were richer and more particularized than those common in Europe at the time, its rhythmic structures of a differently supple complexity. The acoustic power of its instruments themselves differed totally from that of our instruments. But, above all, the poetic imposed itself corrosively (one recalls the adventure of Van Gogh and Japanese painters at almost that same moment).

In that Paris of 1890, Debussy came to know Satie; there often has been talk of Satie's influence upon Debussy (the use of parallel ninth chords and those of superimposed fourths). It even is said that Satie's *Sarabandes* and *Gymnopédies* showed Debussy the way to harmonic discoveries that he would carry to a high degree of refinement. If that influence is occasionally to be felt, it is nonetheless true that Debussy owed the discovery of his harmonic vocabulary to himself. Satie remained in the state of a collector of rare objects: he never succeeded in integrating his "discoveries" into a coherent vocabulary. In orchestrating two of the *Gymnopédies*, Debussy paid a debt out of friendly regard rather than rendered real homage to Satie. From that period on, Debussy's originality was manifest: the composition of the celebrated *Prélude à L'Après-midi d'un faune* dates from 1892–4. Before speaking of that primordial work, I must mention the String Quartet in G, which was composed in 1893 and performed for the first time on December 29 of that year by the Ysaÿe Quartet. It is hard now to comprehend the reservations expressed after its first performance. The quartet then passed for the quintessence of musical art, but the minds of the enthusiasts most capable of enjoying the work were encumbered with a bundle of prejudices linked to memories of the Viennese school (Haydn, Mozart, and, most especially, Beethoven, who had recently been discovered in France). These people were surprised to encounter a work that was not a true quartet—that is, did not make use of the traditional schemas deduced from Viennese masterpieces. The models of that period remained César Franck and Vincent d'Indy—and the *Andantino* of Debussy's quartet contains reminiscences of Franck. Despite the "cyclic" construction that Debussy had adopted, his quartet disturbed serious amateurs by its formal liberty, by the new essence of its harmony, and finally by its instrumental writing, the best pages of which owed nothing to known predecessors. Ernest Chausson himself, then an intimate friend of Debussy, was unable wholly to accept a work that relied, he felt, upon intangible esthetic canons. Paul Dukas, however, did immediate justice to Debussy's quartet, recognizing in it a "melodic essence . . . concentrated but rich in flavor," a "harmonic tissue of penetrating and original poetry," a "harmony never harsh or hard . . . despite great audacities." Dukas added: "M. Debussy is particularly pleased by successions of full-bodied chords, by dissonances without crudity, more harmonious in their complication than consonances themselves . . ." The Quartet is not Debussy's masterpiece, but it heralded an undeniable renewal in the spirit of chamber music, which it pried loose from the rigid structure, congealed rhetoric, and rigoristic esthetic in which Beethoven's successors had shut it up; it introduced "modernity" into one of the forms of musical literature which had been least disposed to it, probably because of the small number and the demands of a caste: the "enlightened amateurs."

That "modernity" was going to triumph easily with a less restricted audience, one above all less prejudiced, one that did not raise pretentions to the point of considering itself privileged, "specialist,"—and that in a field forbidden to most amateurs. The *Prélude à L'Aprés-midi d'un faune*, given for the first time on December 22, 1894, by the Société Nationale under the direction of Gustave Doret, won success immediately; it was so much applauded that it had to be repeated. Undeniably, the *Prélude* gave proof of much greater audacity than the String Quartet; that doubtless was owing in large part to the poem, the extensions of which incited Debussy's thought to free itself of any scholastic impediment. This masterwork of Debussy's rapidly became the most popular of his concert works; it marked the decisive advent of a music merely foreseen by Mussorgsky. It has been said often: the flute of the *Faune* brought new breath to the art of music; what was overthrown was not so much the art of development as the very concept of form itself, here freed from the impersonal constraints of the schema, giving wings to a supple, mobile expressiveness, demanding a technique of perfect instantaneous adequacy. Its use of timbres seemed essentially new, of exceptional delicacy and assurance in touch; the use of certain instruments—flute, horn, and harp—showed the characteristic principles of the manner in which Debussy would employ them in later works. The writing for woodwinds and brasses, incomparably light-handed, performed a miracle of proportion, balance, and transparency. The potential of youth possessed by that score defies exhaustion and decrepitude; and just as modern poetry surely took root in certain of Baudelaire's poems, so one is justified in saying that modern music was awakened by *L'Après-midi d'un faune.* In the beginning, we know, Debussy intended to write a prelude, an interlude, and a final paraphrase of Mallarmé's poem; he acted only upon the idea of the prelude. Mallarmé thanked the young composer by inscribing on a copy of the poem this quatrain to him:

Sylvain d'haleine première
Si ta flûte a réussi,
Ouïs toute la lumière
Q'y soufflera Debussy.

In 1893, Maeterlinck's *Pelléas et Mélisande* was played at the Bouffes-Parisiens. Like the other young intellectuals of the day, Debussy was much struck by this very important manifestation of symbolism. Encouraged by his friends of the time, he resolved to set to music a play that had so impressed him. He sought out Maeterlinck in Belgium to obtain agreement. Pierre Louÿs went with him; in a letter, he gave a very amusing account of that meeting, which did not at all foretell the snarling misunderstanding that was to poison the atmosphere of the first performances of the opera. Maeterlinck's *Pelléas* appeared in the bookshops in 1892, the year that has been assigned to the anecdote of Debussy coming upon one of the recently published copies while browsing in a bookstore and hastening to buy it. As his opera was not performed until 1902, its composition is often said to have required ten years. In fact, Debussy labored for three or four years to give form to the work (a first version of it was finished about 1896); to give it definitive form required a longer effort, which stretched out over the succeeding years. He kept on revising his score ceaselessly up to the date of the *première;* at the last moment, he had to add the interludes to permit the changes of scenery.

In any case, his activity during those years was not limited to *Pelléas*. He composed the *Trois Chansons de Bilitis* (1897) to texts by Pierre Louÿs. These songs displayed his chief preoccupation of the period: the voice. Written as though by-products of the opera, they displayed the flowering of Debussy's melodic genius, far outdistancing the first collections, whether the *Ariettes oubliées* or the *Cinq Poèmes de Baudelaire*.

The three *Nocturnes—Nuages, Fêtes, Sirènes*—date from 1898–9; the third, which requires a female chorus, unhappily is omitted from many performances for economic reasons. (The mutilation of this triptych, performed so often, is true nonsense: it damages the first two pieces by destroying the total balance, breaking up the entire proportion of the group. As a result, the significance of *Fêtes* in particular is diminished.) The *Nocturnes* had originally been projected as a symphonic piece for violin and orchestra meant for the violinist Ysaÿe. Debussy's relations with Ysaÿe having become embittered—one does not know the cause—he later composed the work for orchestra alone in such a way that one would never suspect his first intention. The two first *Nocturnes* were played by Lamoureux on December 9, 1890; on October 27, 1901, Lamoureux also conducted the first integral performance of the work. The pieces owe their group title to the influence of Whistler, a friend of Mallarmé, some of whose pictures bear this title. Debussy described his intentions in a brief commentary:

> The title *Nocturnes* is to be taken here in a very general and, above all, very decorative sense. It does not, then, refer to the usual form of the nocturne, but to what that word contains of impressions and of special lights. *Nuages:* this is the unchangeable aspect of the sky, with the slow, melancholy march of the clouds ending in a gray agony slightly tinged with black. *Fêtes:* this the motion, the dancing rhythm of the atmosphere, with shafts of brusque light; it is also the episode of a cortège (a dazzling, chimerical vision) passing through the fête, becoming mixed with it; but the background remains, persists, and is always the fête and

its mixture of music and of luminous dust participating in a total rhythm. *Sirènes:* it is the sea and its unnumberable rhythm; then, among waves silvered by the moon, is heard, laughing and passing, the mysterious song of the Sirens.

In the *Nocturnes*, Debussy pursued the quest for freedom which he had begun with the *Prélude à L'Après-midi d'un faune:* he renounced traditional symphonic schemas and the thematic obligatory in the material of a work for large orchestra—and did so with a maturity that affirmed the seductions of more complex harmonic texture and more exquisite instrumental color. The English horn of *Nuages* prolongs the flute of the *Faune* by the new breathing that the composer sustains; his esthetic ambition was obliging him to find a new syntax, escaping from the canons and taboos of the Franckist school. The freshness and beauty of inspiration that the *Nocturnes* retain give them a position in the first rank of the contemporary repertoire.

Talk still goes on about the first performance of *Pelléas et Mélisande* and the scandal that it provoked, a scandal that had been preceded long before by that of *Tannhäuser* and was to be followed by that of *Le Sacre du printemps.* Debussy's friends had been trying unsuccessfully for a long time to have *Pelléas* accepted by an opera director. In 1898, André Messager, a convinced admirer of Debussy's music, succeeded in having its staging at the Opéra-Comique accepted in principle, thanks to Albert Carré, then director of that house. A quarrel between Debussy and Maeterlinck intervened on the subject of who was to portray Mélisande. Maeterlinck wanted the role assigned to Georgette Leblanc; Debussy refused. The selection of Mary Garden aroused Maeterlinck's anger; in his fury, he went as far as to wish that the whole thing would fail. Predisposed by numerous stories in the papers and by dubious information, the audiences at the dress rehearsal and at the *première* (respectively April 27 and 30, 1902) reacted in the stupidest of ways; rarely has an audience displayed such aggressive stupidity. Criticism surpassed itself that day: with Camille Bellaigue in the lead, it cumulated in incomprehension, incompetence, pretentiousness, stupidity, ridiculousness, imbecility; an anthology of the criticisms published after the performance of *Pelléas* would be a worthy companion to similar collections devoted to *Le Sacre du printemps* or to *Wozzeck*. The chief complaints formulated? Absence of melody and rhythm, the cacophony of the orchestra. These critiques would not be worth noticing if the spectacle were not repeated in each generation. Despite the sharp attacks of which it was the object, *Pelléas* became a success; the receipts of the Opéra-Comique show that interest in this revolutionary work increased. So many people later boasted of having attended the *première* of *Pelléas* that the occasion would have had to be a triumph; in reality, it was a very turbulent occasion.

At present, the two or three mediocre performances of *Pelléas et Mélisande* given annually by the Opéra-Comique do not attract audiences; they exert no influence because their mediocrity is unable to woo the public away from inveterate idolatries. The music of *Pelléas* has taken rank as a masterpiece, but one cannot say the same of Maeterlinck's text, which has aged terribly; its *démodé* symbolism has become caricature.

Debussy had created a new form of lyric art, which contrasts violently with Wagner's esthetic; certain effusions aside, the radically different vocal writing is presented as recitative discreetly underlined by the orchestra. Debussy has given value just as much to French vocal characteristics as to French prosody. French voices generally dispose of a rather restricted *tessitura*, both because of the ambitus of the language and because of a certain tradition; it tends to approach as closely as possible pure declamation, which evolves within an excessively restricted register. Today, certain defects of *Pelléas* have become clear (perhaps I am mistaken, but I cannot keep from formulating certain complaints): the musical form does not make maximal use of its power of expression and construction;

certain scenes seem to me too visibly made out of fragments joined end to end, their harmonic repetitions and progressions (in combinations of two measures) accentuating the simplistic symmetry of musical ideas from which this treatment evaporates the real emotional strength. Furthermore, one does not grasp the basis for that stubborn insistence upon bringing the vocal line so obstinately toward the condition of spoken declamation, seeing that the "artificial" conventions of sung opera are used: as much in exhausting the virtualities rather than wanting to dissimulate them by too-discreet allusions as in trying, by camouflaging them, to render them "natural"—there lie the reasons why certain scenes in *Pelléas* seem to me no less of doubtful "truth" than the fabricated deliria of *bel canto:* they show an esthetic insufficiently aware of the ambiguities in the convention. It is to the degree to which the musical structure—both vocal and instrumental—assumes full theatrical responsibility that today I find *Pelléas* an irreplaceable masterpiece. On the other hand, the ingenuity of the *infinite recitative* (probably replacing *infinite melody*) rapidly becomes mannered and, far from leading to the natural declamation that Debussy desires, rapidly devolves into irrelevance. This is to say that in my view *Pelléas* has aged because it was unable to dominate unrestrictedly or—because of the contradictions that distort it—to regenerate the exhausted form that opera had become.

After *Pelléas et Mélisande*, Debussy's name signified something to the large public. His fame rapidly became worldwide; each of his later works was awaited, although each was always found disappointing in relation to the preceding work, which—it too—had disappointed in that same way. (That critical method is very monotonous, as it successively demolishes each new work to the benefit of the preceding masterpiece, which had been demolished earlier.)

On January 11, 1902, Ricardo Viñes won a lively success with the suite *Pour le piano* and its remarkable *Sarabande*.

Estampes (1903), *Masques* and *L'Isle joyeuse* (1904), the two books of *Images* (1905–8) marked the flowering of one form of Debussy's pianistic writing, in which *Children's Corner* (1906–8) provided an interlude of rest. An extremely brilliant period in the composer's evolution: he would go no farther in the utilization of the piano's resources, in the specific use of its timbre and colors. With that series of collections, he inaugurated a new way of writing for the instrument, one that most of his listeners would call musical impressionism. Never before had writing for the piano been so fluid, so varied, even so surprising, although one could locate its exact origin in certain pages of Chopin and Liszt. The young Ravel himself, issuing directly from Liszt, unquestionably influenced certain aspects of this piano-writing, and it has often been asserted that the *Soirée dans Grenade* owed much to Ravel's famous *Habanera* (later orchestrated in the *Rhapsodie espagnole*). Some resemblances do not diminish Debussy's genius at all; he transmuted in a totally personal manner what he may have conceived after reading Ravel. That series of piano pieces which he wrote between 1902 and 1908 is one of the monuments of piano literature. It is inconceivable that a composer should remain unaware of it or that a pianist should not assure himself of acquiring the exemplary technique that it demands.

Of the two large orchestral works that followed, *La Mer* was composed in 1904–5 (first performance at the Concerts Colonne on January 19, 1908, with Debussy conducting); the *Images* for orchestra were written between 1910 and 1913; they are in three sections—*Gigues* (first performance at the Concerts Colonne on January 26, 1913), *Ibéria* (first performance at the Concerts Colonne on February 20, 1910), and *Rondes de printemp* (first performance at the Concerts Durand on March 2, 1910).

Except for *Ibéria*, the *Images* remain badly known, and neither *Gigues* nor *Rondes des printemps* is ever played. The three pieces are looked upon as a folkloric triptych in which the failing imagination of Debussy, losing momentum, has had recourse to themes of popular inspiration in an attempt to recover final élan—empty reproaches of lack of originality or of nascent academicism leveled at Debussy by apologists for his youthful works; that triptych, on the contrary, displays a continuous evolution tending ceaselessly to renew the poetic feeling. *Gigues* and *Les Parfums de la nuit* (the second movement of *Ibéria*) seem to me to be the peaks of Debussy's art in that period of his development.

At the same time, new collections of songs appeared, among them *Trois Chansons de France* (1904), the second series of *Fêtes galantes* (1904), *Le Promenoir des deux amants* (1904–10), and finally the *Trois Ballades de Villon* (1910). They have more incisiveness of design than the youthful works; sometimes austere, they announce the intention of his final masterworks. Between 1910 and 1913, Debussy composed the two collections of *Préludes pour le piano*, transitional between the *Estampes* and *Images* on one side and the 1915 *Études* on the other. Not all of these are of equal value: some humoristic pieces become dated, the humor having evaporated. But in them one finds pages that equal the most beautiful poems that the literature of the piano contains.

At about this time, Debussy projected a new theatrical work, but was unstable and hesitant as he faced various possibilities considered. The one that occupied him longest was *La Chute de la Maison Usher*, after Poe's *The Fall of the House of Usher*, a story well designed to seduce him by the rare, fantastic quality of its inspiration. Another aspect of Poe's humor attracted him temporarily to *The Devil in the Belfry*. He also pondered a *Tristan et Yseult* (adapted by Joseph Bédier) and an *Orphée* (to a text by Victor Segalen). None of these projects came to fruition. He finally settled on, but rather because of the sudden accident of a commission than through premeditation and slowly matured conviction, *Le Martyre de Saint-Sébastien*, incidental music for the drama by Gabriele d'Annunzio. The first performance occurred on Monday, May 22, 1911, at the Théâtre du Châtelet, with Ida Rubinstein—who had ordered the music—as the principal interpreter. Even before that *première*, the work was put on the Index by the Archbishop of Paris, who found it unpleasant that the cult of Adonis should be joined to that of Jesus—paganism to Christianism. The reception was mediocre: Ida Rubinstein had larger financial than theatrical means. Furthermore, the work suffers from its genealogy: D'Annunzio's savoir-faire and Debussy's genius are strangely disparate. A gaudy, bloated, and ostentatious text could not be allied profoundly to music of rare distinction and refinement. Nonetheless, the music needs the support of the text; consequently, one cannot conceive of a performance without that balderdash, called poetic. Generally the text is reduced to the indispensable minimum by Draconian cuts. The symphonic fragments, extracted after the fact, probably at the publisher's wish and without Debussy's direct participation in their elaboration, deform the composer's thought because suppression of the vocal element (chorus and soloists), which is very important in the original version, is not at all justified except by the exigencies of publication. Thus, *Le Martyre* always suffers from its hetereogeneity. Jacques Rouche suggested to Debussy that he recast the score, give it coherence and independence, supremacy over a text reduced to a petrified amalgam; he died before undertaking anything of the sort. Recent attempts at performance prove incontestably that only Debussy himself would have been capable of wholly appropriate revision.

In 1912, Diaghilev asked Debussy, then at the zenith of his glory, to compose a ballet for his company; he proposed a story and choreography by Nijinsky on the theme of amorous jealousy among two young girls and a young man, tennis partners. Building up from that *Après-midi d'un faune* in sports clothes, Diaghilev conceived the ballet as a "plastic apologia for the 1913 man." The work was called *Jeux:* "That says conveniently the 'horrors' that pass among these three personages," Debussy then wrote to Stravinsky (the two composers were in regular contact from 1911 to 1914). The first performance took place on May 15, 1913, exactly two weeks before that of *Le Sacre du printemps* (May 29, 1913). *Le Sacre* blotted out Debussy's score, doing so the more easily, furthermore, because Nijinsky appears not to have given it a satisfactory realization. After that first failure, a sort of "curse" hung over *Jeux*, and the score was rarely played until recently, when it was seen to be one of its composer's most remarkable achievements. One has only to read certain critiques of the period to grasp how badly appreciation of it blundered: there is talk of competition with the young Stravinsky, of delitescence of musical ideas, of impotence to develop them; the composer is taxed with a painful diminution of creative faculties. Well, far from being pitifully sectioned, the structure is rich in inventions and of flowing complexity; it is cast in an extremely ductile form of thought founded on the idea of irreversible time. To *understand* it, one must submit to its development, for its constant evolution of thematic ideas disperses any symmetry of architecture (in music, memory of determining auditory landmarks plays somewhat the role of the field of vision in appreciating perspective). *Jeux* announced the achievement of a musical form that, in renewing itself instantaneously, implies a no less instantaneous way of hearing. The instrumentation is a logical outcome of the experiments made in *La Mer* and the *Images* with respect to individualization of timbre and acoustic conception of the orchestral ensemble. The orchestration-raiment, that primary notion, has disappeared in favor of orchestration-invention; the composer's imagination does not confine itself to successive composition of musical text and then its adornment with instrumental attractions; the very fact of orchestrating inflects not only the musical ideas, but also the mode of writing destined to set them forth—original alchemy, not ulterior chemistry. Finally, the general organization of the work is as changeable instant by instant as it is homogeneous in development. A single basic tempo is needed to regulate the evolution of the thematic ideas, a fact that makes interpretation very difficult because one must preserve that fundamental unity while one is casting into relief all the ceaselessly occurring incidents. Although the idiom is, morphologically speaking, less "advanced" than the vocabulary used by the generation that followed Debussy, *Jeux* nonetheless marks a capital date in the history of the contemporary esthetic. That renovation of the esthetic, although it did not coincide with radical questioning of the traditional morphology, was pursued in Debussy's final works, composed beween 1913 and 1917: *Trois Poèmes de Mallarmé* (1913), *Douze Études pour piano* (1915), *En Blanc et noir*, for two pianos (1915), and, finally, the sonatas: for piano and violoncello (1915), for flute, viola, and harp (1915), for piano and violin (1917). In that final group of chamber-music pieces—a genre he had not employed after composing the String Quartet—one sees the musician's drive toward a more delicate, more austere art, freer of immediate seductions but unequaled in richness of inspiration: they go on from *Jeux* in sounding an esthetic truth without visible precedent. These last works of Debussy include pages that belong among the most remarkable that he invented: the distance from the *Prélude à L'Après-midi d'un faune* to the piano *Études* is as great as that between the *Prélude* and the music that antedated it.

From 1910 on, Debussy suffered from a cancer of slow, continuous evolution: he died on March 25, 1918, in a distressed Paris preoccupied with war and bombardments. The event passed all but unnoticed. He was buried in Père-Lachaise on March 28 and later transferred to the Passy Cemetery.

Debussy certainly was not that "*musicien français*" dear to adepts wanting to reduce him to their own paltry dimension, although his belated patriotism willingly accepted that sobriquet. Furthermore, he was not an "impressionist," although he himself furnished pretexts for that limiting designation. The misunderstanding resulted from the titles of his works and from the fact that "Monsieur Croche talked about an orchestral scores as about a picture"—a simple question of antidilettantism. On the other side stands the great force of refusal with which he opposed the Schola: he took the side of "sound-alchemy" against the "beaver-science." He rejected the heritages and followed a dream of vitrified improvisation; he refused to play that game of construction which so often transforms the composer into a child playing architect; in his eyes, form was never a given thing; his pursuit of the unanalyzable was constant, developing so as to admit the rights of surprise and imagination. He had only disdain for the architectural monument, preferring structures mixing rigor and free will; with him, the words, the keys—all the scholarly apparatus—lost their sense and pertinence. Even if one expands the extension of the usual categories of an exhausted tradition, it cannot be applied to his work. He would have suffered in the face of the debauch of "classicism" which took place after his death. There are some hints of Pre-Raphaelitism in the procedure that led him to turn back to Villon and Charles d'Orléans, but that poetic deviation is not comparable to his successors' errors. The title *Hommage à Rameau* was not justified by any considerations of style—the piece is "in the style of a sarabande, but not rigorously." *The Debussy reality* excludes all academicism. Incompatible with any stereotyped order, with all ordering not created at the instant, that reality has remained isolated in Occidental music, the latest evolution of which has remained impermeable by it. The cause of that isolation is only too clear: Debussy rejected all hierarchy outside the musical moment itself. With him, and above all in his final works, musical time often changes in significance. Wanting to create his technique, create his vocabulary, and create his form, he was led to dispense completely with ideas that had remained static up to that time. Motion, the instant, irrupt into his music, not merely an impression of the instant, of the fugitive to which it has been reduced, but really a relative and irreversible conception of musical time and, more generally, of the musical universe. In the organization of sounds, that conception rejected the harmonic hierarchies existing as unique *données* of the sound-world. The relations between object and object were established in the context, following functions that were not constant. As for the rhythmic writing, it partakes of that manifestation no less, of that will toward mobility in the metric concept. In the same way, his experiments with timbre deeply modified the writing, the instrumental combinations, the sonority of the orchestra. Debussy's courage as a voluntary autodidact obliged him to rethink all aspects of musical creation. Doing that, he brought about a radical, though not always spectacular, revolution. The two portraits of M. Croche bear witness to that: in black—"They salute you with sumptuous epithets, and you are nothing but a rogue! something between a monkey and a domestic"; in white—"One must seek discipline in liberty and not in the formulations of a philosophy that has become decrepit and good only for the feeble." In the eyes of the builders, his fatal fault was that he promulgated nothing. There, nonetheless, you have the most fascinating myths. Debussy remains one of the most isolated of all musicians. Although his epoch at times forced him to find fugitive, feline solutions, in view of his incommunicable experience and his sumptuous reserve, he is the only universal French musician, at least during the nineteenth and twentieth centuries. He preserves a power of magical, mysterious seduction. His position at the beginning of the contemporary movement is a position in flux, but solitary. Moved by that "desire always to go farther which for him took the place of bread and wine," he contradicted in advance any attempt to relate him to the old order. We should not forget that Debussy's period was also Cézanne's and Mallarmé's—a triple conjunction that may lie at the root of all modernity, although one cannot exactly find any formulated teaching there. But no doubt it is possible that Debussy wanted it known that he needed to dream his revolution no less than to construct it.

Schoenberg,

ARNOLD, AUSTRIAN COMPOSER
(VIENNA, SEPTEMBER 13, 1874—
LOS ANGELES, JULY 13, 1951)

He was an autodidact in music. Circumstances forced him to interrupt his education very early. At first he cultivated music as an amateur. He learned to play the cello, composed duos, trios, and quartets for chamber groups in which he often played with friends. That spontaneous attraction toward chamber music, thus precociously displayed, would mark his entire activity as a composer. Schoenberg left the Lyceum without having completed his secondary studies; from then on, he devoted himself entirely to music. The only teacher responsible for his education was Alexander von Zemlinsky, his elder by two years, who at that time had an imposing reputation. That friendly instruction, of short duration, was all that Schoenberg ever was to receive; later he gladly claimed the privileges of an autodidact.

Schoenberg's first works, in the Wagner-Brahms tradition, fitted into a certain historical current: in them, tonality is used in an expanded way that is nonetheless traditional: the relationships are very chromatic, but the general tonal structures are respected. From that epoch dates the Sextet, opus 4, entitled *Verklärte Nacht* (*Transfigured Night*), which was composed during the summer of 1899. Shortly afterward, in March 1900, Schoenberg began to compose the *Gurre-Lieder*, a gigantic work that he would not complete until much later; that vast score has all the typically post-Wagnerian characteristics. As a matter of curiosity, I give the scoring here: five solo voices, a reciter, three male choruses in four parts and a mixed chorus in eight parts, four small and four large flutes, three oboes, two English horns, two small clarinets, three clarinets, two bass clarinets, three bassoons, two contrabassoons, ten horns, six trumpets, a bass trumpet, seven trombones, a tuba, six kettledrums, a large percussion section, four harps, a celesta, and a quintet of strings in a number comparable to that of the rest of the forces.

Composition of the *Gurre-Lieder* occupied Schoenberg for a year, but the instrumentation was not completed, following numerous periods of interruption, until 1911, by which time he long had passed beyond the work's esthetic. The mere enumeration of its vocal and instrumental apparatus makes clear that Schoenberg carried to its zenith the excess of romantic orchestration, in which mass effects had taken a preponderant place. Mahler already was engaged in that same enterprise, a kind of flamboyant baroque exasperation of dying romanticism.

Clearly, that composition does not suffice for a judgment of Schoenberg's native talent; it can easily be confused with some work by Richard Strauss and with the turgidity of his style. But Schoenberg already had created *Pelleas und Melisande*, a suite for orchestra after Maeterlinck's drama. It dates from 1902, the year in which Debussy's *Pelléas et Mélisande* was given its first performance, in Paris. The notion of comparing the two scores immediately springs to mind, but that comparison is not justified. One must content oneself with saying that Debussy's esthetic is in a new dispensation, newer than the romantic pathos in which Schoenberg's work again is bathed. In order to emerge from the post-Wagnerian circle, Schoenberg still needed several years more; all his life, however, he remained impregnated with the tradition and taste of the Viennese epoch of 1900, for which, despite certain abrupt aspects of his vocabulary, he essentially went on feeling nostalgia.

After *Pelleas und Melisande* came a series of works among which I shall mention the First Quartet, in D minor, opus 7 (1904–5), the *Kammersymphonie*, opus 9 (1906), and the Second Quartet, in F-sharp minor, opus 10 (1907–8). These pieces marked the gathering-together of Schoenberg's tonal language. Departing from them, he would enter a decisive stage of his creative career.

The *Kammersymphonie* begins with a celebrated motif made up wholly of fourths, which shows Schoenberg's preoccupation with finding a system different from that of thirds employed up to his day. However, this theme in fourths soon is revealed as a thematic constant that in fact does not give rise to the piece's harmony. What seems more interesting to me is the formal elaboration of the pieces, which condenses the traditional four movements into one, thus making the idea of development coincide with that of structural schema. I should remark that opus 9 was composed for fifteen soloistic instruments and that it is extremely difficult because the writing for the winds is very strong and is likely to overpower the strings, which are reduced to the condition of a solo quintet. That explains why the piece often is played in an adaptation in which the strings are reinforced. Even so, the string parts require great virtuosity, and production of a satisfactory ensemble remains uncertain. I have remarked that the instrumental writing of opus 9 demands interpretive virtuosity; almost always, Schoenberg's chamber works call for rare ability on the part of instrumentalist and conductor; for that reason, his works have frequently been betrayed by interpretations deficient even more from the point of view of style than from that of technique.

The Quartet, opus 10, in F-sharp minor, might be considered as articulation between Schoenberg's truly tonal writing and a writing in which the tonal functions would be avoided by the use of "anarchistic" intervals defying all "classified" relation. The fourth movement of opus 10 is especially symptomatic in that respect, for in it the interval often takes precedence over harmonic dependence. Here the major seventh, major ninth, and diminished fifth appear as privileged—intervals of the greatest tenstion; these "dissonant" intervals are joined to "consonant" intervals such as the major or minor third in a manner that does not produce a classified chord; the perfect fifth is quickly avoided out of regard for its great force of tonal attraction.

Now one reaches the most important period of Schoenberg's creative activity. Having temporarily left Vienna, he made several stays in Berlin, where he taught; it was in Berlin that his most important works were created and given their first performance. Numerous pupils began to group themselves around him: Berg and Webern, the first two of his disciples, alone among them would attain celebrity.

Schoenberg's teaching activity was constant; his young students testified to the veritable fascination that he exercised. He wrote several didactic books, among them the famous *Harmonielehre* (1909–11); toward the end of his life, in the United States, he was to publish still more theoretical works, among them *Models for Beginners in Composition* and *Structural Functions of Harmony;* also, a number of articles, courses, and lectures were brought together under the title *Style and Idea.* One might almost say that as Schoenberg grew older, didactic preoccupations weighed upon his work, influencing it in a not always happy way. Listening, for example, to the Variations, opus 31, one seems to be hearing not variations, but the way to make them. This point of view may be too caustic, but I think that it has a real basis.

Let me return to Schoenberg's creative activity from 1908 on. I have considered that period as being of the greatest importance; in fact, the years from 1908 to 1915 produced all of his most striking and most significant works: Three Pieces for Piano, opus 11 (1908); the *Buch des hängenden Gärten*, opus 15, a cycle of songs for piano and voice on poems by Stefan George; Five Pieces for Orchestra, opus 16 (1909); two one-act stageworks—*Erwartung*, opus 17 (1909), and *Die glückliche Hand*, opus 18 (1909–13); Six Small Pieces for Piano, opus 19 (1911); *Herzgewächse*, for voice and three instruments, opus 20 (1911); the celebrated *Pierrot lunaire* for reciter and five instruments, opus 21 (1912); and Four Songs for voice and orchestra, opus 22 (1913–15).

With those titles, all of them glorious, I think that one can sum up Schoenberg's creative personality. It was in that universe—not tonal, but not yet serial—that he showed his most brilliant gifts, his greatest vitality. The power of renovation contained in his language is much more manifest in those works than in the later compositions in which he adopted the serial principle. The writing is highly complex—if not when intended for a single instrument, at least when conceived for chamber ensembles. The counterpoint, freed of tonal restraints, could develop with a baroque richness that romantic music had never attained, all relations except the tonal one being permitted—which is to say that this universe is very rich, but also very anarchic. Schoenberg's only preoccupation was to maintain the permanence of chromatic relations, a fact that allowed no influence of chords—in which, no note being doubled, different intervals accumulate—upon the melodic lines considered among themselves or upon the harmonic construction. It can be asserted, furthermore, that this hyperchromaticism is related to Schoenberg's dramatic and expressionist temperament: the wide intervals, the "dissonances" that so struck his contemporaries, were perfectly integrated into an intellectual and literary context that took them fully into account. They were no less justified musically: the notion of consonance and dissonance as the classic tradition had understood it had become decrepit. Oppositions between tension and relaxation were nonetheless preserved, but by other means and functions.

Tension results, for example, from the value of the interval, from its more or less "anarchistic" quality, from the greater or smaller density of accumulated anarchistic intervals—or, again, from the mixture and dosage of strong and weak intervals, the notion of strength and weakness being related to the variable complexity of their relationships. The Five Pieces for Orchestra, opus 16, show a desire to treat the large orchestra almost like an expanded chamber group. Unlike Debussy's writing, which treats the orchestra "acoustically," Schoenberg's is parceled out among an ensemble of soloists and utilizes the orchestral groups in large, homogeneous ensembles that in a sense play the role of enlarged instruments. That tendency is very sharp in opus 22, which marks one of the apexes of Schoenbergian orchestral writing, as that utilization of homogeneous groups was very rarely exploited later.

The third piece of opus 16 also shows a very particular employment of timbre: in it, Schoenberg puts the ambiguity of a timbre into play in relation to another. The opening of this third piece consists of a five-tone chord, the color of which is constantly renewed by procedures of dissolving linkages; that ambiguity of timbres, furthermore, is functional—which is to say that it assumes the total structure. For the first time, then, one sees timbre employed for its own sake, functionally, not as the result of an instrument.

It was not without intent that Shceonberg entitled that piece *Farben* (*Colors*), for in it, for the first time, color, timbre, was being played upon with extraordinary efficacity. In the third piece of opus 16 this principle of color was applied, as I have said, to a chord. In the fifth piece, entitled *Obligatory Recitative*, that notion was adapted to recitative. This meant that the different periods of a phrase were renewed by instrumentation.

Schoenberg gave the name *Klangfarbenmelodie* to this procedure, which could be defined as a constant alteration of timbre applied to the horizontal dimension of music.

In opus 16, Schoenberg had used an orchestra that may be called normal; in opus 22, on the other hand, the orchestra bears a very exceptional nomenclature: as a result of that instrumentation in groups, certain families of instruments are inordinately amplified here while others are atrophied almost out of existence.

I may cite, for example, the instrumentation of the first of these four songs: it utilizes six clarinets, a trumpet, three trombones, a tuba, bells, a percussion section composed of cymbals, xylophone and tam-tam, twenty-four violins, twelve cellos, and nine doublebasses. One notices immediately, at the very outset, that the twenty-four violins are not divided into first and second violins in the traditional classic way; they both play in unison and are divided in a mobile fashion into from two to six parts. There are no violas. The twelve cellos also vary constantly between unison and division into six parts. The clarinets—one of the most conspicuous phenomena of this song—sometimes play in unison, but also open out brusquely into chords of two, three . . . six sounds, giving the line a sudden thickness, "a fan opened out and then closed." This gives the impression that these chords are more a phenomenon of timbre, have more an acoustic result than a determined function as chords; they are in some way "mutations" comparable to the play of mutations on the organ. The only inherent difficulty in performing these works consists in finding the forces necessary to play them. These do not coincide with the norm of the traditional orchestra, and it is costly to engage numerous supplementary musicians to add to the forces of a constituted orchestra. That is why one rarely hears this opus 22, which is exceptional in all senses of that word.

Erwartung and *Die glückliche Hand* marked Schoenberg's first contact with the stage. Unhappily, the librettos of these works are not in the best taste. The text of *Erwartung*, which brings into play an expressionism of very dubious quality, dates terribly; in a related way, that of *Die glückliche Hand*, oscillating between socially preoccupied realism and second-hand mysticism, has aged considerably. Alas, Schoenberg was not always happy in choosing texts: *Pierrot lunaire* too is erected upon a text of somewhat dated poetic, but the mediocrity of these texts cannot make us forget the exraordinary dramatic quality of the music.

Erwartung certainly was the source of *Wozzeck*. Schoenberg having dealt with a shorter form, *Erwartung* does without the structural prolongations of Berg's opera, but in it one finds, carried to paroxysm, invention in the state of perpetual becoming, freeing itself from all determined formal designs; one might, in fact, consider *Erwartung* as a cycle of songs written for the stage. That improvised aspect doubtless was what gave the greatest impulse to the dramatic act that Schoenberg then accomplished.

Pierrot lunaire is his most celebrated work, a central fact around which all the other works have been ranged. It is certain that, despite the importance of the others, this one is the center of gravity. Its newness results from two chief aspects: the utilization of *Sprechgesang* and the relation of its small form to a restricted instrumental group. After the instrumental excesses that had been Schoenberg's habit, excesses also displayed in the conception of the large form, here we find concentration in thought and in realization indicating a profound renovation of his own views. *Pierrot lunaire* consists of three cycles of seven pieces each, the shortest of them extending only thirteen measures. It is written for a small ensemble that includes a piano, a flute (interchangeable with piccolo), a clarinet alternating with a bass clarinet, a violin alternating with a viola, and a violoncello. Each piece has its own instrumental combination (in that, Schoenberg returned to Bach's conception for the different numbers of his cantatas, Passions, and Mass): this is not a matter of homogeneous, continuous formation, but one of groupings of different organization. What to say about *Sprechgesang*? We must remember that the work was composed at the request of an actress. The poems therefore were to be spoken against a musical background—in sum, a superior "cabaret," the humorous side of which has been neglected too often. Certainly some sections of *Pierrot lunaire* have a tragic dimension, but even that tragedy does not lack *arrière-pensée* and irony. To take these texts at face value seems to me a mistake, one that has given birth to the greatest misunderstandings in the interpretation of this work.

The esthetic of *Pierrot lunaire* is not very distant—all question of temperament, all question of musical characterology aside—from that of some of Debussy's works, such as the Sonata for piano and violoncello. (André Schaeffner in fact has noted this: the preliminary title of the second movement of that Sonata was *Pierrot fêché avec la lune*, the same literary mythology as point of departure.)

Sprechgesang raises theoretical and practical problems. Schoenberg seems not to have made any exact study of the relationships between the vocal, sung register and the speaking register, not only in *tessitura*, but also in length of emission. One can speak on a given pitch for only a very brief time without producing a sung emission; furthermore, for the female voice, the spoken register is deeper and more restricted than the singing register. Wanting to speak *Pierrot lunaire*, one comes to a species of reduction—à la "*jivaro*"—of the written line: the highest intervals are narrowed toward the deeper part, whereas those located there remain almost unchanged. This results in a formal contradiction between the written musical text and its sound-realization. Up to now, to my knowledge, no satisfactory solution has been found to unravel that contradiction. We may believe that Schoenberg himself came to think the problem insoluble, as in later works in which he used

Sprechgesang, he adopted an entirely different notation—as in the *Ode to Napoleon,* for example, or *A Survivor from Warsaw.*

Schoenberg was at the sumit of his inventiveness and originality in the instrumental writing itself: making use of a free idiom, he organized it as functioning in sound-figures of more or less thematic tendencies, simultaneously often using the severest forms of counterpoint. Bizarrely, that utilization of such forms most struck the first listeners, or at least the first "chroniclers" and other accountants; the impulse has been to retain of that writing only its most rigorous elements, whereas they are far from dominant in the work. More especially, *Pierrot lunaire* displays a plenitude of conception which Schoenberg very rarely attained and a utilization—wholly coherent in its freedom—of a language without determining functions, tonal or nontonal. *Pierrot lunaire* made Schoenberg's name famous, arousing a large number of polemics from which, unhappily, little is to be saved, given the feebleness of the points of view and the misunderstanding of the scores which engendered them. I shall content myself with recalling that it supplied the occasion for a glancing meeting, much more "impressionistic" than reasoned, of Stravinsky and Ravel with Schoenberg.

After 1915, Schoenberg's creative activity was suspended for a time: he published nothing more until 1923. That silence of eight years has been interpreted variously. It was not, as so often has been insinuated, owing to a crisis of sterility. Nonetheless, Schoenberg had to conquer the "anarchistic" side of his writing, give it a new coherence destined to replace the former one.

Be that as it may, that interval of eight years was devoted to augmented didactic activity. Schoenberg enlarged his courses in composition. He also organized concerts of the new music: this was the Verein für musikalische Privataufführungen (Association for Private Musical Performances). Works were not only played, but also were introduced and discussed; the audience could, if it wished, attend some rehearsals; as one sees, not even these concerts were without didactic *arrière-pensée.* For Schoenberg the composer, the period was crowded with experiments and groping: he began to write a work, left uncompleted, entitled *Die Jakobsleiter* (*Jacob's Ladder*); in it, for the first time, he approached a more rigorous technique in deployment of sounds. It was found among his papers after his death, and some fragments of it have been performed.

The first composition that Schoenberg published after that eight-year interval was the Five Pieces for piano, opus 23, written in 1923; in it, the strict serial discipline appeared for the first time. In the course of the work, it is made precise in a more and more conscious way, at first having the aspect of an "ultrathematicism" resulting in the series of twelve tones, properly speaking; in the fifth piece—*Walzer*—one finds it employed, though in a simple way. In opus 24, The Serenade, which followed, the technique was reaffirmed, above all during the central, or fourth, movement, which includes a voice and uses a Petrarch sonnet. With opus 25, the Suite for Piano, Schoenberg began really to master it.

What is rather surprising is that, while making his theoretical views precise, Schoenberg used more and more established forms, as if in some way to verify, to prove, the viability of the new technique. The Suite for Piano, in fact, was conceived in the preclassic style; in the same way, a little later, the Suite for Seven Instruments, opus 29, made use of the consecrated forms of the Viennese classic era.

One is justified in finding this return to a certain very nearly academic notion of classicism rather disappointing in a mind as innovating as Schoenberg's. Whence that nostalgia? I find no explanation for it except in purely personal and sentimental considerations, the musical *raison d'être* of which is more difficult to locate. I shall cite one example that seems typical to me: in the three *Satires*, opus 28, Schoenberg brands the compositions as neoclassic and toward that end uses a language making use of forms, reminiscences, classic clichés. If the satirical reference were not announced explicitly in the text, it would be difficult to determine the difference between the caricature in opus 28 and the "classicism" put into play in opus 29.

Also, those "verifications" of the serial technique by the use of old-time forms are what has aged most rapidly in Schoenberg; for my part, they bring on my most formal reservations in appreciating his work after opus 25. Then one notices different metamorphoses, various stages in this "classicism," the most important moment of which remains the Variations for Orchestra, opus 31 (1927–8). These Variations, conceived in a state of mind very close to Brahms, are more interesting for certain technical aspects of their writing than for their esthetic.

Shortly after that, Nazi persecution would oblige Schoenberg to flee Europe and find refuge in the United States, where he was able, after some difficulties, to obtain a class at the University of California at Los Angeles, a position that he kept until he was seventy. His composing in America was divided bizarrely between some purely serial works and works "of conciliation," in which he attempted to synthesize tonal *données* and the demands of the series much as Berg had tried to do, for example, in his Violin Concerto. That explains why Schoenberg's last works appear tainted with a certain futility: their constituents lack homogeneity. There are certain exceptions, such as the Piano Concerto, opus 42, and the String Trio, opus 45, but it must be conceded that as contrasted with the brilliant group of works from opus 11 to opus 23, these cannot arouse undiluted enthusiasm. I shall not dilate upon them further, as for me the essential part of Schoenberg already has been touched upon—the part that can influence future generations or even just remain and have a privileged position in the history of music seems to me to be summed up in that period from 1908 to 1915.

Schoenberg's health was very unstable from 1946 on. The official musical life of the United States absolutely was not designed for a man like him: his integrity and courage were put to rude proof by a discouraging conformism. He lived in isolation, compensated for by the great solicitude of his friends and of *emigrés* from Germany and Austria, who reconstituted a brilliant intellectual circle around him. He died in Los Angeles on July 13, 1951, leaving incomplete his opera *Moses und Aron*, the first performance of which took place some years later. That work is the most important manifestation of the final period of his life; unhappily, in it too the literary quality of the libretto is much inferior to the musical quality of the score. Schoenberg himself wrote it, and in it one finds a rather naïve opposition between materialism, represented by Aaron, and idealism, represented by Moses. The happiest aspect of the opera seems to be its simultaneous employment of sung roles and spoken roles—for both the soloists and the choruses—a procedure of undeniable dramatic quality which permits him to conquer the classic opposition between recitative and aria. As for the stylistic quality of the music, it tells us nothing especially new about Schoenberg's neoclassic evolution.

In sum, Schoenberg's personality is fascinating as long as he is free with regard to language and his postromantic esthetic coincides perfectly with that freedom. But from the time of his discovery of the series, a discovery for which I do not forget our debt to him, there seems to have been a distortion between technique as such and an academic constraint that he felt to be a guarantee. Nonetheless, few men have had so much influence and power over the destiny of music. He is one of the chief figures of twentieth-century music, one of those men who gave the contemporary language its present-day contours.

SCHOENBERG'S PIANO WORKS

In the catalogue of Schoenberg's works, the works for piano are of first importance, for they include five collections—opus 11, opus 19, opus 23, opus 25, and opus 33 (a and b)—of which three are of rather vast dimension. These collections mark dates in their composer's quest in astonishingly precise fashion; each of them marks an important stage in the evolution of his writing and his thought, an evolution that can be symbolized well enough by a parabola, the top of which will be opus 23. In fact, opus 11 and opus 19 propound a denial of the tonal universe in language and in form; the search for vocabulary becomes keener in opus 23, which includes the first piece in twelve tones; opus 25 and opus 33 make use of classic forms as ways of shoring up the morphological construction based upon the series.

To tell the truth, it is curious to note that one of the primordial works in Schoenberg's creative arc, opus 23, was written for the keyboard: Schoenberg was not a pianist, but had worked at the violin and then at the violoncello, the instrument through which, while still young, he was initiated into chamber music. The piano by itself seems to have tempted Berg and Webern much less, for each of them composed only one work for that instrument—the former the Sonata, opus 1, the latter the Variations, opus 27. Nevertheless, one should not decide on the basis of that fact that they thought this form of writing minor: they employed the piano abundantly in chamber groups and in song cycles, as did Schoenberg.

If one approaches Schoenberg's piano music from the point of view of pianistic writing, one must not expect to encounter advantageous clichés that "fit the hands" or any characteristic novelty in unforeseen use of the instrument's resources. Whereas Debussy and Ravel on one hand, Stravinsky and

Bartók on the other, were able, in completely opposite directions, to give radical evolution to the sound-conception and musical treatment of the keyboard, Schoenberg's thought in that domain is directly related to that of Brahms. He varied the vocabulary, the musical materials, the types of chords and arpeggios, for example, but did not modify either the pianistic aspect or the pianistic presentation. Once one has realized that, one sees that Schoenberg's writing for keyboard is only the apogee of a pianistic style that is extremely effective because of the amplitude and certainty of the means put into play. It is perhaps one of the last examples of that "large piano" as the best composers from Schumann to Brahms conceived it, an appanage of the most brilliant and most solid German instrumental tradition.

Opus 11 was composed in 1908, between the composition of opus 15 and that of opus 16 (the opus numbers corresponded to dates of publication, not to those of composition). It was played for the first time in 1909 during an evening organized by the Verein für Kunst and Kultur. Later, Ferruccio Busoni made a "concert" transcription of it. The three pieces of this work mark—as does the *Buch der hängenden Gärten*, the song cycle of opus 15—the effacement of tonality from Schoenberg's writing. A *nonfunctional* harmony makes use of unclassifiable chords as the intermediary of a constantly chromatic writing. The perfect chord is avoided utterly, and the octave is used only as a doubling. On the other hand, there is a profusion of intervals of greater tension, such as the major seventh, the minor ninth, and the augmented fourth. Furthermore, the complimentarity of intervals is used with the aim of attaining a chromatic tonality at each instant. The three pieces differ greatly in character. The first opposes a melodic phrase in moderate tempo to more animated passages consisting of rapid, packed arpeggios. The second piece, the longest in the collection, sets forth a slow, somber theme on an eighth-note *osti-*

nato; then, after two developments leading to a paroxysm in the keyboard's highest register, the first theme returns. The third piece is full of violent contrasts in agitated movement; it is very rhapsodic and is certainly the most interesting of the group from the point of view of writing. In this very free recitative, one can see one of Schoenberg's first attempts—and one of the most conclusive—to create a constantly evolving form.

In its brevity, opus 19, written in 1911, furnishes a contrast to the dimensions of the lyric work *Die glückliche Hand,* composed at the same time. But if one places it alongside the song *Herzgewächse,* opus 20, exactly contemporary with it, one may well say that it is a dress rehearsal for *Pierrot lunaire,* opus 21. In the Six Pieces of opus 19 Schoenberg inaugurated the "small form" that by then already was very characteristic of Webern's production. These are certainly the shortest pieces that he ever composed. Their concision shows one principal aim, that of completely avoiding all repetition by a development that puts identical musical figures into play. Extremely expressive, these pieces rarely reach violence, being held to an essentially intimate sonority in willing reserve, and to exemplary concentration. The sixth of the pieces, which is very slow, superimposes two chords in a funeral-bell effect, and was inspired by the death of Mahler (May 18, 1911), who had been to Schoenberg a benevolent protector and faithful friend.

With opus 23 and the year 1923, we reach a capital phase in Schoenberg's evolution. For eight years he had not published anything; his last work to be revealed had been the collection of Songs for Voice and Orchestra, opus 22. That enclosing silence was long questioned, but one now sees that if during those eight years no work had been completed, the period was nonetheless of first importance in the unfolding of Schoenberg's creation. In a letter to Nicolas Slonimsky, Schoenberg himself wrote: "The method of composition with twelve tones is the fruit of a whole succession of experiences . . . I can cite, among the attempts, the piano pieces, opus 23 . . . Contrary to the fashion in which a musical motif ordinarily is utilized, there I already used the method of the series of twelve tones . . . I take other motifs and themes, different presentations, chords too, despite which the theme is composed of twelve sounds. . . . Still . . . absolute priority remains with some movements of the Suite for Piano [opus 27], composed in the autumn of 1921. It was at that moment that I suddenly became conscious of the real importance of the end toward which I was striving—unity and regularity, to which I had been led unconsciously."

The third and fifth pieces of the collection—which is made up of five pieces—are the most remarkable from that point of view. In the third, a succession of five tones takes on an ultrathematic character and in effect gives birth to all the figures of the work, harmonic as well as melodic, through its various inversions and transpositions. That was the first time that such a technique had been applied with so much consequence. That series of five sounds is manipulated with even more refinement than the series of twelve tones in the works that were to follow immediately, perhaps because of its more practical simplicity and greater malleability. With regard to that, the fifth piece is based on a complete series of twelve tones, but one that is employed only in its original form—that is, without undergoing any modification. Although it was the first really and strictly "dodecaphonic" example, it nonetheless reveals, or at least so one may judge, a lower level of writing than the four other pieces. It is nevertheless of great importance historically speaking.

The Suite, opus 25, published in 1924, the composition of which stretched out over three years from 1921 on, marked a recoil from opus 23. Assuring the supremacy of the series in order to give coherence and solidity to the counterpoint and harmony that thus emerged from some fifteen years of anarchy, Schoenberg felt a need to consolidate the forces of this new instrument with the help of classic and preclassic forms. Thus, this Suite includes a Prelude, a Gavotte followed by a Musette, an Intermezzo, a Minuet with trio, and a Gigue. One can assert that an archaicizing drive clearly lay behind the choice of abandoned forms that had fallen into desuetude. It is evident that these forms were not borrowed in a servile way from the tradition and that they underwent undeniable revitalization. Nevertheless, the rhythmic schemes are perhaps the snag upon which the discrepancy between the new vocabulary and the old-time forms catch. The Gigue, however, brilliantly concludes this brilliant master's exercise.

The Two Pieces, opus 33, were issued by two different publishers, whence the established procedure of adding a letter to each of them: the first, opus 33a, was published in 1929 by Universal Edition in Vienna; the second, opus 33b, appeared in the April 1932 edition of *New Music* in New York. These pieces belong to the period during which Schoenberg was composing two lyric works: *Von Heute auf Morgen*, first presented at Frankfurt-am-Main in 1930, and *Moses und Aron*, which was performed only after the composer's death, in 1954. Between the two operas, of which the second is above all of vast scope, the two pieces appear as a relaxation. They have none of the importance that I have pointed out in other piano works of Schoenberg. In opus 33a, the dodecaphonic technique is managed with evident suppleness at the service of a thought in repose; it is practically a sonata movement, with a first, vigorously asserted theme, to which a second theme, singing and flexible, replies. Opus 33b is clearly more complex in structure, also being constructed of two themes in one unit of time, the first in binary division, the second in ternary. Strength preponderates in the second theme, it being thus opposed to the sweetness that reigns in the first theme. With music that is relaxed and brief, these two pieces are the penultimate stage of Schoenberg's pianistic work: he would use the instrument for the last time as a soloist ten years later—in 1942—in the Concerto for Piano and Orchestra, opus 42.

Performance of these collections faces the virtuoso with difficulties not easily surmounted at first reading: the complexity of the polyphonic writing demands great clarity in establishing the various sound-levels. Schoenberg was, furthermore, very meticulous in choosing his indications, and when he employed certain graphic signals, it was with absolute precision in each case. All the works are preceded by explanatory and very detailed prefaces that end with this significant phrase: "The best fingerings are those which permit exact realization of the text without the aid of the pedal. On the other hand, the soft pedal often renders excellent service." But, beyond the virtuoso's difficulties, Schoenberg's works—and opus 23 especially—require the performer to have clear comprehension of the form, translation of which implies both "unity and regularity." When this double obstacle has been overcome, then the beauty has time to be deployed amply and to inundate the listener. Certain of these pieces, and in particular the third number of opus 11, are among the most extraordinary successes ever to be played on a keyboard.

Webern,

ANTON VON, AUSTRIAN COMPOSER
(VIENNA, DECEMBER 3, 1883—
MITTERSILL, SEPTEMBER 15, 1945)

Webern lived first in Vienna, then in Graz and Klagenfurt. He returned to Vienna to study music under Guido Adler, studies that ended in 1906. He received his doctoral degree from the University of Vienna with a thesis on Heinrich Isaac's *Choralis Constantinus.* Earlier, in 1904, he had met Schoenberg—after, it is said, having tried unsuccessfully to take lessons from Hans Pfitzner!

His first compositions revealed a strong attachment to the postromantic tradition, especially to Mahler, toward whom he kept a memory of great fidelity throughout his life. Thus it was that his Passacaglia, opus 1, in D minor, is in a style that may greatly astonish a listener acquainted with his other works. Written in an expanded tonality as that was conceived in the 1890–1900 Vienna epoch, this work was born under the sign of an esthetic that Webern very quickly caused to disappear from his music, above all as expressed in so direct a manner.

Nonetheless, one already notes in that use of the passacaglia form his tendency to utilize the most rigorous forms, if not the most scholastic ones, in musical writing. I could also point out that in the *a cappella* Chorus, opus 2—which followed the Passacaglia immediately and bore the title *Entfliecht auf liechten Künhen*—Webern used the canon form as the chief organizing principle of the structure of the piece; this canon, though again using intervals strongly tied to the tonal world—and here brought in without excessive ambiguity—nevertheless constituted the debut of a universe that did not rest exclusively upon strictly tonal relationships.

It is with Webern's opus 3 and opus 4 that one notices his immense progress toward a "liberation" outside tonality. Bizarrely, these two works are both groups of *Lieder:* furthermore, we almost always observe the same fact in Webern's development—the chief periods of his creative life were initiated into their evolution by the most frequent, almost exclusive composition of vocal music.

One might say that Webern's style, properly speaking, in the sense in which we understand it now, began with the two cycles of opus 3 and opus 4. Because both of them were composed on poems by Stefan George (opus 2 also had used a text by that poet), they also reveal Webern's literary taste at that time.

Beginning with opus 5, the genius of Webern appears as unprecedented, both for the radicalism of his points of view and for the novelty of his sensibility—a rare amalgam testified to by a series of works that still astonish us. This group includes the Five Movements for String Quartet, opus 5, the Six Pieces for Orchestra, opus 6, and the Pieces for Piano and Violin, opus 7. In these one sees made precise his predilection for the "little form," by which I do not mean a brief form, but a form so highly concentrated that it cannot support long development in time because of the richness of means involved and the poetic governing them.

The Movements, opus 5, and the Six Pieces for Orchestra, opus 6, have now become the most accessible of Webern's compositions; each time they are performed, they win their audience, however prejudiced it may have been in the beginning. In fact, Webern never had been so seductive before and perhaps never would be again. For the baroque charm—in the stylistic sense of the word—emanating from these pieces proved completely transitory in Webern's work. He was to bend his effort toward a rigor that is no less beautiful but is less directly intelligible.

One can, *grosso modo*, organize the elements of his style at that time and make their fundamental characteristics precise: the individual lines are excessively supple; their curve, their unexpectedness, their grace, and their complete lack of heaviness are captivating; the polyphony itself is rarely complex, for most of the pieces consist of a melody—if one will give a large meaning to the term—accompanied by chords that, although they no longer have any tonal function, nonetheless are in close relation (chromatically) with that melody. In another sense, the chromatic universe in which this music moves is again composed of conjunct intervals or, if they are disjunct, intervals disposed in a register sufficiently narrowed so that the ear is able to perceive the continuity at once. Finally, a sensibility extremely close to Debussy's in its refinement, its taste for ellipsis, its delicacy, creates an atmosphere almost familiar to our ears. The use of instrumental color is of so direct a beauty that the listener has no difficulty in enjoying it, although at first it may be so strange to him as to seem a rarefaction of the musical atmosphere. There is no aggressivity in the sonority; on the contrary—an exceptional instance aside—sweetness and transparency are the determining qualities of this group of works.

Now we are in 1911, the time of Stravinsky's first great ballets. (We must not forget that the Pieces, opus 6, are contemporary with *Petrushka.*) In 1911, Webern left Vienna for a time before assuming the post of *Kapellmeister* successively at Danzig, Berlin, and Stettin. In that connection, let us remember that, contrary to certain overdistributed legends, Webern always was a musician of the highest professional conscience; he constantly was in pragmatic rapport with the musical métier—by which I mean to say that he knew perfectly both the vocal and the instrumental possibilities that the Occidental tradition put at his disposition. Not only was he a remarkable theoretician—an excessively rare example of a composer who had studied musicology—but also he was a musician in métier: he never during his life ceased to conduct, either in the theater or in concert, works of the classic and contemporary repertoire. And we find traces of that fact in his music: Webern is never unplayable. He sometimes is difficult ("delicate" would be more exact), but much more because of the stylistic qualities that his interpreter must develop than because of any instrumental difficulty as such. He composed, so to speak, no virtuoso works except, perhaps, some vocal conceptions that for difficulty can be compared to certain roles in *Così fan tutte* or *Die Entführung aus dem Serail.*

But let me go back to Webern's evolution as a composer. In the period from 1910 to about 1914, he went ahead, almost to asphyxia, in exploring the microcosm toward which his temperament already had attracted him. This was the epoch of his shortest works: Six Bagatelles for String Quartet, opus 9; Five Pieces for Chamber Orchestra, opus 10; Three Pieces for Piano and Violoncello, opus 11. In these last, the parallel with the Japanese *haï-kaï* can be established easily: a phrase suffices to place a universe and impose it forcibly. The third piece of opus 11, for example, is restricted to six short measures; the fourth of opus 10 lasts twenty seconds. (It is very difficult to present such works in concert because of their brevity, but even more because of their restricted sound-dynamic, which makes use of nuances at the edge of the audible.) An elementary problem in perception sometimes is posed here: in a large hall, for example, the environing noise has a tendency in itself to cover the dynamic level of the music. The psychological relationship with an audience, what is more, cannot be established on large dimensions unless one disposes of a sufficient margin of time and of hearing; otherwise the contact, scarcely established, is broken off and the effort to re-create a "circuit of hearing" must be made with each new piece. Whence the painful impression for the interpreter that he is not "catching on": he is not given the almost material possibility of taking his public in hand; for, another face of the problem, the great difficulty of these works is to know how to listen to them. Perhaps our Occidental tradition does not predispose us in that direction as much as is necessary; the Occident always has needed a largely explicit gesture in order to understand what is being told to it. If one compares, in the theater, the style of our actors and the style of, for example, Japanese actors or our dancers' style with that of the dancers of India, one sees immediately what I mean. Webern is an innovator, one sees, not only in the esthetic of his works, but also in the physics and gestures of the concert.

Thus Webern moved in a more and more rarefied universe; he sought a way to metamorphose his experiences, never to condemn himself to the sterility of repetition or even to total sterility. I note that, again, vocal music played a very important role in his production. The period from 1914 to 1917—very important in the development of his thinking—contained absolutely nothing but cycles of *Lieder*. These have the opus numbers 13, 14, 15, 16, 17, 18, and 19. I shall add that in order to organize music by the new structures, Webern felt the need to lean on a text that gave him formal bench marks outside properly musical functions; that, furthermore, permitted him to build, despite the brevity of each poem, longer cycles in which characteristics responded from one piece to another.

Finally, Webern disembarrassed himself completely of that typical nineteenth-century concept—piano and voice; instead he amalgamated the voice and shifting groups of instruments in an organic whole. One is no longer dealing with accompanied melody, but with an ensemble in which the voice organizes and "supervises" the distribution. When that use of instrumental groups in relation with the voice is well understood, it is possible to see in it the undeniable influence of Schoenberg's *Pierrot lunaire,* which then was shining in its fresh newness. One must, however, point out that Webern never employed the voice as Schoenberg did in *Pierrot lunaire*—that is to say, in view of a specifically dramatic effect—the *Sprechgesang.* He utilized it in a severely restricted domain, pure "song," willingly ignoring the paramusical resources of which more general usage is prodigal. It nonetheless remains certain that the voice integrated into a small instrumental formation was originally native to Schoenberg and that Webern took up and transcended that dramatic formula invented by his master. It was equally in the course of this phase of his evolution—in his opus 17—that Webern adopted as the organizing principle of his music the series of twelve tones inaugurated by Schoenberg. (The first use of the series, let me recall, went back to the fifth piece of Schoenberg's Pieces for Piano, opus 23.) Here it is well to make clear my point of view about the precedence of that "discovery." By all the evidence, Schoenberg was first, and really codified the employment of the twelve-tone series, and Webern, in the strictest sense, did nothing but follow his example. But his originality bulks large, in the sense that his work showed no break in continuity despite the mutation that his adoption of the new technique of writing brought into it.

The arrival of the series marked no discontinuity in Schoenberg's work either: one finds again the postromantic and neoclassic characteristics of his style—serial or not—because in sum he used the series on the morphological level as a unifying principle; his semantics underwent no decisive modification in the drawing-up of his works posterior to the series.

With Webern, one notices equally that use of the series unifies his vocabulary, gives it more assured cohesion, but does not fundamentally alter the creative thinking: his stylistic was revolutionary before the series and remained so with it. Let me note at the outset that, although all the stylistic antecedents of Webern were preserved, he organized them definitely by greater coherence, more rigorous usage, more developed control of the means of writing. Let me also point out, without entering into technical details, that Webern's evolution played on that primordial ambiguity—the assimilation of rigorous counterpoint to fundamental serial forms, an ambiguity that risked engendering a rather futile academicism, which Webern escaped because, beyond that scholasticism, he definitely engaged the future of music by prolongations that had not been precisely included at first. By this I understand, very particularly, the abolition of the contradiction that formerly existed between the horizontal and vertical phenomena of tonal music. Webern created a new dimension, which we might label diagonal, a sort of distribution of points, or blocs, or figures no longer on the flat space, but in the sound-space. As a result, he would go deeply into the problem of form in pure music—that is, music without text. We are approaching the most ascetic period of Webern's existence, having as its principal works the String Trio, opus 20; the Symphony, opus 21; the Quartet for Clarinet, Tenor Saxophone, Violin, and Piano, opus 22, and the Concerto for Nine Instruments, opus 24, all of which were composed between 1927 and 1934.

Among Webern's works, these were the ones that most violently shocked the amateurs of contemporary music; they have proved to be a profound influence upon young composers of the succeeding generation. Why so? Because, it seems, Webern here had brought his language to its highest degree—the first fruits of the future language—in the clearest way that could be envisaged. In a certain sense, one would be correct in relating these few compositions to *Das musikalisches Opfer* and *Die Kunst der Fuge*, in the sense that they are no less didactic—to use that term in its loftiest sense—than properly musical. If one wishes to define the serial technique at its origins, these works provide an indispensable *summa* to know, to analyze, to understand. In the String Trio, perhaps, one encounters an exaggerated care to make reference to such classic forms as sonata or rondo. Webern, in fact, had not escaped the influence of Schoenberg, who believed that he must "verify" the new method of organizing the language by means of criteria already strongly established and must verify relied-upon forms by a new means of investigation.

In Webern's Trio, we are in the presence of a formal construction and rhythmic structures not at all in accord with the vocabulary itself. This is certainly the work in which one notices the greatest autonomy of the various components of the language and, I might say, the greatest "discrepancy" among the means put into play, on the levels of semantic and rhetoric.

In the Symphony, opus 21, on the other hand, and particularly in its first movement, which, however, utilizes the sonata form, one sees that Webern quickly surmounted those divergences and reached an absolutely remarkable stylistic cohesion. One is faced with a conception in which serial characteristics, classic form, and rigor of preclassic writing are found combined in a unique mixture, laying the foundations of a language totally independent of references.

What seems to be most characteristic at first hearing is an almost constant use of disjunct wide intervals, instrumentation in pure colors, the presence of silences in unaccustomed amplitude. The disjunct intervals are positioned so as to avoid even fortuitous establishment of any tonal rapport. The conjunct intervals show a tendency to agglomerate according to "habitual relations" even though the truly tonal rapport is not present. Each sound becomes a phenomenon in itself, linked to the others, as goes without saying, by a very puissant context. Attention is attracted to the unique place that each takes in the register in which it is located. This is a matter of interrelationships among autonomous phenomena rather than of total relations being exercised over a group as a result of certain *données.*

In that sense, the greatest innovation of the Webernian vocabulary is that of considering each phenomenon as at once autonomous and interdependent, a radically new way of thinking in Occidental music. In order to place that characteristic in relief, Webern accords great importance not only to the register in which a given sound is located, but also to its temporal position in the unfolding of the work, a sound enclosed by silences acquiring by that isolation a much stronger significance than a sound in the matrix of an immediate context. That is why Webern's innovation in the domain of silence seems more relevant to the very morphology of pitches and their sequence than to a rhythmic phenomenon that never greatly preoccupied him. He aerates his positionings in time and space as well as in their instrumental context. He renounces the seductiveness of his first works, the use of coloration from a purely hedonistic point of view, so as to give instrumentation a truly structural function.

This is not a matter of a use of instruments conceived on an acoustic basis in the sense that the acoustic can engender structural phenomena—that was, in particular, the way of the very late Debussy—but a matter of a contrapuntal-instrumental writing in which each timbre traces a structural characteristic of the work.

I should note that in his "orchestral" works, Webern does not employ pure colors in the sense of assigning a pure contrapuntal line to several interchanging instruments, whereas in his "chamber music," an instrument permanently assumes a single contrapuntal line (Trio, opus 20; Quartet for Clarinet, Tenor Saxophone, Violin, and Piano, opus 22). In the "orchestral" works, he thus persisted in the use of *Klangfarbenmelodie*, but developed that principle much more strictly than in his first works, in which the decorative urge is much more manifest than the structural urge.

If, for example, one analyzes the double canon that opens the first movement of the Symphony, opus 21, one notices that each voices passes from instrument to instrument, the very fact of that changing pointing up the truly structural characteristics of the "abstract" melodic phrase. Contrary to what most listeners at first imagined and still often imagine (one could, what is more, compare the case of Mallarmé), the more Webern appears hermetic, the more he becomes clear, the more he tries to be clear.

Nevertheless, it is in the Concerto for Nine Instruments, opus 24, that one finds the clearest, most directly comprehensible example of the Webernian use of the twelve tones; for that purpose, Webern did not select a disymmetrical—that is, anarchistic—series, with each interval pulling in its own direction, but a very strongly hierarchized series in which an organic-basis phenomenon is repeated several times and therefore becomes more easily discernible. The series used in opus 24 is not made up of twelve tones, but of four times three tones, and the relation among the three tones of a cell is exactly the same in all four cells, engendering both the harmonic and contrapuntal relations and the structural functions.

An art that has attained such a degree of naked clarity might appear poor; one has often heard it said, especially of this Concerto, that it lacks substance, or "*pâte*"; it has been criticized for some lack of density, this in comparison with the harmonic music of the nineteenth century.

Nonetheless, it was essential, in order to discover new, clear structural functions, evident in their novelty, that the series should so be limited to a small number of intervallic relations that the form would appear clearly articulated on simple basic principles. It is certain that the exposition of the first movement of opus 24 practically gave birth to serial thought, through the fact that all of its relations are conrolled, and even though those relations seem to us now excessively simplified, they bear the germ of a specific way of thinking that could be extended and diffused, but which, nevertheless, remains fundamental.

After that truly "didactic" period, Webern went on to enlarge the universe that he was to conquer. And, significantly, vocal works again appeared. I shall emphasize as primordial in that period of his life the three cantatas that he wrote on poems by Hildegard Jone: *Das Augenlicht*, opus 26 (1935), First Cantata, opus 29 (1939), and Second Cantata, opus 31 (1943). In those works, he was less preoccupied with placing than with utilizing: more at ease with the vocabulary that he himself had forged, he began to make more supple use of it. But an intelligence like his could not remain inactive in discovery; for that reason, new means of writing appeared.

In this period, however, the vocal works were not alone. We can mention also very important instrumental works such as the Piano Variations, opus 27 (1936); the String Quartet, opus 28 (1938); and the Variations for Orchestra, opus 30 (1940). But it does not seem to me that these works, full of genius as they are, enrich the Webern phenomenon as much as the three cantatas do. In the latter, Webern did not lean upon a text in order to construct a form, but organized his form by integrating the text into it—a very different procedure, in which the musician feels confident of his strengths and imposes his will upon the poem.

Let me add that the poetic texts lend themselves to that treatment, having a literary value much inferior to that of the texts that Webern had selected when younger (one cannot compare Hildegard Jone to Georg Trakl or even Stefan George). What is more, it seems that Webern selected these texts, which satisfied him well, for their somewhat naïve mysticism, their optimistic pantheism, rather than for their true literary qualities: in short, it was a poor substitute for Goethe. That is why I envisage the three cantatas not on the plane of the relation between poetry and music, but rather as music organized on the word. I do not linger over *Das Augenlicht* or the First Cantata because I believe that the Second Cantata, Webern's final work, pushes to the maximum the consequences of such elaboration, marks the boundary of his invention, and sums up the other two works. The Second Cantata seems rich for the future because it puts into play a new manner of thinking and of conceiving musical relations which is in no way didactic. As I have already said, the technique has been made more flexible and therefore is capable of producing more.

Many new ideas are present here: (1) functional harmony beyond previous critieria; (2) begetting by a series of sound-blocs having autonomous life; (3) utilization of classic forms of counterpoint controlled by a pure distribution of intervals; (4) abolition of the frontier between the horizontal and the vertical dimensions by considering that the horizontal function rejoins the vertical function at time zero; (5) utilization of series with symmetrical functions on a much more "naïve" level than in the preceding works; (6) utilization of functions of "mutation" (in the sense in which the word is applied to organ stops), in which the series is somehow thickened by one or more basis intervals; (7) a single temporal function governing the entire work.

One could prolong that list still more. Let me limit myself to the most important characteristics, which were to exercise influence of a decisive sort over the entire future of music. One can cite as an example the sixth movement of the Second Cantata, a revival of the *a cappella* writing of the sixteenth century—that is not what most attracts me in the work, naturally, but because Webern was a capital point of junction, his references to the past are as forceful as his projections into the future are daring. In that sense, his place in the contemporary evolution is historically unique, he having made use of many elements borrowed from the past, even of the remote past, so as to project them into a future that their creators certainly could not have foreseen. I noted above that the cenral ambiguity of his work resides precisely there: that ambiguity is the pivot that permitted the musical language to make a "historic" rotation and inaugurate a period of its evolution which is fundamentally irreducible to the preceding one.

After opus 31, Webern began to compose a chamber concerto, but then transformed that instrumental project by turning aside to a new cantata on a text by Hildegard Jone; then he had to leave Vienna to escape the violent and murderous bombardments that the city was suffering. He took refuge in a small village in the province of Salzburg, at Mittersill, where he thought that he would be able to work in peace until the end of the war. As the result of a stupid misunderstanding, he was shot down by an American sentinel on September 15, 1945. The customary reference to an irreparable loss whenever a celebrated man disappears takes on its full meaning when it deals with a Webern and so absurd a death.

I have not discussed Webern's life very much because, aside from that tragic end, it was not rich in "biographical" elements. I have mentioned his activities as *Kapellmeister* up to 1913 at Stettin. He rejoined the Austrian army in 1915, but was discharged the next year because of his defective eyesight; he passed the season of 1917–18 in Prague as conductor of the orchestra at the Deutsches Landestheater, remaining there until 1920. From 1923 on, he led a workers' choral association, which he had sing the classic repertoire and some works by Mahler and Schoenbreg. He twice was awarded the music prize of the city of Vienna, in 1924 and in 1932. During that period, Webern made some trips abroad (Germany, Switzerland, England) to conduct his own compositions. Later, the Nazi regime having practically forbidden cultural activity in Austria, his existence became very difficult; he found himself very much alone, Berg having died in 1935 and Schoenberg having fled Austria because of racial persecution. Nazism's war against *Kulturbolschevismus*, the unceasing persecutions, the humiliations imposed upon all propagators of "decadent" music little by little made all professional activity impossible for him. The Viennese public had no special taste for facing the future, so Webern did not find there, aside from comprehension by a small group of friends, anything but silence and obstruction, the fate that had been the lot of most illustrious Viennese, whether Mozart, Beethoven, Schubert, Mahler, Berg, Schoenberg, or Webern himself.

The last part of Webern's life, then, was spent in the most complete obscurity. He existed thanks to Universal Edition, for which he did work as a reader and textual editor.

A remarkable fact: while Webern was alive, his work provoked no noisy scandals, no marked blame such as was aroused by *Le Sacre du printemps*, *Pierrot lunaire*, and *Wozzeck*. Even at the time when his compositions were played regularly in Germany (1919–33), they were looked upon as an extremist solution without future, as a closed, isolated domain that one could ignore and need not fight—in a way, a musical Kamchatka.

It was after the Second World War, in 1945, that his work was found bringing to young musicians precisely what they found lacking in the music of the generation that had preceded them. I speak not only of musical qualities but also, it can be said, of the intellectual and moral qualities that they found in it. Webern's name has emerged from the shadow: its radiance no longer needs explanation or justification.

By now, the elements of his vocabulary, properly speaking, have been assimilated by the succeeding generation; it nonetheless remains true that his intellectual rigor, his probity, his courage, his line of conduct, his perseverance remain a unique model for contemporary musical literature.

I believe more than ever what I have already said: Webern remains the threshold of the new music. Any composer who has not deeply felt and understood the ineluctable necessity of Webern is completely futile. Perhaps Webern's music, exactly like Mallarmé's poetry, will never become as "popular" as that of some of his contemporaries. Nonetheless, it will maintain its force as example, its exceptional purity, which will always oblige music to place guidelines in relation to it, and in a much sharper fashion than in relation to any other composer.

Webern has been the master thinker of a whole generation,

in posthumous revenge for the obscurity that hid his existence. As of today, he can be considered one of the greatest of all musicians, an indelible man.

Postface

This volume brings together texts written by Pierre Boulez between 1948 and 1962. The oldest of these, that is to say, were contemporary with his first compositions—the First Sonata, Sonatina for Flute and Piano, *Soleil des eaux;* the most recent date from the period when he was completing the second book of *Structures* and the *Portrait de Mallarmé.* While practicing his métier as a composer, Boulez was led to understand its significance. If, for him, acquiring mastery of his technique was an evident necessity, serving an apprenticeship in musical thinking seemed to him no less essential. For that reason, he applied himself to criticism, a criticism sometimes pushed to polemic.

Inevitably a crisis is produced, Baudelaire already has taught us; *all great poets naturally, fatally, become critics.* Baudelaire said "poets," but he spoke of Wagner as a poet, and one can easily understand it as "musician." That crisis—*in which* (poets, musicians) *desire to reason about their art, to discover the obscure laws in virtue of which they have produced, and to draw a series of precepts from that study*—that crisis, then, began to find resolution toward the years 1954–7. It was expressed at once by the creation of *Le Marteau sans maître,* the *Livre pour quatuor,* the Third Sonata, and by four of the articles grouped here under the general title *In View of a Musical Esthetic.* Although these latter belong among the latest of the texts in this volume, and although they may be considered a summation, they have been placed at the beginning not because they resulted from those years of apprenticeship, but to indicate the levels reached and as an introduction to a future musical esthetic, of which they were, with *A Time for Johann Sebastian Bach*, the first landmarks.

Notes of an Apprenticeship also includes three other sections. *Toward a Technology* brings together musical analyses and technical studies. In *Some Éclats*, Pierre Boulez appears more as a pamphleteer. The chronological order has been followed in these two sections because it seemed most natural. One exception: *A Note on Sprechgesang* has been added to the *Trajectories*, which it completes.

In the final section will be found articles that Pierre Boulez wrote for the *Encyclopédie musicale* published by Fasquelle—first the definitions of general technical terms and the studies of certain school disciplines looked at from a less stratified, more current point of view; then the articles dedicated to some great composers of the end of the nineteenth century and the beginning of the twentieth. To the article on Arnold Schoenberg has been added the study of his works for piano, which adds some supplementary details.

No one will be surprised to find at places in this text ideas put forth in others. Very concrete circumstances evoked most of these articles: *Propositions* was written for a special number (*Le Rhythme musical*) of the review *Polyphonie; Incipit* was an homage to Webern; *Schoenberg Is Dead* was in reaction to the composer's death. It was natural, each time, to return to certain major ideas, to recast certain important remarks. That is why, for example, in *Eventually . . .* Pierre Boulez did not neglect to remark that a certain rhythmic domain was scarcely suspected by the three Viennese, although he had brought up that subject when examining, in *Stravinsky Remains*, the rhythmic phenomenon in that composer. In the same way, the fact that he recalled *Corruption in the Censers* in the encyclopedia article on Claude Debussy is not surprising.

It may be said that the collecting of these texts in a single volume should have been taken as the occasion to rewrite parts of the articles. But then the volume would have lost its essential value as testimony.

During the course of those fifteen years, Pierre Boulez's thinking had been refined and deepened. Read these *Notes* carefully, and you can watch it being transformed. His marked predilection for Webern, increased by his determination to have it agreed to, at first made him unconsciously partial, with regard to Berg, who was too quickly rebuked, for the worst reasons, by that category of musicians who wanted to annex him as a hostage. Of his own accord he reshaped those rough judgments in the article *Alban Berg*—and rendered Berg the most appreciable of homages, in the final account, by conducting the first performance of *Wozzeck* (1963) at the Paris Opéra. Furthermore, had he not already foreshadowed that change in 1948, when he wrote: "I ask myself—beyond passing remorse—why am I so intransigent about Berg"?

As for his passionate severity toward part of Stravinsky's *oeuvre*, that was little by little modified by more lucid admiration—*la connaissance, puis, la re-co(n)naissance.*

P. T.

DATES OF FIRST PUBLICATION OF THE ESSAYS IN THIS VOLUME

DATES OF FIRST PUBLICATION OF THE ESSAYS IN THIS VOLUME

A Time for Johann Sebastian Bach: *Contrepoint*, No. 7, 1951.

Today's Searchings: *Nouvelle Revue française*, No. 23, November 1, 1954.

Corruption in the Censers: *Nouvelle Revue française*, No. 38, December 1, 1956.

Alea: *Nouvelle Revue française*, No. 59, November 1, 1957.

Sound and Word: *Cahiers de la Compagnie Madeleine Renaud-Jean-Louis* Barrault, 22nd & 23rd *cahier*, May 1958.

Proposals: *Polyphonie*, 2nd *cahier*, 1948.

Stravinsky Remains: Volume I of *Musique russe*, Presses Universitaires de France, 1953 (the text was edited in 1951).

Eventually . . . : *Revue musicale*, 1952.

"*Auprès et au loin*": *Cahiers de la Compagnie Madeleine Renaud-Jean-Louis Barrault*, 3rd *cahier*, 1954.

"To the Farthest Reach of the Fertile Country": *Die Reihe*, No. 1, 1955.

Directions in Recent Music: *Revue musicale*, 1957.

Present-day Encounters with Berg: Polyphonie, 2nd *cahier*, 1948.

Trajectories: Ravel, Stravinsky, Schoenberg: *Contrepoint*, No. 6, 1949.

A Note on *Sprechgesang:* with the recording of *Pierrot lunaire* made by Pierre Boulez in 1962.

Schoenberg Is Dead: *The Score*, May 1952.

Incipit: *Domaine musical*, No. 1, 1954.

Of a Conjunction—in Three Bursts: with the *Domaine musical* recording containing Stravinsky's *Canticum Sacrum*, 1957.

Chord, Chromaticism, Concrete (Music), Counterpoint, Béla Bartók, Alban Berg, Claude Debussy, in the volume A–E of the *Encyclopedie de la Musique*, Fasquelle, 1961.

Series, Arnold Schoenberg, Anton Webern, in the volume L–Z of the *Encyclopedie de la Musique*, Fasquelle, 1961.

Schoenberg's Piano Works, with the recording made by Paul Jacobs, 1958.

A NOTE ABOUT THE AUTHOR

Pierre Boulez was born on March 26, 1925, at Montbrison (Loire). Having studied music and higher mathematics at St.-Étienne and Lyon, he continued his musical studies in Paris with René Leibowitz and Olivier Messiaen. As composer, writer, teacher, conductor, and guiding spirit of the Domaine Musical concerts (Paris), Boulez won a position of dominance in the European avant-garde after World War II. More recently, he has become internationally familiar as the conductor of "standard-repertoire" music, and particularly of operas—from *Parsifal* (Bayreuth) to *Wozzeck* (Paris and Frankfurt)—both "live" and on recordings. Perhaps the most familiar of his own numerous compositions is *Le Marteau sans maître*.

A NOTE ON THE TYPE

The text of this book was set on the Linotype in Janson, a recutting made direct from type cast from matrices long thought to have been made by the Dutchman Anton Janson, who was a practicing type founder in Leipzig during the years 1668–87. However, it has been conclusively demonstrated that these types are actually the work of Nicholas Kis (1650–1702), a Hungarian, who most probably learned his trade from the master Dutch type founder Kirk Voskens. The type is an excellent example of the influential and sturdy Dutch types that prevailed in England up to the time William Caslon developed his own incomparable designs from these Dutch faces.

This book was composed by Kingsport Press, Inc., Kingsport, Tennessee, printed by The Universal Lithographers, Lutherville, Maryland, and bound by L. H. Jenkins, Richmond, Virginia. Designed by Anthea Lingeman.

DATE DUE

COPY